D0855079

THE BETRAYAL

OF

MARX

*the text of this book is printed
on 100% recycled paper*

THE BETRAYAL
OF
MARX

EDITED AND WITH INTRODUCTIONS BY

FREDERIC L. BENDER

HARPER TORCHBOOKS
Harper & Row, Publishers
New York, Evanston, San Francisco, London

Published under the editorship of Charles M. Sherover

THE BETRAYAL OF MARX

Copyright © 1975 by Frederic L. Bender

First HARPER TORCHBOOK edition published 1975

LIBRARY OF CONGRESS CATALOG CARD NUMBER: 72-14343

STANDARD BOOK NUMBER: 06-138089-x

CONTENTS

PREFACE

One main obstacle to a clear understanding of Marxism has been the failure to distinguish the views of Marx from those of his epigones, including the most important of these such as Engels, Bernstein, Lenin, and Stalin. It is to clarify the development of Marxism after Marx that the present anthology has been conceived. Limitations of space forbid the inclusion of selections from Marx's own writings, so the most important points are treated in the Introduction and in headnotes, with several references to my earlier anthology, *Karl Marx: The Essential Writings* (New York: Harper and Row, 1972), in which I discussed Marx's use of dialectical thinking and his concept of alienation. The Introduction is designed primarily to provide a basis for evaluating subsequent alterations in Marxist thought.

I can anticipate at least two major lines of criticism. First, there is the claim which can be expected from Communist apologists that my approach artificially divorces the work of Marx from that of his successors, thereby destroying the "historical unity" that is Marxism. The second objection can be expected to emanate from those less concerned with preserving the status' of the prophets of the True Faith but more concerned with political practice as opposed to theoretical study. Their claim would be that my approach in some way fails to do justice to the revolutionary significance of Marxism, such that in dissecting Marxism and in claiming to illustrate its historical degeneration (at least from Engels to Stalin), it weakens Marxism as an ideological weapon of the revolutionary struggle in process today. One can expect to be accused of thereby performing a reactionary service for the corporate bourgeoisie in the archetypal style of the petit-bourgeois philosophy professor for whom ideas, not historical-political reality, are of paramount importance.

The first of these is of less importance to me than the second. As far as the apologists of "official Communism" are concerned, it is quite correct that I direct my comments at many of the characteristic utterances of the pundits of Marxist-Leninist orthodoxy. This is, to my mind, an absolute necessity if we are to understand Marxism (i.e., its development since the later works of Engels) as what it in fact is—viz., the betrayal of Marxian humanism. Although I can hardly claim to be the first such critic of "Marxism" from a Marxian perspective (I would cite Karl Korsch's *Marxism and Philosophy,* Georg Lukacs's *History and Class Consciousness,* and Iring Fetscher's *Marx and Marxism* as landmark efforts), I do see this volume as an attempt to bring such a critical understanding of Marxism in its development to a larger audience than these earlier—and more significant—efforts have reached. In this era of mass ideologies and sophisticated propaganda techniques, the public has too long been fed the view that figures such as Lenin and Stalin are genuine followers of Marx, simply because they have claimed that distinction. It is interesting that this view is received and promulgated by both the Soviet Communist and the American anti-Communist establishments. The willingness to tolerate such a distortion and neutralization of Marx is precisely, I think, the index of the *anti*revolutionary bias of *both* these establishments and of those whose minds they are able to control.

This brings me to the second, and more important, anticipated objection. If it is the case that I stand accused of weakening and undermining the cause of further Marxist revolution (that is, to whatever extent this book succeeds in its critical purpose), I gladly plead guilty *to the extent that* that "revolution" has betrayed both Marx's humanism and the aspirations of the toiling masses and has become simply another means of enslavement in this technological era. If I am said to place theory above practice (and thus to "undermine"), I ask my critics whether they do not in fact place practice so far above theory as to fetishize the former and destroy the latter. Do these apostles of an activism without humanism (in *practice* as well as theory) believe that they can distort the Marxian heritage and still emerge with a revolutionary cause that is worth fighting for? Marx, we may recall, defined his position as the *"unity* of theory and practice," by which it is meant that the goal of the liberation of man as a communal and individual (i.e., a "species") being *demands* a normative understanding of man which not only cannot be ignored in practice but which is in fact the sole justification of that practice.

The further question, as raised by Trotsky and Albert Camus among others, as to whether that ideal does, in fact, justify the means necessary to its attainment, cannot even be raised until the Marxian humanist ideal in its subsequent distortion by the "orthodox" Marxists has been fully understood and, as is necessary, the goal be critically juxtaposed to the "results" achieved thus far. In my own opinion, *nothing* justifies the deeds of a perverse Marxism (e.g., that of Stalin); a proper understanding of Marxian humanism, and its betrayal, in contrast, enables us to raise afresh the question of means and to reevaluate the relevant historical, economic, and political facts. But that is a matter for another study.

FREDERIC L. BENDER

Honolulu, Hawaii
December 1972

ACKNOWLEDGMENTS

Certain ideas incorporated in the Introduction were first developed in my article "Lenin's Revisions of Orthodox Marxism and their Significance for Non-Western Revolution" in *Philosophy East and West,* 23, no. 3, (July 1973). Acknowledgment is made to the editor of that journal for permission to utilize these materials here.

The author takes full responsibility for the interpretatons of the materials in this volume as reflected in the choice of selections and in the introductory essays. He would like to express his gratitude to Mrs. Renate Murray of Educational Resources Corporation and Ms. Millie Owen, the copy editor, for their help in preparing the final manuscript and to Mrs. Jean Motooka and Miss Gayle Maekawa for their assistance in typing sections of the manuscript.

INTRODUCTION: THE BETRAYAL OF MARX

The "betrayal" of Marx of which we shall speak is, in effect, the transformation of Marxian humanism into an ideology in the name of which various political leaders calling themselves Marxists have carried human degradation to some of its greatest extremes.[1] Viewed thematically, these alterations involved major changes in both the philosophical and the political self-understanding of "Marxist" movements developing as either evolutionary or revolutionary in the face of changing economic and political conditions.

Viewed historically, these same alterations fall into several periods, which we can distinguish as follows:

1. Original Marxism, i.e., the Marxian humanist ideal of communism, defined as the overcoming of the general condition of alienation characteristic of capitalist (bourgeois) society, as attained by Marx by 1844.

2. The development by Marx, in collaboration with Friedrich Engels (1820–1895), of the materialist interpretation of history, by which Marxism was transformed into "scientific socialism" and philosophy decisively rejected during the period 1844–1847.

3. Marx's political praxis of 1848–1875, leaving an ambiguous legacy concerning his views on the nature of the proletarian political party, its relation to the proletarian masses, the nature of the social changes necessary for the "regeneration of man" after the revolution, and the role of the state in carrying these out.

4. The grafting of the materialist interpretation of history

---

1. Throughout this volume we shall use "Marxian" to denote the ideas and positions held by Karl Marx and "Marxist" to denote those of his followers, beginning with Friedrich Engels in the period following Marx's death. Thus, it shall be shown that "Marxist" thought and practice often contain elements which distort or add to the original "Marxian" views; in fact this anthology has been conceived so as to illustrate the differences between some of the most important Marxist and "Marxist-Leninist" views and their "Marxian" originals.

onto an allegedly "Marxist" ontology (or ontomythology), the so-called dialectical materialism, which was accomplished primarily by Engels and Plekhanov in the years between Marx's retirement from active political life (roughly 1875) to Engels's death in 1895.

5. The reformist, rather than revolutionary, self-conception of Marxist Social Democracy, dominant in Europe between 1875 and 1914, led by the theoreticians of the German Social Democratic party (SPD), heirs to the "orthodoxy" of Engels.

6. The further transformation of Marxism by V.I. Lenin into an elitist movement of professional revolutionaries, during the fifteen years prior to the outbreak of the Russian Revolution in 1917, and the fact that the first successful socialist government was established in economically underdeveloped Russia.

7. The betrayal of the Russian Revolution and the international proletarian movement by the arch-bureaucrat and tyrant, Joseph Stalin, beginning shortly before Lenin's death in 1924.

In these introductory remarks we shall trace briefly the main outlines of these seven stages in their theoretical and practical implications for the transformation of Marxism and the betrayal of Marx.

THE MARXIAN CONCEPT OF THE ALIENATION OF LABOR AND THE IDEAL OF COMMUNISM

I have traced the early development of Marx's concept of alienation in the Introduction to *Karl Marx: The Essential Writings*[2] and thus refer the reader to that discussion, as well as to Parts I and II of that volume. Briefly, what was discussed there was Marx's appropriation of Feuerbach's analysis of religious alienation and his application of it to political alienation as found in, first, Hegel's depiction of the "rational state" in *The Philosophy of Right;* second, the so-called Christian State, i.e., the Prussia of the early 1840s; and, third, the state in general, even the fully democratic state. This last view, that even in a participatory democracy the citizen is an alienated human being, owing to the inner division between "man" and "citizen"—

2. New York: Harper and Row, 1972, pp. 5–11. I shall on occasion refer the reader to the selections contained in that volume.

between private economic agent or member of civil society, on the one hand, and as citizen and member of the commonweal, on the other—led Marx in turn to distinguish radically between "human" and "merely political" emancipation:

> Political emancipation is a reduction of man, on the one hand, to a member of civil society, an *independent* and *egoistic* individual, and on the other hand, to a *citizen*, to a moral person.
> Human emancipation will only be complete when the real, individual man has absorbed into himself the abstract citizen; when as an individual man, in his everyday life, in his work, and in his relationships, he has become a *species-being*, and when he has recognized and organized his own powers as *social* powers so that he no longer separates this social power from himself as *political* power.[3]

On the basis of this distinction, Marx was led, both in his researches and in his observations of the life of the industrial laborers (once he had reached Paris in early 1844 and had been introduced into some workers' circles), to develop the concept of the *alienation of labor,* from the perspective of which he was able to define his own position as "communist." Drawing upon his understanding of Hegel, as well as his newly begun study of bourgeois economic relations (largely stimulated by Friedrich Engels's article "Outline of the Critique of National Economy," which Marx had edited in 1843 for the *Deutsch-Französische Jahrbücher*), Marx recognized the importance of industrialization and its implications for the laboring class. Referring to the importance of alienated labor in Hegel's philosophy, Marx noted:

> The outstanding achievement of Hegel's *Phenomenology*—the dialectic of negativity as the moving and creating principle—is, first, that Hegel grasps the self-creation of man as a process, objectification [*Vergegenständlichung*] as loss of the object [*Entgegenständlichung*], as alienation [*Entäusserung*] and transcendence [*Aufhebung*] of this alienation, and that he, therefore, grasps the nature of *labor*, and conceives objective man (true, because real man) as the result of *his own labor*. The *real*, active orientation of man to himself as a species-being [*Gattungswesen*], or the affirmation of himself as a real species-being (i.e. as a human being) is only possible so far as he really brings forth all his species-powers (which is only possible through the co-operative endeavors of mankind and as an outcome of history) and treats these powers as objects, which can only be done at first in the form of alienation [*Entfremdung*]. . . .

3. Marx, "On the Jewish Question," trans. T. B. Bottomore, in *Karl Marx: Early Writings* (New York: McGraw-Hill, 1964), p. 31. Cf. also *Karl Marx: The Essential Writings*, p. 66.

Hegel's standpoint is that of modern political economy. He conceives *labor* as the *essence,* the self-confirming essence of man; he observes only the positive side of labor, not its negative side. Labor is *man's coming to be for himself* within *alienation* [*Entäusserung*] or as an *alienated* man. Labor as Hegel understands and recognizes it is *abstract mental labor.*[4]

The reference is clearly to the section of Hegel's *Phenomenology* entitled "Lordship and Bondage,"[5] in which Hegel analyzes the relation in which the labor performed by one man (the bondsman, i.e., servant or slave) for another (the master) is seen as alienated labor wherein, as noted by Marx, Hegel conceives man (here, the laborer or bondsman) as a self-consciousness instead of, as Marx will have it, a real, historically situated, being.

Let us follow Hegel's analysis in detail here, and then return to evaluate the passage by Marx just cited. It is important to bear in mind that the following discussion of the dialectical relation between master and bondsman represents, for Hegel—and in a more generalized form for Marx as well—the formally constitutive structure of society, i.e., the fundamental relation between two or more human individuals who have risen above their merely natural urge to biological survival. In this sense, the relationship between master and bondsman for Hegel, or that between the exploiting and exploited classes for Marx, is the fundamental condition for the existence of society, i.e., of human existence as such. Conceiving self-consciousness (the ego) as essentially the striving for infinitude, i.e., as seeking to make its own all that would stand over against it, one self-consciousness must perceive in another self-consciousness an object to be dominated, lest *it* become dominated by the other. The striving for infinitude, according to Hegel, makes inevitable the life-and-death struggle between any two egos. One possible outcome of this struggle would be the death of one of the egos, but this would leave the victor with only the *abstract* infinitude of his solitude, as he would be the sole survivor. Alternatively, and more *concretely,* the life-and-death struggle between the two egos may end in the vanquishing of one by the other in which the

4. Marx, "Critique of Hegel's Dialectic and Philosophy as a Whole," *ibid.,* pp. 202–203. The passage in question appears in *Karl Marx: The Essential Writings,* p. 133.
5. Hegel, *The Phenomenology of Mind,* trans. J. B. Baillie (London: George Allen and Unwin, 1961), pp. 229–240.

vanquished's plea for life is honored at the price of his abandoning his claim to infinitude (i.e., abandoning his selfhood) and his accepting an existence in bondage to the other ego, now to be acknowledged as master and veritable *self* of the vanquished. In the context of Hegel's analysis, for any self-consciousness the loss of life is perceived as the supreme evil to be avoided at *all* costs, and accordingly the highest good is the security gained by vanquishing all potential rivals and the concretization of the ego's striving for infinite power by his having them work as his slaves, thereby producing whatever is needed to fulfill the desires of his master's will. It should be obvious that Marx's comment to the effect that Hegel occupies the position of the classical political economists reflects the indebtedness of these economists to Hobbes's conception of the so-called natural state of mankind. Although, for Hobbes, this analysis of "lordship and bondage" (read: sovereignty and the "covenant" of the subjects) is his fullest conception of the nature of the social bond, Hegel, on the contrary, saw this relationship as ultimately to be transcended in a more concrete conception of the relation of the individual to society based upon the voluntary subordination of egoistic interests to the common good. Nonetheless, for Hegel as well as for Hobbes and the classical political economists (e.g., Smith, Malthus, Ricardo), *at least the foundation* of the social bond is the security achieved through the (temporary) cessation of the struggle among egos (Hobbes's "war of each against all"), such that the relation of lordship and bondage is thereby implicit in all social relations.

The bondsman, for Hegel, is understood to *be* (not merely to *have,* as for Marx) a dependent self-consciousness whose existence is *to labor* at the command of his master, i.e., to "mediate" nature for his master. At this stage of the analysis, then, the bondsman has no self-consciousness of his own (except his desire for the continuance of his biological existence regardless of the human cost); it is the will of the master which provides him with the goals of all his actions. His activity is his enslaved labor and *the social relation* is, for Hegel, that of *the labor of one man for another.* We may, to anticipate, speak of the labor of the bondsman as his alienated existence, in that he *is* no more than a tool of his master's will, and his labor is at the command of, and simply for the satisfaction of, the will of another rather than his own.

The alienation of the bondsman's labor places him in a necessary relation to nature as the field of the objects for his labor. In his labor, as he objectified himself (for both Hegel and Marx characteristic of all activity), he really objectifies his master, for he *has* no self; thus, he alienates himself in his labor, in that his labor, i.e., his life, and its products, all belong to and express the will of another man. However, argued Hegel, it is only through labor that the bondsman has the opportunity to emancipate himself (as opposed to availing himself of the illusory satisfactions of stoicism and religion) and to overcome his alienation by becoming the master of his master. This is made possible only *through* his labor, in that he thus makes his master entirely dependent upon *his* labors, thereby, at least potentially, gaining mastery over his master through the threat or actuality of withholding that labor. That is, through his labor he masters nature, including his own slavish nature, and thereby develops skills which become indispensable to his master and which endow him with the self-confidence necessary to renew the life-and-death struggle. It is with this slowly evolving realization that it is only through his labor that the master can *be* master, the bondsman comes to experience himself as not merely a bondsman but also as self-consciousness; and with this realization his alienation—i.e., his lacking of self-consciousness—is held by Hegel to be thereby transcended.

Marx, however, regarded this newly won self-consciousness as only a necessary condition for the overcoming of alienation, because the bondage of the real human individual—or class—can be ended only through revolutionary action, not merely in self-consciousness. This, of course, reflects the abstract character of Hegel's analysis as contrasted with that of Marx. But for Hegel, at any rate, this newly won self-consciousness of the bondsman is gained only through the "discipline of service and obedience" and through the growth of the bondsman's power through his mastery of nature and of his own fears.

Labor . . . is desire restrained and checked . . . in other words, labor shapes and fashions the thing. . . . This activity giving shape and form, is at the same time the individual existence, the pure self-

existence of that consciousness, which now in the work it does is externalized and passes into the condition of permanence. The consciousness that toils and serves accordingly attains by this means the direct apprehension of that independent being as its self. . . .
   The bondsman becomes thereby aware of himself as factually and objectively self existent. . . . Thus precisely in labor where there seemed to be merely some outsider's mind and ideas involved, the bondsmen becomes aware, through this re-discovery of himself by himself, of having and being a "mind of his own."[6]

We can now make sense of Marx's comment that Hegel "conceived objective man [although Hegel speaks rather of self-consciousness] as the product of *his own labor*," in that the process underlying the development of civilization (Hegel would say of "Spirit") consists in the labor performed by those who, or whose forefathers, were once bondsmen. Periodic reversals of station within the universal formal relationship of master to bondsman, combined with growth in productive capacity and its qualitative change, have produced the characteristically different contents (e.g., laws, customs, ideologies) of different societies and different epochs, depending upon the self-consciousness attained by those who have most recently installed themselves, after a victorious struggle, as the current masters of society. Thus, in Marx's words, "all history has been the history of class struggles."

For Hegel, however, it is not exclusively this reversal of roles which constitutes the attainment of freedom for the hitherto alienated laborer, but rather his self-expression and self-objectification *within* his alienated labor.

   The repressed and subordinated type of consciousness . . . becomes, in the formative activity of work, an object to itself. . . . [and] . . . thinghood, which received its shape and form through labor, is no other substance than consciousness . . . a type of consciousness which takes on the form of infinitude. . . . It is one who *thinks* or is free self-consciousness. . . . In thinking I am free, because I am not in an other, but remain simply and solely in touch with myself, and the object which for me is essential reality, is in undivided unity with my self-existence; and my procedure in dealing with notions [*Begriffen*] is a process within myself.[7]

We must note again that, for Hegel, this freedom is achieved only in thought, for he conceives the bondsman as a self-

6. *Ibid.*, pp. 238–239.
7. *Ibid.*, pp. 242–243.

conscious ego, and not a real and concretely situated human being. On this basis we may return to Marx's evaluation of Hegel's position: clearly, Hegel has grasped that labor is the "self-confirming essence" of man. Marx's charge that, in conceiving man as self-consciousness, Hegel conceives of labor as "abstract mental labor" constitutes a misunderstanding of Hegel which is not directly relevant to our theme here. Suffice it to say that for Marx, concretizing Hegel, labor must be, in the Europe of the 1840s, conceived as industrial labor under the economic, political, and legal presuppositions of bourgeois civil society. In industrial labor, which, incidentally, was just beginning to emerge as the form of labor which would dominate a new age, Marx conceived of five specific forms of alienation:

1. The wage laborer is alienated from the product of his labor. This is to distinguish alienation from objectification, in that any laborer, whether industrial or not, objectifies himself in his product; whereas it is further the case that under the conditions of industrial capitalism the product is taken from him under the legal sanction of the "freedom of contract," which constitutes the specific form of the master-slave relation, i.e., the bond (which is at the same time the struggle) between the capitalist and his wage laborer, characteristic of bourgeois society. This arises out of the peculiarity of the capitalist system that the product legally belongs not to the laborer or laborers who made it, but to the capitalist who has hired the laborer for wages and has provided him with raw materials and, in some cases, tools (machinery). These products, however, act as further constraints upon the laborer, for they now serve as objects of desire, for which he must return a (large) portion of his wage (after heavy taxation to support the government, which in turn protects the relationship of wage labor), and thus he must resume his labors in order to acquire sufficient money with which to purchase his own products. In addition, during those frequent periodic intervals in which an unplanned surplus of commodities has been produced beyond the capacities of the market to absorb them, these surplus products of the laborers' activities now force many workers out of their jobs and leave them idle and in danger of starvation.

2. The wage laborer is alienated from his activity itself, for the

actions which he performs while in the hire of the capitalist reflect the will of the latter (i.e., the capitalist's desire for pecuniary profit), not the laborer's own. Thus the laborer is reduced from a man to a tool for the production of profit; to an appendage of the machinery owned by the capitalist; his lot is not to use his capacities for judgment or to involve himself in the decisions and responsibilities regarding the production process; he is simply required to do as he is told. Considering that the major portion of the worker's waking hours are spent at his job (up to sixteen hours daily in Marx's era), we can speak here also of his being alienated from his potentiality to develop himself into the kind of human being he would choose to be, were he able to exercise such choice.

3. In terms of the types of human beings who are developed under the conditions of the capitalist mode of production, we find the wage laborer is generally trained in the most efficient fashion, that is, in only one operation, which is generally of no intrinsic significance to him as a person, but merely serves as a means by which he may earn the wage so vital to his survival. He is most often left in a state of functional or actual illiteracy, and he hardly participates in the benefits and achievements of mankind's collective power to modify and improve its quality and style of life. That is to say, the laborer is a stunted and warped creature hardly fit to be called "human," and in this sense he may be considered to be "alienated" from that which it has been shown to be within the potential of humanity to achieve.

4. The foregoing aspects of alienated wage labor would hardly be accepted voluntarily by the worker were he to understand the extent of his alienation. However, in a society in which he has the "choice" of hiring himself out to a capitalist or of starving— that is, in a society whose values are encapsulated in the money economy and the cash transaction between individuals—it is small wonder that there is a virtually inexhaustible supply of labor power. But as a direct result of this, all men are forced to become competitors with one another, as capitalist against other capitalists through competition, as worker against worker (for the relatively scarce number of jobs), as well as capitalist against worker and worker against capitalist (over wages, working condi-

tions, etc.). Thus each individual struggles against the rest of humanity in the purely individual effort to ensure his own survival and that of his dependents. That is, under the conditions characterizing bourgeois civil society, each man is radically alienated from all others. This should be contrasted with Marx's normative conception of man as a "species being," an anthropological and philosophical concept adopted from Feuerbach, by which the individual is conceived as both a part of, and as equally aware of and concerned for, humanity as a whole.[8] It is this equally descriptive and normative concept of man which underlies the concept of alienation and which provides the basis of the Marxian conception of communism, which is defined as the overcoming of the alienation of labor and the alienation of man from man.

5. Under the conditions of bourgeois industrial production, the laborer is alienated from nature, as labor becomes increasingly abstracted from the natural environment and becomes a process in which machines, not men, act directly on nature; while at the same time the laborer performs his activities upon the machines. Further, nature is conceived, for capitalism, as a storehouse of raw materials to be plundered at will by the capitalist who happens to "own" a piece of the earth to the exclusion of all other men.

In contrast to this generalized condition of alienation under capitalism, Marx conceived communism as that condition in which the social bond would no longer be defined in terms of the relation of master to bondsman, and would thus no longer be based upon the alienation of the bondsman's labor. In this sense, and not necessarily in that of who has the most money or material possessions, Marxian communism is defined as a *classless society*.

Communism is the *positive* abolition of *private property*, of *human self-alienation*, and thus the real *appropriation* of *human* nature through and for man. It is, therefore, the return of man himself as a *social*, i.e., really human, being, a complete and conscious return which assimilates all the wealth of previous development. Communism as a fully developed naturalism is humanism and as a fully developed

8. Cf. *Karl Marx: The Essential Writings*, pp. 91–92.

humanism is naturalism. It is the *definitive* resolution of the antagonism between man and nature, and between man and man. It is the true solution of the conflict between existence and essence, between objectification and self-affirmation, between freedom and necessity, between individual and species. It is the solution of the riddle of history and knows itself to be this solution.[9]

There is no other concept of communism to be found in Marx's writings; any society which fails to meet these criteria, defined in terms of the alienation of labor and of man from his essence as a "species being," or which in fact abandons the progress along the path to these goals once the proletariat has attained political power, *is not communistic in Marx's sense.* As we shall see below, it is in abandoning the means necessary to attain these goals and obscuring the goals themselves that the betrayal of Marx, both by the nineteenth-century Social Democrats and by the Bolsheviks of pre- and post-Revolutionary Russia, is to be found.

THE MATERIALIST INTERPRETATION OF HISTORY AND "SCIENTIFIC SOCIALISM"

On the basis of the concept of the alienation of labor, which he had formulated by mid-1844, Marx, with the collaboration of Engels, in the following year developed the basic principles of the materialist interpretation of history, which interprets history by regarding the socially prevalent form of production as determinant of the conditions of such other activities as art, religion, politics, law, and philosophy. Marx and Engels regarded the materialist interpretation of history as "scientific" on five grounds:

1. The materialist interpretation recognizes that any human social group (society) is compelled to satisfy its so-called material needs; that is, it must provide itself with sufficient food, clothing, and shelter to maintain and perpetuate its existence. These are simply taken to be the necessary conditions of human survival. Other activities, such as art and so on, mentioned above, are among the sufficient conditions of existence, which are grouped

9. Marx, "Private Property and Communism," trans. by T. B. Bottomore, in *Karl Marx: Early Writings,* p. 155. Cf. also *Karl Marx: The Essential Writings,* p. 89.

by Marx and Engels under the heading "superstructure," as distinguished from the productive "base."

2. The materialist interpretation is—allegedly—empirical, for it regards all products and artifacts of society as indicative of the relations of production prevalent therein, without the study of which history remains speculative. Thus, in opposition to the so-called idealist interpretations of history, based upon the assumptions that activities such as religion, philosophy, or politics are the "foundations" of society, the materialist interpretation begins with the necessary—which Marx and Engels term the "real"—conditions of history.

3. In the spirit of the sciences, the materialist interpretation reduces the myriad phenomena comprising the "superstructure" to effects of productive relations, which are themselves seen as determined by the laws characteristic of the various forms of production (e.g., feudal, capitalist, socialist). The materialist interpretation thus introduces a uniform principle of organization into the study of history, and claims the ability to extrapolate to predictions of future history. It should be emphasized that the materialist interpretation makes no ontological claims or commitments, and that Marx regarded metaphysics as having been definitively superseded by the materialist interpretation of history and its conception of the relation of philosophy to production.[10]

4. The materialist interpretation is dialectical rather than causal in its method, conceiving all previous history as the struggle of opposing forces (i.e., social classes) and as developing through a series of stages, each one the "negation" of the one previous, ultimately developing toward the complete negation of private property and alienated labor in future Communist society. That is, the materialist interpretation preserves the Hegelian sense of "science" (*Wissenschaft*), as distinguished from its positivistic sense.

5. Finally, to reinforce the prediction of capitalism's demise, Marx devoted himself to the analysis of the laws of capitalist production and, in *Capital,* ventured the thesis that, owing to

10. Cf. pp. 17–28 below.

the allegedly demonstrable tendency of the average social rate of profit under advanced capitalism to decline, a capitalist economy would eventually stagnate, thereby creating the conditions for the revolution of the starving industrial wage laborers, or "proletariat."

It follows from this that: (a) Communism is, for Marx, possible only on the basis of the prior achievement of a high degree of industrialization under capitalism, with its attendant conditions of generalized alienation. (b) In so increasing alienated production, the bourgeoisie also increases the size and class consciousness of the proletariat, the class that will eventually overthrow it. The achievement of these two conditions Marx termed the "historical mission" of the bourgeoisie. (c) A successful proletarian revolution requires a prolonged industrial crisis induced by unplanned overproduction, which would be characterized by mass unemployment and general poverty of the proletariat. Such a crisis would also result in the ruin of many nonproletarian elements of society and thus intensify class antagonisms as society increasingly divides into two hostile camps. (d) It is to be expected that the bourgeoisie will utilize every means at its command to forestall these developments. Among these measures would be the planned perpetual increase in the consumers' "needs" and the opening of foreign markets to dispose of excess production and eventually the imperialist domination of these markets to protect them from competition from other capitalist nations. This would bring the entire world into one vast relation of production and exchange. (e) Ultimately, however, after all the bourgeoisie's attempts to forestall the inevitable decline of the rate of profit have failed, faced with the two extreme alternatives of starvation or revolution, the proletariat will have no choice but to seize control of the means of production and to organize them socialistically. (f) The resulting stage of "socialism" or the "dictatorship of the proletariat," is conceived by Marx as a relatively brief period of "transition to communism," since nearly all of society would have already become proletarianized under advanced capitalism and would thus, with the demise of the latter, be essentially (although not completely) classless. The final formation of a classless society would be, according to Marx, tantamount to the foundation of Communism and the solution to the problem of alienation.

MARX'S CONCEPTION OF THE ROLE OF PHILOSOPHY AND ENGELS'S RETURN TO AN UNCRITICAL ONTOLOGY

The question to be dealt with in this section is: What is the role of philosophy in Marx's materialist interpretation of history, or revolutionary "unity of theory and practice"? The answer depends upon first examining certain aspects of traditional Western philosophy. The Western tradition has been guided from its beginnings by the fundamental concern of inquiring into the True, the Real, and the Right, giving birth to the philosophical disciplines of logic, ontology, and ethics. The third of these is the domain in which the philosopher specifically intends to describe and prescribe a rational, or "examined," life, providing a conscious guide to action based upon the critical use of reason. In the classical period of Greek philosophy, ethics included prescription for both private and political action; in fact, the separation of these two was to emerge only in the Hellenistic period. For both Plato and Aristotle, there is an identity of individual and political "ethics," as it was assumed that man is essentially, as Aristotle put it, a "political being" ($\pi o \lambda \iota \tau \iota \kappa \grave{o} \nu$ $\zeta \hat{\varphi} o \nu$). For Plato, the philosopher is assigned (against his will) the task of guiding the *polis* of the Idea; whereas, for Aristotle, the "great-souled" man is, first and foremost, an active member of his *polis*. Yet, this unity of ethical and political philosophy, and therefore of philosophy and political practice, was strained in the Hellenistic period (in Stoicism, for example), as concerns for the life of the soul became increasingly preeminent, and this unity was shattered altogether in Christian philosophy with the separation of the soul's *principal* concern with the "City of God" from the problems arising owing to the station of the body in the "City of Men." There followed, even in the Thomistic tradition of Christian philosophy, a separation of "ethics" from "political philosophy" which has prevailed in the "modern" period in philosophy inaugurated by Descartes and Hobbes through Kant. It is noteworthy that for Hobbes, the foremost of the bourgeois political thinkers, the state is understood to be an artificial product of human action logically consequent upon men's *ethical* failings in their "natural" state. It was not to be until Hegel, and especially until the Young Hegelians and Marx, that *man is seen* once again, as previously in Plato and Aristotle, *as fundamentally a political being,* such that the purely "ethical" problems are seen as a consequence of the "abstraction" of man conceived as an isolated individual. It is to fall, further, to Marx to self-consciously seek to repair the break between individual and political action, taking as his point of departure the recognition that all action, because it is the action of a historically and socially situated being, issues in public consequences and therefore must be examined from the viewpoint of its consequences for the encompassing political and historical situation of the agent *as well as* in terms of its individual intention and motivation. Further, as we shall see below, Young Hegelianism strives to base this necessarily political action upon what it takes to be the critical use of (dialectical) reason, thereby retransforming "ethics" into "politics" and speculative into "critical" philosophy, while the characteristic positions of Marxian thought—i.e., those based on the concept of the alienation of labor under capitalism and of the materialist interpretation of history—are conceived in opposition to all philosophy, speculative or critical alike.

Dialectics, in its primary sense for Young Hegelianism, refers to the assessing of the historically given by inquiring into its "rationality." In this sense, a dialectical philosophy *compares* the actual with the rational and "critically" delineates the necessity for change to the extent that it finds actuality to be irrational. This conception of a *critical philosophy* was originally outlined, and concealed from his critics, by Hegel; the *locus classicus* of critical philosophy lying in the proposition: "What is rational is actual and what is actual is rational."[11] Although this dictum was taken by Hegel's first readers to be a justification of the status quo,[12] it was to fall to the second generation of his followers, the so-called Young Hegelians (among whom were

11. Hegel, *The Philosophy of Right,* trans. T. M. Knox (Oxford: Oxford University Press, 1952) , p. 10.
12. Especially when followed by the statement that "to recognize reason as the rose in the cross of the present . . . is the rational insight which reconciles us to the actual." *Ibid.*

Marx's teachers and closest associates during his student days, 1837–1841), who were to see in it the demand that, since that which is actual can be shown to be only *partially* rational, and that only the *fully* rational *deserves* recognition as the real, philosophy must criticize the actual in the name of reason and supply the understanding of and grounds for the transformation of the actual in the direction of greater rationality (which, for the Hegelian tradition in general, is indicative of freedom). Thus, in a manner reminiscent of the "critical philosophy" implicit in Plato's *Republic,* in which reason is invoked to provide the grounds for the *polis* of the Idea of justice by which Athens is to be judged, it is the responsibility of philosophy to describe the need for, and prescribe the direction of, progressive political action, precisely insofar as only philosophy is able to contrast actuality with the Idea.[13] Hence Hegelian critical philosophy demands that praxis be directed toward the rationalization (and therefore liberation) of human *historical* existence.

Thus, in a world which is—for the Hegelian philosopher—preeminently historical, i.e., a world which is "revolutionary" to the core, it is recognized that struggle and revolution is the encompassing condition of human social existence. Hence, for the Young Hegelian, the critical philosopher must play the preeminent role of pundit of the revolution; any "revolution" which is without reason is merely a meaningless conflict, whereas one with and for reason is the necessary means of "progress in the consciousness of freedom." We must recall, however, that Hegel himself explicitly drew this conclusion only in his youth (recognizing that the French Revolution was precisely such a liberating event on a world-historical scale). But he carefully refrained from elucidating this conclusion in the works which he published in his lifetime. From the perspective of the Young Hegelians, who did not flinch from enunciating this conclusion, Hegel therefore appeared as a reactionary figure. For the later Hegel himself, philosophy was to be assigned a merely speculative and historically passive role: "The Owl of Minerva" (philosophy) flies allegedly only at dusk; i.e., only *after* the sheer struggle of those who, unwittingly, perform the bidding of Reason.[14]

13. Plato, *Eidos;* Hegel, *Begriff.*
14. Hegel, *The Philosophy of Right,* p. 13.

The crucial factor in this analysis is thus the distinction between speculative and critical philosophy. It was to fall to Marx to push this distinction so far that it collapsed; for him, after first accepting but later criticizing the Young Hegelian notion of a critical philosophy, *all* philosophy assumes the aspect of *ideology,* and the motive force of historical development is located no longer in the influence of ideas upon the men who make events, but in the struggle of classes insofar as they are involved in labor and in the struggle for ownership of the means of production. For Marx, the "leading ideas" become by definition the ideas of the "leading class," and philosophy becomes an ideological apologia for the status quo and a diversionary tactic of the owners of the means of production who hire and support the ideologists.

Writing as early as 1843, Marx noted that "philosophy can only be fulfilled as it is transcended and abolished *(aufgehoben)* ."[15] It becomes "transcended and abolished" precisely in abandoning its claim to speak (even "critically") in the name of an ahistorical (i.e., abstract) reason and, rather, adopts itself to the concrete struggles of that class of society which represents the cause of human emancipation (the bourgeoisie in the eighteenth century, the proletariat in the nineteenth century) .

In short, then, from the Marxian point of view, *philosophy* (of *either* the critical or the speculative variety) *has no intrinsic relation to revolution,* except insofar as it "finds its material weapons in the proletariat," and this class in turn finds its "spiritual weapons in philosophy." But in so transforming itself, philosophy becomes an interpretation of society and history (rather than of the eternal truths of reason) . The inquiry into the True, the Real, and the Right is now transformed into the unity of theory and practice subordinated to the historically given "humanist revolution" to be effected by the proletariat.

This *rejection of philosophy* is best exemplified by Marx's wholesale attack on philosophy of 1844–1845, as the materialist interpretation of history was germinating in his (and Engels's) mind. Implicit in the following argumentation is the division of all philosophy into two opposing camps, those of idealism (as

15. Marx: "Contribution to the Critique of Hegel's *Philosophy of Right,"* trans. by T. B. Bottomore, in *Karl Marx: Early Writings,* p. 50.

most fully represented by Hegel) and materialism (as best represented by the eighteenth-century French Philosophies and, in an "anthropological" rather than mechanistic form, by Feuerbach). We shall now trace Marx's rejection of *all* sides of this metaphysical dispute, *including ontological materialism.*

Whereas Marx had earlier embraced the ideal of a critical philosophy, in the Paris Manuscripts of 1844 and *The Holy Family* (written with Engels, 1844–1845) he rejected the idealist assumptions of such philosophy, i.e., its claim to know the eternal ideas and to be able to critically contrast historical reality with these. Speaking in 1844 of the standpoint of idealist philosophy, i.e., that of self-consciousness, Marx noted that it follows therefrom that idealism must conceive the "thing" as the product of such consciousness, i.e., as consciousness's own objectification. He pointed out that, for idealism, it is this "alienation of self-consciousness" which "establishes thinghood." Yet, on this basis, how could objects of sense perception (i.e., "things") be distinguished from objects of imagination, hallucination, dreaming, and so on? Rather than beginning within self-consciousness as does idealism, a "naturalistic" outlook would recognize that these differences must be assumed as given and justified in theory. He remarks:

. . . it is quite understandable that a living, natural being endowed with objective (i.e. material) faculties should have *real natural objects* of its being, and equally that its self-alienation should be an establishment of a *real,* objective world, but in the form of externality, as a world which does not belong to, and dominates, its being. . . . But it is equally clear that a self-consciousness, i.e. its alienation, can only establish "thinghood," i.e. only an abstract thing, a thing created by abstraction and not a real thing. It is clear, moreover, that "thinghood" is totally lacking in *independence,* in being, vis a vis self-consciousness; it is a mere *construct* established by self-consciousness.[16]

What Marx was after here, in opposition to idealism, was a revaluation of the given in sensory experience, rather than the introduction of another "category" of consciousness called "thinghood," as Hegel had done. The roots of such abstraction lie in Hegel's having sought the universal, i.e., the rational, in the Idea (*Begriff*), which was then alleged to be instantiated in

16. Marx, "Critique of Hegel's Dialectic and Philosophy as a Whole," *ibid.,* pp. 205–206.

the concrete (and historical) particular. This idealist mode of philosophizing, for Marx, is based upon the false identification of thought and being, insofar as the ideas (universals) are, for Hegel, supposed to account for the being, i.e., the real existence, of the sensory particulars.

If from real apples, pears, strawberries and almonds I form the general idea "Fruit," if I go further and *imagine* that my abstract idea "Fruit," derived from real fruit, is an entity existing outside me, is indeed the *true* essence of the pear, the apple, etc.; then, in the *language of speculative* philosophy I am declaring that "Fruit" is the *substance* of the pear, the apple, the almond, etc. I am saying, therefore, that to be a pear is not essential to the pear, that to be an apple is not essential to the apple; that which is essential to these things is not their real being, perceptible to the senses, but the essence of my ideal "Fruit." I therefore declare apples, pears, almonds, etc. to be mere forms of existence, *modes* of "Fruit." My finite understanding supported by my senses does, of course, *distinguish* an apple from a pear and a pear from an almond; but by speculative reason declares these sensuous differences unessential, indifferent. It sees in the apple *the same* as in the pear, and in the pear the same as in the almond, namely "Fruit." Particular and real fruits are no more than semblances whose true essence is "the Substance"—"Fruit."[17]

Marx's much-vaunted "materialism" is not itself an ontology, but is rather the rejection of such metaphysical hypostatization as in the passage just cited and an assertion of a return to the phenomenal world as it is given in experience without contrasting it to the supposedly "real" world which may only be thought. Similarly, his experiencing subject is *real concrete man,* not man as a merely cognizing subject, an abstract consciousness. Thus, the actions of such real men are *themselves* objective, not the mythical "objectifications" of an abstract self-consciousness.

When real corporeal *man,* with his feet firmly planted on the solid ground, inhaling and exhaling all the powers of nature, *posits* his real objective faculties, as a result of his alienation, as alien objects, the *positing* is not the subject of this act but the subjectivity of *objective* faculties whose action must also, therefore, be *objective.* An objective being acts objectively, and it would not act objectively if objectivity were not part of its essential being. It creates and establishes *only objects, because* it is established by objects, and because it is fundamentally natural. In the act of establishing it does not descend from its "pure activity" to the *creation of objects;* its *objective* activity

17. Marx and Engels, *The Holy Family,* trans. R. Dixon (Moscow: Foreign Languages Publishing House, 1956), pp. 78–79. This passage was written by Marx. Cf. also *Karl Marx: The Essential Writings,* p. 141.

as an objective product simply confirms its *objective* activity, as an objective, natural being.[18]

Marx claims that his own "consistent materialism or humanism is distinguished from both materialism and idealism, and at the same time constitutes their unifying truth."[19] This "humanism" accepts the real existence of objects as given, thereby denying consciousness any role in "deriving" the particulars from concepts. What it does recognize, in opposition to the passive epistemology characteristic of empiricism and materialism, is that it is real active men, not blank tablets or passive minds (brains), that perceive and sense. Thus, for Marx, perception is the result of the dialectical interaction of an object with an active "subject," in a historical-social-human situation, in which the concrete subjectivity of the perceiver plays a constitutive role in the perception of the meaning of the object. That is, the subject's *activities* provide the ground of the signification of the perceived object within the horizon of the human world; while the object, however, has its existence, but not its significance, independently of this "positing" by the subject. It is this view of man and his world which Marx calls "naturalism," for in it the "natural" and the "human" coincide.

> *Man* is directly a *natural being* . . . as a living natural being he is, on the one hand, endowed with *natural powers* and faculties, which exist in him as tendencies and abilities, as *drives*. On the other hand, as a natural, embodied, sentient, objective being he is a *suffering*, conditioned and limited being, like animals and plants. The *objects* of his drives exist outside himself as *objects*, independent of him, yet they are *objects* of his *needs*, essential *objects* which are indispensable to the exercise and confirmation of his faculties. The fact that man is an *embodied*, living, real, sentient, objective being with natural powers, means that he has *real, sensuous objects* as the objects of his being, or that he can only express his being in real, sensuous objects. *To be* objective, natural, sentient, and at the same time to have objects, nature and sense outside oneself, or to be oneself object, nature and sense for a third person, is the same thing. *Hunger* is a natural need; it requires, therefore, a *nature* outisde itself, an *object* outside itself, in order to be satisfied and stilled. . . .[20]

18. Marx, "Critique of Hegel's Dialectic and Philosophy as a Whole," trans. T. B. Bottomore, in *Karl Marx: Early Writings*, p. 206. Cf. also *Karl Marx: The Essential Writings*, p. 134.

19. *Ibid.*

20. *Ibid.*, pp. 206–207. Cf. also *Karl Marx: The Essential Writings*, pp. 134–135.

It is important to realize that Marx is not claiming that man is merely a natural being; his concept of man also includes man as a "species being," i.e., as a being who is essentially involved with other men, as well as with natural objects.

But man is not merely a natural being; he is a *human* natural being. He is a being for himself, and, therefore, a *species-being;* and as such he has to express and authenticate himself in being as well as in thought. Consequently, *human* objects are not natural objects as they present themselves directly, nor is *human sense,* as it is immediately and objectively *given, human* sensibility and human objectivity. Neither objective nature nor subjective nature is directly presented in a form adequate to the *human* being. And as everything natural must have its *origin* so *man* has his process of genesis, *history,* which is for him, however, a conscious process and thus one which is consciously self-transcending.[21]

The aspect of man as "for himself," as a being *for his species,* differentiates him from other beings, and is based upon the introduction of human meanings into a natural world which would otherwise seem to be the mere product of the play of meaningless (efficient) causes. Insofar as man sees all objects as "for man," they cease to be merely "natural" objects in themselves and become also "human" objects. As a species being, man must express himself in language and common action—which is Marx's way of rejecting the definition of man as an isolated active self-consciousness (idealism) or an isolated passively cognizing subject (empiricism and materialism). Man's knowledge arises out of the interaction of an *already* socially developed consciousness, not a blank tablet, with the object of the new experience.

Marx's critique of materialism also stems from 1844–1845, appearing in a chapter he contributed to *The Holy Family* entitled "Critical Battle against French Materialism," in which the materialist ontology of that period, and its foundations in Descartes, Hobbes, Locke, and Condillac, is subjected to criticism on the grounds that it is an abstract metaphysics, i.e., that such materialism denies the meaning of the given in sense experience and replaces it with the mythology of sensory qualities which allegedly impinge upon an isolated and essentially passive epistemological subject.

21. *Ibid.,* p. 208. Cf. also *Karl Marx: The Essential Writings,* p. 136.

Marx begins the discussion by noting that the French materialism of the eighteenth century was primarily a reaction against the metaphysical speculation of the seventeenth, and was thus also a reaction against theology and religion. To this extent *only,* it is to be considered "progressive." Marx seeks to draw a parallel between this criticism and the work of Feuerbach and himself vis-à-vis nineteenth-century German metaphysics, claiming that *"speculative metaphysics* and *metaphysics in general* . . . will be defeated forever by materialism which has now [i.e., in the *nineteenth* century] been perfected by the work of *speculation* itself [i.e., the Hegelian and Young Hegelian return to the historical and humanist standpoints] and which coincides with humanism."[22] Thus, the difference between eighteenth-century French materialism and Feuerbachian-Marxian "modern materialism" lies in the fact that whereas the former reduced man to the resultant of external stimuli, the latter recognizes that man is self-creative, and his world is essentially a "human"—i.e., a *social*—world. The earlier materialism was abstract and speculative itself, and thus, while it served as a progressive ideological weapon of the rising bourgeoisie in its struggle against feudalism in the eighteenth century, it now appears as an antihumanist, i.e., reactionary, philosophy in the nineteenth.

The abstract character of metaphysical materialism, which, we note, is to be found in an extreme form in Lenin's epistemology,[23] was seen by Marx as due, first of all, to the predominant influence of Descartes's mechanically *materialist* physics, rather than his *dualistic* metaphysics, upon the metaphysics of the eighteenth century. The project of transferring to man the Cartesian view of animals as machines was inaugurated by Regius (whose work Descartes protested) and continued through La Mettrie and Cabanis a century later. This, plus the general indifference of the Enlightenment to metaphysics (owing largely to the work of Bayle) and the rapid progress of Newtonian science, led to the triumph of the mechanistic conception of man within a century of Descartes's death.

The linchpin of this transformation of the concept of man was

22. Marx and Engels, *The Holy Family,* p. 168. Cf. also *Karl Marx: The Essential Writings,* p. 145.
23. Cf. Selection 14, below.

the introduction of Locke's psychology (i.e., his *Essay Concerning Human Understanding*) into France (1700), thereby showing the possibility of explaining mental events, as well as bodily movements (as had already been done by Descartes and Hobbes), as the products of proximate efficient causes. Thus, Marx recognized Locke's empiricism, and English nominalism dating back to Duns Scotus, as legitimizing the presuppositions of materialism. Marx cites Francis Bacon as the first member of the nominalist tradition who attempted to turn nominalism into a *scientific* philosophy. He notes that

the real founder of *English materialism* and all *modern* experimental science [*sic*] was *Bacon*. For him natural science was true science and *physics* based on perception was the most excellent part of natural science. . . . According to his teaching the *senses* are infallible and are the source of all knowledge. Science is *experimental* and consists in applying a *rational method* to the data provided by the senses. Induction, analysis, comparison, observation and experiment are the principle requisites of the rational method. The first and most important of the inherent qualities of matter is *motion,* not only *mechanical* and *mathematical* movement, but still more *impulse, vital life-spirit tension,* or to use Jacob Boehme's expression the *throes [Qual]* of matter.[24]

At the same time, Marx sees Bacon as the *last* of the *nonreductive* materialists:

In *Bacon,* its first creator, materialism contained latent and still in a naïve way the germs of all-round development. Matter smiled at man with poetical sensuous brightness. The aphoristic doctrine itself, on the other hand, was full of the inconsistencies of theology. In its further development, materialism became *one-sided.*[25]

Now, if "materialism contained latent . . . the germs of [its] all-round development" in Bacon, its *first creator,* then Marx's observation that "in its further development materialism became one-sided" must be understood as a thoroughgoing criticism of Bacon's successors, including Hobbes, Locke, and Locke's French followers. Thus Marx criticizes the French materialism of the eighteenth century with respect to both its mechanistic origins in Descartes's physics and its one-sided, i.e., passive, empiricist psychology originating in nominalism.

Thus, we see that Marx can be legitimately considered a

---

24. Marx and Engels, *The Holy Family,* p. 172. Cf. also *Karl Marx: The Essential Writings,* pp. 147–148.
25. *Ibid.* Cf. also *Karl Marx: The Essential Writings,* p. 148.

"materialist" in *only one sense:* his wholehearted opposition to the idealist abstraction of consciousness from its embodiment in a historically and socially situated human being. He is, equally, *not at all a materialist* in any sense which would equate his thought with the *mechanistic materialism* of the Enlightenment. Marx's "materialism" is, simply, a *humanism,* i.e., the placing of real men at the center of the study of history and of the structures of the social world. That is, the "materialist" interpretation of history is not an ontology, nor is it *derived* from an ontology. Insofar as the previous materialists were abstract mechanists, Marx opposes their antihumanism just as much as he opposes the abstractions of the idealists. Marx's "materialism" is decidedly not an ontology placed in opposition to idealism; it is the transcendence of the materialist-idealist dichotomy (i.e., the transcendence of speculative *philosophy*) in the humanist-historical perspective of revolutionary praxis.

This is illustrated in Marx's critique of the development of materialism after Bacon, which is seen as parallel to the *decreasing* sense of the uniqueness of human *activities* considered vis-à-vis physical *processes.* According to Marx, Bacon had made materialism into a naturalism; physics and geometry turned naturalism into mechanism. Hobbes, Bacon's successor and the clearest spokesman for bourgeois political theory, turned the mechanistic interpretation of nature into a hedonistic psychology of human experience which he based upon a mechanistic interpretation of human sensibility, thereby conceiving all human social life as simply a matter of efficiency in the preservation of the life and goods of isolated, egoistic individuals. Marx adds that

in its further development, materialism became one-sided. Hobbes was the one who *systematized* Bacon's materialism. Sensuousness lost its bloom and became the abstract sensuousness of the *geometrician. Physical* motion was sacrificed to the *mechanical* or *mathematical, geometry* was proclaimed the principal science. Materialism became hostile to humanity. . . .

If man's senses are the source of all his knowledge, Hobbes argues, proceeding from Bacon, then conception, thought, imagination, etc., are nothing but phantoms of the material world more or less divested of its sensuous form. . . . Every human passion is a mechanical motion ending or beginning. The objects of impulses are what is called good.

Man is subject to the same laws as nature; might and freedom are identical.[26]

Marx's most penetrating critique of ontological materialism is found in his "Theses on Feuerbach" (1845). These notebook jottings, first published by Engels in 1888, document Marx's complete break now not only with the mechanistic materialism of the seventeenth and eighteenth centuries but with Feuerbach's "anthropological materialism" as well. The "Theses" signify Marx's complete repudiation of traditional philosophy, i.e., of both materialism and idealism, as one-sided abstractions. Since these "Theses" were written at the same time that Marx and Engels were working on their first presentation of the materialist interpretation of history, the new viewpoint in their eyes supersedes philosophy and reduces all philosophy (including materialism) to the status of mere ideology.

In the first of the "Theses," Marx notes that

the chief defect of all previous materialism (including Feuerbach's) is that the object, actuality, sensuousness, is conceived only in the form of the *object or perception,* but not as sensuous human *activity, practice,* not subjectively. Hence in opposition to materialism the active side was developed by idealism—but only abstractly since idealism naturally does not know actual, sensuous activity as such. Feuerbach wants sensuous objects actually different from thought objects; but he does not comprehend human activity itself as objective. Hence in *The Essence of Christianity* he regards only the theoretical attitude as the truly human attitude, while practice is understood and fixed only in its dirty . . . form of appearance. Consequently he does not comprehend the significance of "revolutionary," of "practical-critical" activity.[27]

Marx's primary objection to "all previous materialism," thus, is directed toward its mechanistic character, conceiving as it does that human sensory experience involves a mechanically causal relation between two *objects,* the perceived object and the passively perceiving object. Further, such materialism assumed the priority of the perceived object ("sensuousness is conceived only in the form of the object or perception, but not as sensuous human activity"), that is, the perceived object was seen as determining the form of consciousness and the "subject," which is in materialism reduced to a perceiving *object,* is regarded as

26. *Ibid.*
27. Cf. *Karl Marx: The Essential Writings,* pp. 152–153.

the passive recipient of such "sensuousness." Thus, what is lost in materialist epistemology is the full wealth of human powers, valuations, and experience. Man is reduced to another mechanical object, a complicated machine which registers the effects of the external causes which are operating on him. Given this abstraction common to Cartesian materialism and the empiricism of Bacon, Hobbes, and Locke, the side of the active aspect of the human subject, i.e., consciousness, was taken by the idealists (e.g., Kant, Fichte, and Hegel), who, however, conceived man as an abstract epistemological consciousness and reduced the perceived object to an "object in consciousness." Hence perception was reduced by idealism to ideation.

Although hitherto Marx had been a follower of Feuerbach, he now saw Feuerbach's dilemma as essentially the same as that of Kant; these two idealists (as Marx now saw even Feuerbach) begin within a perspective in which the perceiving subject allegedly organizes its data only in accordance with purely *theoretical* categories. In both cases the object is given only to *perception,* not to the *activity* of a historically and socially active being; i.e., even though formally active, Feuerbach's subject is abstract and undifferentiated "man." Thus, even for Feuerbach, the subject is not a really active species being in relation to its object, for his standpoint is still that of pure cognition. For Marx, on the contrary, since an object "in itself" is always an abstraction of speculative thought, a real object is always dealt with and therefore known "in and for itself," i.e., as existing within the horizon of human practical interest, not that of pure cognition. Thus there is no need to begin with trying to establish the relation, which is in fact already given, between the subject and its object. For Marx, the object both exists and has meaning in accordance with *"human* sensuousness" based upon *practice.* Thus the conception of perception in its pure disinterested state, no matter how "active" the perceiver is supposed to be, is merely a one-sided conception, that is, Feuerbach "regards only the theoretical attitude as the truly human attitude." Given this prejudice for knowledge as the paradigmatic human relation to the world, practice necessarily appears to philosophy as "dirty," i.e., to idealism and materialism alike. It follows, then, that Feuerbach, or anyone else assuming the priority of knowing over doing, would regard practical attempts to alter the mode of man's concrete social existence as of at best secondary importance to philosophy. That is, philosophy cannot "comprehend the significance of . . . practical-critical [i.e., revolutionary] activity."

The Ninth Thesis reads: "The highest point attained by perceptual materialism, that is, materialism that does not comprehend sensuousness as practical activity, is the view of separate individuals and civil society."[28] That is, abstract materialism, based as it is upon the assumed priority of the epistemological over the practical subject, must of necessity begin with man conceived as an isolated individual upon whom various physical causes are registering their effects. As we have seen above, such an isolated individual is in fact conceived not as a subject, i.e., as an agent in social intercourse with others, but as an object poised across a gulf separating him from the world of natural objects. That is, abstract materialism sees man as surrounded by a world of perceivable "things," whereas Marx sees him alongside other men, in a world of useful objects which labor has brought from nature to dwell within the human horizon. The standpoint of all materialism, including that of Feuerbach, since it is that of cognition, leads to the conception of action as individual in which each will is in isolation from, and (usually) in conflict with, other wills. Materialism, in its most characteristic representatives such as Hobbes and Helvetius, could never transcend the dichotomy of the individual versus the universal (the latter conceived, e.g., as society, state, or community), for it always found its sociological point of departure precisely where it had found its epistemological one, in the abstract "subjectivity" of the isolated ego, i.e., in the conception of society as the "civil society" of a plurality of egoists.

The Tenth Thesis notes that "the standpoint of the old materialism is civil society; the standpoint of the new is human society or socialized humanity."[29] That is, Marx sees the materialism of the seventeenth and eighteenth centuries (in Great Britain and France, respectively) as the philosophy of the then rising, virile bourgeoisie in their struggle against the remnants of the feudal nobility and the clergy. This once "progressive" philosophy

28. *Ibid.*, p. 155.
29. *Ibid.*

(which included the "scandalous" works of Hobbes, La Mettrie, and Diderot) speaks to, and of, the world of the bourgeoisie, i.e., that of civil society. But the impending social revolution to be directed *against* the bourgeoisie, which has in the meantime assimilated most of the intellectual and religious trappings of a ruling class, demands, as Marx sees it, a new "materialism" which surmounts the standpoint of bourgeois materialism by having surmounted its presupposition of the isolated, egoistic subject.

Marx's complete condemnation of philosophy is found in the Eleventh Thesis: "The philosophers have only *interpreted* the world in various ways; the point is, to *change* it."[30] What Marx now requires, and which he attempts in the materialist interpretation of history, is a new unity of theory and practice which parts completely from the assumed priority of cognition and thus from the idealist-materialist dichotomy to which such a presupposition leads.

It was Engels who, during the years between Marx's death in 1883 and his own in 1895, attempted to provide an ontological framework for Marxism, under the pressure of the criticism of its philosophical "naïveté." This step was to prove decisive for the subsequent transformation of Marxist politics which, now once again a "philosophy," was also to be transformed by Engels into a democratic reformism, much as it had been for Marx prior to 1844. Engels's "dialectical materialism" departs from Marx's antiphilosophy on the following major points: (a) Whereas Marx understood the materialist interpretation of history to be the supersession of philosophy, and therefore scrupulously abstained from making any ontological pronouncements, Engels argued that "being" is "material" and is active in relation to consciousness, which is the passive "reflection of being."[31] (b) Whereas Marx had criticized traditional materialism for its assuming the orientation of the isolated individual standing mutely in "awe" of (or "comprehending") the world, Engels defines the subject matter of philosophy as the study of "pieces of matter" in motion.[32] That is, what for Marx is at most an implicit "realism," i.e., belief in the existence of objects inde-

---

30. *Ibid.*
31. Cf. Selection 2, below.
32. Cf. Selections 2 and 4, below

pendent of human cognition, is transformed by Engels into "dialectical materialism." It should be stressed that since Engels this distinction between "materialism" and "realism" is regarded as being without validity by nearly all Marxist philosophers who, following Engels, divide philosophy (like bourgeois society) into the so-called two great camps, the "materialists" and the "idealists." Marx, for them, is then blithely placed among the former. (c) Whereas Marx had drawn considerably from his study of the classical political economists and of history, Engels assimilated "materialist dialectics" to the *natural* sciences (mainly physics, chemistry, and biology), with no consideration of the distinction implicit in Hegel (and certainly not lost on Marx) between the natural and "spiritual" sciences (*Naturwissenschaften* and *Geisteswissenschaften*). In overlooking this distinction, and in believing dialectical materialism to possess the formal laws of a deterministic universe which were corroborated by the advances of the natural sciences of his day, Engels transformed historical materialism into a specific "application" of his ontology. (d) Engels, whom we shall see below had lost his awareness of the proletariat's *revolutionary* role, apparently conceived communism largely in terms of equality, leisure, sufficiency of goods, and the rational planning of production, without the emphasis on freedom and self-creation of the individual and society which had so motivated Marx.[33]

THE AMBIGUOUS LEGACY OF MARX'S POLITICAL PRAXIS

The year 1844 marked Marx's decisive turn toward communism and revolution. He and Engels made it their first task to begin a series of polemical attacks upon rival revolutionary writers, and thereby was established a pattern of intolerance of differing, "unscientific" socialist views which would remain a hallmark of their style of intellectual work. *The Holy Family* (1845) was a scathing assault upon the idealism of Marx's former mentor Bruno Bauer; *The German Ideology* (1846), most noteworthy for containing the first formulation of the materialist interpretation of history, was literally a series of baiting taunts

33. These sweeping changes in the self-conception of Marxism will be documented in the selections which comprise Part I.

directed against both the persons and views of Feuerbach, Bauer, Max Stirner, and the so-called "True Socialists"—Karl Grün, Moses Hess, Georg Kuhlmann, Lorenz von Stein, and Wilhelm Weitling. *The German Ideology,* in short, was designed to discredit all rival German theorists of socialism and to castigate them as "petit-bourgeois" or "idealist." *The Poverty of Philosophy* (1847) was a similar attack directed at the very influential Pierre Proudhon, whom Marx had defended only two years previously. Characteristic of Marx's intolerance of disagreement was a desire to drive his competitors out of revolutionary politics. These efforts reached fruition when, in November 1847, Marx was asked by the Communist League to draft its Manifesto. Marx took advantage of the situation and composed a stirring document equally calling the proletariat to revolutionary arms and damning for all time non-Marxian conceptions of socialism. The immense success (by the 1870s) of the *Manifesto* eventually established Marx's claim to being the leading theoretician of proletarian revolution in the nineteenth century. Marx's desire to turn the Communist League into a monolithic party was to succeed with the League's decimation and reorganization in the aftermath of the German Revolution of 1848–1849.

Marx's activities in 1848–1849 consisted primarily in his founding and editing the *Neue Rheinische Zeitung,* a newspaper distinguished for the consistency of its radical position. Marx's and Engels's many articles of this period heaped scorn on the heads of the politicians in the Frankfurt Assembly as much as they heaped invective on the monarchy in Berlin. It must be said, however, that the incompetence of the Frankfurt Assembly was indeed scandalous. Once back in London, however, Marx and Engels assumed the leadership of the remnants of the Communist League and drafted their famous "Letter of the Central Committee to the Communist League" of March 1850, in which they outlined the underground strategy to be followed by the League cadres remaining in Germany. This document subsequently assumed great importance owing to Lenin's using it as an illustration of proper Communist party tactics in a prerevolutionary period. According to the Letter, the Party is small, secret, hierarchically organized and tightly disciplined, the decisions of the

Central Committee being carried out without question by the lower echelons. The plan of action in March 1850, was to reorganize the scattered forces of the League and to place into effect a program of consistently undermining the parliamentary regime which it was thought would soon become a reality following renewed revolutionary uprisings. The Communist party should make demands upon the liberal bourgeois and petit-bourgeois democratic parties and governments which these latter could not possibly accept. At the same time, since the main strength of the Communist party would lie in the workers whom it would organize, the liberals and democrats would be compelled to yield to these demands. The working class would provide the means of constantly fomenting unrest for the bourgeois governments, thereby increasing their isolation from, and opposition to, the working class. This, and the repression which could be expected to follow upon the workers' unrest, would in turn be used to bring still more workers and workers' organizations under the control of the Communist party. All along, the Party would press for the weakening of the standing army and police force, and would carry out the arming of the workers. It would also agitate for such measures as universal suffrage and a steeply graduated income tax, by which further pressure could be placed on the bourgeoisie. The constant turmoil which only it could control would eventually make the Communist party stronger than the government, and eventually, the government would have either to repress forcefully or to capitulate to the Communists' demands (which would immediately be replaced by more radical ones). Eventually, the continual chaos would bring about the collapse of the bourgeois governments and enable the Communists to seize control of the state. At such a time, all democratic pretensions would be abandoned and the Communist party would attempt to rule absolutely on the basis of the support of the armed workers.

What is significant about this scenario is that it is so nakedly a plan to seize state power and so utterly devoid of Marx's earlier repudiation of the alienation of man in the external state. In fact, this plan is the first blueprint of the totalitarian state, although Marx understandably does not dwell upon this fact.

There can thus be small wonder why Marx would try to discredit those socialists who advocated socialist democracy and the preservation (or expansion) of human rights and those "anarchists" advocating the abolition of the state, as Marx had himself advocated in 1843–1844. For Marx the revolutionary, everything is subordinated to the seizure of state power. It was, however, Engels who first formulated the theory of the eventual "withering away" of the state,[34] by which the revolutionary state, i.e., the state power in the hands of the Communist party, would be gradually diminished as the "need" for the state, that is, the class divisions within society, would be gradually decreased. But this eventual elimination of the state depends, of course, on the Central Committee of the Communist party to self-destruct its own exclusive power. Insofar as the concept of "withering away" can be attributed to Marx (who had certainly abandoned that of the state's being "abolished"), he was accepting a mechanistic theory of the state in which the state is conceived to be a "machine" used by the ruling class (in this case the proletariat through its "representative," the Communist party), which this class is supposed to cease to use under certain optimal conditions. That is, the concept of "withering away" conceals a commitment to a totalitarian view of the period before the "withering" begins. What Marx's view lacks entirely is an appreciation of the dialectics (and psychodynamics) of the struggle for, and consolidation of, power and of the subservience of those who are ruled. Despite the claim that the Party will gradually surrender its privileged position as society becomes classless and individuals and social relations more rational, such a doctrine in fact in no way provides for any checks upon the use (and abuse) of absolute power. Such a conception of the dictatorship of the proletariat, indeed, is a

materialist doctrine that men are the products of circumstances and upbringing and that, therefore, changed men are products of other circumstances and changed upbringing, [which] forgets that it is men

34. Engels's remark appears in *Anti-Duhring* (1880) where it is said that the state "will not be abolished, it will wither away" (*der Staat wird nicht 'abgeschafft,' er stirbt ab*). Marx, on the other hand, wrote in 1843 of the "abolition and transcendence" (*Aufhebung*) of the state. Cf. Shlomo Avineri, *The Social and Political Thought of Karl Marx* (Cambridge: Cambridge University Press, 1969), pp. 202–203. Cf. also p. 265, below.

that change circumstances and that the educator himself needs educating. Hence, this doctrine necessarily arrives at dividing society into two parts, of which one is superior to society. . . .[35]

It may be noted that such a dialectic of power was in principle available to Marx in Hegel's discussion of the dialectic of the relation between master and slave, in which the slave frees himself by becoming stronger than the master; but this would yield a blueprint for the succession of revolutions and not that of the promised end of revolution and of the state itself.

The crucial difficulty in Marx's political praxis, which was to become even more obvious in that of Lenin, lies in replacing the revolutionary force of the proletariat itself by that of an elite party which, among other things, *uses* the proletariat for its allegedly "real" or "objective" interests. This distinction, lost on the later Engels and the Social Democrats (except Rosa Luxemburg), effectively eliminated the *revolutionary* character of the proletariat. For Lenin, with Nechayev's conception of the conspiratorial party[36] in the background, such a view of the Party is said to be the necessary alternative to Social Democracy's conception of the passive Party and for the discipline in practice necessary to carry out a successful revolution in backward Russia. But Lenin and the Social Democrats both began from the idea of the passive proletariat. Thus, in Marxism-Leninism, i.e., in the Marxist theory of the Party as practiced by Lenin, the proletariat exchanges its alienation in the bourgeois state for its alienation in the Party state, regardless of the claim that the Party acts on the basis of its "scientific" knowledge of the laws of history and the "objective" interests of the proletariat. Even if these claims are true (as they sometimes were in Lenin's praxis), the passive proletariat remains an alienated proletariat.[37]

But Marx's conception of the Party and its role in revolution is not as unambiguous as that of Lenin after him. We also find Marx at times advocating the direct revolutionary rule of the proletariat, without the domination of a "Marxist" party. With

35. Marx, Third "Thesis" on Feuerbach, as edited by Engels. Cf. Karl Marx and Friedrich Engels, *Selected Works*, Vol. I (Moscow: Co-operative Publishing Society of Foreign Workers in the U.S.S.R., 1935) p. 472. The totalitarian nightmare, of course, was inaugurated in Lenin's regime and realized in Stalin's.

36. Cf. pp. 187–188, below.

37. Cf. selections 10, 12, and 18, below.

respect to the brief success of the Paris Commune of 1871, Marx, who had opposed the rising of Paris prior to its occurrence, came to its journalistic defense by penning a stirring tribute to its memory once the Commune had been destroyed by the army of the bourgeois Third Republic. *The Civil War in France* is Marx's monument to the Commune, and in it he extolled what he took to be the proletariat's first attempt at direct control of society. He was most impressed by such features of the Commune as the decentralization of administration, the rise of the citizens' milita, the subordination of the police to the will of the people, the direct election and recall of local leaders and representatives, the active role (which, however, Marx exaggerates) of the proletariat in the shaping of policy, and the exhilarating freedom permeating the liberated city. However, the Commune in fact had no Marxist leaders, for there had been no large socialist political organization in France during and immediately after the reign of Napoleon III. It was led, instead, by artisans and shopkeepers, i.e., the much despised petit bourgeoisie. It is this fact, coupled with his intelligent guess that the Commune would be unable to rally all of France to its side, which accounts, presumably, for Marx's initial reluctance to support the Commune. But the tens of thousands of martyrs to revolution, many from the working class but only a few industrial proletarians among them, had the effect of leading Marx to overlook that the Commune was indeed a spontaneous rising and not the result of Communist planning. As Lichtheim points out, Marx's claim that the Commune was the leading element in the proletarian revolution implies the view, which Marx never held, that France was the most advanced capitalist nation.[38] The Commune was, rather, the latest in a series of dramatic French barricade rebellions, which Marx, in the enthusiasm of the moment, turned into a mythological proletarian uprising. Be that historical judgment as it may, however, Marx's idealization of the Commune was greatly influential, and is also indicative of that aspect of his thinking about the nature of the proletarian revolution which contradicts the one just discussed.

Marx saw in the Commune the revolution of the proletariat

38. George Lichtheim, *Marxism: An Historical and Critical Study* (New York: Frederick A. Praeger, 1969) , p. 113.

not only against the bourgeoisie, but, more importantly, against the very power of the state itself, and thus we find once again the early Marxian theme of the decisive struggle to overcome political alienation and to abolish the state.

> The true antithesis to the *Empire itself*—that is to the state power, the centralized executive . . . —was *the Commune*. This state power forms in fact the creation of the middle class, first a means to break down feudalism, then a means to crush the emancipatory aspirations of the producers, of the working class. All reactions and all revolutions had only served to transfer that organized power—that organized force of the slavery of labor—from one hand to the other, from one fraction of the ruling classes to the other. . . . [The Commune] was, therefore, a Revolution not against this or that, legitimate, constitutional, republican or Imperialist form of State Power. It was a Revolution against the *State* itself, of this supernaturalist abortion of society, a resumption by the people for the people of its own social life. It was not a revolution to transfer it from one fraction of the ruling classes to the other, but a Revolution to break down this horrid machinery of Class-domination itself.[39]

That is, for the Marx of 1871, the state and the class domination upon which it rests, is smashed immediately, within the first upsurge of the proletarian revolution, by the proletarians themselves, *sans* Party.

> The *Commune*—the reabsorption of the State power by society as its own living forces instead of as forces controlling and subduing it, by the popular masses themselves, forming their own force instead of the organized force of their suppression—the political form of their social emancipation, instead of the artificial force (appropriated by their oppressors) . . . of society wielded for their oppression by their enemies.[40]

Indeed, if we take this view as Marx's definitive one on this subject, the proletarian revolution is itself the abolition of the state; the so-called "withering away" of the state of Engels and Lenin is but a dogma to excuse the "transfer of organized power—that organized force of the slavery of labor—from one hand to another," i.e., into the hands of the Party.

The key to the evaluation of the Commune lay, for Marx, in the matter of the relations of production, i.e., the nature and conditions of labor, by which it was characterized. Thus, the Commune, to Marx, was merely the "political form" of the prole-

---

39. Marx's first draft of *The Civil War in France,* in *The Civil War in France* (Peking: Foreign Languages Press, 1966) , pp. 165–166. Cf. also *Karl Marx: The Essential Writings,* pp. 290–291.
40. *Ibid.,* p. 168. Cf. also *Karl Marx: The Essential Writings,* p. 293.

tarian revolution, for it did not take sufficient steps to inaugurate a socialist social system. It was thus criticized by Marx. The
Commune was only

> *the political form of the social emancipation,* of the liberation of labor
> from the usurpations (slaveholding) of the monopolists of the means
> of labor, created by the laborers themselves or forming the gift of na-
> ture. . . . The Commune is not the social movement of the working
> class and therefore of a general regeneration of mankind, but the or-
> ganized means of action. The Commune does not do away with class
> struggles, through which the working classes strive to the abolition of
> all classes [class rule] (because it does not represent a peculiar inter-
> est . . .), but it affords the rational medium in which that class
> struggle can run through its different phases in the most rational and
> humane way. . . . It begins the *emancipation of labor*—its great goal—
> by doing away with the unproductive and mischievous work of the
> state parasites. . . .
> The working classes know that they have to pass through different
> phases of class-struggle. They know that the superseding of the eco-
> nomical conditions of the slavery of labor by the conditions of free and
> associated labor can only be the progressive work of time, . . . that
> they require not only a change of distribution, but a new organization
> of production, or rather the delivery (setting free) of the social forms
> of production in present organized labor, of their present class
> character. . . .[41]

That is, the "general regeneration of mankind" requires both the
emancipation of labor, which is the social revolution, and the
abolition of the state, which is the fundamental political revolution as distinguished from the mere transfer of state power to a
new group of "state parasites." We shall attempt to illustrate
that the "Marxist-Leninist" Soviet Union has failed utterly to
carry out Marx's program for the "regeneration of mankind"
through the creation of the conditions of "free and associated
labor" and the abolition of the state.[42]

Yet, we should not assume that Marx's writings on the Commune represented an unambiguous reaffirmation of his earliest
concept of Communism as the overcoming of alienation. In his
response to the 1875 program of the German Social Democrats, or
"Critique of the Gotha Program," Marx argued that the immediate result of the proletarian revolution will not be a Commune,
but a proletarian-controlled state dictatorship, although he said
nothing about single-party control. It should be noted that by

41. *Ibid.,* pp. 171–172.
42. Cf. selections 20, 21, 24, and 27, below.

1875 the Communist League had long since been abandoned. The Gotha program was adopted by the German Social Democrats at their founding congress and reflected the failure of Marx's followers to defeat the trades-union followers of Ferdinand Lasalle. Hence Marx no longer "had" a party in the image of the Communist League, so he could hardly have specified a conception of the proletarian state similar to that of 1848–1850. Only in an eventual "higher phase" of Communist society, after

the enslaving subordination of the individual to the division of labor, and therewith also the antithesis between mental and physical labor, has vanished; after labor has become not only a means of life but life's prime want; after the productive forces have also increased with the all-round development of the individual, and all the springs of cooperative wealth flow more abundantly—only then can the narrow horizon of bourgeois right be crossed in its entirety and society inscribe on its banners: From each according to his ability, to each according to his needs![43]

That is, as in 1844, Marx again saw the key to the "regeneration of mankind" lying in the emancipation of labor. But in this instance he supported the idea of the state-form of the proletarian dictatorship and implied only the *eventual* diminution of the powers of the state, in contrast to his position in 1843–1844 and in the writings on the Commune of 1871. On the other hand, Marx's epigones in the U.S.S.R. have consistently avoided abolishing the "enslaving subordination of the individual to the divsion of labor" and therewith have failed to take the necessary first step toward the overcoming of the alienation of labor, the abolition of the state, and the founding of the "higher stage" of Communism—which is precisely what Marx as early as 1844 had defined Communism to be—and from which point of view he excoriated the so-called "vulgar communists." That the extraordinarily low stage of economic development of Russia following the Civil War of 1918–1920 may be said to have "necessitated" the sacrifices of generations in order to lay the groundwork in productivity for the *eventual* overcoming of the "subordination of the individual to the division of labor" may well have been the case; but it serves at the same time to demonstrate the vast abyss separating the conditions, policies, and practices of the

43. Marx, "Critique of the Gotha Program." Cf. also *Karl Marx: The Essential Writings*, p. 281.

Soviet state from Marxian communism. The promise, made by a totalitarian police-state, of an eventual "withering away" of the state, must ring quite hollow in the ears of those who have little but promises to live on.

Thus, Marx's practical ideal of the Party and his changing pronouncements on the nature of the proletarian revolution and the so-called stages of Communism represented an ambiguous legacy.

To the extent that he embraced the monolithic party and the concept of the indefinite postponement of the abolition of the state, Marx, too, must be said to have contributed to the "betrayal of Marx."

ENGELS'S SHAPING OF SOCIAL DEMOCRACY AND THE DECLINE OF MARXISM AS A REVOLUTIONARY MOVEMENT

Finding himself cast in the role of elder statesman to the Social Democratic party of Germany (*Sozialdemokratische Partei Deuschlands,* or SPD), whose inaugural program Marx had so bitterly excoriated in 1875,[44] Engels lived to see the SPD grow into the largest political party in one of the most advanced industrial nations, as well as to see similar movements active in the other industrialized countries of Europe. In addition, he witnessed the social reforms of Bismarck, the German government's artificial stimulation of its economy, and Germany's active role in the era of global imperialist expansion. In short, the later Engels was aware of a decidedly higher stage of capitalist development than Marx had seen; and he revised strategy accordingly. These social developments accelerated the tendency (among nonmilitant socialists) to rely upon a legal socialist party's gaining political dominance through the ballot, disregarding Marx's tenet that governments rule only in the interest of the ruling class and thereby make impossible the peaceful transfer of power to another class. Nonetheless, parliamentary socialism appeared in the last two decades of the nineteenth century as a convenient and nonviolent shortcut to power as, numerically, the population was becoming increasingly prole-

44. Cf. Marx, "Critique of the Gotha Program." Cf. also *Karl Marx: The Essential Writings,* pp. 273–286.

tarianized, although, unknown to the socialist politicians, the proletariat's revolutionary vigor was being sapped by its newly found prosperity. In his more sanguine moments, however, Engels recognized that the proletarian seizure of power could also occur in the aftermath of a climactic war among the leading imperialist states. Engels never departed from Marx in believing that socialist revolution would occur first in the most advanced countries, which, in turn, would assure a relatively short transition stage, or "dictatorship of the proletariat." In sum, the turn of the century saw Marxism as the philosophy of the transformation of fully developed bourgeois society into socialist society, with hardly a second thought given to the vast industrially undeveloped regions of the globe. It was considered sufficient that revolution would succeed in the developed nations, and the rest of the world could be expected soon to follow.

Thus the Social Democrats, led by Engels, saw hope that not only could socialism be achieved following the working class's seizure of power, but that the rapidly growing proletariat (especially in Germany) could assume this power peacefully, by means of the ballot. The history of Social Democracy until 1914 is the history of how these hopes were to remain unfulfilled, not the least because the Social Democrat politicians blinded themselves to the facts that the proletariat had lost the "will" to revolution and that the factional divisions in the SPD would serve to paralyze the proletarian cause.

What was really happening remained hidden from all "Orthodox" Social Democrat followers of Engels (but not from Rosa Luxemburg and Lenin), i.e., that the classical competitive stage of capitalism was rapidly becoming superseded by a state-regulated monopoly capitalism, supported by the successes of Empire, which was creating a "workers' aristocracy" in the major industrial states of Europe, especially Great Britain, Germany, and France. As ignorant of the causes of this process as were his colleagues, nonetheless the phenomenal form of this new prosperity and the changes in the working class did become apparent to Eduard Bernstein, who saw that the income of the proletariat was rising steadily within the prevailing bourgeois order. In light of the fact that Engels and his appointed successor, Karl Kautsky, had earlier approved the nonrevolutionary strategy of "parliamentary socialism" (while, however, retaining the Marxian revolutionary rhetoric), it remained for Bernstein to conclude that Social Democracy should simply abandon the "outmoded" theory of economic crises and the central role they were allegedly to play in the revolutionary road to power, and to replace them with the presumably more appealing advocacy of the gradual improvement of the living and working conditions of the proletariat, which were to be guaranteed by the steady democratization of bourgeois political institutions. Thus, Bernstein's "Revisionism" ignored entirely the matter of seizing control of the means of production and of ending the exploitation of labor. At the turn of the century, it served to reinforce the nonrevolutionary self-consciousness of the vast majority of trade-union members (in Germany and elsewhere) and tended to force Social Democracy to turn even further away from any "adventurist" policy that would alienate the movement from the trade-union masses whose desires for security and comfort were so well understood by Bernstein. Thus, despite the appearance of controversy between the "Revisionist" Bernstein and the "Orthodox" leadership of Kautsky, there was little to choose between them *in practice,* although the orthodoxy still adhered to the rhetoric of revolution, despite their parliamentary strategy.

But "parliamentary socialism" served further to accelerate the transformation of Marxism, owing to its elitist conception of the role of the socialist politicians as representatives who were to speak *for* the masses. The political leaders soon became the sole driving forces of the Social Democratic movement, with the rank and file caring only about the tangible economic gains that could be won. Although the Kautskyan orthodoxy continued to delude itself into thinking that it was a revolutionary party which had adopted parliamentarism only as a tactic, the working class increasingly identified itself with these efforts at democratic reform and became increasingly limited to the standpoint of its immediate economic interests, with the overriding historical goal of Marxism—the humanist remaking of mankind—remaining little more than a somewhat stale reminder of the "heroic" past. Of all the Social Democratic leaders, it would be only Rosa Luxemburg who would see that unless the trend to parliamentarism were buttressed by continual *mass economic action for political purposes* (e.g., the perpetual mass strike), the working class would become incapable of its historical mission, even if by some miracle the capitalist regime should collapse. The leadership of both the Orthodox Center and Revisionist Right of the SPD, however, dismissed her criticisms as dangerously radical and outdated.

Thus, while both economic and political changes were working to divert the proletariat from its goal, the clinching factor in Social Democracy's loss of its Marxian heritage was its ideological self-conception as a "scientific" socialism. It saw itself as the party which possessed "scientific" knowledge of the inevitable workings of the "laws of history" which "derived" from dialectical materialism. This meant that (a) because the bloodshed of revolution was now "unnecessary" to achieve the inevitable transformation to socialism, it would suffice to await the inevitable collapse of the capitalist economic system and then to step in the name of humanity and civilization to end the misery of the overwhelming mass of the population; and (b) because, after all, Marxism was a "science," and since science only *describes* phenomena and makes it possible to *predict* future events, never confusing these with the *prescription* of action, Social Democracy must look elsewhere (i.e., to Kantianism) for its prescriptive ethics. With the prominence of these two philosophical trends, the "unity of theory and praxis" of Marx was shattered; there no longer could be found any sufficient reason why the knowledge of the laws governing social evolution should issue in any imperatives for political action. Thus, the panegyric to bourgeois democracy was in fact nothing more than an excuse for Social Democracy to fail to will the means necessary to overthrow the bourgeoisie. Thus there was in effect no longer any *allegiance to the goal of Marxian communism.*[45] The lost humanism of Marx was all the more easily forgotten because, under the influence of Engels, an entire generation of Social Democrats had imbibed the doctrines that (a) there is nothing in the universe but matter; (b) therefore man is material, i.e., a collection of atoms and molecules which are in motion solely in accordance with the laws of physics;

---

45. It was Bernstein who said that "the movement means everything for me and what is usually called 'the final aim of socialism' is nothing." Cf. p. 139, below.

(c) therefore man is not and could never become free;[46] and (d) since capitalism will collapse anyway, we socialist politicians shall await that event, await the reins of government falling into our hands, then nationalize the means of production, proceed to increase the living standard of everyone (except the bourgeoisie, of course), and *that* will constitute socialism! The only difference between the "Orthodox" and the "Revisionists" was that the latter openly avowed themselves Kantians in morality and declared they would refuse to violate the categorical imperative to treat all men as ends before or after the collapse of capitalism, while the former (following the lead of Engels) grudgingly admitted that *after* power were to fall into their hands they might have to reprimand a few recalcitrant bourgeoisie so that the peaceful transition to socialism might not be delayed.[47]

THE THEORETICAL FOUNDATIONS OF LENINISM

The link between Social Democratic Marxism and Stalinist totalitarianism is to be found in Leninist theory and practice, the uniqueness of which is due primarily to the fact that the revolution in Russia occurred in an isolated country at only the beginning of its capitalist development. This in turn led to Lenin's alterations of both Marxist theory and practice; he was the first to seize upon the possibility of carrying out a proletarian revolution in an industrially undeveloped country without awaiting the prior revolution in the advanced (Western) nations, although he expected that they would not lag very far behind. Lenin's characteristic transformation of both the Marxian and the Social Democratic traditions, the former of which he didn't know and the latter of which he despised, are fourfold: (a) his further "development" of Engels's dialectical materialism, (b) his concept of the Communist party as the elite "vanguard" of the proletariat, (c) his evolving views on the role to be played by the poor peasantry (or "rural proletariat") in the democratic

46. Bernstein remarked that "the materialist is a Calvinist without God." Cf. p. 141, below.
47. These far-reaching changes in "Marxist" theory and political practice are illustrated in Parts I and II, respectively.

revolution which was expected to occur in Russia, and (d) his conception of the role of imperialism in creating revolutionary conditions in the world's colonized or semicolonized regions.[48] Following the initial successes of the October Revolution (1917), to these were added the following: (e) the facts that Lenin's personal domination of events was irreplaceable by any form of "collective leadership," and the momentum of the steps toward the militarization of Soviet society which were forced upon the Revolution by foreign invasion and protracted civil war, (f) the growth of the bureaucracy, which became increasingly infused with nonrevolutionary elements, including many officials of the former regime as well as the parvenu cadres who flocked to the banner of the Revolution in hopes of personal advancement, and the continued scarcities (including famine) which made the central administration and continued bureaucratization of the economy a necessity and, finally, (g) the megalomania and paranoia of Joseph Stalin, the man who embodied the unchecked growth of the authoritarian trends initiated by Lenin and whose rule brought these to total victory over both the previously revolutionary masses and the revolutionary elements among the Bolsheviks themselves.[49]

Lenin's Revisions of Dialectical Materialism

For Lenin, dialectical materialism unquestionably provided the "scientific" foundation of the Marxist theory of society and history. Drawing heavily upon Engels (whose views he never questioned as but being identical with those of Marx), Lenin disputed the epistemology of the Russian social democratic followers of Ernst Mach, and enunciated a so-called materialist epistemology in his *Materialism and Empiriocriticism* (1909); he dogmatically assumed the validity of the "copy" theory of perception, despite the view of his teacher, G. V. Plekhanov, that the representation is only a "hieroglyph" or clue to the external world. Lenin uncritically claimed that it was "obvious" to anyone who takes seriously the progress of modern science that

48. These are illustrated in Part III.
49. These are illustrated in Parts IV and V.

perceptions are merely copies, like photographs of material bodies, induced in the brain by isolated processes occurring in the sense organs and nerve cells. Lenin thus accelerated the decline of Marxism by substituting causal for dialectical relationships in his theory of knowledge, and by reinforcing the mechanistic and thus antihumanistic conception of man.

Lenin also embraced a determinist ontology and subsumed under it an equally determinist philosophy of history, thereby obfuscating the insight of Hegel and Marx that men make history through their creative acts. He totally ignored the point that it is the freeing of human activity—i.e., labor—that is precisely the ideal of Marxian communism. Nonetheless, to justify his characteristic style of revolutionary praxis, Lenin sought philosophical grounds for the leading role to be played by the "party of a new type," as is illustrated in the following passage:

> The idea of determinism, which postulates that human acts are necessitated and rejects the absurd tale about free will, in no way destroys man's reason or conscience, or appraisal of his actions. . . . The idea of historical necessity does not in the least undermine the role of the individual in history: all history is made up of the actions of individuals who are undoubtedly active figures. The real question that arises in appraising the social activity of an individual is: what conditions insure the success of his actions, what guarantee is there that these actions will not remain an isolated act lost in a welter of contrary acts?[50]

This idea of historical necessity and the quasi-utilitarian evaluation of individual human actions thus replaces Marx's normative foundation of the Communist ideal, and serves to justify Lenin's tactics as well as his use and abuse of those whose choice is not to act in accordance with the "scientifically demonstrated" laws of historical necessity.

The Communist Party as the "Vanguard" of the Proletariat

Implicit in the passage just cited is a further aspect of Lenin's conception of political practice, one which at first sight appears inconsistent with his historical determinism: in terms of strategy and tactics, Lenin was an extreme voluntarist. Accepting Plekha-

50. Lenin, "Who the 'Friends of the People' Are," *Collected Works*, I (Moscow: Foreign Languages Publishing House, 1963), p. 159.

nov's view—which Bernstein had denied—that there is a fundamental difference between conformity to historical law and blind fatalism, the certainty of the proletarian revolution (implied in Lenin's determinist rereading of the materialist interpretation of history) was combined with the voluntaristic and quasiutilitarian conception of action (i.e., everything that aids the revolution is good and vice versa). It yielded the conception of the Party as comprised of a small and tightly disciplined band of professional revolutionaries whose role as "vanguard" is to dictate to, and lead, the proletariat, often against its immediate inclinations, on the basis of the "scientific" knowledge of historical evolution possessed by the Party elite. Lenin thus emphasized aspects of Marx's writings stressing the tight organization of the Party and its independence of the momentary desires of the proletarian masses. This view is continually illustrated by Lenin's frequent polemics against the parliamentarism of both the "renegade" Kautsky and the "opportunist" Bernstein, as well as against all forms of "left-wing" proletarian "spontaneity," the first of which he held would lead to the working class sacrificing its political mission for token improvements in its present economic conditions, and the second to a disorganized and self-defeating adventurism. Thus, Lenin rejected all three trends in Western Social Democracy and substituted his notion of the "vanguard" party. It is precisely in this conception of the nature and function of the Party that is to be found the incipient divorce of the Party from the proletarian masses which was later to become evident in the devotion demanded of the party cadres to the Stalinist "line," as well as the arrogance and authority of the Party toward the non-Party masses whose interests it was supposed to foster.

The Peasantry and the Proletariat

In 1899, Lenin published *The Development of Capitalism in Russia,* in which he argued that Russia had by that time attained a relatively advanced stage of capitalist development. and was thus ready for a proletarian revolution. As late as 1905, Lenin, along with all other Marxists, still saw Russia's revolutionary future dependent upon the success of bourgeois development.

His thesis in *Development* is that, in the four decades since the emancipation of the serfs, Russian agriculture had evolved from the feudal to the capitalist form, thereby creating a large home market for capitalist manufactures which was to be the primary spur to Russia's industrial development, which, in turn, would make possible a revolution of the workers in the industrial centers. The formation of the "rural proletariat," which proceeded apace with the capitalization of agriculture, was seen as accelerating the flow of jobless peasants into the urban centers, in turn further exacerbating the economic (and hence, political) confrontation of the bourgeoisie and the industrial proletariat. That is—and numerous parallel passages are cited by Lenin from *Capital*—it is the migration of the poor peasantry, providing a growing supply of unemployed and unskilled labor, which is, as Marx had shown, the basic condition of capitalist accumulation. What Lenin overlooked, however, is that Marx had recognized these developments as being characteristic of only the *earliest* stages of capitalism, having begun in Western Europe as early as the fourteenth and fifteenth centuries. But Lenin, who was already assured of the inevitable triumph of the Russian proletariat through his understanding of the "laws" of history, and who was not to be bound to awaiting the spontaneous rising of revolutionary class consciousness, believed that sufficient revolutionary potential already existed which should be enflamed by the "vanguard" party to induce what was, in effect, premature proletarian revolution.

Marx and Engels had argued that the total transformation of society from feudalism to industrial Communism involves two distinct stages: first, the development of capitalism from feudalism (which took three centuries in Britain, one century in France, and fifty years in Germany) and which requires a "bourgeois-democratic" revolution; and, second, the distinctively proletarian revolution, occurring only once the conditions created by advanced capitalist industrialization had been met, which would take the form of a "revolutionary dictatorship of the proletariat" and transform bourgeois society into classless, Communist society (Marx: the supersession [*Aufhebung*] of the state; Engels: the withering away [*Absterbung*] of the state).

What Russia lacked in 1905 was precisely a bourgeois-democratic revolution of lasting significance; she was still only in the earliest stage of the transformation from feudalism into capitalism and, politically, still an absolute monarchy (the state form which Marx had recognized as most suited for the consolidation of a national economy necessary for the *beginning* of capitalist industrialization). Marx had realized from his studies of the English and French revolutions that even though it was always the propertyless classes which bore the brunt of the fighting for the bourgeoisie against the nobility, the bourgeoisie was nonetheless able to secure the gains won and, by its guile and intellectual superiority, able to reap the benefits of the struggle and keep the proletariat from sharing them. The gains of the revolution fought jointly by the bourgeoisie and proletariat were consolidated for the former against the latter precisely through bourgeois parliamentary democracy, which would then create the conditions for a subsequent proletarian revolution.[51]

The outbreak of revolution in Russia early in 1905 demonstrated the extent of proletarian *and peasant* revolutionary will directed against the monarchy, but the docility of the Russian bourgeoisie soon resulted in the triumph of reaction. The experience of 1905, including the spontaneous creation of the "workers' and peasants' soviets" (councils) as the preeminent form of local revolutionary organization, led Leon Trotsky, who had led the St. Petersburg Soviet, to advocate the doctrine of "permanent revolution," whereby the proletariat would recognize that it must make the democratic revolution *for* the bourgeoisie and then continue it "in permanence" until it becomes a socialist revolution, not allowing the consolidation of bourgeois power and thus avoiding a lengthy capitalist stage. At the time, even Lenin dismissed this proposal as verging on anarchism, although he was ready, by July 1905, to insist that the proletariat must become the leader of the democratic revolution (for the bourgeoisie) and the democratic revolution in Russia would have to

51. Cf. Marx, "Address of the Central Committee to the Communist League," March 1850, in Karl Marx and Friedrich Engels, *Selected Works*, Vol. II (Moscow: Co-operative Publishing Society of Foreign Workers in the U.S.S.R., 1936), pp. 154–168. Cf. also *Karl Marx: The Essential Writings*, pp. 264–272.

be the revolution of the peasantry as well as the industrial proletariat, both dragging the bourgeoisie through its historical mission. Of course, Lenin made no secret that he had no lasting interest in programs of vital importance to the peasantry (primarily the breaking up of estates and the granting of small holdings) or, for that matter, in the spontaneous desires of the proletariat either; but he regarded it as necessary to achieve a well-controlled peasant revolution which would do the work of Russia's missing bourgeois revolution. In short, Lenin wanted revolution any way he could get it; and it was clear to him that the peasantry, not the bourgeoisie, was going to provide its issues and its main forces.

Imperialism and Revolution in Underdeveloped Countries

At the turn of the century, Russia occupied an ambiguous position in the world: on the one hand she was an imperial power, occupying vast regions in Asia populated by non-Russian peoples and exploiting them for the benefit of the Russian aristocracy and bourgeoisie. On the other hand, much of her industry, which was far less than that of the Western countries, was controlled by Western European, primarily French and German, capital. In this latter respect, although politically independent, Russia was nonetheless an economic colony of imperialist Europe. In short, the Russia of this period was both an imperialist power and a semicolony. Although Lenin, in his *Imperialism: The Highest Stage of Capitalism* (1917), emphasized the former aspect (arguing that the then current world war was essentially an imperialist struggle for world domination among the European powers, including Russia, which should be transformed eventually into a proletarian revolution throughout Europe), his economic analysis of imperialism also indicated an awareness of the potentially revolutionary situation in the colonized and semicolonized regions, such that the struggle against capitalist imperialism is now seen as a worldwide struggle in which the *weakest* link in the capitalist chain (i.e., Russia) might be expected to be the first to break, precisely because of its economic backwardness. Thus Lenin no longer accepted the Marxian concept of proletarian revolution occurring first in the most advanced countries.

Lenin's Improvisations in the Early Years of the Bolshevik Revolution

The collapse of the czarist regime in March 1917 (the so-called February Revolution, according to the old-style Julian calendar) did not lead to an immediate victory for Lenin's Bolsheviks, but Lenin drove his party to a successful coup d'état by November of that year (i.e., the so-called October Revolution). Then, finding himself master of a sprawling, chaotic, and backward country, wracked by three years of an indecisive war which had led to general social collapse, and without any specific guidelines from the heritage of Marx and Engels, Lenin improvised for the five years of his dictatorial rule over Soviet Russia. These "improvisations" were in fact policies dictated by necessity which Lenin himself often embraced only half-heartedly. The factors determining the policies adopted by the Soviet government included: the occupation of vast areas of Russia by German forces, which the peace of March 1918 recognized by the cession of the Baltic states, Poland, Bessarabia, and the Ukraine to Germany; the Allied invasions of Russia following the end of the world war; the uprisings against Bolshevik rule in 1918, which became, by the middle of that year, an open civil war in which the "White" armies were directly aided by numerous foreign governments; the large-scale drop in production caused by the civil war as well as by the resistance of most of the technical and managerial elite; and widespread famine, to name a few. Far from being the relatively easy expropriation of a solidly based industrial economy, the Bolshevik Revolution in its first years presided over the diminution of industrial and agricultural output on an economy hitherto hardly very highly developed. In the face of these threats to continued Bolshevik rule, it was little more than the energy of Lenin alone which held the Party, and then the nation, together. But to enable the Revolution to survive, Lenin had to adopt policies which were inevitably to sap its dynamism and, eventually, to bring it to an exhausted halt, easy prey for the counterrevolution of Stalin. For one thing, Lenin's personal domination of the Party, effected primarily through persuasion, was irreplaceable by any combination of collective leadership; and when Trotsky refused to attempt to dominate the Revolution while Lenin lay dying (1923–1924), the way was open for Stalin, by far the most ruthless of the Bolsheviks, to amass supreme power by taking control of the Party. With the growing scarcity of goods, it became necessary that the proletarian dictatorship be severe, that the countryside be systematically plundered (at least prior to 1921) to feed the starving urban population. This resulted in the rampant growth of the bureaucracy (the source of Stalin's power) required to administer the nationwide economy. Under these permanent wartime conditions, it became necessary to use whatever means were necessary to control the masses, thereby demanding the rapid growth of governmental and Party control over society. Despite Lenin's growing awareness as he lay dying that something had gone drastically wrong, it was by then impossible to prevent the Soviet State from becoming self-perpetuating not only at the cost of the Marxian humanist ideal (which was of little concern to the Bolsheviks anyway), but of even that freedom that had been attained by the bourgeois regimes of the West. By the time that he became aware of the grave danger of Stalin's drive for personal power, Lenin lay powerless to prevent those tendencies, which he had himself begun as "temporary" expediencies, from providing the basis for both Stalin's power and his dictatorial methods.

THE GROWTH OF THE BUREAUCRACY AND THE ORIGINS OF THE STALIN TERROR

Owing to the Bolsheviks' small numbers at the time of the October Revolution, and to the fact that many Bolsheviks were killed fighting in the Red army during the civil war (1918–1920), it became inevitable that the ranks of the expanding bureaucracy would become inundated with individuals who saw participation in the new order as the road to personal power and well-being. This was true of both proletarian and nonproletarian elements, as the bureaucracy and then the Party itself became swollen with the sons and daughters of petty officials of the old regime. This was a new breed of administrators, for whom survival and upward mobility depended upon their being able to rigidly control their subordinates and the populace entrusted to their control, and who were thus an antirevolutionary class *par excellence*. Long before, Marx had portrayed the bureaucrat as motivated by a "crass materialism, the materialism of passive obedience, of faith in authority, of the mechanism of fixedly formal activity, fixed principles, views and traditions," for whom "public service" means nothing but his private purpose of hunting for higher positions and making a career for himself.[52] This text lay as a closed book in the Marx-Engels Archive in Moscow. The administration of the nationalized economy, as well as the enforced obedience of the masses, i.e., the very survival of the Soviet state, demanded that the powers of the bureaucracy and secret police be increasingly expanded; and it was thus that this "new class" of political bureaucrats began to reinforce *its own* authority as its supreme mission, and in the process to betray the Revolution.

The bureaucracy, however, needed a spokesman, and they found their man in Joseph Stalin. For here was an old Bolshevik who had gained a reputation as a flawless administrator and to whom the radical humanism of Marx had never been known. Stalin was a man obsessed with the dream of winning and maintaining absolute power, and thus was not only the creator, but even more the creature, of the bureaucracy. His skillful maneuverings and his easy elimination of his Bolshevik rivals were just the reflection of the increasing power of the bureaucratic apparatus over both Party and national life; were Stalin not around, the bureaucracy would have created a facsimile to have served in his stead. By this time the only "force" that might have thwarted the impending triumph of state bureaucratization was a militant proletariat determined, like the Communards of Paris, to shape their own destiny in the light of the ideal of the "regeneration of man" by overcoming the institutionalized division of labor and the authoritarian state which imposed it. But these goals of Marx were utterly neglected by the Bolsheviks (despite Lenin's futile attempts in the days of his final illness and Trotsky's later claims on behalf of the Opposition), had been long forgotten by the

52. Marx, "Critique of Hegel's *Philosophy of Right*." See *Karl Marx: The Essential Writings*, pp. 33–34.

Social Democrats before them, and had still earlier been compromised by Marx himself. The proletariat of semifeudal Russia was no more equal to its task than the proletariat of industrialized Germany, to whom Lenin (but not Stalin) continually looked for support, was equal to its. The totalitarianism of Hitler's Germany, victorious in part due to the connivance of Stalin, was more than matched in barbarity by that of Stalin's Russia. With that dubious achievement the betrayal of Marx was complete.

PART I
FOUNDATIONS OF DIALECTICAL MATERIALISM

Friedrich Engels (1820–1895) was Marx's closest collaborator for almost forty years, until the latter's death in 1883. Although there can be no question but that they shared many concepts basic to the development of Marxist socialism, it is by no means correct to assume the identity of their every view, nor to uncritically attribute the views of one or the other man to "Marx and Engels" combined. A critical approach to the question of the relation of the thought of Engels to that of Marx is significant in view of the widespread assumption among "Marxist-Leninists" to the contrary in both respects. Owing to Marx's earlier death, Engels inherited the mantle of leadership of German Social Democracy which, by the 1870s, had begun to develop along lines which were anathema to Marx.[1] Engels was Marx's literary executor; thus his interpretations of his friend's works were soon acknowledged by Marxists as authoritative, and his abilities as a political leader and theoretician in his own right facilitated this assimilation of his views of the 1880s and 1890s to those of Marx. It is thus our first task to ferret out those ideas uniquely characteristic of the "later" Engels and to distinguish them from those of Marx.

We shall see in this chapter that Engels departed from Marx in a number of important respects, which may be traced to the economic, political, and intellectual situations of Social Democracy in the closing two decades of the century. In brief, this was

1. Cf. Marx, "Critique of the Gotha Program." Cf. *Karl Marx: The Essential Writings*, pp. 273–286.

the era of the unprecedented growth of the Social Democratic party of Germany (SPD) in both electoral strength and parliamentary representation. This growth was spurred by rapid strides in industralization which occurred under the guidance of Bismarck, chancellor of the Reich from 1862 to 1890. Increasing industrialization brought in its wake the weakening of the lower middle classes and the peasantry and the increasing proletarianization of the working classes. The German bourgeoisie, in their turn, were largely content to allow Bismarck and the Junkers to play the leading political role, as their policies proved to be of great benefit to the economic interests of the bourgeoisie.

In addition, the 1870s and 1880s saw European capital gain control of most of the globe. Germany, one of the last European powers to enter imperialist competition, nonetheless rapidly expanded her influence abroad and deemed it necessary to surpass France and to challenge the hegemony of Great Britain in world politics. Although it was not to be until 1907 that the theoreticians of Social Democracy would begin to develop an explicit theory of imperialism, it had become apparent as early as the 1890s that the day-to-day existence of the European proletariat was becoming more, instead of less, bearable, in contrast to the so-called predictions of Marx.[2] It was to be this changing economic trend, and the consequent decline in the radicalism of large segments of the working class, that was eventually to split Social Democracy, throughout Europe, into "Orthodox" and "Revisionist" wings.[3] At this point, however, we shall consider only Engels's leading role as creator of the philosophy of Social Democratic Marxism, and thus as the ultimate source of both these trends within Social Democracy in the era prior to the outbreak of World War I in 1914.

Although the SPD was the largest and most successful socialist party of the era, it was by no means the only one. The year 1889 saw the founding of the Second, or "Socialist," International, an organization which united the socialist parties of all leading industrial nations, with the SPD—and thus Engels—as its guiding

2. Cf. *Capital,* especially Vol. I, chaps. 32 and 33, and Vol. II, Part 3, excerpts from which may be found in *Karl Marx: The Essential Writings,* pp. 386–418.
3. Cf. Part II, below.

force. Thus, as it appeared, Marxism had entered a new stage of of its political existence, in which bullets would be replaced by ballots, and which, moreover, promised victory over the bourgeoisie in the most advanced countries, especially Germany, within a reasonably short time. To this end, it was felt that Social Democracy needed an ideology which would provide it with intellectual respectability. The historical significance of the "later" Engels's contribution lies in fulfilling this task.

Thus, we must consider the "later" Engels as the key transitional figure between Marx and Lenin. We shall see in the selections comprising this section that his "dialectical materialism" laid the foundation for the Social Democrats' and Lenin's reinterpretations of Marx. That Social Democracy developed a comprehensive world view, to which it assimilated natural science in an unsuccessful attempt to refute positivism and neo-Kantianism; that it became in deed if not in word a reformist rather than a revolutionary party; and that it ultimately proved powerless to effect a peaceful transition to socialism but fell instead easy victim to national chauvinism are all ultimately to be traced to those elements of Engels's philosophy which served to blunt the radical humanism of Marx, as much as to the improvement in the standard of living of the European proletariat.

1. ENGELS:
SCIENTIFIC SOCIALISM
AND DIALECTICS

In the first part of his Socialism: Utopian and Scientific *(1880), Engels discussed the utopian socialisms of Saint-Simon (1760–1825), Fourier (1772–1837), and Owen (1771–1858) as reactions to the growth of capitalism and the failure of bourgeois society to measure up to the aspirations of the French Revolution. These three utopian thinkers are pictured by Engels as the first serious critics of bourgeois society. Their "utopian" character lies in their criticisms remaining on the level of the effects (e.g., poverty, inequality, injustice) of bourgeois society rather than seeking the grounds of these effects in the economic preconditions of the capitalist production process upon which bourgeois society is based. Limitations of space prevent us from excerpting this material.*

Engels then goes on to expound his famous distinction between "metaphysical" and "dialectical" thinking, holding that it is only the use of the latter which makes a doctrine truly scientific, even though the particular sciences, as they have developed since the founding work of Galileo and Newton, have been largely responsible for the apparent triumph of the "metaphysical" mode of thinking. Thus, in what follows, we shall bear in mind that it is the use of dialectical thinking, rather than the adoption of this or that theory current in the sciences, which, for Engels, defines a social or political doctrine as "scientific." This distinction is basically that between (1) studying phenomena in isolation, taking them as fixed and assuming that investigating things as they are (i.e., as stationary and in the present) offers us an adequate knowledge of them and (2) studying the relations among things, recognizing their genesis and more importantly their ongoing development and their potential future changes, respectively.

Engels then discusses the historical role played by Hegel's philosophy in demonstrating the superiority of dialectical to metaphysical thinking. It should be stressed that Engels is here using the term "meta-

SOURCE: From Friedrich Engels, *Socialism: Utopian and Scientific*, in Karl Marx and Friedrich Engels, *Selected Works*, Vol. I (Moscow: Co-operative Publishing Society of Foreign Workers in the U.S.S.R., 1935).

physical" to describe a mode of thinking which includes "sound common sense." Thus, as used in this context, "metaphysics" blurs the distinction between this common sense and metaphysical philosophy properly understood; for Engels the former is just as "metaphysical" as the latter. Hegel, on the other hand, is for Engels a "dialectician" (regardless of the fact that he expounded an idealist metaphysics), and what is usually referred to as Hegel's "metaphysics" is called by Engels his "System." Thus, Engels wishes to separate Hegel's dialetical "method" (which is his "epochmaking service") from his "System," which is, for Engels, an "ideological miscarriage."

The selection concludes with Engels's observation that Marx's analysis of the capitalist mode of production is a "dialectical" analysis, in that it locates the essential characteristics of capitalism in the production of surplus value and then utilizes this concept in tracing the genesis and future development of capitalism to its supersession in socialism. This use, then, of the "dialectical method" is what serves to define Marxism as "scientific socialism" for Engels.

We thus witness the origins of Engels's "re-Hegelianizing" of Marxism. This consists in his isolating the "dialectical method" from the idealist systematic "content" in Hegel. Marxism, as "scientific," is then held to derive its dialectical method from Hegel while abandoning the idealist System to the dustbin of the history of ideological confusions. Henceforth Marxist theory will divide along the lines of the acceptance or rejection of Engels's "re-Hegelianizing": i.e., between the "re-Hegelianizing" followers of Engels (including Plekhanov, Lenin, and Stalin) who claim to be dialecticians and to possess in dialectics the "laws" which govern all phenomena and the "de-Hegelianizing" (or antidialectical Neo-Kantian, or quasi-positivist) school headed by Kautsky and Bernstein, who wish to abandon dialectics and who see Marxism become "scientific" not in Engels's sense but only insofar as it is allegedly modeled upon the natural sciences. Thus, both camps turned "Marxism" into a "pure theory," whether they saw Hegel as a great scientific thinker because he "invented" dialectics or as the arch antiscientific speculative philosopher because he tried to compress modern science into his speculative System. Thus, it is possible for both trends to claim the mantle of "Marxist" Orthodoxy on the grounds that they adopt one or the other aspect of Engels's (but not Marx's) view of Hegel. But the more fundamental question still remains: Can one legitimately isolate "method" from "System" in Hegel's philosophy? That is, are the dialectic and the systematic content distinct or even distinguishable? Yet no "Orthodox" Marxist ever raises this question, because it became a major point of "Orthodoxy" to accept uncritically

Engels's interpretation of Hegel, whereas no unbiased student of Hegel could conceivably answer these questions in the affirmative.

In the light of examining Marx's real relation to Hegel,[1] we can at least begin to elucidate the mistakes of both camps. The antidialecticians would have Marx reject the "mysteries" of Hegel's dialectic altogether, whereas the dialecticians would have him be a follower of Hegel. But the point is that Marx was never an "Hegelian," i.e., an orthodox follower of Hegel, but was merely a follower of the extreme left Young Hegelians (especially Bauer and Feuerbach), who were themselves radically different from Hegel and his immediate followers (the so-called Old Hegelians). Bearing this in mind, we can see that the Marxian materialist interpretation of history is in fact the supersession of Marx's own earlier Young Hegelianism and liberalism. Marx, in thereby going beyond Hegel and all other Hegelians, nonetheless remains within the orbit of his great predecessor's thought, as he was himself to acknowledge as late as 1873.[2] We may thus surmise that there is no Marxian treatise on dialectics (although there is one by Engels) because it is not only dialectics (as Engels thought) that Marx adopts from Hegel. Although rejecting much of Hegel's philosophy, Marx still recognizes that Hegel was "the first to grasp the self-alienation of man, . . . the notion of labor, and . . . [who] . . . conceives objective man . . . as the result of his own labor."[3] It is in this sense, rather than in that of the abstract alternatives of "method" and "System," that Marx retained and developed such Hegelian insights as the struggle between master and slave as forming the constituent social relationship under the conditions of private property and the notion of the division between civil society and the state as ultimately based upon the alienation of labor. Further, Hegel's statement that "what is rational is actual and what is actual is rational"[4] became, in Marx's hands, the manifesto of the radical critique of bourgeois society which, of course, Marx never abandoned. Thus, the distinction between the "re-" and the "de-" Hegelianizing Marxists, based upon Engels's erroneous perspective of Hegel, is in turn based upon the abstract separation of "method" and "System" in Hegel is foreign to Marx. And, despite Engels's usually correct efforts on behalf of dialectics as a method, even the so-called re-Hegelianizing trend within Marxism, especially as represented subsequently by Lenin and Stalin,[5] in fact so distorts Marx

1. Cf. pp. 3–8, 15–21, above.
2. Cf. pp. 237, 239, and 386, below.
3. Cf. pp. 3–11, above.
4. Cf. p. 15, above.
5. Cf. Selections 14, 15, and 26, below.

that it was ultimately to adopt a thoroughly undialectical theory of per-
ception[6] and to assimilate the so-called "laws" of dialectics[7] to the
strictly causal analyses of the natural sciences and positivistic philosophy.
Thus, both trends carry "Marxism" even further away from Marxian
humanism, insofar as they both fail to grasp the nature of the Hegel-
Marx relationship owing to the ubiquitous mediation of Engels.

. . . When we reflect on nature or the history of mankind or
our own intellectual activity, the first picture presented to us is of
an endless maze of relations and interactions in which nothing
remains what, where, and as it was, but everything moves,
changes, comes into being, and passes out of existence. We see,
therefore, at first the picture as a whole, in which the details are
still kept more or less in the background; we pay more attention
to the movement, the transitions, the interconnections than to
what it is that moves, changes, or is connected. This primitive,
naïve, yet intrinsically correct conception of the world was that
of ancient Greek philosophy, and was first clearly formulated by
Heraclitus: everything is and also is not, for everything is in flux,
is constantly changing, constantly coming into being and passing
away. But this conception, correctly as it covers the general
character of the picture of phenomena as a whole, is yet inadequate to explain the details of which this total picture is composed; and so long as we do not understand these, we also have
no clear idea of the picture as a whole. In order to understand
these details, we must detach them from their natural or historical connections, and examine each one separately, as to its
nature, its special causes and effects, etc. This is primarily the
task of natural science and historical research; branches of science which the Greeks of the classical period, on very good
grounds, relegated to a merely subordinate position, because they
had first of all to collect materials for these sciences to work
upon. . . . The beginnings of the exact investigation of nature
were first developed by the Greeks of the Alexandrian period,
and later on in the Middle Ages were further developed by the

6. Cf. Selections 2 and 15, below.
7. Cf. Selections 3 and 26, below.

Arabs. Real natural science, however, dates only from the second half of the fifteenth century, and from then on it has advanced with constantly increasing rapidity. The analysis of nature into its individual parts, the grouping of the different natural processes and natural objects in definite classes, the study of the internal anatomy of organic bodies in their manifold forms— these were the fundamental conditions of the gigantic strides in our knowledge of nature which have been made during the last four hundred years. But this method of investigation has also left us as a legacy the habit of observing natural objects and natural processes in their isolation, detached from the whole vast interconnection of things; and therefore not in their motion, but in their repose; not as essentially changing, but as fixed constants; not in their life, but in their death. And when, as was the case with Bacon and Locke, this way of looking at things was transferred from natural science to philosophy, it produced the specific narrow-mindedness of the last century, the metaphysical mode of thought.

To the metaphysician, things and their mental images, ideas, are isolated, to be considered one after the other, apart from each other, rigid, fixed objects of investigation given once for all. He thinks in absolutely discontinuous antitheses. . . . For him a thing either exists, or it does not exist; it is equally impossible for a thing to be itself and at the same time something else. Positive and negative absolutely exclude one another; cause and effect stand in an equally rigid antithesis one to the other. At first sight this mode of thought seems to us extremely plausible, because it is the mode of thought of so-called sound common sense. But sound common sense, respectable fellow as he is within the homely precincts of his own four walls, has most wonderful adventures as soon as he ventures out into the wide world of scientific research. Here the metaphysical mode of outlook, justifiable and even necessary as it is in domains whose extent varies according to the nature of the object under investigation, nevertheless sooner or later always reaches a limit beyond which it becomes one-sided, limited, abstract, and loses its way in insoluble contradictions. And this is so because in considering individual things it loses sight of their connections; in contemplating their existence it forgets their coming into being and passing away; in looking at them at rest it leaves their motion out of account; because it cannot see the wood for the trees. For everyday purposes we know, for example, and can say with certainty whether an animal is alive or not; but when we look more closely we find that this is often an extremely complex question. . . . In the same way every organic being is at each moment the same and not the same; at each moment it is assimilating matter drawn from without, and excreting other matter; at each moment the cells of its body are dying and new ones are being formed; in fact, within a longer or shorter period the matter of its body is completely renewed and is replaced by other atoms of matter, so that every organic being is at all times itself and yet something other than itself. Closer investigation also shows us that the two poles of an antithesis, like positive and negative, are just as inseparable from each other as they are opposed, and that despite *all* their opposition they mutually penetrate each other. It is just the same with cause and effect; these are conceptions which only have validity in their application to a particular case as such, but when we consider the particular case in its general connection with the world as a whole they merge and dissolve in the conception of universal action and interaction, in which causes and effects are constantly changing places, and what is now or here an effect becomes there or then a cause and vice versa.

None of these processes and methods of thought fits into the frame of metaphysical thinking. But for dialectics, which grasps things and their images, ideas, essentially in their interconnection, in their sequence, their movement, their birth and death, such processes as those mentioned above are so many corroborations of its own method of treatment. Nature is the test of dialectics, and it must be said for modern natural science that it has furnished extremely rich and daily increasing materials for this test, and has thus proved that in the last analysis nature's process is dialectical and not metaphysical; that she does not move in the eternal oneness of a perpetually repeated cycle, but goes through a real historical evolution. Here, before all others, mention should be made of Darwin, who dealt the metaphysical conception of nature the heaviest blow by his proof that the whole of organic nature today, plants, animals and therefore also man, is the product of a process of evolution which has gone on through millions of years. But the scientists who have learned to think dialectically are still few and far between, and hence the conflict between the discoveries made and the old traditional mode of thought. . . .

[The] newer German philosophy culminated in the Hegelian system, in which for the first time—and this is its great merit—the whole natural, historical and spiritual world was presented as a process, that is, as in constant motion, change, transformation and development; and the attempt was made to show the internal interconnections in this motion and development. From this standpoint the history of mankind no longer appeared as a confused whirl of senseless deeds of violence, all equally condemnable before the judgment seat of the now matured philosophic reason, and best forgotten as quickly as possible, but as the process of development of humanity itself. It now became the task of thought to follow the gradual stages of this process through all its devious ways, and to trace out the inner regularities running through all its apparently fortuitous phenomena.

That Hegel did not succeed in this task is here immaterial. His epochmaking service was that he propounded it. It is indeed a task which no individual will ever be able to solve. Although Hegel—with Saint-Simon—was the most encyclopedic mind of his age, yet he was limited, in the first place, by the necessarily restricted compass of his own knowledge, and, secondly, by the similarly restricted scope and depth of the knowledge and ideas of his age. But there was also a third factor. Hegel was an idealist, that is to say, the thoughts within his mind were to him not the more or less abstract images of real things and processes, but on the contrary, things and their development were to him only the images made real of the "idea" existing somewhere or other already before the world existed. This mode of thought placed everything on its head, and completely reversed the real connections of things in the world. And although Hegel grasped correctly and with insight many individual interconnections, yet, for the reasons just given, there is also much that in point of detail also is botched, artificial, labored, in a word, wrong. The Hegelian system as such was a colossal miscarriage—but it was also the last of its kind. It suffered, in fact, from an internal and insoluble contradiction. On the one hand, its basic assumption was the historical outlook that human history is a process of evolution, which by its very nature cannot find intellectual finality in the discovery of any so-called absolute truth; but on the other hand, it laid claim to being the very sum total of precisely this absolute truth. A system of natural and historical knowledge which is all-embracing and final for all time is in contradiction to the fundamental laws of dialectical thinking; which, however, far from excluding, on the contrary includes, the idea that the systematic knowledge of the external universe can make giant strides from generation to generation.

The realization of the entire incorrectness of previous German idealism led necessarily to materialism, but, it must be noted, not to the simple metaphysical and exclusively mechanical materialism of the eighteenth century. Instead of the simple and naïvely revolutionary rejection of all previous history, modern materialism sees history as the process of the evolution of humanity, and its own problem as the discovery of the laws of motion of this process. . . . Modern materialism embraces the more recent advances of natural science, according to which nature also has its history in time, the celestial bodies, like the organic species which under favorable circumstances people them, coming into being and passing away. . . . In both cases modern materialism is essentially dialectical, and no longer needs any philosophy standing above the other sciences. As soon as each separate science is required to get clarity as to its position in the great totality of things and of our knowledge of things, a special science dealing with this totality is superfluous. What still independently survives of all former philosophy is the science of thought and its laws—formal logic and dialectics. Everything else is merged in the positive science of nature and history.

While, however, the revolution in the conception of nature could only be carried through to the extent that research furnished the corresponding positive materials of knowledge, already much earlier certain historical facts had occurred which led to a decisive change in the conception of history. . . . The class struggle between proletariat and bourgeoisie came to the front in the history of the most advanced European countries, in proportion to the development there, on the one hand, of large-scale industry, and on the other, of the newly won political domination of the bourgeoisie. Facts more and more forcibly stamped as lies the teachings of bourgeois economics as to the identity of the interests of capital and labor, as to the universal harmony and universal prosperity that free competition brings. All these things could no longer be ignored, any more than the French and English socialism which was their theoretical, even though extremely imperfect, expression. But the old idealist conception of history, which was not yet displaced, knew nothing of class struggles based on material interests, in fact knew nothing at all of material interests; production and all economic relations appeared in it only as incidental, subordinate elements in the "history of civilization."

The new facts made imperative a new examination of all past history, and then it was seen that *all* past history, with the exception of primitive conditions, was the history of class struggles, that these warring classes of society are always the products of the conditions of production and exchange, in a word, of the *economic* conditions of their time; that therefore the economic structure of society always forms the real basis from which, in the last analysis, is to be explained the whole superstructure of legal and political institutions, as well as of the religious, philosophical, and other conceptions of each historical period. Hegel had freed the conception of history from metaphysics, he had made it dialectical—but his conception of history was essentially idealistic. Now idealism was driven from its last refuge, the philosophy of history; now a materialist conception of history was propounded, and the way found to explain man's consciousness by his being, instead of, as heretofore, his being by his consciousness.

Henceforward socialism no longer appeared as the accidental discovery of this or that brilliant mind, but as the necessary outcome of the struggle between two historically developed classes—the proletariat and the bourgeoisie. Its task was no longer to manufacture a system of society as perfect as possible, but to investigate the historical, economic succession of events from which these classes and their antagonism had of necessity sprung and to discover in the economic position thus created the means for solving the conflict. But the socialism of earlier days was just as incompatible with this materialist conception of history as the French materialist conception of nature was with dialectics and modern natural science. It is true that the earlier socialism criticized the existing capitalist mode of production and its consequences, but it could not explain them, and so also could not get the mastery over them; it could only simply reject them as evil. . . . But what had to be done was to show this capitalist mode of production on the one hand in its historical sequence and in its inevitability for a definite historical period, and therefore also the inevitability of its downfall; and on the other hand also to lay bare its essential character, which was still hidden. This was done by the discovery of *surplus value*. It was shown that the appropriation of unpaid labor is the basic form of the capitalist mode of production and of the exploitation of the worker effected through it; that even if the capitalist buys the labor power of his laborer at its full value as a commodity on the market, he yet extracts more value from it than he paid for; and that in the ultimate analysis this surplus value forms those sums of value from which are heaped up the constantly increasing masses of capital in the hands of the possessing classes. The process both of capitalist production and of the production of capital was explained.

These two great discoveries, the materialist conception of history and the revelation of the secret of capitalist production by means of surplus value, we owe to Marx. With these discoveries socialism became a science, which had in the first place to be developed in all its details and relations.

2. ENGELS:
THE BASIC CONCEPTS OF
DIALECTICAL MATERIALISM

The following selection, taken from Engels's Ludwig Feuerbach and the Close of Classical German Philosophy *(1888), presents in detail his ideas on the nature of philosophy and of the "epochal significance" of Hegel. This crucial text includes Engels's most lucid presentation of "materialist dialectics" (the term "dialectical materialism" was first used by G. V. Plekhanov in 1891) and becomes the basis of all subsequent "Orthodox" Marxist philosophy. We shall see many of Engels's characteristic arguments reappear in the works of Lenin and Stalin, among others, as Engels's return to philosophy, as opposed to Marx's rejection and transcendence of it, becomes a central dogma of later "Marxism."*

In one sense, Engels argues that philosophy must abandon its pretensions to absolute knowledge and yield to the progressively increasing relative truths of the particular sciences. Philosophy's role is thus reduced by Engels from that of the critical use of reason in social existence (which had been Marx's conception of what is valid in philosophy) to that of the guardian of the laws of formal logic and dialectics. Yet, Engels also argues that Marxism is a form of ontological materialism, and thus he returns to the dogmatic standpoint characteristic of pre-Kantian speculative metaphysics which Marx, following the criticisms of Hegel and Feuerbach, had declared to be purely ideological.[1] Thus Engels's conception of philosophy is thoroughly at odds with that of Marx, for whom philosophy (even when he had accepted it as legitimate) is essentially criticism rather than speculation and which Marx, of course, eventually abandoned as ideological. For Marx, a dialectical philosophy is one which contrasts the actual with the rational in order to find the actual wanting and which thereby guides the struggles of

SOURCE: From Friedrich Engels, *Ludwig Feuerbach and the Close of Classical German Philosophy*, in Karl Marx and Friedrich Engels, *Selected Works*, Vol. I. (Moscow: Co-operative Publishing Society of Foreign Workers in the U.S.S.R., 1935).

1. Cf. pp. 17–28, above.

actuality toward rational ends. But Engels simply turns to a dogmatic materialism.

Engels's materialism, as presented below in his famous "two great camps" argument, contains important inconsistencies. "Materialism" is defined in that place variously as: (1) the conception of "nature as the sole reality"; (2) the view that "nothing exists outside nature and man"; (3) the belief in the "primacy" of nature over spirit; (4) the view that "mind itself is merely the highest product of matter"; (5) the conception of economics as the foundation of philosophy; (6) the relentless decision "to sacrifice every idealist fancy which could not be brought into harmony with the facts conceived in their own and not in a fantastic connection," which is to be "carried through consistently . . . in all domains of knowledge"; and (7) the "copy" theory of perception, such that the "materialist" comprehension of concepts is defined as viewing them as "images of real things". That is, Engels here defines "materialism" variously as (1) a consistent naturalistic ontology; (2) an inconsistent naturalism, i.e., a dualism, implying that man is a being apart from nature; (3) a dualism claiming the priority of nature over spirit, it never being specified whether this priority is ontological, epistemological, or both; (4) an epiphenomenalism; (5) a "vulgar Marxism," i.e., the reduction of all social products to their alleged economic causes; (6) a dogmatic reductionism; and (7) a passive sensationism. We simply wish to note the seventh of these: it is the basis of the naïvely "materialist" (i.e., mechanistic) epistemology that was later to be adopted by Lenin and which thus serves as the starting point of all Soviet Marxist philosophy.

HEGEL AND HIS INFLUENCE

. . . No philosophical proposition has earned more gratitude from narrow-minded governments and wrath from equally narrow-minded liberals than Hegel's famous statement: "All that is real is rational: and all that is rational is real." That was tangibly a sanctification of things that be, a philosophical benediction bestowed upon despotism, police government . . . and censorship. That is how Frederick William III and his subjects understood it. But according to Hegel everything that exists is certainly not also *real,* without further qualification. For Hegel the attribute of reality belongs only to that which at the same time is necessary: "The reality proves itself to be the necessary in the course of its development." A particular governmental act— Hegel himself cites the example of "a certain tax regulation"—is therefore for him by no means real without qualification. That which is necessary, however, proves itself in the last resort to be also rational; and, applied to the Prussian state of that time, the Hegelian proposition therefore merely means: this state is rational, it corresponds to reason insofar as it is necessary; and if it nevertheless appears to us to be evil, but still, in spite of its evil character, it continues to exist, then the evil character of the government is explained and justified by the corresponding evil character of the subjects. The Prussians of that day had the government that they deserved.

Now, according to Hegel, reality is, however, in no way an attribute of any given state of affairs, social or political, in all circumstances and for all time . . . in the course of development, all that was previously real becomes unreal, loses its necessity, its right of existence, its rationality. And in the place of moribund reality comes a new reality capable of living—peacefully if the old has enough intelligence to go to its death without a struggle: forcibly if it resists this necessity. Thus the Hegelian proposition turns into its opposite through Hegelian dialectics itself: All that is real in the sphere of human history becomes irrational in the process of time and is therefore irrational already by its destination, is tainted beforehand with irrationality, and everything which is rational in the minds of men is destined to become real, however much it may contradict the apparent reality of existing conditions. In accordance with all the rules of the Hegelian method of thought, the proposition of the rationality of everything which is real resolves itself into the other proposition: All that exists deserves to perish.

But precisely here lay the true significance and the revolutionary character of the Hegelian philosophy, that it once and for all dealt the deathblow to the finality of all products of human thought and action. Truth, the cognition of which is the business of philosophy, became in the hands of Hegel no longer an aggregate of finished dogmatic statements, which once discovered, had merely to be learned by heart. Truth lay now in the process of cognition itself, in the long historical development of science, which mounts from lower to ever higher levels of knowledge without ever reaching, by discovering so-called absolute truth, a point at which it can proceed no further and where it would have nothing more to do than to fold its hands and admire the absolute truth to which it had attained. And what holds good for the realm of philosophic knowledge holds good also for that of every other kind of knowledge and also for practical affairs. Just as knowledge is unable to reach a perfected termination in a perfect, ideal condition of humanity, so is history unable to do so; a perfect society, a perfect "state," are things which can only exist in imagination. On the contrary, all successive historical situations are only transitory stages in the endless course of development of human society from the lower to the higher. Each stage is necessary, therefore justified for the time and conditions to which it owes its origin. But in the newer and higher conditions which gradually develop in its own bosom, each loses its validity and justification. It must give way to a higher form which will also in its turn decay and perish. . . . It reveals the transitory character of everything and in everything; nothing can endure before it except the uninterrupted process of becoming and of passing away, of endless ascendency from the lower to the higher. And dialectical philosophy itself is nothing more than the mere reflection of this process in the thinking brain. It has, of course, also a conservative side: it recognizes that definite stages of knowledge and society are justified for their time and circumstances. . . . The conservatism of this mode of outlook is relative; its revolutionary character is absolute—the only absolute it admits. . . .

But what must, in fact, be said here is this: that in Hegel the above development is not to be found in such precision. It is a necessary conclusion from his method, but one which he himself never drew with such explicitness. And this, indeed, for the simple reason that he was compelled to make a system, and, in accordance with all the traditional requirements, a system of philosophy must conclude with some sort of absolute truth. . . . In this way, however, the whole dogmatic content of the Hegelian system is declared to be absolute truth, in contradiction to his dialectical method, which dissolves all dogmatism. Thus the revolutionary side becomes smothered beneath the overgrowth of the conservative side. . . .

But all this did not prevent the Hegelian system from covering an incomparably greater domain than any earlier system; nor from developing in this domain a wealth of thought which is astounding even today. . . . And as he was not only a creative genius but also a man of encyclopedic erudition he played an epoch-making role in every sphere. It is self-evident that owing to the needs of the "system" he very often had to resort to those forced constructions about which his pigmy opponents make such a terrible fuss even today. But these constructions are only the frame and scaffolding of his work. If one does not loiter here needlessly, but presses on further into the immense building, one finds innumerable treasures which today still possess undiminished value. With all philosophers it is precisely the "system" which is perishable; and for the simple reason that it springs from an imperishable desire of the human mind—the desire to overcome all contradictions. But if all contradictions are once and for all disposed of, we shall have arrived at so-called absolute truth: world history will be at an end. And yet it has to continue, although there is nothing more left for it to do—thus, a new insoluble contradiction arises. As soon as we have once realized—and in the long run no one has helped us to realize it more than Hegel himself—that the task of philosophy thus stated means nothing but the task that a single philosopher should accomplish that which can only be accomplished by the entire human race in its progressive development—as soon as we realize that, there is an end of all philosophy in the hitherto accepted sense of the word. One leaves alone "absolute truth," which is unattainable along this path or by any single individual; instead, one pursues attainable, relative truths along the path of the positive sciences, and the summation of their results by means of dialectical thinking. At any rate, with Hegel philosophy comes to an end: on the one hand, because in his system he comprehended its whole development in the most splendid fashion; and on the other hand, because, even if unconsciously, he showed us the way out of the labyrinth of "systems" to real positive knowledge of the world.

One can imagine what a tremendous effect this Hegelian system must have produced in the philosophy-tinged atmosphere of Germany. It was a trumphal procession which lasted for decades and which by no means came to a standstill on the death of Hegel. On the contrary, from 1830 to 1840 Hegelianism reigned most exclusively, and to a greater or less extent infected even its opponents. . . .

We will not go into the decomposition process of the Hegelian school. More important for us is the following: the main body of the most determined Young Hegelians was, by the practical necessities of its fight against positive religion, driven back to Anglo-French materialism. This brought it into conflict with its school system. While materialism conceives nature as the sole reality, nature in the Hegelian system represents merely the "alienation" of the absolute idea, so to say, a degradation of the idea. In all circumstances thinking and its thought-product, the idea, is here the primary, nature the derived element, which only exists at all by the condescension of the idea. And in this contradiction they [i.e., the followers of Hegel] floundered as well or as ill as they could.

Then came Feuerbach's *Essence of Christianity*. With one blow it pulverized the contradiction, in that without circumlocutions it placed materialism on the throne again. Nature exists independently of all philosophy. It is the foundation upon which we human beings, ourselves products of nature, have grown up. Nothing exists outside nature and man, and the higher beings our religious fantasies have created are only the fantastic reflection of our own essence.

The spell was broken. The "system" was exploded and cast aside. And the contradiction, shown to exist only in our imagination, was dissolved. One must himself have experienced the liberating effect of this book to get an idea of it. Enthusiasm was general; we all became at once Feuerbachians. How enthusiastically Marx greeted the new conception, and in spite of all critical reservations he was influenced by it. . . .

IDEALISM AND MATERIALISM

The great basic question of all philosophy, especially of modern philosophy, is that concerning the relation of thinking and being. From the very early times when men, still completely ignorant of the structure of their own bodies, under the stimulus of dream apparitions came to believe that their thinking and sensation were not activities of their bodies, but of a distinct soul which inhabits the body and leaves it at death . . . men have been driven to reflect about the relation between this soul and the outside world. If in death it took leave of the body and lived on, there was no occasion to invent yet another distinct death for it. . . . Not religious desire for consolation, but the quandary arising from the common universal ignorance of what to do with this soul (once its existence had been accepted) after the death of the body—led in a general way to the tedious notion of personal immortality. In an exactly similar manner the first gods arose through the personification of natural forces. And these gods in the further development of religions assumed more and more an extramundane form, until finally by a process of abstraction . . . occurring naturally in the course of man's intellectual development, out of the many more or less limited and mutually limiting gods there arose in the minds of men the idea of the one exclusive god of the monotheistic religions.

Thus the question of the relation of thinking to being, the relation of spirit to nature—the paramount question of the whole of philosophy—has, no less than all religion, its roots in the narrow-minded and ignorant notions of savagery. But this question could for the first time be put forward in its whole acuteness, could achieve its full significance, only after European society had awakened from the long hibernation of the Christian Middle Ages. The question of the position of thinking in relation to being, a question which, by the way, had played a great part also in the scholasticism of the Middle Ages, the question: which is primary, spirit or nature—that question, in relation to the Church, was sharpened into this: "Did god create the world or has the world been in existence eternally?"

The answers which the philosophers gave to this question split them into two great camps. Those who asserted the primacy of spirit to nature and, therefore, in the last instance, assumed world creation in some form or other—and among the philosophers, Hegel, for example, this creation often becomes still more intricate and impossible than in Christianity—comprised the camp of idealism. The others, who regarded nature as primary, belong to the various schools of materialism.

These two expressions, idealism and materialism, primarily signify nothing more than this; and here also they are not used in any other sense. What confusion arises when some other meaning is put into them will be seen below.

But the question of the relation of thinking and being has yet another side: in what relation do our thoughts about the world surrounding us stand to this world itself? Is our thinking capable of the cognition of the real world? Are we able in our ideas and notions of the real world to produce a correct reflection of reality? In philosophical language this question is called the question of the "identity of thinking and being," and the overwhelming majority of philosophers give an affirmative answer to this question. With Hegel, for example, its affirmation is self-evident; for what we perceive in the real world is precisely its thought content—that which makes the world a gradual realization of the absolute idea, which absolute idea has existed somewhere from eternity, independent of the world and before the world. But it is manifest without more ado that thought can know a content which is from the outset a thought-content. It is equally manifest that what is here to be proved is already tacitly contained in the presupposition. . . .

In addition there is yet another set of different philosophers—those who question the possibility of any cognition (or at least of an exhaustive cognition) of the world. To them, among the moderns, belong Hume and Kant, and they have played a very important role in philosophical development. What is decisive in the refutation of this view has already been said by Hegel—insofar as this was possible from an idealist standpoint. The materialistic additions made by Feuerbach are more ingenious than profound. The most telling refutation of this as of all other philosophical fancies is practice, *viz.*, experiment and industry. If we are able to prove the correctness of our conception of a natural process by making it ourselves, bringing it into being out of its conditions and using it for our own purposes into the bargain, then there is an end of the Kantian incomprehensible "thing-in-itself." The chemical substances produced in the bodies of plants and animals remained just such "things-in-themselves" until organic chemistry began to produce them one after another, whereupon the "thing-in-itself" became a thing for us, as, for instance, alizarin, the coloring matter of the madder, which we no longer trouble to grow in the madder roots in the field, but produce much more cheaply and simply from coal tar. For three hundred years the Copernican solar system was a hypothesis with a hundred, a thousand, or ten thousand chances to one in its favor, but still always a hypothesis. But when Leverrier, by means of the data provided by this system, not only deduced the necessity of the existence of an unknown planet, but also calculated the position in the heavens which this planet must necessarily occupy, and when Galle really found this planet, the Copernican system was proved. . . .

But during this long period from Descartes to Hegel and from Hobbes to Feuerbach, the philosophers were by no means impelled, as they thought they were, solely by the force of pure reason. On the contrary, what really pushed them forward was the powerful and ever more rapidly onrushing progress of natural science and industry. Among the materialists this was plain on the surface, but the idealist systems also filled themselves more and more with a materialist content and attempted pantheistically to reconcile the antithesis between mind and matter. Thus, ultimately, the Hegelian system represents merely a materialism idealistically turned upside down in method and content. . . .

The course of evolution of Feuerbach is that of a Hegelian—a never quite orthodox Hegelian, it is true—into a materialist; an evolution which at a definite stage necessitates a complete rupture with the idealist system of his predecessor. With irresistible force Feuerbach is finally forced to the realization that the Hegelian premundane existence of the "absolute idea," the "preexistence of the logical categories" before the world existed, is nothing more than the fantastic survival of the belief in the existence of an extramundane creator; that the material, sensuously perceptible world to which we ourselves belong is the only reality; and that our consciousness and thinking, however suprasensuous they may seem, are the product of a material, bodily organ, the brain. Matter is not a product of mind, but mind itself is merely the highest product of matter. This is, of course, pure materialism. But, having got so far, Feuerbach stops short. He cannot overcome the customary philosophical prejudice not against the thing but against the name materialism. . . .

Feuerbach lumps together the materialism that is a general world outlook resting upon a definite conception of the relation between matter and mind, and the special form in which this world outlook was expressed at a definite stage of historical development, *viz.,* in the eighteenth century. . . .

The materialism of the last century was predominantly mechanical, because at that time, of all natural sciences, mechanics and indeed only the mechanics of solid bodies—celestial and terrestrial in short, the mechanics of gravity, had come to any definite close. Chemistry at that time existed only in its infantile, phlogistic form. Biology still lay in swaddling clothes; vegetable and animal organisms had been only roughly examined and were explained as the result of purely mechanical causes. As the animal was to Descartes, so was man a machine to the materialists of the eighteenth century. This exclusive application of the standards of mechanics to processes of a chemical and organic nature—in which processes, it is true, the laws of mechanics are also valid, but are pushed into the background by other and higher laws—constitutes a specific but at that time inevitable limitation of classical French materialism.

The second specific limitation of this materialism lay in its inability to comprehend the universe as a process—as matter developing in a historical process. This was in accordance with the level of the natural science of that time, and with the metaphysical, i.e., antidialectical manner of philosophizing connected with it. Nature, it was known, was in constant motion. But according to the ideas of that time, this motion turned eternally in a circle and therefore never moved from the spot; it produced the same results over and over again. This conception was at that time inevitable. The Kantian theory of the origin of the solar system had been put forward but recently and was regarded merely as a curiosity. The history of the development of the earth, geology, was still totally unknown, and the conception that the animate natural beings of today are the result of a long sequence of development from the simple to the complex could not at that time scientifically be put forward at all. The unhistorical view of nature was therefore inevitable. . . .

This same unhistorical conception prevailed also in the domain of history. Here the struggle against the remnants of the

Middle Ages blurred the view. The Middle Ages were regarded as a mere interruption of history by a thousand years of universal barbarism. The great progress made in the Middle Ages—the extension of the area of European culture, the bringing into existence there of great nations, capable of survival, and finally the enormous technical progress of the fourteenth and fifteenth centuries—all this was not seen. Consequently a rational insight into the great historical interconnections was made impossible, and history served at best as a collection of examples and illustrations for the use of philosophers. . . .

Feuerbach is quite correct in asserting that the exclusively natural-scientific materialism was indeed "the foundation of the edifice of human . . . knowledge, but . . . not . . . the building itself." For we live not only in nature but also in human society, and this also no less than nature has its history of development and its science. It was therefore a question of bringing the science of society (i.e., the sum total of the so-called historical and philosophical sciences) into harmony with the materialist foundation, and of reconstructing it thereupon. . . .

DIALECTICAL MATERIALISM

. . . Out of the dissolution of the Hegelian school, there developed the only [tendency] which has borne real fruit. And this tendency is essentially connected with the name of Marx.

The separation from the Hegelian school was here also the result of a return to the materialist standpoint. That means it was resolved to comprehend the real world—nature and history—just as it presents itself to everyone who approaches it free from preconceived idealist fancies. It was decided relentlessly to sacrifice every idealist fancy which could not be brought into harmony with the facts conceived in their own and not in a fantastic connection. And materialism means nothing more than this. But here the materialistic world outlook was taken really seriously for the first time and was carried through consistently—at least in its basic features—in all domains of knowledge concerned.

Hegel was not simply put aside. On the contrary, one started out from his revolutionary side described above, from the dialectical method. But in its Hegelian form this method was unusable. According to Hegel, dialectics is the self-development of the concept. The absolute concept does not only exist—where unknown—from eternity, it is also the actual living soul of the whole existing world. It develops into itself through all the preliminary stages which are treated at length in the *Logic* and which are all included in it. Then it "alienates" itself by changing into nature, where, without consciousness of itself, disguised as the necessity of nature, it goes through a new development and finally comes again to self-consciousness in man. This self-consciousness then elaborates itself again in history from the crude form until finally the absolute concept again comes to itself completely in the Hegelian philosophy. According to Hegel, therefore, the dialectical development apparent in nature and history, i.e., the causal interconnection of the progressive movement from the lower to the higher, which asserts itself through all zigzag movements and temporary setbacks, is only a miserable copy of the self-movement of the concept going on from eternity, no one knows where, but at all events independently of any thinking human brain. This ideological reversal had to be done away with. We comprehended the concepts in our heads once more materialistically—as images of real things instead of regarding the real things as images of this or that stage of development of the absolute concept. Thus dialectics reduced itself to the science of the general laws of motion—both of the external world and of human thought—two sets of laws which are identical in substance, but differ in their expression insofar as the human mind can apply them consciously, while in nature and also up to now for the most part in human history, these laws assert themselves unconsciously in the form of external necessity in the midst of an endless series of seeming accidents. Thereby the dialectic of the concept itself became merely the conscious reflex of the dialectical motion of the real world and the dialectic of Hegel was placed upon its head; or rather, turned off its head, on which it was standing before, and placed upon its feet again. . . .

In this way, however, the revolutionary side of Hegelian philosophy was again taken up and at the same time freed from the idealist trammels which in Hegel's hands had prevented its consistent execution. The great basic thought that the world is not to be comprehended as a complex of ready-made *things*, but as a complex of *processes*, in which the things apparently stable no less than their mind-images in our heads, the concepts, go through an uninterrupted change of coming into being and passing away, in which, in spite of all seeming accidents and of all temporary retrogression, a progressive development asserts itself in the end. . . . If . . . investigation always proceeds from this standpoint, the demand for final solutions and eternal truths ceases once for all; one is always conscious of the necessary limitation of all acquired knowledge, of the fact that it is conditioned by the circumstances in which it was acquired. On the other hand, one no longer permits oneself to be imposed upon by the antitheses, insuperable for the still common old metaphysics, between true and false, good and bad, identical and different, necessary and accidental. One knows that these antitheses have only a relative validity; that that which is recognized now as true has also its latent false side which will later manifest itself, just as that which is now regarded as false has also its true side by virtue of which it could previously have been regarded as true. One knows that what is maintained to be necessary is composed of sheer accidents and that the so-called accidental is the form behind which necessity hides itself—and so on.

The old method of investigation and thought which Hegel calls "metaphysical," which preferred to investigate *things* as given, as fixed and stable, a method the relics of which still strongly haunt people's minds, had a good deal of historical justification in its day. It was necessary first to examine things before it was possible to examine processes. One had first to know what a particular thing was before one could observe the changes going on in connection with it. And such was the case with natural science. The old metaphysics which accepted things as finished objects arose from a natural science which investigated dead and living things as finished objects. But when this investigation had progressed so far that it became possible to take the decisive step forward of transition to the systematic investigation of the changes which these things undergo in nature itself, then the last hour of the old metaphysics sounded in the realm of philosophy also. And, in fact, while natural science up to the end of the last century was predominantly a *collecting* science, a science of finished things, in our century it is essentially a *classifying science,* a science of the processes, of the origin and development of these things and of the interconnection which binds all these natural processes into one great whole. Physiology, which investigates the processes occurring in plant and animal organisms; embryology, which deals with the development of individual organisms from germ to maturity; geology, which investigates the gradual formation of the earth's surface—all these are the offspring of our century.

But, above all, there are three great discoveries which have enabled our knowledge of the interconnection of natural processes to advance by leaps and bound: first, the discovery of the cell as the unit from whose multiplication and differentiation the whole plant and animal body develops—so that not only is the development and growth of all higher organisms recognized to proceed according to a single general law, but also, in the capacity of the cell to change, the way is pointed out by which organisms can change their species and thus go through a more than individual development. Second, the transformation of energy, which has demonstrated that all the so-called forces operative in the first instance in inorganic nature—mechanical force and its complement, so-called potential energy, heat, radiation (light or radiant heat) , electricity, magnetism and chemical energy—are different forms of manifestation of universal motion, which pass into one another in definite proportions so that in place of a certain quantity of the one which disappears, a certain quantity of another makes its appearance and thus the whole motion of nature is reduced to this incessant process of transformation from one form into another. Finally, the proof which Darwin first developed in connected form that the stock of organic products of nature surrounding us today, including mankind, is the result of a long process of evolution from a few original unicellular germs, and that these again have arisen from protoplasm or albumen which came into existence by chemical means.

Thanks to these three great discoveries and the other immense advances in natural science, we have now arrived at the point where we can demonstrate as a whole the interconnection between the processes in nature not only in particular spheres but also in the interconnection of these particular spheres themselves, and so can present in an approximately systematic form a comprehensive view of the interconnection in nature by means of the facts provided by empirical natural science itself. . . . Today, when one needs to comprehend the results of natural scientific investigation only dialectically, that is, in the sense of their own interconnections, in order to arrive at a "system of nature" sufficient for our time; when the dialectical character of this interconnection is forcing itself against their will even into the metaphysically trained minds of the natural scientists, today this natural philosophy is finally disposed of. Every attempt at resurrecting it would be not only superfluous but a *step backwards*.

But what is true of nature, which is hereby recognized also as a historical process of development, is also true of the history of society in all its branches and of the totality of all sciences which occupy themselves with things human (and divine). Here, too, the philosophy of history, of law, of religion, etc., has consisted in the substitution of an interconnection fabricated in the mind of the philosopher for the actual interconnection to be demonstrated in the events; and in the comprehension of history as a whole as well as in its separate parts, as the gradual realization of ideas. . . . Here, therefore, just as in the realm of nature, it was necessary to do away with these fabricated, artificial interconnections by the discovery of the real ones; a task which ultimately amounts to the discovery of the general laws of motion which assert themselves as the ruling ones in the history of human society.

In one point, however, the history of the development of society proves to be essentially different from that of nature. In nature—insofar as we ignore man's reactions upon nature—there are only blind unconscious agencies acting upon one another and out of whose interplay the general law comes into operation. . . . In the history of society, on the other hand, the actors are all endowed with consciousness, are men acting with deliberation or passion, working toward definite goals; nothing happens without a conscious purpose, without an intended aim. But this distinction . . . cannot alter the fact, that the course of history is governed by inner general laws. For here, also, on the whole, in spite of the consciously desired aims of all individuals, accident apparently reigns on the surface. That which is willed happens but rarely; in the majority of instances the numerous desired ends cross and conflict with one another, or these ends themselves are from the outset incapable of realization or the means of attaining them are insufficient. Thus the conflict of innumerable individual wills and individual actions in the domain of history produces a state of affairs entirely analogous to that in the realm of unconscious nature. The ends of the actions are intended, but the results which actually follow from these actions are not intended; or when they do seem to correspond to the end intended, they ultimately have consequences quite other than those intended. Historical events thus appear on the whole to be likewise governed by chance. But where on the surface accident holds sway, there actually it is always governed by inner, hidden laws and it is only a matter of discovering these laws.

Men make their own history, whatever its outcome may be, in that each person follows his own consciously desired end, and it is precisely the resultant of these many wills operating in different directions and of their manifold effects upon the outer world that constitutes history. Thus it is also a question of what the many individuals desire. The will is determined by passion or deliberation. But the levers which immediately determine passion or deliberation are of very different kinds. Partly they may be external objcts, partly ideal motives, ambition, "enthusiasm for truth and justice," personal hatred or even purely individual whims of all kinds. . . . But, on the one hand, we have seen that the many individual wills active in history for the most part produce results quite other than those they intended—often quite the opposite; their motives therefore in relation to the total result are likewise of only secondary significance. On the other hand, the further question arises: What driving forces in turn stand behind these motives? What are the historical causes which transform themselves into these motives in the brains of the actors?

The old materialism never put this question to itself. Its conception of history, insofar as it has one at all, is therefore essentially pragmatic; it judges everything according to the motives of the action. . . .

3. ENGELS:
THE THREE LAWS
OF DIALECTICS

This selection, taken from Engels's unfinished Dialectics of Nature, *illustrates his attempt to develop a comprehensive ontology which would allegedly demonstrate that all natural processes occur according to the three "laws" of dialectics: (1) the law of the transformation of quantity into quality and vice versa; (2) the law of the interpenetration of opposites; and (3) the law of the negation of the negation. These three "laws" are then illustrated with examples taken from the natural science of Engels's day—with which, incidentally, he was thoroughly acquainted. The obvious purpose of these examples is to show that all natural science unknowingly presupposes these three dialectical laws, thereby making possible a "scientific" ontology from which the dialectics of history (i.e., the materialist interpretation of history) could be derived, thereby endowing the various "Marxist" predictions of future history with "scientific" status. In so conceiving the materialist interpretation of history as derivative of his materialist ontology, Engels helps to further undermine Marx's humanism with respect to historical development and social struggle. Without the humanist perspective which underlies all of Marx's work, however, communism becomes just another in a succession of social systems and thereby ceases to be the decisive overcoming of alienation and the start of man's "true" history as Marx conceived it.*

It must be conceded, however, that Engels's enumeration of the three "laws" of dialectics represents with a fair degree of accuracy the dialectical elements which were presupposed, without formal exposition, by Marx. What is strange, however, from the Marxian perspective, is the attempt to apply these to nature taken in itself, i.e., independently of human social appropriation through labor. Engels overlooks the fact that Marx considered such an uncritical naturalism as decisively superseded by the materialist interpretation of history, rather than as presupposed by it, for it is only nature taken as within the horizon of human social appropriation (i.e., labor) which is considered as meaningful by Marx. Marx's entire perspective, as has been shown

SOURCE: From Friedrich Engels, *The Dialectics of Nature,* trans. Clemens Dutt (Moscow: Progress Publishers, 1966).

above,[1] *is a humanist one; i.e., it is grounded in human social existence and the latter's basis in labor. The philosophy of nature, whether in the idealist form of Hegel or in the materialist form of Engels, is, for Marx, simply another instance of philosophy, i.e., ideology.*

It is from the history of nature and human society that the laws of dialectics are abstracted. For they are nothing but the most general laws of these two aspects of historical development, as well as of thought itself. And indeed they can be reduced in the main to three:

The law of the transformation of quantity into quality and vice versa;

The law of the interpenetration of opposites;

The law of the negation of the negation.

All three are developed by Hegel in his idealist fashion as mere laws of *thought:* the first, in the first part of his *Logic,* in the Doctrine of Being; the second fills the whole of the second and by far the most important part of his *Logic,* the Doctrine of Essence; finally the third figures as the fundamental law for the construction of the whole system. The mistake lies in the fact that these laws are foisted on nature and history as laws of thought, and not deduced from them. This is the source of the whole forced and often outrageous treatment; the universe, willy-nilly, has to conform to a system of thought which itself is only the product of a definite stage of evolution of human thought. If we turn the thing around, then everything becomes simple, and the dialectical laws that look so extremely mysterious in idealist philosophy at once become simple and clear as noonday. . . .

We are not concerned here with writing a handbook of dialectics, but only with showing that the dialectical laws are real laws of development of nature, and therefore are valid also for theoretical natural science. Hence we cannot go into the inner interconnection of these laws with one another.

THE TRANSFORMATION OF QUANTITY INTO QUALITY AND VICE VERSA

For our purpose, we can express this by saying that in nature, in a manner exactly fixed for each individual case, qualitative

1. Cf. pp. 2–11.

changes can only occur by the quantitative addition or quantitative subtraction of matter or motion (so-called energy).

All qualitative differences in nature rest on differences of chemical composition or on different quantities or forms of motion (energy) or, as is almost always the case, on both. Hence it is impossible to alter the quality of a body without addition or subtraction of matter or motion, i.e., without quantitative alteration of the body concerned. In this form, therefore Hegel's mysterious principle appears not only quite rational but even rather obvious.

It is surely hardly necessary to point out that the various allotropic and aggregational states of bodies, because they depend on various groupings of the molecules, depend on greater or lesser amounts of motion communicated to the bodies.

But what about change of form of motion, or so-called energy? If we change heat into mechanical motion or vice versa, is not the quality altered while the quantity remains the same? Quite correct. . . . Change of form of motion is always a process that takes place between at least two bodies, of which one loses a definite amount of motion of one quality (e.g., heat), while the other gains a corresponding quantity of motion of another quality (mechanical motion, electricity, chemical decomposition). Here, therefore, quantity and quality mutually correspond to each other. So far it has not been found possible to convert motion from one form to another inside a single isolated body.

We are concerned here in the first place with nonliving bodies; the same law holds for living bodies, but it operates under very complex conditions and at present quantitative measurement is still often impossible for us.

If we imagine any nonliving body cut up into smaller and smaller portions, at first no qualitative change occurs. But this has a limit: if we succeed, as by evaporation, in obtaining the separate molecules in the free state, then it is true that we can usually divide these still further, yet only with a complete change of quality. The molecule is decomposed into its separate atoms, which have quite different properties from those of the molecule. In the case of molecules composed of different chemical elements, atoms or molecules of these elements themselves make their appearance in the place of the compound molecule; in the case of molecules of elements, the free atoms appear, which exert quite distinct qualitative effects: the free atoms of nascent oxygen are easily able to effect what the atoms of atmospheric oxygen, bound together in the molecule, can never achieve.

But the molecule is also qualitatively different from the mass of the body to which it belongs. It can carry out movements independently of this mass and while the latter remains apparently at rest, e.g., heat vibrations; by means of a change of position and of connection with neighboring molecules it can change the body into an allotrope or a different state of aggregation.

Thus we see that the purely quantitative operation of division has a limit at which it becomes transformed into a qualitative difference: the mass consists solely of molecules, but it is something essentially different from the molecule, just as the latter is different from the atom. It is this difference that is the basis for the separation of mechanics, as the science of heavenly and terrestrial masses, from physics, as the mechanics of molecules, and from chemistry, as the physics of atoms.

In mechanics, no qualities occur; at most, states such as equilibrium, motion, potential energy, which all depend on measurable transference of motion and are themselves capable of quantitative expression. Hence, insofar as qualitative change takes place here, it is determined by a corresponding quantitative change.

In physics, bodies are treated as chemically unalterable or indifferent; we have to do with changes of their molecular states and with the change of form of motion, which in all cases, at least on one of the two sides, brings the molecule into action. Here every change is a transformation of quantity into quality, a consequence of the quantitative change of the amount of motion of one form or another that is inherent in the body or communicated to it.

Similarly, a definite minimum current strength is required to cause the platinum wire of an electric incandescent lamp to glow; and every metal has its temperature of incandescence and fusion, every liquid its definite freezing and boiling point at a given pressure—insofar as our means allow us to produce the temperature required; finally also every gas has its critical point at which it can be liquefied by pressure and cooling. In short, the so-called physical constants are for the most part nothing but designations of the nodal points at which quantitative addition or subtraction of motion produces qualitative change in the state of the body concerned, at which, therefore, quantity is transformed into quality.

The sphere, however, in which the law of nature discovered by Hegel celebrates its most important triumphs is that of chemistry. Chemistry can be termed the science of the qualitative changes of bodies as a result of changed quantitative composition. That was already known to Hegel himself. . . . As in the case of oxygen: if three atoms unite into a molecule, instead of the usual two, we get ozone, a body which is very considerably different from ordinary oxygen in its odor and reactions. And indeed the various proportions in which oxygen combines with nitrogen or sulfur, each of which produces a substance qualitatively different from any of the others! How different is laughing gas (nitrogen monoxide N_2O) from nitric anhydride (nitrogen pentoxide, N_2O_5) ! The first is a gas, the second at ordinary temperatures a solid crystalline substance. And yet the whole difference in composition is that the second contains five times as much oxygen as the first, and between the two of them are three more oxides of nitrogen (NO, N_2O_3, NO_2), each of which is qualitatively different from the first two and from one another.

This is seen still more strikingly in the homologous series of carbon compounds, especially of the simpler hydrocarbons. Of the normal paraffins, the lowest is methane, CH_4; here the four linkages of the carbon atom are saturated by four atoms of hydrogen. The second, ethane, C_2H_6, has two atoms of carbon joined together and the six free linkages are saturated by six atoms of hydrogen. And so it goes on, with C_3H_8, C_4H_{10}, etc. according to the algebraic formula C_nH_{2n+2}, so that by each addition of CH_2 a body is formed that is qualitatively distinct from the preceding one. The three lowest members of the series are gases, the highest known, hexadecane, $C_{16}H_{34}$, is a solid body with a boiling point of 278°C. Exactly the same holds good for the series of primary alcohols with the formula $C_nH_{2n+2}O$, derived (theoretically) from the paraffins, and the series of monobasic fatty acids (formula $C_nH_{2n}O_2$). What qualitative difference can be caused by the quantitative addition of C_3H_6 is taught by experience if we consume ethyl alcohol, C_2H_6O, in any drinkable form without addition of other alcohols, and on another occasion take the same ethyl alcohol but with a slight addition of amyl alcohol, $C_5H_{12}O$, which forms the main constituent of the abominable fusel oil. One's head will certainly be aware of it the next morning, much to its detriment; so that one could even say that the intoxication, and subsequent "morning after" feeling, is also quantity transformed into quality, on the one hand of ethyl alcohol and on the other hand of this added C_3H_6.

In these series we encounter the Hegelian law in yet another form. The lower members permit only of a single mutual arrangement of the atoms. If, however, the number of atoms united into a molecule attains a size definitely fixed for each series, the grouping of the atoms in the molecule can take place in more than one way; so that two or more isomeric substances can be formed, having equal numbers of C, H, and O atoms in the molecule but nevertheless qualitatively distinct from one another. We can even calculate how many such isomers are possible for each member of the series. Thus, in the paraffin series, for C_4H_{10} there are two, for C_5H_{12} there are three; among the higher members the number of possible isomers mounts very rapidly. Hence once again it is the quantitative number of atoms in the molecule that determines the possibility and, insofar as it has been proved, also the actual existence of such qualitatively distinct isomers.

Still more. From the analogy of the substances with which we are acquainted in each of these series, we can draw conclusions as to the physical properties of the still unknown members of the series and, at least for the members immediately following the known ones, predict their properties, boiling point, etc., with fair certainty.

Finally, the Hegelian law is valid not only for compound substances but also for the chemical elements themselves. We now know that "the chemical properties of the elements are a periodic function of their atomic weights" (Roscoe-Schorlemmer, *Ausführliches Lehrbuch der Chemie,* II, p. 823), and that, therefore, their quality is determined by the quantity of their atomic weight. And the test of this has been brilliantly carried out. Mendeleyev proved that various gaps occur in the series of related elements arranged according to atomic weights indicating that here new elements remain to be discovered. He described in advance the general chemical properties of one of these unknown elements, which he termed eka-aluminum, because it follows after aluminum in the series beginning with the latter, and he predicted its approximate specific and atomic weight as well as its atomic volume. A few years later, Lecoq de Boisbaudran actually discovered this element, and Mendelyev's predictions fitted with only very slight discrepancies. Eka-aluminum was realized in gallium (*ibid.*, p. 828). By means of the—unconscious—application of Hegel's law of the transformation of quantity into quality, Mendeleyev achieved a scientific feat which it is not too bold to put on a par with that of Leverrier in calculating the orbit of the until then unknown planet Neptune.

In biology, as in the history of human society, the same law holds good at every step, but we prefer to dwell here on examples from the exact sciences, since here the quantities are accurately measurable and traceable. . . .

THE INTERPENETRATION OF OPPOSITES

Hard and fast lines are incompatible with the theory of evolution. Even the borderline between vertebrates and invertebrates is now no longer rigid, just as little is that between fishes and amphibians, while that between birds and reptiles dwindles more and more every day. Between *Compsognathus* and *Archaeopteryx* only a few intermediate links are wanting, and birds' beaks with teeth crop up in both hemispheres. "Either-or" becomes more and more inadequate. Among lower animals the concept of the individual cannot be established at all sharply. Not only as to whether a particular animal is an individual or a colony, but also where in development *one* individual ceases and the other begins. . . .

For a stage in the outlook on nature where all differences become merged in intermediate steps, and all opposites pass into one another through intermediate links, the old metaphysical method of thought no longer suffices. Dialectics, which likewise knows no hard and fast lines, no unconditional, universally valid "either-or" and which bridges the fixed metaphysical differences, and besides "either-or" recognizes also in the right place "both this—and that" and reconciles the opposites, is the sole method of thought appropriate in the highest degree to this stage. Of course, for everyday use, for the small change of science, the metaphysical categories retain their validity.

The law of identity in the old metaphysical sense is the fundamental law of the old outlook: $a = a$. Each thing is equal to itself. Everything was permanent, the solar system, stars, organisms. This law has been refuted by natural science bit by bit in each separate case, but theoretically it still prevails and is still put forward by the supporters of the old in opposition to the new: a thing cannot simultaneously be itself and something else. And yet the fact that true, concrete identity includes difference, change, has recently been shown in detail by natural science (see above).

Abstract identity, like all metaphysical categories, suffices for *everyday* use, where small dimensions or brief periods of time are in question; the limits within which it is usable differ in almost every case and are determined by the nature of the object; for a planetary system, where in ordinary astronomical calculation the ellipse can be taken as the basic form for practical purposes without error, they are much wider than for an insect that completes its metamorphosis in a few weeks. (Give other examples, e.g., alteration of species, which is reckoned in periods of thousands of years.) For natural science in its comprehensive role, however, even in each single branch, abstract identity is totally inadequate, and although on the whole it has now been abolished in practice, theoretically it still dominates people's minds, and most natural scientists imagine that identity and difference are irreconcilable opposites, instead of one-sided poles which represent the truth only in their reciprocal action, in the inclusion of difference *within* identity.

Dialectics, so-called *objective* dialectics, prevails throughout nature, and so-called subjective dialectics, dialectical thought, is only the reflection of the motion through opposites which asserts itself everywhere in nature, and which by the continual conflict of the opposites and their final passage into one another, or into higher forms, determines the life of nature. Attraction and repulsion. Polarity begins with magnetism; it is exhibited in one and the same body; in the case of electricity it distributes itself over two or more bodies which become oppositely charged. All chemical processes reduce themselves to processes of chemical attraction and repulsion. Finally, in organic life the formation of the cell nucleus is likewise to be regarded as a polarization of the living protein material, and from the simple cell onward the theory of evolution demonstrates how each advance up to the most complicated plant on the one side, and up to man on the other, is effected by the continual conflict between heredity and adaptation. . . .

THE NEGATION OF THE NEGATION

Let us take a grain of barley. Billions of such grains of barley are milled, boiled, and brewed and then consumed. But if such a grain of barley meets with conditions which are normal for it, if it falls on suitable soil, then under the influence of heat and moisture it undergoes a specific change; it germinates; the grain as such ceases to exist, it is negated, and in its place appears the plant which has arisen from it, the negation of the grain. But what is the normal life process of this plant? It grows, flowers, is fertilized and finally once more produces grains of barley, and as soon as these have ripened the stalk dies, is in its turn negated. As a result of this negation of the negation we have once again the original grain of barley, but not as a single unit, but ten-, twenty- or thirty-fold. Species of grain change extremely slowly, and so the barley of today is almost the same as it was a century ago. But if we take a plastic ornamental plant, for example a dahlia or an orchid, and treat the seed and the plant which grows from it according to the gardener's art, we get as a result of this negation of the negation not only more seeds, but also qualitatively improved seeds, which produce more beautiful flowers, and each repetition of this process, each fresh negation of the negation, enhances this process of perfection.

With most insects, this process follows the same lines as in the case of the grain of barley. Butterflies, for example, spring from the egg by a negation of the egg, pass through certain transformations until they reach sexual maturity, pair, and are in turn negated, dying as soon as the pairing process has been completed and the female has laid its numerous eggs. . . . The negation of the negation *really does take place* in both kingdoms of the organic world. Furthermore, the whole of geology is a series of negated negations, a series of successive shatterings of old and deposits of new rock formations. First the original earth crust brought into existence by the cooling of the liquid mass was broken up by oceanic, meteorological, and atmospherico-chemical action, and these fragmented masses were stratified on the ocean bed. Local upheavals of the ocean bed above the surface of the sea subject portions of these first strata once more to the action of rain, the changing temperature of the seasons and the oxygen and carbonic acid of the atmosphere. These same influences act on the molten masses of rock which issue from the interior of the earth, break through the strata, and subsequently cool off. In this way, in the course of millions of centuries, ever new strata are formed and in turn are for the most part destroyed, ever anew serving as material for the formation of new strata. But the result of this process has been a very positive one: the creation of a soil composed of the most varied chemical elements and mechanically fragmented, which makes possible the most abundant and diversified vegetation. . . .

It is the same in history, as well. All civilized peoples begin with the common ownership of the land. With all peoples who have passed a certain primitive stage, this common ownership becomes in the course of the development of agriculture a fetter on production. It is abolished, negated, and after a longer or shorter series of intermediate stages is transformed into private property. But at a higher stage of agricultural development, brought about by private property in land itself, private property conversely becomes a fetter on production, as is the case today with both small and large landownership. The demand that it, too, should be negated, that it should once again be transformed into common property, necessarily arises. But this demand does not mean the restoration of the aboriginal common ownership, but the institution of a far higher and more developed form of possession in common which, far from being a hindrance to production, on the contrary for the first time will free production from all fetters and enable it to make full use of modern chemical discoveries and mechanical inventions.

Or let us take another example: the philosophy of antiquity was primitive, natural materialism. As such, it was incapable of clearing up the relation between mind and matter. But the need to get clarity on this question led to the doctrine of a soul separable from the body, then to the assertion of the immortality of this soul, and finally to monotheism. The old materialism was therefore negated by idealism. But in the course of the further development of philosophy, idealism, too, became untenable and was negated by modern materialism. This modern materialism, the negation of the negation, is not the mere reestablishment of the old, but adds to the permanent foundations of this old materialism the whole thought-content of two thousand years of development of philosophy and natural science, as well as of the history of these two thousand years. It is no longer a philosophy at all, but simply a world outlook which has to establish its validity and be applied not in a science of sciences standing apart, but in the positive sciences. Philosophy is therefore "sublated" here, that is, "both overcome and preserved"; overcome as regards its form, and preserved as regards its real content. . . .

And so, what is the negation of the negation? An extremely general—and for this reason extremely far-reaching and important—law of development of nature, history, and thought; a law which, as we have seen, holds good in the animal and plant kingdoms, in geology, in mathematics, in history and in philosophy. . . . When I say that all these processes are a negation of the negation, I bring them all together under this one law of motion, and for this very reason I leave out of account the specific peculiarities of each individual process. Dialectics, however, is nothing more than the science of the general laws of motion and development of nature, human society, and thought.

But someone may object: the negation that has taken place in this case is not a real negation: I negate a grain of barley also when I grind it, an insect when I crush it underfoot, or the positive quantity a when I cancel it, and so on. Or I negate the sentence: the rose is a rose, when I say: the rose is not a rose; and what do I get if I then negate this negation and say; but after all the rose is a rose?

These objections are in fact the chief arguments put forward by the metaphysicians against dialectics, and they are wholly worthy of the narrow-mindedness of this mode of thought. Negation in dialectics does not mean simply saying no, or declaring that something does not exist, or destroying it in any way one likes. Long ago Spinoza said: *Omnis determinatio est negatio*— every limitation or determination is at the same time a negation. And further: the kind of negation is determined, firstly, by the general and, secondly, by the particular nature of the process. I must not only negate, but also sublate the negation. I must therefore so arrange the first negation that the second remains or becomes possible. How? This depends on the particular nature of each individual case. If I grind a grain of barley, or crush an insect, I have carried out the first part of the action, but have made the second part impossible. Every kind of thing therefore has a peculiar way of being negated in such a manner that it gives rise to a development, and it is just the same with every kind of conception or idea. The infinitesimal calculus involves a form of negation which is different from that used in the formation of positive powers from negative roots. This has to be learned, like everything else. The bare knowledge that the barley plant and the infinitesimal calculus are both governed by negation of negation does not enable me either to grow barley successfully or to differentiate and integrate; just as little as the bare knowledge of the laws of the determination of sound by the dimensions of the strings enables me to play the violin. . . .

4. ENGELS:
THE TWO CONCEPTIONS
OF MATTER

The numerous conceptions and definitions of "matter" and "materialism" that we found in Selection 2, above, are reduced by Engels to two, as illustrated in the brief passages taken here from The Dialectics of Nature.

Essentially, Engels wishes to define matter ontologically as both (1) the purely abstract creation of thought and (2) the "stuff" of the universe, i.e., the substratum of all motion and change.

As we saw above, Engels's epistemological definitions are variations on the theme of the primacy (in cognition) of matter over thought; i.e., the assumption that thought is a product of various interactions of matter as defined in (2) above.

MATTER AS A CONCEPTUAL ABSTRACTION

Matter as such is a pure creation of thought and an abstraction. We leave out of account the qualitative differences of things in lumping them together as corporeally existing things under the concept matter. Hence matter as such, as distinct from definite existing pieces of matter, is not anything sensuously existing. When natural science directs its efforts to seeking out uniform matter as such, to reducing qualitative differences to merely quantitative differences in combining identical smallest particles, it is doing the same thing as demanding to see fruit as such instead of cherries, pears, apples, or the mammal as such instead of cats, dogs, sheep, etc., gas as such, metal, stone, chemical compound as such, motion as such. . . . As Hegel has already shown, this view, this "one-sided mathematical view," according to which matter must be looked upon as having only quantitative determination, but, qualitatively, as identical originally, is "no other standpoint than that" of the French materialism of the

SOURCE: From Friedrich Engels, *The Dialectics of Nature*, trans. Clemens Dutt (Moscow: Progress Publishers, 1966) .

eighteenth century. It is even a retreat to Pythagoras, who regarded number, quantitative determination, as the essence of things.

MATTER AS THE REAL SUBSTRATUM OF CHANGE

Reciprocal action is the first thing that we encounter when we consider matter in motion as a whole from the standpoint of modern natural science. We see a series of forms of motion, mechanical motion, heat, light, electricity, magnetism, chemical union and decomposition, transitions of states of aggregation, organic life, all of which, if *at present* we *still* make an exception of organic life, pass into one another, mutually determine one another, are in one place cause and in another effect, the sum total of the motion in all its changing forms remaining the same. . . . Mechanical motion becomes transformed into heat, electricity, magnetism, light, etc., and vice versa. Thus natural science confirms what Hegel has said, that reciprocal action is the true *causa finalis* of things. We cannot go back further than to knowledge of this reciprocal action, for the very reason that there is nothing behind to know. If we know the forms of motion of matter (for which it is true there is still very much lacking, in view of the short time that natural science has existed), then we know matter itself, and therewith our knowledge is complete. . . . Only from this universal reciprocal action do we arrive at the real causal relation. In order to understand the separate phenomena, we have to tear them out of the general interconnection and consider them in isolation, and *then* the changing motions appear, one as cause and the other as effect.

. . . It is an eternal cycle in which matter moves, a cycle that certainly only completes its orbit in periods of time for which our terrestrial year is no adequate measure, a cycle in which the time of highest development, the time of organic life and still more that of the life of beings conscious of nature and of themselves, is just as narrowly restricted as the space in which life and self-consciousness come into operation; a cycle in which every finite mode of existence of matter, whether it be sun or nebular vapor, single animal or genus of animals, chemical combination or dissociation, is equally transient, and wherein nothing is eternal but eternally changing, eternally moving matter and the laws according to which it moves and changes. But however often, and however relentlessly, this cycle is completed in time and space; however many millions of suns and earths may arise and pass away; however long it may last before, in one solar system and only on *one* planet, the conditions for organic life develop; however innumerable the organic beings, too, that have to arise and to pass away before animals with a brain capable of thought are developed from their midst, and for a short span of time find conditions suitable for life, only to be exterminated later without mercy—we have the certainty that matter remains eternally the same in all its transformations, that none of its attributes can ever be lost, and therefore, also, that with the same iron necessity that it will exterminate on the earth its highest creation, the thinking mind, it must somewhere else and at another time again produce it.

5. ENGELS:
THE DIALECTICAL MATERIALIST
CONCEPTION OF MAN

In this selection, taken from a fragment entitled "The Part Played by Labor in the Transition from Ape to Man" found in the manuscript of The Dialectics of Nature, *Engels attempts to distinguish several stages of human evolution according to the changing types of labor by which primitive man was able at various stages of evolution to modify his natural environment while at the same time undergoing changes which further adapted him to this modified milieu. Engels's stress on labor and man's use of tools serves him as a point of contact for the theories of Marx and Darwin, by which he attempts to apply the materialist interpretation of history to the prehistory of the human species, i.e., to the long period prior to the origin of society.*[1] *But, since Marx's theoretical position is precisely the materialist interpretation of* history, *which, as we have seen above, requires private property and the class struggle,*[2] *such speculation about* prehistory, *i.e., about the period prior to the emergence of the class struggle and private property, is irrelevant. If there ever were such a thing as "primitive communism," it certainly was not part of history, i.e., of the dialectical march toward the "regeneration of man" in industrial communism. On the other hand, ethnological reports of so-called "primitive" tribes only reinforce the thesis that known human society is always hierarchical, even when based upon kinship relations or totem-identification rather than on private property.*

Engels's basic assumption, on the other hand, that man as a historical being evolved within nature prior to the emergence of private property and hierarchy (if not actual classes), reveals a misunderstanding of Marx's view of man's uniqueness due to his species consciousness and his ability to master nature through social labor and thus to create history. But to master nature through social labor is, as indicated above, to have already established the dialectical struggle-bond between lord and

SOURCE: From Friedrich Engels, *The Dialectics of Nature,* trans. Clemens Dutt (Moscow: Progress Publishers, 1966) .

1. Cf. Selection 6, below, for a further discussion of this point. .
2. Cf. pp. 4–7, above.

bondsman. This relationship is precisely what makes society *possible, i.e., it makes possible the organized production that enables the "material needs" to be met. Marx differed from Hegel on this point only in emphasizing the class character of this relationship (i.e., that it involves societies of real men) rather than, as in Hegel's view, considering it to be a relation between two consciousnesses. Hegel's underlying idea was that the central social relationship (which for Marx is the class struggle) is based upon the master's (but not the slave's) ability to conquer nature within himself by overcoming his fear of death and by risking his life for recognition by the other, and the slave's (but not the master's) subsequently learned ability to conquer external nature at the order of the master and thus to remake himself through his labor. In both aspects, human society depends on the conquest of nature; it would even be fair to say that, for Hegel, man is human, i.e., self-creative and hence historical, precisely because he conquers nature in this two-fold manner.[3] For Marx, in a similar vein, man is human precisely insofar as he labors, i.e., masters nature. Yet this "humanism" is at the same time a "naturalism" for Marx in the sense that man is not understood to possess any sort of supernatural faculty or ability:*

> *Man is not merely a natural being; he is a* human *natural being. He is a being for himself, and therefore a* species-*being; and as such he has to express and authenticate himself in being [i.e. through labor] as well as in thought. Consequently,* human *objects are not natural objects as they present themselves directly.*[4]

What distinguishes communism, according to Marx, from all previous stages of history, is that it will create the conditions for the full development of mankind's potential, i.e., it will overcome all forms of social alienation by overcoming the alienation of labor. As such, communism will not be the "end" of history, but rather will be the beginning of "truly human" history. Only under such conditions will it be possible to overcome the division between man and nature, i.e., to end the exploitation of nature for pecuniary profit, because only then will the social bond no longer be that of master to slave, exploiting class to exploited class:

> *Communism is the* positive *abolition of* private *property, of human self-alienation, and thus the* real *appropriation of* human *nature through and for man. It is, therefore, the return of man himself*

3. Cf. Alexandre Kojeve, *Introduction to the Reading of Marx,* trans. James H. Nichols, Jr. (New York: Basic Books, 1969), pp. 8–9.

4. Marx, "Critique of Hegel's Dialectic and Philosophy in General," in *Karl Marx: Early Writings,* trans. T. B. Bottomore (New York: McGraw-Hill, 1964) , p. 208. Cf. also *Karl Marx, The Essential Writings,* p. 136.

as a social, *i.e., really human, being, a complete and conscious return which assimilates all the wealth of previous development. Communism as a fully developed naturalism is humanism and as a fully developed humanism is naturalism. It is the* definitive *resolution of the antagonism between man and nature, and between man and man. . . . It is the solution to the riddle of history and knows itself to be this solution.*[5]

But such Marxian "naturalism" is by no means the scientistic naturalism of late nineteenth-century biology, as is assumed by Engels in the present selection. The properly Marxian conception of the origin of human society, which has always been class society ("all previous history has been the history of class struggles") is to be found in labor and the class (or master-slave) division or struggle, which is, dialectically, also a bond. It is not to be found in the evolution of the hand, brain, or speech organs, as for Engels. Marx says:

as *society itself produces* man *as man, so it is* produced *by him. Activity and mind are social in their content as well as in their* origin; *they are* social *activity and* social *mind. The* human *significance of nature only exists for* social *man, because only in this case is nature a* bond *with other* men, *the basis of his existence for others and of their existence for him. Only then is nature the* basis *of his own* human *experience and a vital element of human reality. The* natural *existence of man has here become human for him. Thus* society *is the accomplished union of man with nature, the veritable resurrection of nature, the realized naturalism of man and the realized humanism of nature.*[6]

Marx differs in this regard from Hegel, for whom humanity consists essentially in the conquest of bios *or the will to live ("desire"). Engels's failure to understand Marx is evidenced in this selection by his habit of referring to society and its origins with no mention whatever of the class struggle. But in so doing, Engels reveals his greater reliance upon naturalistic science, which is "bourgeois" precisely because it omits any reference to the historical ubiquity of the class struggle and pretends that its findings are "neutral" with respect to that struggle, than upon Marxian thought, for which man's interaction with nature (under the rule of private property, i.e., throughout all of history) has been the conquest and exploitation of nature based precisely upon the struggle of the classes within society.*

Labor is the source of all wealth, the political economists assert. And it really is the source—next to nature, which supplies

5. Marx, "Private Property and Communism," in *Karl Marx: Early Writings,* trans. by T. B. Bottomore (New York: McGraw-Hill, 1964), p. 154. Cf. also *Karl Marx: The Essential Writings,* p. 89.
6. *Ibid.* Cf. also *Karl Marx: The Essential Writings,* pp. 90–91.

it with the material that it converts into wealth. But it is even infinitely more than this. It is the prime basic condition for all human existence, and this to such an extent that, in a sense, we have to say that labor created man himself.

Many hundreds of thousands of years ago, during an epoch, not yet definitely determinable, of that period of the earth's history known to geologists as the Tertiary period, most likely toward the end of it, a particularly highly developed race of anthropoid apes lived somewhere in the tropical zone—probably on a great continent that has now sunk to the bottom of the Indian Ocean. Darwin has given us an approximate description of these ancestors of ours. They were completely covered with hair, they had beards and pointed ears, and they lived in bands in the trees.

Climbing assigns different functions to the hands and the feet, and when their mode of life involved locomotion on level ground, these apes gradually got out of the habit of using their hands [in walking] and adopted a more and more erect posture. This was *the decisive step in the transition from ape to man. . . .*

It stands to reason that if erect gait among our hairy ancestors became first the rule and then, in time, a necessity, other diverse functions must, in the meantime, have devolved upon the hands. Already among the apes there is some difference in the way the hands and the feet are employed. In climbing, as mentioned above, the hands and feet have different uses. The hands are used mainly for gathering and holding food in the same way as the forepaws of the lower mammals are used. Many apes use their hands to build themselves nests in the trees or even to construct roofs between the branches to protect themselves against the weather, as the chimpanzee, for example, does. With their hands they grasp sticks to defend themselves against enemies, and with their hands they bombard their enemies with fruits and stones. In captivity they use their hands for a number of simple operations copied from human beings. It is in this that one sees the great gulf between the undeveloped hand of even the most manlike apes and the human hand that has been highly perfected by hundreds of thousands of years of labor. The number and general arrangement of the bones and muscles are the same in both hands, but the hand of the lowest savage can perform hundreds of operations that no simian hand can imitate—no simian hand has ever fashioned even the crudest stone knife.

The first operations for which our ancestors gradually learned to adapt their hands during the many thousands of years of transition from ape to man could have been only very simple ones. The lowest savages, even those in whom regression to a more animallike condition with a simultaneous physical degeneration can be assumed, are nevertheless far superior to these transitional beings. Before the first flint could be fashioned into a knife by human hands, a period of time probably elapsed in comparison with which the historical period known to us appears insignificant. But the decisive step had been taken, *the hand had become free* and could henceforth attain ever greater dexterity; the greater flexibility thus acquired was inherited and increased from generation to generation.

Thus the hand is not only the organ of labor, *it is also the product of labor.* Labor, adaptation to ever new operations, the inheritance of muscles, ligaments, and, over longer periods of time, bones that had undergone special development and the ever-renewed employment of this inherited finesse in new, more and more complicated operations, have given the human hand the high degree of perfection required to conjure into being the pictures of a Raphael, the statues of a Thorwaldson, the music of a Paganini.

But the hand did not exist alone; it was only one member of an integral, highly complex organism. And what benefited the hand benefited also the whole body it served; and this in two ways.

In the first place, the body benefited from the law of correlation of growth, as Darwin called it. This law states that the specialized forms of separate parts of an organic being are always bound up with certain forms of other parts that apparently have no connection with them. . . . The gradually increasing perfection of the human hand, and the commensurate adaptation of the feet for erect gait, have undoubtedly, by virtue of such correlation, reacted on other parts of the organism. However, this action has not as yet been sufficiently investigated for us to be able to do more here than to state the fact in general terms.

Much more important is the direct, demonstrable influence of the development of the hand on the rest of the organism. It has already been noted that our simian ancestors were gregarious; it is obviously impossible to seek the derivation of man, the most social of all animals, from nongregarious immediate ancestors. Mastery over nature began with the development of the hand, with labor, and widened man's horizon at every new advance. He was continually discovering new, hitherto unknown properties in natural objects. On the other hand, the development of labor necessarily helped to bring the members of society closer together by increasing cases of mutual support and joint activity, and by making clear the advantage of this joint activity to each individual. In short, men in the making arrived at the point where *they had something to say* to each other. Necessity created the organ; the undeveloped larynx of the ape was slowly but surely transformed by modulation to produce constantly more developed modulation, and the organs of the mouth gradually learned to pronounce one articulate sound after another. . . .

First labor, after it and then with it speech—these were the two most essential stimuli under the influence of which the brain of the ape gradually changed into that of man, which for all its similarity is far larger and more perfect. Hand in hand with the development of the brain went the development of its most immediate instruments—the senses. Just as the gradual development of speech is inevitably accompanied by a corresponding refinement of the organ of hearing, so the development of the brain as a whole is accompanied by a refinement of all the senses. The eagle sees much farther than man, but the human eye discerns considerably more in things than does the eye of the eagle. The dog has a far keener sense of smell than man, but it does not distinguish a hundredth part of the odors that for man are definite signs denoting different things. And the sense of touch, which the ape hardly possesses in its crudest initial form, has been developed only side by side with the development of the human hand itself, through the medium of labor.

The reaction on labor and speech of the development of the brain and its attendant senses, of the increasing clarity of consciousness, power of abstraction and of conclusion, gave both labor and speech an ever-renewed impulse to further development. This development did not reach its conclusion when man finally became distinct from the ape, but on the whole made further powerful progress, its degree and direction varying among different peoples and at different times, and here and there even being interrupted by local or temporary regression. This further development has been strongly urged forward, on the one hand, and guided along more definite directions, on the other, by a new element which came into play with the appearance of fully fledged man, namely, *society*.

Hundreds of thousands of years—of no greater significance in the history of the earth than one second in the life of man—certainly elapsed before human society arose out of a troupe of tree-climbing monkeys. Yet it did finally appear. And what do we find once more as the characteristic difference between the troupe of monkeys and human society? *Labor.* The ape herd was satisfied to browse over the feeding area determined for it by geographical conditions or the resistance of neighboring herds; it undertook migrations and struggles to win new feeding grounds, but it was incapable of extracting from them more than they offered in their natural state, except that it unconsciously fertilized the soil with its own excrement. As soon as all possible feeding grounds were occupied, there could be no further increase in the ape population; the number of animals could at best remain stationary. But all animals waste a great deal of food, and, in addition, destroy in the germ the next generation of the food supply. Unlike the hunter, the wolf does not spare the doe which would provide it with the young the next year; the goats in Greece, that eat away the young bushes before they grow to maturity, have eaten bare all the mountains of the country. This "predatory economy" of animals plays an important part in the gradual transformation of species by forcing them to adapt themselves to other than the usual food, thanks to which their blood acquires a different chemical composition and the whole physical constitution gradually alters, while species that have remained unadapted die out. There is no doubt that this predatory economy contributed powerfully to the transition of our ancestors from ape to man. In a race of apes that far surpassed all others in intelligence and adaptability, this predatory economy must have led to a continual increase in the number of plants used for food and to the consumption of more and more edible parts of food plants. In short, food became more and more varied, as did also the substances entering the body with it, substances that were the chemical premises for the transition to man. But all that was not yet labor in the proper sense of the word. Labor begins with the making of tools. And what are the most ancient tools that we find—the most ancient judging by the heirlooms of prehistoric man that have been discovered, and by the mode of life of the earliest historical peoples and of the rawest of contemporary savages? They are hunting and fishing implements, the former at the same time serving as weapons. But hunting and fishing presuppose the transition from an exclusively vegetable diet to the concomitant use of meat, and this is another important step in the process of transition from ape to man. A *meat diet* contained in an almost ready state the most essential ingredients required by the organism for its metabolism. By shortening the time required for digestion, it also shortened the other vegetative bodily processes that correspond to those of plant life, and thus gained further time, material and desire for the active manifestation of animal life proper. And the farther man in the making moved from the vegetable kingdom the higher he rose above the animal. Just as becoming accustomed to a vegetable diet side by side with meat converted wild cats and dogs into the servants of man, so also adaptation to a meat diet, side by side with a vegetable diet, greatly contributed toward giving bodily strength and independence to man in the making. The meat diet, however, had its greatest effect on the brain, which now received a far richer flow of the materials necessary for its nourishment and development, and which, therefore, could develop more rapidly and perfectly from generation to generation. With all due respect to the vegetarians man did not come into existence without a meat diet, and if the latter, among all peoples known to us, has led to cannibalism at some time or other (the forefathers of the Berliners, the Weletabians or Wilzians, used to eat their parents as late as the tenth century), that is of no consequence to us today.

The meat diet led to two new advances of decisive importance—the harnessing of fire and the domestication of animals. The first still further shortened the digestive process, as it provided the mouth with food already, as it were, half-digested; the second made meat more copious by opening up a new, more regular source of supply in addition to hunting, and moreover provided, in milk and its products, a new article of food at least as valuable as meat in its composition. Thus both these advances were, in themselves, new means for the emancipation of man. It would lead us too far afield to dwell here in detail on their indirect effects notwithstanding the great importance they have had for the development of man and society.

Just as man learned to consume everything edible, he also learned to live in any climate. He spread over the whole of the habitable world, being the only animal fully able to do so of its own accord. The other animals that have become accustomed to all climates—domestic animals and vermin—did not become so independently, but only in the wake of man. And the transition from the uniformly hot climate of the original home of man to colder regions, where the year was divided into summer and winter, created new requirements—shelter and clothing as protection against cold and damp, and hence new spheres of labor, new forms of activity, which further and further separated man from the animal.

By the combined functioning of hands, speech organs, and brain, not only in each individual but also in society, men became capable of executing more and more complicated operations, and were able to set themselves, and achieve, higher and higher aims. The work of each generation itself became different, more perfect and more diversified. Agriculture was added to hunting and cattle raising; then came spinning, weaving, metalworking, pottery, and navigation. Along with trade and industry, art and science finally appeared. Tribes developed into nations and states. Law and politics arose, and with them that fantastic reflection of human things in the human mind—religion. In the face of all these images, which appeared in the first place to be products of the mind and seemed to dominate human societies, the more modest productions of the working hand retreated into the background, the more so since the mind that planned the labor was able, at a very early stage in the development of society (for example, already in the primitive family) , to have the labor that had been planned carried out by other hands than its own. All merit for the swift advance of civilization was ascribed to the mind, to the development and activity of the brain. Men became accustomed to explain their actions as arising out of thoughts instead of their needs (which in any case are reflected and perceived in the mind) ; and so in the course of time there emerged that idealistic world outlook which, especially since the fall of the world of antiquity, has dominated men's minds. It still rules them to such a degree that even the most materialistic natural scientists of the Darwinian school are still unable to form any clear idea of the origin of man, because under this ideological influence they do not recognize the part that has been played therein by labor.

Animals, as has already been pointed out, change the environment by their activities in the same way, even if not to the same extent, as man does, and these changes, as we have seen, in turn react upon and change those who made them. In nature nothing takes place in isolation. Everything affects and is affected by every other thing, and it is mostly because this manifold motion and interaction is forgotten that our natural scientists are prevented from gaining a clear insight into the simplest things. We have seen how goats have prevented the regeneration of forests in Greece; on the island of St. Helena, goats and pigs brought by the first arrivals have succeeded in exterminating its old vegetation almost completely, and so have prepared the ground for the spreading of plants brought by later sailors and colonists. But animals exert a lasting effect on their environment unintentionally and, as far as the animals themselves are concerned, accidentally. The further removed men are from animals, however, the more their effect on nature assumes the character of premeditated, planned action directed toward definite preconceived ends. The animal destroys the vegetation of a locality without realizing what it is doing. Man destroys it in order to sow field crops on the soil thus released, or to plant trees or vines which he knows will yield many times the amount planted. He transfers useful plants and domestic animals from one country to another and thus changes the flora and fauna of whole continents. More than this. Through artificial breeding both plants and animals are so changed by the hand of man that they become unrecognizable. The wild plants from which our grain varieties originated are still being sought in vain. . . .

It goes without saying that it would not occur to us to dispute the ability of animals to act in a planned, premeditated fashion. On the contrary, a planned mode of action exists in embryo wherever protoplasm, living albumen, exists and reacts, that is, carries out definite, even if extremely simple, movements as a result of definite external stimuli. Such reaction takes place even where there is yet no cell at all, far less a nerve cell. There is something of the planned action in the way insect-eating plants capture their prey, although they do it quite unconsciously. In animals the capacity for conscious, planned action is proportional to the development of the nervous system, and among mammals it attains a fairly high level. While fox hunting in England one can daily observe how unerringly the fox makes use of its excellent knowledge of the locality in order to elude its pursuers, and how well it knows and turns to account all favorable features of the ground that cause the scent to be lost. Among our domestic animals, more highly developed thanks to association with man, one can constantly observe acts of cunning on exactly the same level as those of children. For, just as the development history of the human embryo in the mother's womb is only an abbreviated repetition of the history, extending over millions of years, of the bodily evolution of our animal ancestors, starting from the worm, so the mental development of the human child is only a still more abbreviated repetition of the intellectual development of these same ancestors, at least of the later ones. But all the planned action of all animals has never succeeded in impressing the stamp of their will upon the earth. That was left for man.

In short, the animal merely *uses* its environment, and brings about changes in it simply by its presence; man by his changes makes it serve his ends, *masters* it. This is the final, essential distinction between man and other animals, and once again it is labor that brings about this distinction.

Let us not, however, flatter ourselves overmuch on account of our human victories over nature. For each such victory nature takes its revenge on us. Each victory, it is true, in the first place brings about the results we expected, but in the second and third places it has quite different, unforeseen effects which only too often cancel the first. The people who, in Mesopotamia, Greece,

Asia Minor and elsewhere, destroyed the forests to obtain cultivable land, never dreamed that by removing along with the forests the collecting centers and reservoirs of moisture they were laying the basis for the present forlorn state of those countries. When the Italians of the Alps used up the pine forests on the southern slopes, so carefully cherished on the northern slopes, they had no inkling that by doing so they were cutting at the roots of the dairy industry in their region; they had still less inkling that they were thereby depriving their mountain springs of water for the greater part of the year, and making it possible for them to pour still more furious torrents on the plains during the rainy seasons. Those who spread the potato in Europe were not aware that with these farinaceous tubers they were at the same time spreading scrofula. Thus at every step we are reminded that we by no means rule over nature like a conqueror over a foreign people, like someone standing outside nature—but that we, with flesh, blood and brain, belong to nature, and exist in its midst, and that all our mastery of it consists in the fact that we have the advantage over all other creatures of being able to learn its laws and apply them correctly.

And, in fact, with every day that passes we are acquiring a better understanding of these laws and getting to perceive both the more immediate and the more remote consequences of our interference with the traditional course of nature. In particular, after the mighty advances made by the natural sciences in the present century, we are more than ever in a position to realize, and hence to control, even the more remote natural consequences of at least our day-to-day production activities. But the more this progresses the more will men not only feel but also know their oneness with nature, and the more impossible will become the senseless and unnatural ideal of a contrast between mind and matter, man and nature, soul and body, such as arose after the decline of classical antiquity in Europe and obtained its highest elaboration in Christianity.

Natural science, like philosophy, has hitherto entirely neglected the influence of men's activity on their thought; both know only nature on the one hand and thought on the other. But it is precisely *the alteration of nature by men,* not solely nature as such, which is the most essential and immediate basis of human thought, and it is in the measure that man has learned to change nature that his intelligence has increased. The natural- istic conception of history, as found, for instance, to a greater or lesser extent in Draper and other scientists, as if nature exclu- sively reacts on man, and natural conditions everywhere exclu- sively determined his historical development, is therefore one- sided and forgets that man also reacts on nature, changing it and creating new conditions of existence for himself. There is devil- ishly little left of "nature" as it was in Germany at the time when the Germanic peoples immigrated into it. The earth's surface, climate, vegetation, fauna, and the human beings themselves have infinitely changed, and all this owing to human activity, while the changes of nature in Germany which have occurred in this period of time without human interference are incalculably small.

6. PLEKHANOV:
THE DARWINIZATION
OF MARXISM

G. V. Plekhanov (1856–1918), the founder of Russian Social Democracy, takes second place only to Engels as the most important Marxist philosopher of the period of the Second International. Initially active in the Narodnik, or "Populist," movement, Plekhanov later came to study the works of Marx and Engels; he abandoned Narodnism for Marxism by 1883 and from that time became responsible for the popularization of Marxist ideas among an entire generation of Russian intelligentsia. Thereafter, Plekhanov remained a staunch opponent of all Narodnik theories of Russia's possibly avoiding its period of capitalist development. For almost thirty years his writings formed the core of the theoretical outlook of Russian Social Democracy.

Following the split of the Russian Social Democratic Labor party in 1903,[1] Plekhanov supported the Menshevik faction and thus reaffirmed his stand with the "Orthodoxy" of the SPD and the Second International, opposing Lenin and the Bolsheviks in their repudiation of Western European Social Democracy.[2] Upon Plekhanov's death, nonetheless, Lenin was to pay him the tribute of always having upheld the cause of Marxism in philosophy, despite their fundamental differences on questions of organization and tactics.

Plekhanov was the first to use the term "dialectical materialism" (in 1891) and to formulate a comprehensive Marxist philosophy, something which even Engels had never completed. Characteristic features of his thought are the presentation of dialectical materialism as the ontological ground of the materialist interpretation of history, the attempted unification of Marxism and Darwinism, a renewed emphasis on the role of social consciousness (especially in psychology and art) in the interpretation of historical events, skepticism with respect to the "copy" theory of perception of Engels and Lenin, the doctrine of "logical dualism" (i.e., the subordination—and hence the recognition of the

SOURCE: From G. V. Plekhanov, *The Development of the Monist View of History*, trans. Andrew Rothstein, in *G. V. Plekhanov—Selected Philosophical Works* (Moscow: Foreign Language Publishing House, n.d.).

1. Cf. Selections 12 and 13, below.
2. Cf. Selections 13 and 17, below.

limited validity—of formal logic to dialectical logic, whereas Engels had repudiated the former) and the working out of the most sophisticated Marxist solution to the problem of the seemingly voluntary action of individuals in the context of the "Orthodox" belief in historical determinism.

In this selection, we illustrate Plekhanov's modifications of the materialist interpretation of history along Darwinian lines. Plekhanov, who claims that Darwin's theory of evolution is dialectical because it is historical, discusses the causal influence of the geographical environment upon man via the social environment. Thus, for Plekhanov, both nature and human social existence are held to be equally describable in naturalistic terms. He then develops his notion that the human consciousness of these laws of historical development—if translated by the proletariat into class-conscious political action—will make possible the subordination of natural necessity (as it has operated hitherto in history, i.e., beyond the control of man) to human action; and this is precisely what Plekhanov considers to be the goal of socialism. There is no mention in Plekhanov of the overcoming of alienation as essential to the Marxian conception of socialism or communism; and, as Lenin was exposed to Marxism through the works of Plekhanov, it becomes somewhat understandable why the concept of alienation plays no role in the Leninist conception of Marxism.

It is, of course, well known that Marx at one time offered to dedicate Capital *to Darwin, so much was he affected by the impact of Darwin's theory of organic evolution. Yet even a casual reading of Darwin makes it obvious that theoretically he is grounded in British empiricism and Malthusian economics, arguing that it is the pressure of the increasing population of a species upon its natural food supply that leads to its eventually evolving first into new varieties of the same species and then into different, but related, species. It is also well known that Marx despised Malthus's theory of population and also rejected his famous theory of the inevitable and perpetual poverty of the masses.*

The reasons for this apparent inconsistency may be (1) that Darwin's theory of evolution is, of course, developmental, and thus bears at least a superficial resemblance to Marx's historical approach to all social questions, although whereas Darwin speaks of the struggles of individual members of a species for *survival,* Marx speaks of the struggle among classes for social *domination; and (2) that in the battles that raged over Darwin's work, he and Marx had many of the same enemies. It is thus only to have been expected that, in the heat of the debates of the 1860s, the apparent similarities of the two theories should have appeared more pronounced than their differences.*

But Darwin was certainly not a Hegelian, and he had nothing to say about human society. This is what fundamentally separates him from Marx and which makes their theories incompatible (even Engels attacked such "Social Darwinists" as Spencer and Huxley). For Marx sees man as a historically self-creative and purposeful being (although he agrees with Hegel that the individual generally lacks much power to determine his existence), whereas Darwin conceives Homo sapiens as just another animal species which has evolved as a result of the blind necessity which prevails throughout nature. Marx, we might say, is not interested in a naturalistic conception of man, but rather in a humanistic conception of nature, i.e., of nature as within the horizon of human social labor.

Darwin is, additionally, a nominalist; only the individual organisms are real for him; the "species" are nothing more than convenient fictions for ease of scientific classification. For Marx, on the contrary, the classes are real entities, the very subjects of history (whereas Hegel had held that the subjects of history are states), although it is to be admitted that at times Marx does sound like a nominalist. Yet, without a realist theory of classes, the class struggle could not be an essential feature of social existence, let alone the motive force of "all previous history"; and the goal of attaining a classless society (i.e., a communist one) could not serve to distinguish radically the "realm of freedom" from that of "necessity."[3] Marx, in fact, regards the isolation of individuals in bourgeois society (i.e., the alienation of man from man and from human "species existence") as precisely the dehumanization of mankind characteristic of capitalism, whereas it is this "social nominalism" which is the presupposition of Malthus's theories.

Plekhanov's attempt to modify Marxism along Darwinian lines is, of course, grounded in the assumption that, as "scientific," Marxism must be able to incorporate into itself the latest theoretical advances of the natural sciences. A major scientific breakthrough such as Darwin's theory of organic evolution, however, exerts more attraction upon Marxism than vice versa, and thus we would have expected the theoretical distortions of the latter to become acute. Essentially, it is only the desire to turn Marxism into a comprehensive "scientific" world view that propels this assimilation; strictly speaking, the issues raised by Darwin have nothing to do with those raised by Marx, which are solely those arising from his interpretation of human history and which are required to provide the proletariat with the self-consciousness necessary to emancipate itself from alienation by the overthrow of the

3. Cf. *Capital*, Vol. III (Moscow: Progress Publishers, 1965), p. 820 and *Karl Marx: The Essential Writings*, p. 430.

bourgeoisie. But this intimate relation between Marxist theory and its revolutionizing practice becomes strained the more it becomes a speculative system. Thus, for Social Democracy, Marxian "scientific socialism" falls increasingly under the sway of the natural sciences and their ideologies, i.e., the allegedly "value-free" neo-Kantianism and positivism, and Plekhanov's "Darwinization" of Marxism serves to hasten Marxism's abandoning its original humanist commitment, as it reintegrates man into nature conceived in itself and theory becomes thereby increasingly divorced from revolutionary practice.

. . . Our anthropoid ancestors, like all other animals, were in complete subjection to *nature*. All their development was that completely unconscious development which was conditioned by adaptation to their environment, by means of natural selection in the struggle for existence. This was the dark kingdom of *physical necessity*. At that time even the *dawn of consciousness*, and therefore of *freedom*, was not breaking. But physical necessity brought man to a stage of development at which he began, little by little, to separate himself from the remaining animal world. He became a *toolmaking animal*. The tool is an organ with the help of which man acts on nature to achieve his ends. It is an organ which subjects *necessity* to the human *consciousness*, although at first only to a very weak degree. . . . *The degree of development of the productive forces determines the measure of the authority of man over nature.*

The development of the productive forces is itself determined by the qualities of the geographical environment surrounding man. In this way nature itself gives man the means for its own subjection.

But man is not struggling with nature individually: the struggle with it is carried on, in the expression of Marx, by social man (*der Gesellschaftsmensch*), i.e., a more or less considerable social union. The characteristics of *social* man are determined at every given time by the degree of development of the productive forces, because on the degree of the development of those forces depends the entire structure of the social union. Thus, this structure is determined in the long run by the characteristics of the geographical environment, which affords men a greater or lesser possibility of developing their productive forces. But once definite social relations have arisen, their further development takes place according to *its own inner laws,* the operation of which accelerates or retards the development of the productive forces which conditions the historical progress of man. The dependence of man on his geographical environment is transformed from *direct* to *indirect.* The *geographical environment* influences man *through the social* environment. But *thanks to this,* the relationship of man with his geographical environment becomes extremely changeable. At every new stage of development of the productive forces it proves to be different from what it was before. The geographical environment influenced the Britons of Caesar's time quite otherwise than it influences the present inhabitants of Great Britain. . . .

The development of the social environment is subjected to its own laws. This means that its characteristics depend just as little on the will and consciousness of men as the characteristics of the geographical environment. The productive action of man on nature gives rise to a new form of dependence of man, a new variety of his slavery: *economic necessity.* And the greater grows man's authority over nature, the more his productive forces develop, the more stable becomes this new slavery: *with the development of the productive forces the mutual relations of men in the social process of production become more complex;* the course of that process completely slips from under their control, *the producer proves to be the slave of his own creation* (as an example, the capitalist anarchy of production) .

But just as the nature surrounding man itself gave him the first opportunity to develop his productive forces and, consequently, gradually to emancipate himself from nature's yoke—so the relations of production, social relations, by the very logic of their development bring man to realization of the causes of his enslavement by *economic* necessity. This provides the opportunity for a new and final triumph of *consciousness* over *necessity,* of *reason* over blind *law.*

Having realized that the cause of his enslavement by his own creation lies in the anarchy of production, the producer ("social man") organizes that production and thereby subjects it to his will. Then terminates the kingdom of *necessity,* and there begins the reign of *freedom,* which itself proves to be *necessity.* The prologue of human history has been played out, history begins.*

Thus dialectical materialism not only does not strive, as its opponents attribute to it, to convince man that it is absurd to revolt against economic necessity, but it is the first to point out *how to overcome* the latter. Thus is eliminated the *inevitably fatalist* character inherent in *metaphysical materialism*. And in exactly the same way is eliminated every foundation for pessimism. . . . The individual personality is only foam on the crest of the wave, men are subjected to an iron law which can only be discovered, but which cannot be subjected to the human will, said Georg Büchner. No, replies Marx: once we have *discovered* that iron law, it depends on us to overthrow its yoke, it depends on us to make *necessity* the obedient slave of *reason*. . . .

Dialectical materialism† says that human reason could not be the demiurge of history, because it is itself the *product of history*. But once that product has appeared, it *must* not—and in its nature it *cannot*—be obedient to the reality handed down as a heritage by previous history; of necessity it strives to transform that reality after its own likeness and image, *to make it reasonable*. . . .

* . . . it will be clear, we hope, what is the relation between the teaching of Marx and the teaching of Darwin. Darwin succeeded in solving the problem of how there originate vegetable and animal species in the struggle for existence. Marx succeeded in solving the problem of how there arise different types of social organization in the struggle of men for their existence. Logically, the investigation of Marx begins precisely where the investigation of Darwin ends. Animals and vegetables are under the influence of their *physical* environment. The physical environment acts on social man through those social relations which arise on the basis of the productive forces, which at first develop more or less quickly according to the characteristics of the physical environment. Darwin explains the origin of species not by an allegedly *innate* tendency to develop in the animal organism, as Lamarck did, but by the adaptation of the organism to the conditions existing outside it: not by the *nature of the organism* but by the influence of *external nature*. Marx explains the historical development of man not by the *nature of man*, but by the characteristics of those social *relations* between men which arise when social man is acting on *external nature*. The spirit of their research is absolutely the same in both thinkers. That is why one can say that Marxism is Darwinism in its application to social science (we know that *chronologically* this is not so, but that is unimportant) . . . .

† We use the term "dialectical materialism" because it alone can give an accurate description of the philosophy of Marx. Holbach and Helvetius were *metaphysical* materialists. They fought against *metaphysical* idealism. Their materialism gave way to *dialectical idealism*, which in its turn was overcome by *dialectical materialism*. The expression "economic materialism" is extremely inappropriate. Marx never called himself an economic materialist.

PART II
MARXIST
SOCIAL
DEMOCRACY

During the years between the deaths of Marx and Engels (1883–1895), the Social Democratic party of Germany (SPD) gained such political strength, despite the fact that it was outlawed from 1878 to 1890, that its prestige in the Second International (founded in 1889) became overwhelming. Among the younger generation of the party's leadership (only Engels remained of the generation of 1848), no one individual was more promising than Karl Kautsky (1854–1938), who was chosen by Engels to be his and Marx's literary executor. This explicit "anointing" followed many years of cooperation between Engels and Kautsky and reflected their agreement on major matters of strategy, especially the repudiation of the revolutionary practice of Marx.

Throughout his long career at the head of the SPD, Kautsky attempted to steer a middle course between the reform-oriented "Revisionists," led by Eduard Bernstein (1850–1932), who sought to abandon the goal of communism and to cooperate instead with the bourgeoisie in pursuing social reform, and the militant "Radicals," led by Rosa Luxemburg (1871–1919), who advocated continual revolutionary pressure (e.g., the mass political strike) and the subordination of the socialist politicians to the spontaneously expressed will of the proletariat.

The SPD had been, since its founding in 1875, more or less openly split between followers of Marx and Engels on the left and followers of Ferdinand Lasalle (1825–1864) on the right. Having been formed by the amalgamation of two parties, one

Marxist and the other Lasallean, the SPD at its founding congress at Gotha adopted a program which was designed to please both factions and which was thus bitterly attacked by Marx for its concessions to the reformism of the trades unions and the Lasalleans. This polemic, the famous Critique of the Gotha Program, *remained unpublished for sixteen years, guarded after Marx's death by Engels. Following the eleven years of the antisocialist laws (1878–1890), on the eve of the newly legalized party's congress at Erfurt, Engels and Kautsky published Marx's* Critique *in hope of seeing the party's new program reflect a thoroughly Marxist line (as they interpreted this). The stratagem worked, and it was Kautsky who was assigned the task of drafting the theoretical part of the program. The acceptance of the Erfurt Program thus established the SPD's ostensible adherence to Marxist principles, at least in regard to its analysis of the nature of capitalism and of the revolutionary role to be played by the political party of the proletariat. On the other hand, the immediately practical part of the Erfurt Program was drafted by Bernstein and thus reflects the latter's reformist positions, which Engels himself, incidentally, was to endorse within four years.[1] Thus, even in its official programs, the SPD displayed its internal division and the gap between its revolutionary theory and its reformist practice which was ultimately to paralyze it. Nonetheless, the rise of Kautsky appeared at the time to be a Marxist victory over trade-union "opportunism" (i.e., cooperation with the bourgeoisie), but Kautsky's and Engels's increasingly nonrevolutionary positions were in fact to signal the ebb of the left wing until the extreme revisionist opportunism of Bernstein and his followers, beginning in 1898, plus the significant albeit only temporary successes of the revolutionary risings in Russia (1905–1906), brought the left wing back to life under the leadership of Rosa Luxemburg.*

Kautsky published a detailed commentary on the Erfurt Program[2] soon after its adoption, in which he demonstrated his abilities as a theoretician, although he too embraced the strategy of the parliamentary "road to power." Thus his leadership, even

1. Cf. Selection 8, below.
2. Published in English as *The Class Struggle,* trans. William E. Bohn (New York: Norton, 1971).

before the factional fights surrounding the Revisionist Contro-
versy (beginning in 1898),[3] *turned it into a party of democratic*
reform based upon the faith that the scientifically demonstrable
inevitability of capitalism's demise guaranteed the eventual elec-
toral success of the Social Democrats. This optimistic, almost
fatalistic,[4] *belief in their eventual success made it possible for*
Kautsky and Bernstein alike to repudiate direct class action on
the part of the proletariat and to replace it with the parliamen-
tary maneuvers of the Social Democratic politicians.

This eventual divorce of the professional socialist politician
from the proletarian masses is reflected in the scholasticism of the
SPD leadership, most of whom were intellectuals rather than
workers, for whom Marxist theory ceased to be an effective guide
to political action. For Kautsky, the relation between "the moral
ideal, the ethical indignation against exploitation and class
domination," becomes a merely contingent one, i.e., it is no
longer inherent in Marxism conceived as "scientific *socialism."*
He adds:

it is true that in the case of a socialist the thinker is also a fighter, and
no one can be artificially cut in two halves having nothing to do with
each other; hence there appears occasionally [!] even in Marx's scientific
work the impact of a moral ideal. But he always [!] and rightly [!]
attempted to eliminate it so far as possible [!]. For in science the moral
ideal becomes a source of error if it presumes to prescribe the goal.[5]

Thus, despite occasional obeisances in the direction of Hegel and
the dialectic (which Bernstein had no difficulty discarding),
Kautsky's "Orthodox" Marxism in fact became a form of neo-
Kantianism, for which ethical action, i.e., commitment to the
proletarian revolutionary cause, could be only an ideal *which is*
never demonstrable *by "value-neutral" social science.*

This dualism of theory and practice, established by Engels's
approach to positivism and Kautsky's approach to neo-Kantian-
ism, was carried to its extreme conclusion by Rudolf Hilferding,
the movement's outstanding economist, who, in his monumental
Das Finanzkapital *(a rereading of Marxist economics in light of*

3. Cf. Selections 9 and 10, below.
4. Bernstein defines the "materialist" as "a Calvinist without God." Cf.
p. 141, below.
5. *Ethik und materialistische Geschichtsauffassung* (Stuttgart, 1906), p. 141.

the triumph of finance capital, monopoly, and imperialism by the turn of the century) states that

there is a . . . widespread but false tendency to identify Marxism with socialism [!]. Because in logical terms, considered merely as a scientific system . . . Marxism is simply a theory of the laws of movement of society which . . . applies Marxist economics to the epoch of the production of commodities. . . . Insight into the validity of Marxism . . . is certainly not a statement of value or an instruction to practical conduct[!]. For acceptance of a necessity [i.e., of historical evolution] and acting in the service of this necessity are two quite different things.[6]

Thus, we see that Kautsky's neo-Kantian orientation contributed considerably to the misinterpretation of Marxism. This separation of theory from practice rests ultimately upon Engels's misreading of Hegel and of the relation of Marxism to the natural sciences.[7]

Kautsky's conscious choice of the middle position between reform and revolution, i.e., his creating of an "Orthodoxy" which could not decide between the two and which rather supported its revolutionary rhetoric with merely reformist deeds, was often difficult for him to justify. The attacks upon him from both sides became increasingly strident in the years nearing the debacle of 1914, until he finally lost all credibility as a socialist leader upon the outbreak of the First World War. With the collaboration of the SPD in the German war effort, none of its leading politicians except Rosa Luxemburg was able to emerge untarnished. Both Kautsky and Bernstein opposed the war on pacifist, i.e., Kantian, grounds. Similarly, all other European Social Democrat parties had splits between their larger pro war right and center and their smaller but vocal antiwar left. This pattern was broken only in Russia, where the left wing, i.e., Lenin's Bolsheviks, supported the war and adopted the strategy of "revolutionary defeatism," whereby they sought to accelerate the collapse of the monarchy through sowing the seeds of revolution among the proletarian and peasant elements in the imperial army.

6. Hilferding, *Das Finanzkapital* (Berlin, 1901), p. 4.
7. Cf. Selections 1–5, above.

7. ENGELS:
THE PROLETARIAN REVOLUTION
AND ADVANCED CAPITALISM

Here we see Engels summarize the economic developments which have led to a stage of capitalism more advanced than that analyzed by Marx and which Engels still sees as ripe for revolution. This passage was first written for Anti-Dühring *in 1877, and was revised with little change for republication in* Socialism: Utopian and Scientific *in 1880. Engels defines the contradiction between "social production and capitalist appropriation" as the underlying cause of periodic industrial crises ("depressions") which, ever growing in magnitude and effect, will eventually bring about the collapse of the capitalist economic order and its political functionaries. The clarity of this popular presentation of the basic argument of Marxism accounts in large measure for the widespread success of* Socialism: Utopian and Scientific.*

The reader should carefully note the closing paragraphs, wherein Engels analyzes monopoly capitalism, which was touched upon only briefly by Marx (whose studies reflect a period prior to the widespread growth of monopoly production). These lines reflect Engels's growing awareness that capitalism was evolving from an anarchic competitive system into one which introduces its own type of "rationalization" into economic life through trusts, cartels, and state regulation of the economy. Engels's arguments, however, still adhere to the thesis that this new "monopoly capitalism" is to be the last *stage of capitalist development; and it is this optimistic assessment of Engels's which underlies Social Democracy's belief in the imminent demise of its adversary which was to be largely responsible for its failure to seize power in the era prior to the outbreak of World War I.*

. . . In the trusts, freedom of competition changes into its opposite—into monopoly, the planless production of capitalist society capitulates before the planned production of the invading socialist society. Certainly this is still at first to the benefit and

SOURCE: From Friedrich Engels, *Socialism: Utopian and Scientific,* in Karl Marx and Friedrich Engels, *Selected Works,* Vol. I (Moscow: Co-operative Publishing Society of Foreign Workers in the U.S.S.R., 1935).

advantage of the capitalists. But in this case the exploitation is so palpable that it must break down. No nation would put up with production conducted by trusts, with such a bare-faced exploitation of the community by a small band of coupon clippers.

In one way or another, with trusts or without, the official representative of capitalist society, the state, is finally constrained to take over the management of production.* This necessity of conversion into state property makes itself evident first in the big institutions for communication: the postal service, telegraphs, and railways.

If the crises revealed the incapacity of the bourgeoisie any longer to control the modern productive forces, the conversion of the great organizations for production and communication into joint stock companies, trusts, and state property shows that for this purpose the bourgeoisie can be dispensed with. All the social functions of the capitalist are now carried out by salaried employees. The capitalist has no longer any social activity save the pocketing of revenues, the clipping of coupons, and gambling on the stock exchange, where the different capitalists fleece each other of their capital. Just as at first the capitalist mode of production displaced the workers, so now it displaces the capitalists, relegating them, just as it did the workers, to the superfluous population, even if in the first instance not to the industrial reserve army.

But neither conversion into joint-stock companies and trusts, nor conversion into state property deprives the productive forces of their character as capital. In the case of joint-stock companies and trusts this is obvious. And the modern state, too, is only the organization with which bourgeois society provides itself in order to maintain the general external conditions of the capitalist mode of production against encroachments either by the workers or by individual capitalists. The modern state, whatever its form, is an essentially capitalist machine; it is the state of the capi-

---

* I say *is constrained to*. For it is only when the means of production or communications have *actually* outgrown management by share companies, and therefore their transfer to the state has become inevitable from an economic standpoint—it is only then that this transfer to the state, even when carried out by the state of today, represents an economic advance, the attainment of another preliminary step toward the taking over of all productive forces by society itself. Recently, however, since Bismarck adopted state ownership, a certain spurious socialism has made its appearance . . . which declares that *all* taking over by the state, even the Bismarckian kind, is in itself socialistic. . . .

talists, the ideal collective body of all capitalists. The more productive forces it takes over, the more it becomes the real collective body of all the capitalists, the more citizens it exploits. The workers remain wage earners, proletarians. The capitalist relationship is not abolished; it is rather pushed to an extreme. But at this extreme it is transformed into its opposite. State ownership of the productive forces is not the solution of the conflict, but it contains within itself the formal means, the key to the solution.

This solution can only consist in the recognition in practice of the social nature of the modern productive forces, in bringing, therefore, the mode of production, appropriation, and exchange into accord with the social character of the means of production. And this can only be brought about by society, openly and without deviation, taking possession of the productive forces, which have outgrown all control other than that of society itself. Thereby the social character of the means of production and of the products—which today operates against the producers themselves, periodically breaking through the mode of production and exchange and enforcing itself only as a blind law of nature, violently and destructively—is quite consciously asserted by the producers, and is transformed from a cause of disorder and periodic collapse into the most powerful lever of production itself.

The forces operating in society work exactly like the forces operating in nature: blindly, violently, destructively, so long as we do not understand them and fail to take them into account. But when once we have recognized them and understood how they work, their direction and their effects, the gradual subjection of them to our will and the use of them for the attainment of our aims depends entirely upon ourselves. And this is quite especially true of the mighty productive forces of the present day. So long as we obstinately refuse to understand their nature and their character—and the capitalist mode of production and its defenders set themselves against any such attempt—so long do these forces operate in spite of us, against us, and so long do they control us. . . . But once their nature is grasped, in the hands of the producers working in association they can be transformed from demoniacal masters into willing servants. This is the difference between the destructive force of electricity in the lightning of a thunderstorm and the tamed electricity of the telegraph and the arc light; the difference between a conflagration and fire in the service of man. Such treatment opens the way to the replacement of the anarchy of social production by a socially planned regulation of production in accordance with the needs both of society as a whole and of each individual. The capitalist mode of appropriation, in which the product enslaves first the producer, and then also the appropriator, will thereby be replaced by the mode of appropriation of the product based on the nature of the modern means of production themselves: on the one hand direct social appropriation as a means to the maintenance and extension of production, and on the other hand direct individual appropriation as a means to life and pleasure.

By more and more transforming the great majority of the population into proletarians, the capitalist mode of production brings into being the force which, under penalty of its own destruction, is compelled to carry out this revolution. By more and more driving toward the conversion of the vast socialized means of production into state property, it itself points the way for the carrying through of this revolution. *The proletariat seizes the state power and transforms the means of production in the first instance into state property.* But in doing this, it puts an end to itself as the proletariat, it puts an end to all class differences and class antagonisms; it puts an end also to the state as the state. Former society, moving in class antagonisms, had need of the state, that is, an organization of the exploiting class at each period for the maintenance of its external conditions of production; that is, therefore, for the forcible holding down of the exploited class in the conditions of oppression (slavery, villeinage or serfdom, wage labor) determined by the existing mode of production. The state was the official representative of society as a whole, its embodiment in a visible corporation; but it was this only insofar as it was the state of that class which itself, in its epoch, represented society as a whole; in ancient times, the state of the slave owning citizens; in the Middle Ages, of the feudal nobility; in our epoch, of the bourgeoisie. When ultimately it becomes really representative of society as a whole, it makes itself superfluous. As soon as there is no longer any class of society to be held in subjection, as soon as, along with class domination and the struggle for individual existence based on the former anarchy of production, the collisions and excesses arising from these have also been abolished, there is nothing more to be repressed which would make a special repressive force, a state, necessary. The first act in which the state really comes forward as the representative of society as a whole—the taking possession of the means of production in the name of society—is at the same time its last independent act as a state. The interference of the state power in social relations becomes superfluous in one sphere after another, and then ceases of itself. The government of persons is replaced by the administration of things and the direction of the processes of production. The state is not "abolished," *it withers away.* . . .

The seizure of the means of production by society puts an end to commodity production, and therewith to the domination of the product over the producer. Anarchy in social production is replaced by conscious organization on a planned basis. The struggle for individual existence comes to an end. And at this point, in a certain sense, man finally cuts himself off from the animal world, leaves the conditions of animal existence behind him, and enters conditions which are really human. The conditions of existence forming man's environment, which up to now have dominated man, at this point pass under the dominion and control of man, who now for the first time becomes the real conscious master of nature, because and insofar as he has become master of his own social organization. The laws of his own social activity, which have hitherto confronted him as external, dominating laws of nature, will then be applied by man with complete understanding, and hence will be dominated by man. Men's own social organization, which has hitherto stood in opposition to them as if arbitrarily decreed by nature and history, will then become the voluntary act of men themselves. The objective, external forces which have hitherto dominated history, will then pass under the control of men themselves. It is only from this point that men, with full consciousness, will fashion their own history; it is only from this point that the social causes set in motion by men will have, predominantly and in constantly increasing measure, the effects willed by men. It is humanity's leap from the realm of necessity into the realm of freedom. . . .

8. ENGELS:
REPUDIATION OF REVOLUTION

In this selection, taken from Engels's introduction to the 1895 edition of Marx's The Class Struggle in France, *we see clearly the "revolution" that has occurred in his conception of the proletarian road to power. Now, fifteen years after giving the argument presented in the preceding selection, reflecting upon the electoral successes of the German Social Democrats, Engels bolsters the trend toward exclusive parliamentarism by bestowing upon it his "Orthodox" sanction. Thus, the material contained in this selection is in fact the epitaph of the proletarian revolution of the nineteenth century and effectively precluded any Orthodox Marxist party from engaging in revolutionary practice during the period prior to the outbreak of the First World War.*

Thus, Engels gives his blessing to the reformist tendency within the SPD and the Second International. Thenceforth, the lines of division among Social Democrats will emerge as follows: (1) the "Orthodox" center, led by Kautsky, which retains the revolutionary slogans of a bygone era while in fact adopting a nonrevolutionary parliamentary program; (2) the "Revisionist" right, led by Bernstein, which argues for the elimination of all revolutionary pretensions and the revision of Marxist theory in terms of the economic realities of advanced capitalism, the emergence of a workers' aristocracy whose condition was demonstrably improving and the seeming efficacy of parliamentary reforms; and at a somewhat later date (3) the "Radical" left, led by Rosa Luxemburg, which demands a return to perpetual revolutionary activity and the subordination of parliamentarism to the spontaneous insurrection of the masses. The temporary victory of the SPD right during the years following Germany's defeat in World War I was ultimately to place German Social Democracy at the feet of the Nazis and, with the complicity of the Communists, to lead to the final destruction of Marxist Social Democracy in Europe.

. . . History has proved us, and all who thought like us, wrong. It has made it clear that the state of economic develop-

SOURCE: From Friedrich Engels, "Introduction" to Marx's *The Class Struggle in France,* in Karl Marx and Friedrich Engels, *Selected Works,* Vol. II (Moscow: Co-operative Publishing Society of Foreign Workers in the U.S.S.R., 1935).

ment on the Continent at that time [1848–1850] was not, by a long way, ripe for the removal of capitalist production; it has proved this by the economic revolution which, since 1848, has seized the whole of the Continent, has really caused big industry for the first time to take root in France, Austria, Hungary, Poland and, recently, in Russia, while it has made Germany positively an industrial country of the first rank—all on a capitalist basis, which in the year 1848, therefore, still had great capacity for expansion. But it is just this industrial revolution which has everywhere for the first time produced clarity in the class relationships, which has removed a number of transition forms handed down from the manufacturing period and in Eastern Europe even from guild handicraft, and has created a genuine bourgeoisie and a genuine large-scale industrial proletariat and has pushed them into the foreground of social development. But owing to this, the struggle of these two great classes, which, apart from England, existed in 1848 only in Paris and, at the most, in a few big industrial centers, has been spread over the whole of Europe and has reached an intensity such as was unthinkable in 1848. . . . At that time the many obscure evangels of the sects, with their panaceas; today the *one* generally recognized, transparently clear theory of Marx, sharply formulating the final aims of the struggle. At that time the masses, sundered and differing according to locality and nationality, linked only by the feeling of common suffering, undeveloped, tossed to and fro in their perplexity from enthusiasm to despair; today a great international army of socialists, marching irresistibly on and growing daily in number, organisation, discipline, insight and assurance of victory. If even this mighty army of the proletariat has still not reached its goal, if, a long way from winning victory with *one* mighty stroke, it has slowly to press forward from position to position in a hard, tenacious struggle, this only proves, once and for all, how impossible it was in 1848 to win social transformation by a simple surprise attack.

It was believed that the militant proletariat had been finally buried with the Paris Commune. But, completely to the contrary, it dates its most powerful advance from the Commune and the Franco-Prussian War. The recruitment of the whole of the population able to bear arms into armies that could be counted in millions, and the introduction of firearms, projectiles, and explosives of hitherto undreamt of efficacy created a complete revolution in all warfare. This, on the one hand, put a sudden end to the Bonapartist war period and insured peaceful industrial development, since any war other than a world war of unheard of cruelty and absolutely incalculable outcome had become an impossibility. On the other hand it caused military expenditure to rise in geometrical progression and thereby forced up taxes to exorbitant levels and so drove the poorer classes of people into the arms of socialism. . . .

The war of 1870–1871 and the defeat of the Commune had transferred the center of gravity of the European workers' movement for the time being from France to Germany, as Marx foretold. In France it naturally took years to recover from the bloodletting of May 1871. In Germany, on the other hand, where industry was, in addition, furthered by the blessing of the French milliards and developed more and more quickly, Social Democracy experienced a rapid and enduring growth. Thanks to the understanding with which the German workers made use of the universal suffrage introduced in 1866 the astonishing growth of the Party is made plain to all the world by incontestable figures: 1871, 102,000; 1874, 352,000; 1877, 493,000 Social Democratic votes. Then came recognition of this advance by high authority in the shape of the Anti-Socialist Law: the Party was temporarily disrupted; the number of votes sank to 312,000 in 1881. But that was quickly overcome, and then, though oppressed by the Exceptional Law, without press, without external organization, and without the right of combination or meeting, the rapid expansion really began: 1884, 550,000; 1887, 763,000; 1890, 1,427,000 votes. Then the hand of the state was paralyzed. The Anti-Socialist Law disappeared; socialist votes rose to 1,787,000, over a quarter of all the votes cast. The government and the ruling classes had exhausted all their expedients—uselessly, to no purpose, and without success. . . .

But the German workers rendered a second great service to their cause in addition to the first, which they performed by their mere existence as the strongest, best-disciplined, and most rapidly growing Socialist party. They supplied their comrades of all countries with a new weapon, and one of the sharpest, when they showed them how to use universal suffrage. . . .

The Communist Manifesto had already proclaimed the winning of universal suffrage, of democracy, as one of the first and most important tasks of the militant proletariat. . . . The franchise has been . . . transformed from a means of deception, which it was heretofore, into an instrument of emancipation. And if universal suffrage had offered no other advantage than that it allowed us to count our numbers every three years; that by the regularly established, unexpectedly rapid rise in the number of votes it increased in equal measure the workers' certainty of victory and the dismay of their opponents, and so became our best means of propaganda . . . then it would still have been more than enough. But it has done much more than this. In election agitation it provided us with a means, second to none, of getting in touch with the mass of the people, where they still stand aloof from us; of forcing all parties to defend their views and actions against our attacks before all the people; and, further, it opened to our representatives in the Reichstag a platform from which they could speak to their opponents in parliament and to the masses without. . . .

With this successful utilization of universal suffrage . . . it was found that state institutions . . . offer still further opportunities for the working class to fight these very state institutions. They took part in elections . . . they contested with the bourgeoisie for every post in the occupation of which a sufficient part of the proletariat had a say. And so it happened that the bourgeoisie and the government came to be much more afraid of the legal than of the illegal action of the Workers' party, of the results of elections than of those of rebellion.

For here, too, the conditions of the struggle had essentially changed. Rebellion in the old style, the street fight with barricades, which up to 1848 gave everywhere the final decision, was to a considerable extent obsolete.

Let us have no illusions about it: a real victory of an insurrection over the military in street fighting, a victory as between two armies, is one of the rarest exceptions. . . .

The numerous successes of the insurgents up to 1848 were due to a great variety of causes. In Paris in July 1830 and February 1848, as in most of the Spanish street fights, there stood between the insurgents and the military a citizens' guard which either directly took the side of the insurrection, or else by its lukewarm, indecisive attitude caused the troops likewise to vacillate, and supplied the insurrection with arms into the bargain. Where this citizens' guard opposed the insurrection from the outset, as in June 1848 in Paris, the insurrection was vanquished. In Berlin in 1848, the people were victorious partly through a considerable accession of new fighting forces during the night and the morning of the 19th, partly as a result of the exhaustion and bad victualing of the troops, and, finally, partly as a result of the paralyzed command. But in all cases the fight was won because the troops failed to obey, because the officers lost their power of decision, or because their hands were tied.

Even in the classic time of street fighting, therefore, the barricade produced more of a moral than a material effect. It was a means of shaking the steadfastness of the military. If it held out until this was attained, then victory was won; if not, there was defeat. This is the main point, which must be kept in view, likewise when the chances of contingent future street fights are examined.

The chances, however, were in 1849 already pretty poor. Everywhere the bourgeoisie had thrown in its lot with the governments, "culture and property" had hailed and feasted the military moving against the insurrections. The spell of the barricade was broken; the soldier no longer saw behind it "the people," but rebels, agitators, plunderers, levelers, the scum of society. . . .

But since then there have been very many more changes, and all in favor of the military. . . .

On the other hand, all the conditions on the insurgents' side have grown worse. An insurrection with which all sections of the people sympathize will hardly recur; in the class struggle all the middle sections will never group themselves around the proletariat so exclusively that the reactionary parties gathered around the bourgeoisie well nigh disappear. The "people," therefore, will always appear divided, and with this a powerful lever, so extraordinarily effective in 1848, is lacking. . . . Does that mean that in the future the street fight will play no further role? Certainly not. It only means that the conditions since 1848 have become far more unfavorable for civil fights, far more favorable for the military. A future street fight can therefore only be victorious when this unfavorable situation is compensated by other factors. Accordingly, it will occur more seldom in the beginning of a great revolution than in its further progress, and will have to be undertaken with greater forces. . . .

Does the reader now understand why the ruling classes decidedly want to bring us to where the guns shoot and the sabers slash? Why they accuse us today of cowardice, because we do not betake ourselves without more ado into the street, where we are certain of defeat in advance? Why they so earnestly implore us to play for once the part of cannon fodder?

The gentlemen pour out their prayers and their challenges for nothing, for nothing at all. We are not so stupid. . . . The time of surprise attacks, of revolutions carried through by small conscious minorities at the head of unconscious masses, is past. Where it is a question of a complete transformation of the social organization, the masses themselves must also be in it, must themselves already have grasped what is at stake, what they are going in for with body and soul. The history of the last fifty years has taught us that. But in order that the masses may understand what is to be done, long persistent work is required, and it is just this work which we are now pursuing, and with a success which drives the enemy to despair. . . .

Everywhere the unprepared onslaught has gone into the background (except where the government has openly provoked it) everywhere the German example of utilizing the suffrage, of winning all posts accessible to us, has been imitated . . . even in France the Socialists are realizing more and more that no lasting victory is possible for them, unless they first win the great mass of people, i.e., in this case, the peasants. Slow propaganda work and parliamentary activity are being recognized here, too, as the most immediate tasks of the Party. . . . We will get in, that is certain, the only question still in dispute is: By which door? . . .

Of course, our foreign comrades do not renounce their right to revolution. The right to revolution is, after all, the only real "historical right," the only right on which all modern states without exception rest. . . .

But whatever may happen in other countries, German Social Democracy has a special situation and therewith, at least in the first instance, a special task. The two million voters whom it sends to the ballot box, together with the young men and women who stand behind them as nonvoters, form the most numerous, most compact mass, the decisive *"shock force"* of the international proletarian army. This mass already supplies over a fourth of the recorded votes; and . . . it increases uninterruptedly. Its growth proceeds as spontaneously, as steadily, as irresistibly, and at the same time as tranquilly as a natural process. All government intervention has proved powerless against it. We can count even today on two and a half million voters. If it continues in this fashion, by the end of the century we shall conquer the greater part of the middle section of society, petty bourgeois and small peasants, and grow into the decisive power in the land, before which all other powers will have to bow, whether they like it or not. To keep this growth going without interruption until of itself it gets beyond the control of the ruling governmental system, not to fritter away this daily increasing shock force in advance guard fighting, but to keep it intact until the day of the decision, that is our main task. And there is only one means by which the steady rise of the socialist fighting forces in Germany could be momentarily halted, and even thrown back for some time: a clash on a big scale with the military, a bloodbath like that of 1871 in Paris. In the long run that would also be overcome. To shoot out of the world a party which numbers millions—all the magazine rifles of Europe and America are not enough for this. But the normal development would be impeded; the shock force would, perhaps, not be available at the critical moment, the decisive struggle would be delayed, protracted, and attended by heavy sacrifices.

The irony of world history turns everything upside down. We, the "revolutionaries," the "rebels"—we are thriving far better on legal methods than on illegal methods and revolt. The parties of order, as they call themselves, are perishing under the legal conditions created by themselves. They cry despairingly [that] legality is the death of us; whereas we, under this legality, get firm muscles and rosy cheeks and look like eternal life. And if we are not so crazy as to let ourselves be driven into street fighting in order to please them, then nothing else is finally left for them but themselves to break through this legality so fatal to them.

Let them put through their antirevolt bills . . . they will achieve nothing but a new proof of their impotence. . . . They can only hold in check the Social Democratic revolt which is just now doing so well by keeping within the law, by revolt on the part of the parties of order, which cannot live without breaking the laws. . . .

9. BERNSTEIN:
THE MANIFESTO OF REVISIONISM

*In 1898, Eduard Bernstein, the author of the second, i.e., "practical,"
part of the Erfurt Program, published two articles in which he advocated
the "revising" of Marxist theory on the basis of the latest developments
of capitalism. Arguing that the anticipated increase in the misery of
the proletariat had failed to materialize, but that the three decades since
the publication of Capital had evidenced the general improvement in
its condition, Bernstein proposed that Marxism as a political movement
should abandon the theory of periodic and worsening economic catastrophes ("depressions") and the alleged necessity of worsening economic conditions to propel the working class to revolutionary action.
Noting, as well, that the SPD was making great strides through the
electoral process, and that this strategy had in fact been endorsed
by Engels, he proposed the abandoning of the theories of the class
struggle and proletarian revolution and their replacement by the ideal
of cooperation between the proletariat and the bourgeois classes in order
to win for Germany a fully democratic political life without requiring
the overthrow of the bourgeoisie and the abolition of capitalism. This
"petit-bourgeois radicalism" was immediately recognized by Bernstein's
critics (foremost among them Rosa Luxemburg and Lenin) as tantamount to abandoning the ultimate goal of socialism. The "Revisionist
Controversy" was thus, by 1899, on in full.*

*The theoretical errors underlying Bernstein's arguments are too
numerous to be properly treated here. But what must be said in his
favor is that he at least had the temerity plainly to advocate officially
adopting a course of action which was in fact if not in theory already
party policy, yet the full significance of which had not yet dawned upon
Kautsky and the party leadership. Thus, the "opportunist" trend (as it
was called by its opponents) was in fact symptomatic of the antirevolutionary, neo-Kantian, and anti-Marxian malady which had begun to
beset Social Democracy from the time of the hegemony of Engels.*

For one thing, Bernstein wished to recognize in theory what Engels

SOURCE: From Eduard Bernstein, *Evolutionary Socialism*, trans. Edith C.
Harvey, introduction by Sidney Hook (New York: Schocken Books, 1961).
Reprinted by permission of Schocken Books, Inc.

and Kautsky had already accepted in practice: that the SPD should set as its goal the utilization of bourgeois democracy to gain political influence in an autocratic Germany and to use this influence to vanquish the autocracy. The unique feature of Bernstein's course lay in his openly avowing that this presumably proximate goal of supporting the growth of democratic institutions within bourgeois society should replace the "ultimate goal" of socialism, whereas Kautsky still repeatedly reaffirmed the "ultimacy" of socialism although he ignored it in practice.

Foremost among Bernstein's goals (most of which had already been written into the Erfurt Program) were the separation of the SPD leadership from the working masses, the adoption of trade-union goals such as the amelioration of the poverty of the unemployed, improvement in living and working conditions, universal suffrage, and so on, and the replacing of the revolutionary struggle of the working class by the parliamentary maneuverings of its political representatives. "Revisionism" thus accelerated the derevolutionizing of the German (and hence the entire European) proletariat by denying it the revolutionary class consciousness which, emerging from its experience in the open class struggle, alone would have made it both capable and worthy of becoming the "gravedigger" of the bourgeoisie and the maker of a new and greater society. Both Engels's and Kautsky's "Orthodoxy" and Bernstein's "Revisionism" failed to perceive the profound illusion contained in the belief that the parliamentary struggle is identical with the class struggle. It is as if they expected the bourgeoisie and the Junkers to hand over governmental power (i.e., first their class privileges and then ultimately their class existence) simply because the SPD, or a coalition of politicians which it led, managed to hold majorities in various legislative assemblies! It was to be only Rosa Luxemburg in Germany and Lenin in Russia who would see that general economic collapse was, more than ever, necessary to the proletarian revolution and that this collapse would require many years of preparation through "premature" (from the "scientific" point of view) revolutionary agitation to thwart capitalist development and to revolutionize the proletariat itself.

For the rest, Bernstein's arguments concerning the separation of "pure" from "applied" Marxism are complete nonsense—especially his bid to abandon the central concept of the class struggle and replace it with Kantian morality. But here too, he is only carrying to its logical conclusion the policies, if not the rhetoric, of Engels and Kautsky.

Lastly, we note that Bernstein, like his disciple Hilferding,[1] had no

1. Cf. pp. 119–120, above.

use for Marxism as the "unity of theory and practice." For Bernstein, Marx's Capital *contained an unacceptable "dualism" which consisted in its attempt to be, on the one hand, a "scientific inquiry" while, on the other, it is a means used "to prove a theory laid down before its drafting." In Bernstein, then, we see not merely a separation of theory from practice, but also a restriction of "theory" to "scientific inquiry" and the exclusion of all "philosophical brain weaving" (the phrase is that of Franz Mehring, Social Democratic biographer of Marx). Bernstein's predilection for the "eternal validity" of the Kantian ethic in place of the unscientific prejudice for the class struggle forbids, in principle, any serious proletarian political action. The dialectic of historical development propelled by the class struggle is abandoned, and replaced—if at all —by the idealism of the categorical imperative forbidding treating others, including class enemies, merely as means, while "theory" is sacrificed to the idol of neo-Kantian scientific neutrality in practical matters. It is thus that, after the influence of Engels and Kautsky had eaten into its heart, finally at Bernstein's hands Social Democracy completely ceased even to pretend to be a revolutionary movement.*

It has been maintained in a certain quarter that the practical deductions from my treatises would be the abandonment of the conquest of political power by the proletariat organized politically and economically. That is quite an arbitrary deduction, the accuracy of which I altogether deny.

I set myself against the notion that we have to expect shortly a collapse of the bourgeois economy, and that social democracy should be induced by the prospect of such an imminent, great, social catastrophe to adapt its tactics to that assumption. That I maintain most emphatically.

The adherents of this theory of a catastrophe base it especially on the conclusions of the *Communist Manifesto*. This is a mistake in every respect.

The theory which the *Communist Manifesto* sets forth of the evolution of modern society was correct as far as it characterized the general tendencies of that evolution. But it was mistaken in several special deductions, above all in the estimate of the *time* the evolution would take. The last has been unreservedly acknowledged by Friedrich Engels, the joint author with Marx of the *Manifesto,* in his preface to the *Class Struggle in France*.[2] But

2. Cf. Selection 8, above.

it is evident that if social evolution takes a much greater period of time than was assumed, it must also take upon itself *forms* and lead to forms that were not foreseen and could not be foreseen then.

Social conditions have not developed to such an acute opposition of things and classes as is depicted in the *Manifesto*. It is not only useless, it is the greatest folly to attempt to conceal this from ourselves. The number of members of the possessing classes is today not smaller but larger. The enormous increase of social wealth is not accompanied by a decreasing number of large capitalists but by an increasing number of capitalists of all degrees. The middle classes change their character, but they do not disappear from the social scale.

The concentration in productive industry is not being accomplished even today in all its departments with equal thoroughness and at an equal rate. . . .

In all advanced countries we see the privileges of the capitalist bourgeoisie yielding step by step to democratic organizations. Under the influence of this, and driven by the movement of the working classes which is daily becoming stronger, a social reaction has set in against the exploiting tendencies of capital, a counteraction which, although it still proceeds timidly and feebly, yet does exist, and is always drawing more departments of economic life under its influence. Factory legislation, the democratizing of local government, and the extension of its area of work, the freeing of trade unions and systems of cooperative trading from legal restrictions, the consideration of standard conditions of labor in the work undertaken by public authorities—all these characterize this phase of the evolution.

But the more the political organizations of modern nations are democratized the more the needs and opportunities of great political catastrophes are diminished. He who holds firmly to the catastrophic theory of evolution must, with all his power, withstand and hinder the evolution described above, which, indeed, the logical defenders of that theory formerly did. But is the conquest of political power by the proletariat simply to be by a political catastrophe? Is it to be the appropriation and utilization of the power of the State by the proletariat exclusively against the whole nonproletarian world?

He who replies in the affirmative must be reminded of two things. In 1872 Marx and Engels announced in the preface to the new edition of the *Communist Manifesto* that the Paris Commune had exhibited a proof that "the working classes cannot simply take possession of the ready-made State machine and set it in motion for their own aims." And in 1895 Friedrich Engels stated in detail in the preface to *The Class Struggle in France* that the time of political surprises, of the "revolutions of small conscious minorities at the head of unconscious masses" was today at an end, that a collision on a large scale with the military would be the means of checking the steady growth of social democracy and of even throwing it back for a time—in short, that social democracy would flourish far better by lawful than by unlawful means and by violent revolution. And he points out in conformity with this opinion that the next task of the party should be "to work for an uninterrupted increase of its votes" or to carry on a slow *propaganda of parliamentary activity.*

Thus Engels, who, nevertheless, as his numerical examples show, still somewhat overestimated the rate of process of the evolution! Shall we be told that he abandoned the conquest of political power by the working classes, because he wished to avoid the steady growth of social democracy secured by lawful means being interrupted by a political revolution?

If not, and if one subscribes to his conclusions, one cannot reasonably take any offense if it is declared that for a long time yet the task of social democracy is, instead of speculating on a great economic crash, "to organize the working classes politically and develop them as a democracy and to fight for all reforms in the State which are adapted to raise the working classes and transform the State in the direction of democracy."

That is what I have said in my impugned article and what I still maintain in its full import. As far as concerns the question propounded above it is equivalent to Engels's dictum, for democracy is, at any given time, as much government by the working classes as these are capable of practicing according to their intellectual ripeness and the degree of social development they have attained. Engels, indeed, refers at the place just mentioned to the fact that the *Communist Manifesto* has "proclaimed the conquest of the democracy as one of the first and important tasks of the fighting proletariat." . . .

No one has questioned the necessity for the working classes to gain the control of government. The point at issue is between the theory of a social cataclysm and the question whether with the given social development in Germany and the present advanced state of its working classes in the towns and the country, a sudden catastrophe would be desirable in the interest of the social democracy. I have denied it and deny it again, because in my judgment a greater security for lasting success lies in a steady advance than in the possibilities offered by a catastrophic crash. . . .

In this sense I wrote the sentence that the movement means everything for me and that what is *usually* called "the final aim of socialism" is nothing; and in this sense I write it down again today. Even if the word "usually" had not shown that the proposition was only to be understood conditionally; it was obvious that it *could* not express indifference concerning the final carrying out of socialist principles, but only indifference—or, as it would be better expressed, carelessness—as to the form of the final arrangement of things. I have at no time had an excessive interest in the future, beyond general principles; I have not been able to read to the end any picture of the future. My thoughts and efforts are concerned with the duties of the present and the nearest future, and I only busy myself with the perspectives beyond so far as they give me a line of conduct for suitable action now.

The conquest of political power by the working classes, the expropriation of capitalists, are no ends in themselves but only means for the accomplishment of certain aims and endeavors. As such they are demands in the program of social democracy and are not attacked by me. Nothing can be said beforehand as to the circumstances of their accomplishment; we can only fight for their realization. But the conquest of political power necessitates the possession of political *rights;* and the most important problem of tactics which German social democracy has at the present time to solve appears to me to be to devise the best ways for the extension of the political and economic rights of the German working classes.

In all sciences a distinction can be drawn between a pure and an applied science. The first consists of principles and of a knowledge, which are derived from the whole series of corresponding experiences and therefore looked upon as universally valid. They form the element of stability in the theory. From the application of these principles to single phenomena or to particular cases of practical experience is formed an applied science; the knowledge won from this application put together in propositions forms the principles of the applied science. These form the variable element in the structure of a science. . . .

When we separate the fabric of the Marxist doctrine . . . we are able to estimate the import of its separate propositions to the whole system. With every proposition of the pure science a portion of the foundation would be torn away and a great part of the whole building would be robbed of its support and fall down. But it is otherwise with the propositions of the applied science. These could fall without shaking the foundations in the least. A whole series of propositions in the applied science could fall without dragging down the other parts in sympathy. . . .

It suffices for my purpose to denote as the chief parts of what in my opinion is the building of the pure science of Marxism, the program of historical materialism, the theory (the germ of which is already contained therein) of the wars of the classes in general and the class war between bourgeoisie and proletariat in particular, as well as the theory of surplus value with that of the method of production in a bourgeois society and the description of the tendencies of the development of this society. Like the propositions of the applied science, those of the pure science are of different values to the system.

No one will deny that the most important element in the foundation of Marxism, the fundamental law so to say which penetrates the whole system, is its specific philosophy of history which bears the name of the materialist interpretation of history. With it Marxism stands or falls in principle; according to the measure in which it suffers limitations will the position of the other elements toward one another be affected in sympathy.

Every search into its validity must, therefore, start from the question whether or how far this theory is true.

"We had to emphasize face to face with our opponents the chief principle (the economic side) denied by them, and there was not always time, place, and opportunity to do justice to the other considerations concerned in and affected by it" (Friedrich Engels, Letter of 1890 reprinted in the *Sozialistischen Akademiker*, October, 1895).

The question of the correctness of the materialist interpretation of history is the question of the determining causes of historic necessity. To be a materialist means first of all to trace back all phenomena to the necessary movements of matter. These movements of matter are accomplished according to the materialist doctrine from beginning to end as a mechanical process, each individual process being the necessary result of preceding mechanical facts. Mechanical facts determine, in the last resort, all occurrences, even those which appear to be caused by ideas. It is, finally, always the movement of matter which determines the form of ideas and the directions of the will; and thus these also (and with them everything that happens in the world of humanity) are inevitable. The materialist is thus a Calvinist without God. If he does not believe in a predestination ordained by a divinity, yet he believes and must believe that starting from any chosen point of time all further events are, through the whole of existing matter and the directions of force in its parts, determined beforehand.

The application of materialism to the interpretation of history means then, first of all, belief in the inevitableness of all historical events and developments. The question is only in what manner the inevitable is accomplished in human history, what element of force or what factors of force speak the decisive word, what is the relation of the different factors of force to one another, what part in history falls to the share of nature, of political economy, of legal organizations, of ideas.

Marx . . . gives the answer, that he designates as the determining factor, the material productive forces and the conditions of production among men at the time.

The method of production of the material things of life settles generally the social, political, and spiritual process of life. It is not the consciousness of men that determines their mode of existence, but on the contrary their social existence that determines [the nature of] their consciousness. At a certain stage in their development the material productive forces of society come into opposition with the existing conditions of production or, which is only a legal expression for it, with the relations of property within which they have hitherto moved. From forms of development of the forces of production, these relations change into fetters. Then enters an epoch of social revolution. With the change of the economic foundation the whole gigantic superstructure (the legal and political organizations to which certain social forms of consciousness correspond) is more slowly or more quickly overthrown. One form of society never perishes before all the productive forces are evolved for which it is sufficiently comprehensive, and new or higher conditions of production never step on to the scene before the material conditions of existence of the same have come to light out of the womb of the old society. The bourgeois relations of production are the last antagonistic form of the social process of production . . . but the productive forces developing in the heart of the bourgeois society create at the same time the material conditions for the solution of this antagonism. The previous history of human society, therefore, terminates with this form of society.*

In the preface to the first volume of *Capital* we come across a sentence savoring no less of predestination. "We are concerned," it reads, with reference to the "natural laws" of capitalist production, "with these tendencies working and forcing their way with iron necessity." And yet just when he was speaking of *law,* a milder concept comes forward—that of tendency. And on the next page stands the sentence so often quoted, that society can "shorten and soften" the birth pains of phases of development in conformity with nature. . . .

In his later works Engels limited the determining force of the conditions of production—most of all in two letters reprinted in the *Sozialistischen Akademiker* of October 1895, the one written in the year 1890, the other in the year 1894. There, "forms of law," political, legal, philosophical theories, religious intuitions or dogmas are enumerated as forces which influence the course of historical struggles and in many cases "are factors preponderating in the determination of their form." "There are then innumerable forces thwarting one another," we read, "an endless

* *A Contribution to the Critique of Political Economy,* Preface. Cf. also *Karl Marx: The Essential Writings,* pp. 161–163.

group of parallelograms of forces, from which one resultant—the historical event—is produced which itself can again be looked upon as the product of a power working as a whole without consciousness or will. For what every single man wills is hindered by every other man, and the result of the struggle is something which no one had intended" (Letter of 1890). "The political, legal, philosophical, religious, literary, artistic evolution rests on the economic evolution. But they all react on one another and on the economic basis" (Letter of 1895). It must be confessed that this sounds somewhat different from the passage from Marx quoted above.

It will, of course, not be maintained that Marx and Engels at any time overlooked the fact that noneconomic factors exercise an influence on the course of history. Innumerable passages from their early writings can be quoted against such suppositions. But we are dealing here with a question of proportion—not whether ideologic factors were acknowledged, but what measure of influence, what significance for history were ascribed to them, and in this respect it cannot be denied that Marx and Engels originally assigned to the noneconomic factors a much less influence on the evolution of society, a much less power of modifying by their action the conditions of production than in their later writings. . . .

In a letter to Conrad Schmidt dated October 27, 1890, Friedrich Engels showed in an excellent manner how from being products of economic development, social institutions become independent social forces with actions of their own, which in their turn may react on the former, and according to circumstances, promote or hinder them or turn them into other directions. He brings forward in the first place the power of the state as an example, when he completes the definition of the state mostly given by him—as the organ of the *government of the classes* and of *repression*—by the very important derivation of the state from the social division of labor. Historical materialism by no means denies every autonomy to political and ideologic forces—it combats only the idea that these independent actions are unconditional, and shows that the development of the economic foundations of social life—the conditions of production and the evolution of classes—finally exercises the stronger influence on these actions.

But in any case the multiplicity of the factors remains, and it is by no means always easy to lay bare the relations which exist among them so exactly that it can be determined with certainty where in given cases the strongest motive power is to be sought. The purely economic causes create, first of all, only a disposition for the reception of certain ideas, but how these then arise and spread and what form they take depend on the cooperation of a whole series of influences. More harm than good is done to historical materialism if at the outset one rejects as eclecticism an accentuation of the influences other than those of a purely economic kind, and a consideration of other economic factors than the technics of production and their foreseen development. . . .

But because men pay ever greater attention to economic factors it easily appears as though these played a greater part today than formerly. That, however, is not the case. The deception is only caused because in many cases the economic motive appears freely today where formerly it was concealed by conditions of government and symbols of all kinds. Modern society is much richer than earlier societies in ideologies which are not determined by economics and by nature working as an economic force. Sciences, arts, a whole series of social relations are today much less dependent on economics than formerly, or, in order to give no room for misconception, the point of economic development attained today leaves the ideological, and especially the ethical, factors greater space for independent activity than was formerly the case. In consequence of this the interdependency of cause and effect between technical, economic evolution and the evolution of other social tendencies is becoming always more indirect, and from that the necessities of the first are losing much of their power of dictating the form of the latter.

"The Iron Necessity of History" receives in this way a limitation, which, let me say at once, signifies in regard to the practice of social democracy no lessening but an increasing and qualifying of its social political tasks.

Thus we see the materialist conception of history today in another form than it was presented at first by its founders. It has gone through a development already, it has suffered limitations in absolutist interpretation. That is the history of every theory. It would be the greatest retrogression to go back from the ripe form which Engels has given it in the letters to Conrad Schmidt to the first definitions and to give it a "monistic" interpretation based on these. . . .

In its first form it could become in the hand of a Marx a lever of mighty historical discoveries, but even his genius was led by it to all kinds of false conclusions. . . .

An economic interpretation of history does not necessarily mean that only economic forces, only economic motives, are recognized; but only that economics forms an ever recurring decisive force, the cardinal point of the great movements in history. To the words "materialist conception of history" still adhere all the misunderstandings which are closely joined with the conception of materialism. Philosophic materialism, or the materialism of natural science, is in a mechanical sense deterministic. The Marxist conception of history is not. It allots to the economic foundation of the life of nations no unconditioned determining influence on the forms this life takes.

. . . To me the chapter [on the "Historical Tendency of Capitalist Accumulation" in Vol. I of *Capital*] illustrates a dualism which runs through the whole monumental work of Marx . . . a dualism which consists in this, that the work aims at being a scientific inquiry and also at proving a theory laid down long before its drafting; a formula lies at the basis of it in which the result to which the exposition should lead is fixed beforehand. The return to the *Communist Manifesto* points here to a real residue of Utopianism in the Marxist system. Marx had accepted the solution of the Utopians in essentials, but had recognized their means and proofs as inadequate. He therefore undertook a revision of them. . . .

For the general sympathy with the strivings for emancipation of the working classes does not in itself stand in the way of the scientific method. But, as Marx approaches a point when that final aim enters seriously into the question, he becomes uncertain and unreliable. Such contradictions then appear as were shown in the book under consideration, for instance, in the section on the movement of incomes in modern society. It thus appears that this great scientific spirit was, in the end, a slave to a doctrine. To express it figuratively, he has raised a mighty building within the framework of a scaffolding he found existing, and in its erection he kept strictly to the laws of scientific architecture as long as they did not collide with the conditions which the construction of the scaffolding prescribed, but he neglected or evaded them when the scaffolding did not allow of their observance. Where the scaffolding put limits in the way of the building, instead of destroying the scaffolding, he changed the building itself at the cost of its right proportions and so made it all the more dependent on the scaffolding. Was it the consciousness of this irrational relation which caused him continually to pass from completing his work to amending special parts of it? However that may be, my conviction is that wherever that dualism shows itself the scaffolding must fall if the building is to grow in its right proportions. In the latter, and not in the former, is found what is worthy to live in Marx.

Nothing confirms me more in this conception than the anxiety with which some persons seek to maintain certain statements in *Capital,* which are falsified by facts. It is just some of the more deeply devoted followers of Marx who have not been able to separate themselves from the dialectical form of the work—that is the scaffolding alluded to—who do this. At least, that is only how I can explain the words of a man, otherwise so amenable to facts as Kautsky, who, when I observed in Stuttgart that the number of wealthy people for many years had increased, not decreased, answered: "If that were true then the date of our victory would not only be very long postponed, but we should never attain our goal. If it be capitalists who increase and not those with no possessions, then we are going ever further from our goal the more evolution progresses, then capitalism grows stronger, not socialism."

That the number of the wealthy increases and does not diminish is not an invention of bourgeois "harmony economists," but a fact established by the boards of assessment for taxes, often to the chagrin of those concerned, a fact which can no longer be disputed. But what is the significance of this fact as regards the victory of socialism? Why should the realization of socialism depend on its refutation? Well, simply for this reason: because the dialectical scheme seems so to prescribe it; because a post threatens to fall out of the scaffolding if one admits that the social surplus product is appropriated by an increasing instead of a decreasing number of possessors. But it is only the speculative theory that is affected by this matter; it does not at all affect the actual movement. Neither the struggle of the workers for democracy in politics nor their struggle for democracy in industry is touched by it. The prospects of this struggle do not depend on the theory of concentration of capital in the hands of a diminishing number of magnates, nor on the whole dialectical scaffolding of which this is a plank, but on the growth of social wealth and of the social productive forces, in conjunction with general social progress, and, particularly, in conjunction with the intellectual and moral advance of the working classes themselves.

Suppose the victory of socialism depended on the constant shrinkage in the number of capitalist magnates, social democracy, if it wanted to act logically, either would have to support the heaping up of capital in ever fewer hands, or at least to give no support to anything that would stop this shrinkage. As a matter of fact it often enough does neither the one nor the other. These considerations, for instance, do not govern its votes on questions of taxation. From the standpoint of the catastrophic theory a great part of this practical activity of the working classes is an undoing of work that ought to be allowed to be done. It is not social democracy which is wrong in this respect. The fault lies in the doctrine which assumes that progress depends on the deterioration of social conditions. . . .

. . . Is [the question] not rather a rejection of certain remains of Utopianism which adhere to Marxism, and which are the cause of the contradictions in theory and practice which have been pointed out in Marxism by its critics? . . .

It is evident at the first glance that great differences exist in the latter respect. But they are usually found to be this: that law, or the path of legislative reform, is the slower way, and revolutionary force the quicker and more radical. But that only is true in a restricted sense. Whether the legislative or the revolutionary method is the more promising depends entirely on the nature of the measures and on their relation to different classes and customs of the people.

In general, one may say here that the revolutionary way (always in the sense of revolution by violence) does quicker work as far as it deals with removal of obstacles which a privileged minority places in the path of social progress: that its strength lies on its negative side.

Constitutional legislation works more slowly in this respect as a rule. Its path is usually that of compromise, not the prohibition, but the buying out of acquired rights. But it is stronger than the revolution scheme where prejudice and the limited horizon of the great mass of the people appear as hindrances to social progress, and it offers greater advantages where it is a question of the creation of permanent economic arrangements capable of lasting; in other words, it is best adapted to positive social-political work. . . .

As soon as a nation has attained a position where the rights of the propertied minority have ceased to be a serious obstacle to social progress, where the negative tasks of political action are less pressing than the positive, then the appeal to a revolution by force becomes a meaningless phrase. One can overturn a government or a privileged minority, but not a nation. When the working classes do not possess very strong economic organizations of their own, and have not attained, by means of education on self-governing bodies, a high degree of mental independence, the dictatorship of the proletariat means the dictatorship of club orators and writers. . . .

One has not overcome Utopianism if one assumes that there is in the present, or ascribes to the present, what is to be in the future. We have to take working men as they are. And they are neither so universally pauperized as was set out in the *Communist Manifesto,* nor so free from prejudices and weaknesses as their courtiers wish to make us believe. They have the virtues and failings of the economic and social conditions under which they live. And neither these conditions nor their effects can be put on one side from one day to another. . . .

We cannot demand from a class, the great majority of whose members live under crowded conditions, are badly educated, and have an uncertain and insufficient income, the high intellectual and moral standard which the organization and existence of a socialist community presupposes. We will, therefore, not ascribe it to them by way of fiction. Let us rejoice at the great stock of intelligence, renunciation, and energy which the modern working class movement has partly revealed, partly produced; but we must not assign, without discrimination to the masses, the millions, what holds good, say, of hundreds of thousands. . . . Just because I expect much of the working classes I censure much more everything that tends to corrupt their moral judgment than I do similar habits of the higher classes, and I see with the greatest regret that a tone of literary decadence is spreading here and there in the working class press which can only have a confusing and corrupting effect. A class which is aspiring needs a sound morale and must suffer no deterioration. Whether it sets out for itself an ideal ultimate aim is of secondary importance if it pursues with energy its proximate aims. The important point is that these aims are inspired by a definite principle which expresses a higher degree of economy and of social life, that they are an embodiment of a social conception which means in the evolution of civilization a higher view of morals and of legal rights.

From this point of view I cannot subscribe to the proposition: "The working class has no ideas to realize." I see in it rather a self-deception, if it is not a mere play upon words on the part of its author.

And in this mind, I, at the time, resorted to the spirit of the great Königsberg philosopher, the critic of pure reason, against the cant which sought to get a hold on the working class movement and to which the Hegelian dialectic offers a comfortable refuge. I did this in the conviction that social democracy required a Kant who should judge the received opinion and examine it critically with deep acuteness, who should show where its apparent materialism is the highest—and is therefore the most easily misleading—ideology, and warn it that the contempt of the ideal, the magnifying of material factors until they become omnipotent forces of evolution, is a self-deception, which has been and will be exposed as such at every opportunity by the action of those who proclaim it. Such a thinker could show what is worthy and destined to live in the work of our great champions, and what must and can perish. . . .

10. LUXEMBURG:
BALLOT BOX OR MASS STRIKE?

Rosa Luxemburg's article "Reform or Revolution?" published in 1898 was the most thorough critique of Bernstein's work to emerge from the ranks of German Social Democracy. Her argument cuts deeply into the errors of Bernstein's shortsighted evaluation of the course of capitalist development (although it would take the debate on imperialism, which would begin only in 1907, to uncover the reasons underlying modern capitalism's ability to survive) and showed that the political consequence of Bernstein's position would be the end of the SPD as a socialist party. This article immediately established her as one of the party's leading theoreticians, but she was not to become the leading spokesman for the left wing until 1906 with her criticism of Kautsky's timid position on the question of the mass strike. Basic to Rosa Luxemburg's drive to revitalize the SPD was her campaign to have the proletarian political movement adopt the mass strike as its primary weapon. Writing in 1906, she openly criticized the leadership on this issue, and was henceforth branded a dangerous radical, whose views were considered alien to, and destructive of, Marxism.

The controversy over the mass strike centered on three points. First, it had been condemned as an exclusively anarchist tactic by both Marx and Engels, at a time when anarchism was indeed a threat to the hegemony of Marxism in the workers' movement. Second, in 1905, the SPD had made it its policy to strike only in the event that the Kaiser's government attempted to suspend the right to vote, this being, of course, the basis of the SPD's claim to existence. But even worse than this purely defensive policy, which aimed only to secure bourgeois rights within the prevailing social order, was the German Trades Union Congress's unconditional rejection of even this mild and conditional acceptance of the general strike, and its decision not even to discuss such a "dangerous" matter any further. Third, the startling success of the revolutionary risings occurring in Russia (1905–1906), which arose from the persistent use of the mass strike during the previous four years, made it obvious to Rosa Luxemburg and her followers that the Western

SOURCE: From Rosa Luxemburg, "The Mass Strike," trans. Patrick Lavin, in *Rosa Luxemburg Speaks*, ed. Mary Alice Waters (New York: Pathfinder Press, 1970). Reprinted by permission.

European Social Democrats needed to reconsider their "Orthodox" parliamentarianism which conceived of socialist praxis as simply propaganda and vote gathering, and to raise anew the question of "reform or revolution." This time the Kautskyan center was forced to defend the course of reform, and it was thus finally exposed for what it truly was—a party of petit-bourgeois democrats masquerading as socialists.

But to Rosa Luxemburg, even more important than the question of tactics was the need to prepare the working class to assume their revolutionary responsibilities, and this seemed to her to require not only the responsiveness of the socialist politicians to the masses whom they claimed to represent but also the instilling—to be gained through experience—*of a revolutionary class consciousness in the workers themselves. This last point, she saw, could be accomplished only in the daily struggle of the entire working class against the bourgeoisie and their political representatives. An unheard voice in the wilderness, Rosa Luxemburg, almost alone among Social Democratic leaders of the period, championed the idea of the* unity *of Marxist social and economic theory and the revolutionary practice of the proletariat.*

Almost all works and pronouncements of international socialism on the subject of the mass strike date from the time before the Russian Revolution [of 1905], the first historical experiment on a very large scale with this means of struggle. It is therefore evident that they are, for the most part, out of date. Their standpoint is essentially that of Engels, who in 1873 wrote as follows in his criticism of the revolutionary blundering of the Bakuninists in Spain:

The general strike, in the Bakuninists' program, is the lever which will be used for introducing the social revolution. One fine morning all the workers in every industry in a country, or perhaps in every country, will cease work, and thereby compel the ruling classes either to submit in about four weeks, or to launch an attack on the workers so that the latter will have the right to defend themselves, and may use the opportunity to overthrow the old society. The proposal is by no means new. French and Belgian socialists have paraded it continually since 1848, but for all that it is of English origin. During the rapid and powerful development of Chartism among the English workers that followed the crisis of 1837, the "holy month"—a suspension of work on a national scale—was preached as early as 1839, and was received with such favor that in July 1842 the factory workers of the north of England attempted to carry it out. And at the Congress of the Alliancists at Geneva on September 1, 1873, the general strike played a great part, but it was admitted on all sides that to carry it out it was necessary to have a perfect organization of the working class and a full war chest. And this is the crux of the question. On the one hand, the government, especially if they are encouraged by the workers' abstention from political action, will never allow the funds of the workers to become large enough, and on the other hand, political events and the encroachments of the ruling classes will bring about the liberation of the workers long before the proletariat gets the length of forming this ideal organization and this colossal reserve fund. But if they had these, they would not need to make use of the roundabout way of the general strike in order to attain their object.

Here we have the reasoning that was characteristic of the attitude of international social democracy toward the mass strike in the following decades. It is based on the anarchist theory of the general strike—that is, the theory of the general strike as a means of inaugurating the social revolution, in contradistinction to the daily political struggle of the working class—and exhausts itself in the following simple dilemma: either the proletariat as a whole are not yet in possession of the powerful organization and financial resources required, in which case they cannot carry through the general strike; or they are already sufficiently well organized, in which case they do not need the general strike. This reasoning is so simple and at first glance so irrefutable, that, for a quarter of a century, it has rendered excellent service to the modern labor movement as a logical weapon against the anarchist phantom and as a means of carrying the idea of political struggle to the widest circles of the workers. The enormous strides taken by the labor movement in all capitalist countries during the last twenty-five years are the most convincing evidence of the value of the tactics of political struggle, which were insisted upon by Marx and Engels in opposition to Bakuninism. . . .

The Russian Revolution has now effected a radical revision of the above piece of reasoning. For the first time in the history of the class struggle it has achieved a grandiose realization of the idea of the mass strike and . . . has even matured the general strike and thereby opened a new epoch in the development of the labor movement. It does not, of course, follow from this that the tactics of political struggle recommended by Marx and Engels were false or that the criticism applied by them to anarchism was incorrect. On the contrary, it is the same train of ideas, the same method, the Engels-Marxian tactics, which lay at the foundation of the previous practice of the German social democracy, which now in the Russian Revolution are producing new factors and new conditions in the class struggle. The Russian Revolution, which is the first historical experiment on the model of the mass strike, not merely does not afford a vindication of anarchism, but actually means *the historical liquidation of anarchism*. . . .

Russia, in particular, appeared to have become the experimental field for the heroic deeds of anarchism. A country in which the proletariat had absolutely no political rights and extremely weak organizations, a many-colored complex of various sections of the population, a chaos of conflicting interests, a low standard of education among the masses of the people, extreme brutality in the use of violence on the part of the prevailing regime—all this seemed as if created to raise anarchism to a sudden if perhaps short-lived power. And finally, Russia was the historical birthplace of anarchism. But the fatherland of Bakunin was to become the burial place of its teachings. Not only did and do the anarchists in Russia not stand at the head of the mass strike movement; not only does the whole political leadership of revolutionary action and also of the mass strike lie in the hands of the social democratic organizations, which are bitterly opposed as "bourgeois parties" by the Russian anarchists . . . the anarchists simply do not exist as a serious political tendency in the Russian Revolution. . . .

Anarchism has become in the Russian Revolution, not the theory of the struggling proletariat, but the ideological signboard of the counterrevolutionary lumpenproletariat, who, like a school of sharks, swarm in the wake of the battleship of the revolution. And therewith the historical career of anarchism is well nigh ended.

On the other hand, the mass strike in Russia has been realized not as means of evading the political struggle of the working class, and especially of parliamentarism, not as a means of jumping suddenly into the social revolution by means of a theatrical coup, but as a means, firstly, of creating for the proletariat the conditions of the daily political struggle and especially of parliamentarism. The revolutionary struggle in Russia, in which mass strikes are the most important weapon, is, by the working people, and above all by the proletariat, conducted for those political rights and conditions whose necessity and importance in the struggle for the emancipation of the working class Marx and Engels first pointed out, and in opposition to anarchism fought for with all their might in the International. Thus . . . the mass strike which, as the opposite of the political activity of the proletariat, was combated appears today as the most powerful weapon of the struggle for political rights. Therefore, the Russian Revolution makes imperative a fundamental revision of the old standpoint of Marxism on the question of the mass strike. . . .

For the anarchist there exist only two things as material suppositions of his "revolutionary" speculations—first, imagination, and, second, good will and courage to rescue humanity from the existing capitalist vale of tears. This fanciful mode of reasoning sixty years ago gave the result that the mass strike was the shortest, surest, and easiest means of springing into the better social future. The same mode of reasoning recently gave the result that the trade union struggle was the only real "direct action of the masses" and also the only real revolutionary struggle—which, as is well known, is the latest notion of the French and Italian "syndicalists." The fatal thing for anarchism has always been that the methods of struggle improvised in the air were not only a reckoning without their host, that is, they were purely utopian, but that they, while not reckoning in the least with the despised evil reality, unexpectedly became in this evil reality, practical helps to the reaction. . . .

On the same ground of abstract, unhistorical methods of observation stand those today who would, in the manner of a board of directors, put the mass strike in Germany on the calendar on an appointed day, and those who, like the participants in the trade union congress at Cologne, would by a prohibition of "propaganda" eliminate the problem of the mass strike from the face of the earth. Both tendencies proceed on the common purely anarchistic assumption that the mass strike is a purely technical means of struggle which can be "decided" at pleasure and strictly according to conscience, or "forbidden"—a kind of pocket knife which can be kept in the pocket clasped "ready for any emergency," and according to decision, can be unclasped and used. . . .

The "practical politicians" [of the SPD] . . . couple the mass strike chiefly with the fate of universal suffrage from which it follows that they can believe two things—first, that the mass strike is of a purely defensive character, and second, that the mass strike is even subordinate to parliamentarism, that is, has been turned into a mere appendage of parliamentarism. . . .

[But] the mass strike, as the Russian Revolution shows it to us, is such a changeable phenomenon that it reflects all phases of the political and economic struggle, all stages and factors of the revolution. Its adaptability, its efficiency, the factors of its origin are constantly changing. Political and economic strikes, mass strikes and partial strikes, demonstrative strikes and fighting strikes, general strikes of individual branches of industry and general strikes in individual towns, peaceful wage struggles and street massacres, barricade fighting—all these run through one another, run side by side, cross one another, flow in and over one another—it is a ceaselessly moving, changing sea of phenomena. . . .

Strike action itself does not cease for a single moment. It merely alters its forms, its dimensions, its effect. It is the living pulsebeat of the revolution and at the same time its most powerful driving wheel. In a word, the mass strike, as shown to us in the Russian Revolution, is not a crafty method discovered by subtle reasoning for the purpose of making the proletarian struggle more effective, *but the method of motion of the proletarian mass,* the phenomenal form of the proletarian struggle in the revolution. . . .

In this general picture the purely political demonstration strike plays quite a subordinate role—isolated small points in the midst of a mighty expanse. Thereby, temporarily considered, the following characteristic discloses itself: the demonstration strikes which, in contradistinction to the fighting strikes, exhibit the greatest mass of party discipline, conscious direction and political thought, and therefore must appear as the highest and most mature form of the mass strike, play in reality the greatest part in the *beginnings* of the movement. . . .

But with the development of the earnest revolutionary struggle the importance of such demonstrations diminishes rapidly. It is precisely those factors which objectively facilitate the realization of the demonstration strike after a preconceived plan and at the party's word of command—namely, the growth of political consciousness and the training of the proletariat—make this kind of mass strike impossible; today the proletariat in Russia, the most capable vanguard of the masses, does not want to know about mass strikes; the workers are no longer in a mood for jesting and will now think only of a serious struggle with all its consequences. . . .

But the movement on the whole does not proceed from the economic to the political struggle, nor even the reverse. Every great political mass action, after it has attained its political highest point, breaks up into a mass of economic strikes. And that applies not only to each of the great mass strikes, but also to the revolution as a whole. With the spreading, clarifying and involution of the political struggle, the economic struggle not only does not recede, but extends, organizes, and becomes involved in equal measure. Between the two there is the most complete reciprocal action.

Every new onset and every fresh victory of the political struggle is transformed into a powerful impetus for the economic struggle, extending at the same time its external possibilities and intensifying the inner urge of the workers to better their position, and their desire to struggle. . . . And conversely. The workers' condition of ceaseless economic struggle with the capitalists keeps their fighting energy alive in every political interval; it forms, so to speak, the permanent fresh reservoir of the strength of the proletarian classes, from which the political fight ever renews its strength, and at the same time leads the indefatigable economic sappers of the proletariat at all times, now here and now there, to isolated sharp conflicts, out of which political conflicts on a large scale unexpectedly explode.

In a word: the economic struggle is the transmitter from one political center to another; the political struggle is the periodic fertilization of the soil for the economic struggle. Cause and effect here continually change places; and thus the economic and the political factor in the period of the mass strike, now widely removed, completely separated or even mutually exclusive, as the theoretical plan would have them, merely form the two interlacing sides of the proletarian class struggle in Russia. And *their unity* is precisely the mass strike. If the sophisticated theory proposes to make a clever logical dissection of the mass strike for the purpose of getting at the "purely political mass strike," it will by this dissection, as with any other, not perceive the phenomenon in its living essence, but will kill it altogether.

Finally, the events in Russia show us that the mass strike is inseparable from the revolution. The history of the Russian mass strikes is the history of the Russian Revolution. When, to be sure, the representatives of our German opportunism hear of "revolution," they immediately think of bloodshed, street fighting or powder and shot, and the logical conclusion thereof is: the mass strike leads inevitably to the revolution, therefore we cannot have it. . . . The revolution, however, is something other and something more than bloodshed. In contradiction to the police interpretation, which views the revolution exclusively from the standpoint of street disturbances and rioting, that is, from the standpoint of "disorder," the interpretation of scientific socialism sees in the revolution above all a thoroughgoing internal reversal of social class relations. And from this standpoint an altogether different connection exists between revolution and mass strike in Russia from that contained in the commonplace conception that the mass strike generally ends in bloodshed. . . .

In Germany the most violent, most brutal collisions between the workers and employers take place every year and every day without the struggle overleaping the bounds of the individual departments or individual towns concerned, or even those of the individual factories. . . . And when they grow into isolated mass strikes, which have without question a political coloring, they do not bring about a general storm. . . .

And conversely, only in the period of the revolution, when the social foundations and the walls of the class society are shaken and subjected to a constant process of disarrangement, any political class action of the proletariat can arouse from their passive condition in a few hours whole sections of the working class who have hitherto remained unaffected, and this is immediately and naturally expressed in a stormy economic struggle. The worker, suddenly aroused to activity by the electric shock of political action, immediately seizes the weapon lying nearest his hand for the fight against his condition of economic slavery: the stormy gesture of the political struggle causes him to feel with unexpected intensity the weight and the pressure of his economic chains. And while, for example, the most violent political struggle in Germany—the electoral struggle or the parliamentary struggle on the customs tariff—exercised a scarcely perceptible direct influence upon the course and the intensity of the wage struggles being conducted at the same time in Germany, every political action of the proletariat in Russia immediately expresses itself in the extension of the area and the deepening of the intensity of the economic struggle. . . .

If the mass strike is not an isolated act but a whole period of the class struggle, and if this period is identical with a period of revolution, it is clear that the mass strike cannot be called at will, even when the decision to do so may come from the highest committee of the strongest social democratic party. As long as social democracy has not the power to stage and countermand revolutions according to its fancy, even the greatest enthusiasm and impatience of the social democratic troops will not suffice to call into being a real period of mass strike as a living, powerful movement of the people. . . . A mass strike born of pure discipline and enthusiasm will, at best, merely play the role of an episode, of a symptom of the fighting mood of the working class upon which, however, the conditions of a peaceful period are reflected.

Of course, even during the revolution, mass strikes do not exactly fall from heaven. They must be brought about in some way or another by the workers. The resolution and determination of the workers also play a part and indeed the initiative and the wider direction naturally fall to the share of the organized and most enlightened kernel of the proletariat. . . .

Further, there are quite definite limits set to initiative and conscious direction. During the revolution it is extremely difficult for any directing organ of the proletarian movement to foresee and to calculate which occasions and factors can lead to explosions and which cannot. Here also initiative and direction do not consist in issuing commands according to one's inclinations, but in the most adroit adaptability to the given situation, and the closest possible contact with the mood of the masses. The element of spontaneity . . . plays a great part in all Russian mass strikes without exception, be it as a driving force or as a restraining influence. This does not occur in Russia, however, because social democracy is still young or weak, but because in every individual act of the struggle so very many important economic, political and social, general and local, material and psychical, factors react upon one another in such a way that no single act can be arranged and resolved as if it were a mathematical problem. The revolution, even when the proletariat, with the social democrats at their head, appear in the leading role, is not a maneuver of the proletariat in the open field, but a fight in the midst of the incessant crashing, displacing and crumbling of the social foundation. In short, in the mass strikes in Russia the element of spontaneity plays such a predominant part, not because the Russian proletariat are "uneducated," but because revolutions do not allow anyone to play the schoolmaster with them. . . .

Instead of puzzling their heads with the technical side, with the mechanism, of the mass strike, the social democrats are called upon to assume *political* leadership in the midst of the revolutionary period.

To give the cue for, and the direction to, the fight; to so regulate the tactics of the political struggle in its every phase and at its every moment that the entire sum of the available power of the proletariat which is already released and active, will find expression in the battle array of the party; to see that the tactics of the social democrats are decided according to their resoluteness and acuteness and that they never fall below the level demanded by the actual relations of forces, but rather rise above it—that is the most important task of the directing body in a period of mass strikes. . . . A consistent, resolute progressive tactic on the part of the social democrats produces in the masses a feeling of security, self-confidence, and desire for struggle; a vacillating weak tactic, based on an underestimation of the proletariat, has a crippling and confusing effect upon the masses. . . .

The plan of undertaking mass strikes as a serious political class action with organized workers only is absolutely hopeless. If the mass strike, or rather, mass strikes, and the mass struggle are to be successful they must become a real *people's movement,* that is, the widest sections of the proletariat must be drawn into the fight. Already in the parliamentary form the might of the proletarian class struggle rests not on the small organized group, but on the surrounding periphery of the revolutionary-minded proletariat. If the social democrats were to enter the electoral battle with their few hundred thousand organized members alone, they would condemn themselves to futility. And although it is the tendency of social democracy wherever possible to draw the whole great army of its voters into the party organization, its mass of voters after thirty years experience of social democracy is not increased through the growth of the party organization, but on the contrary, the new sections of the proletariat, won for the time being through the electoral struggle, are the fertile soil for the subsequent seed of organization. Here the organization does not supply the troops for the struggle, but the struggle, in an ever growing degree, supplies recruits for the organization.

In a much greater degree does this obviously apply to direct political mass action than to the parliamentary struggle. If the social democrats, as the organized nucleus of the working class, are the most important vanguard of the entire body of the workers and if the political clarity, the strength, and the unity of the labor movement flow from this organization, then it is not permissible to visualize the class movement of the proletariat as a movement of the organized minority. Every real, great class struggle must rest upon the support and cooperation of the widest masses, and a strategy of class struggle which does not reckon with this cooperation, which is based upon the idea of the finely stage-managed march out of the small, well-trained part of the proletariat is foredoomed to be a miserable fiasco. . . .

In the case of the enlightened German worker the class consciousness implanted by the social democrats is *theoretical and latent*: in the period ruled by bourgeois parliamentarism it cannot, as a rule, actively participate in a direct mass action. . . . In the revolution when the masses themselves appear upon the political battlefield this class consciousness becomes *practical and active*. A year of revolution has therefore given the Russian proletariat that "training" which thirty years of parliamentary and trade union struggle cannot artificially give to the German proletariat. . . .

11. LUXEMBURG:
REQUIEM FOR SOCIAL DEMOCRACY

On August 4, 1914, the SPD delegates to the Reichstag voted unanimously to support the war credits requested by the government, and in that one act destroyed the Second International and its fight in each European nation to avoid the holocaust which was shortly to descend upon them all. For many years prior to that ignominious date, amid the recurrent political crises among the imperialist states of Europe, the Second International, with the SPD at its head, had resolutely vowed to prevent the outbreak of war. In the months immediately preceding August 1914, the socialist parties redoubled their opposition to their respective governments' war preparations, although they were powerless to prevent these preparations from rapidly approaching the point of no return.

On August 4 the German government announced to the Reichstag that its armies had already invaded Belgium and that war between Austria (Germany's major ally) and Russia had begun, and it requested ratification of the war-credits bills, without which it would have been unable to pursue its war aims. The SPD delegates lined up to a man in support of the bill and issued a proclamation (the first of many such) urging the working class to support the German war effort and acquiesce in all governmental and managerial demands, thereby stunning the working class of all of Europe. Lenin, at the time in exile in Switzerland, on reading a newspaper account of these events, declared it to obviously be a forgery, a trick of the German and Russian police, for the SPD simply could never join in the declaration of such a war! Immediately, the other socialist parties rallied to the support of "their" respective governments' call for "national defense," and shortly thereafter the working class of Europe, until so recently united in its opposition to the impending war, was bayoneting and gassing itself to death on the battlefield. The war which was to bring classical European civilization to an end was under way, its first casualty having been the Second International and the ideal of the brotherhood and solidarity of the working class.

SOURCE: From Rosa Luxemburg, "The Junius Pamphlet," in *Rosa Luxemburg Speaks*, ed. Mary Alice Waters (New York: Pathfinder Press, 1970). Reprinted by permission.

Among the leading figures of European Social Democracy, only Rosa Luxemburg, her close associate Karl Liebknecht, and Lenin were able to resist the rising tide of national chauvinism: Luxemburg and Liebknecht with regrets over the demise of Social Democracy; Lenin with eager anticipation of the chaos the war would bring in its wake.

After having been arrested shortly after the outbreak of hostilities, Rosa Luxemburg was soon convicted of antiwar activities and began serving her prison sentence by February 1915. She immediately set to work on a pamphlet in which she forced herself to face for the first time the full rottenness of the SPD and in which she explored the underlying causes of the war which the socialist parties of the International had been powerless to prevent. The pamphlet, completed by April 1915 and entitled The Crisis of German Social Democracy, *was smuggled out of her cell and published under the pseudonym "Junius" a year later. As unquestionably the outstanding socialist document to emerge from the war, the "Junius Pamphlet" became the nucleus around which the isolated socialist opponents of the war were slowly to begin their arduous task of regrouping the remnants of Europe's revolutionary proletariat.*

The scene has thoroughly changed. The six weeks' march to Paris has become world drama. Mass murder has become a monotonous task, and yet the final solution is not one step nearer. Capitalist rule is caught in its own trap, and cannot ban the spirit that it has invoked.

Gone is the first mad delirium. Gone are the patriotic street demonstrations, the chase after suspicious-looking automobiles, the false telegrams, the cholera-poisoned wells. Gone the mad stories of Russian students who hurl bombs from every bridge of Berlin, or Frenchmen flying over Nuremberg; gone the excesses of a spy-hunting populace, the singing throngs, the coffee shops with their patriotic songs; gone the violent mobs, ready to denounce, ready to persecute, women ready to whip themselves into a delirious frenzy over every wild rumor. . . .

The show is over. The curtain has fallen on trains filled with reservists, as they pull out amid the joyous cries of enthusiastic maidens. We no longer see their laughing faces, smiling cheerily from the train windows upon a war-mad population. Quietly they trot through the streets, with their sacks upon their shoulders. And the public, with a fretful face, goes about its daily task.

Into the disillusioned atmosphere of pale daylight there rings a different chorus; the hoarse croak of the hawks and hyenas of the battlefield. Ten thousand tents, guaranteed according to specifications, 100,000 kilos of bacon, cocoa powder, coffee substitute, cash on immediate delivery. Shrapnel, drills, ammunition bags, marriage bureaus for war widows, leather belts, war orders—only serious propositions considered. And the cannon fodder that was loaded upon the trains in August and September is rotting on the battlefields of Belgium and the Vosges, while profits are springing, like weeds, from the fields of the dead.

Business is flourishing upon the ruins. Cities are turned into shambles, whole countries into deserts, villages into cemeteries, whole nations into beggars, churches into stables; popular rights, treaties, alliances, the holiest words and the highest authorities have been torn into scraps; every sovereign by the grace of God is called a fool, an unfaithful wretch, by his cousin on the other side; every diplomat calls his colleague in the enemy's country a desperate criminal; each government looks upon the other as the evil genius of its people, worthy only of the contempt of the world. Hunger revolts in Venetia, in Lisbon, in Moscow, in Singapore, pestilence in Russia, misery and desperation everywhere.

Shamed, dishonored, wading in blood and dripping with filth, thus capitalist society stands. Not as we usually see it, playing the roles of peace and righteousness, of order, of philosophy, of ethics—as a roaring beast, as an orgy of anarchy, as a pestilential breath, devastating culture and humanity—so it appears in all its hideous nakedness.

And in the midst of this orgy a world tragedy has occurred: the capitulation of social democracy. To close one's eyes to this fact, to try to hide it, would be the most foolish, the most dangerous thing that the international proletariat could do. . . . The goal of its journey, its final liberation, depends entirely upon the proletariat, on whether *it* understands to learn from *its* own mistakes. Self-criticism, cruel, unsparing criticism that goes to the very root of the evil is life and breath for the proletarian movement. The catastrophe into which the world has thrust the socialist proletariat is an unexampled misfortune for humanity. But socialism is lost only if the international proletariat is unable to measure the depths of the catastrophe and refuses to understand the lesson that it teaches.

The last forty-five years in the development of the labor movement are at stake. . . .

The bearer, the defender, the protector of this new method was German social democracy. The war of 1870 and the downfall of the Paris Commune had shifted the center of gravity of the European labor movement to Germany. Just as France was the classic country of the first phase of the proletarian class struggle, as Paris was the torn and bleeding heart of the European working class of that time, so the German working class became the vanguard of the second phase. By innumerable sacrifices in the form of agitational work, it has built up the strongest, the model organization of the proletariat, has created the greatest press, has developed the most effective educational and propaganda methods. It has collected under its banners the most gigantic labor masses, and has elected the largest representative groups to its national parliament.

German social democracy has been generally acknowledged to be the purest incarnation of Marxian socialism. It has held and wielded a peculiar prestige as teacher and leader in the Second International. . . . German social democracy was . . . the jewel of the organization of the class-conscious proletariat. In its footsteps the French, the Italian, and the Belgian social democracies, the labor movements of Holland, Scandinavia, Switzerland, and the United States, followed more or less eagerly. The Slav nations, the Russians, and the social democrats of the Balkans looked up to the German movement in boundless, almost unquestioning admiration. In the Second International German social democracy was the determining factor. In every congress, in the meetings of the International Socialist Bureau, everything waited upon the opinion of the German group.

Particularly in the fight against militarism and war the position taken by German social democracy has always been decisive. "We Germans cannot accept that," was usually sufficient to determine the orientation of the International. Blindly confident, it submitted to the leadership of the much admired, mighty German social democracy. It was the pride of every socialist, the horror of the ruling classes of all countries.

And what happened in Germany when the great historical crisis came? The deepest fall, the mightiest cataclysm. Nowhere was the organization of the proletariat made so completely subservient to imperialism. Nowhere was the state of siege so uncomplainingly borne. Nowhere was the press so thoroughly gagged, public opinion so completely choked off, nowhere was the political and industrial class struggle of the working class so entirely abandoned as in Germany.

But German social democracy was not only the strongest body, it was the thinking brain of the International as well. Therefore the process of self-analysis and appraisement must begin in its own movement, with its own case. It is in honor bound to lead the way to the rescue of international socialism, to proceed with the unsparing criticism of its own shortcomings. . . .

One thing is certain. It is a foolish delusion to believe that we need only live through the war, as a rabbit hides under the bush to await the end of a thunderstorm, to trot merrily off in his old accustomed gait when all is over. The world war has changed the condition of our struggle, and has changed *us* most of all. Not that the laws of capitalist development or the life-and-death conflict between capital and labor have been changed or minimized. . . . But evolution has received a mighty forward impetus through the outbreak of the imperialist volcano. The enormity of the tasks that tower before the socialist proletariat in the immediate future make the past struggles of the labor movement seem but a delightful idyll in comparison. . . .

Have we ever had a different conception of the role to be played by the working class in the great world war? Have we forgotten how we were wont to describe the coming event, only a few short years ago?

Then will come the catastrophe. All Europe will be called to arms, and sixteen to eighteen million men, the flower of the nation, armed with the best instruments of murder will make war upon each other. But I believe that behind this march there looms the final crash. Not we, but they themselves will bring it. They are driving things to the extreme, they are leading us straight into a catastrophe. They will harvest what they have sown. The *Götterdämmerung* of the bourgeois world is at hand. Be sure of that. It is coming.

Thus spoke Bebel, the speaker of our group in the Reichstag in the Morocco debate. . . .

When in the summer of 1911, the *Panther* made its spring to Agadir, and the noisy clamor of German imperialists brought Europe to the precipice of war,* an international meeting in London, on the fourth of August, adopted the following resolution:

The German, Spanish, English, Dutch and French delegates of labor organizations hereby declare their readiness to oppose every declaration of war with every means in their power. Every nationality here represented pledges itself, in accordance with the decisions of its national and international congresses to oppose all criminal machinations on the part of the ruling classes.

But when in November 1912 the International Peace Congress met at Basel,† when the long train of labor representatives entered the Minster, a presentiment of the coming hour of fate made them shudder and the heroic resolve took shape in every breast.

The cool, skeptical Victor Adler cried out: "Comrades, it is most important that we here, at the common source of our strength, that we, each and every one of us, take from hence the strength to do in his country what he can, through the forms and means that are at his disposal, to oppose this crime of war, and if it should be accomplished, if we should really be able to prevent war, let this be the cornerstone of our coming victory. That is the spirit that animates the whole International.

"And when murder and arson and pestilence sweep over civilized Europe—we can think of it only with horror and indignation, and protests ring from our hearts. And we ask, are the

---

* In July 1911 the German gunboat *Panther* sailed to Agadir, Morocco, "to protect German interests," i.e., to secure sources of iron ore for Mannesmann Steel. War almost broke out between France and Germany, but on the threat of British intervention, Germany withdrew. At the Treaty of Berlin, November 1911, Germany was given a slice of the Cameroons and gave up her claims to Morocco.

† The Peace Congress at Basel, Switzerland, was held at the Basel Minster on November 24 and 25, 1912. The immediate occasion was the fear of general European war, as Montenegro had declared war on Turkey in October, embroiling the Balkans. It was the last prewar general meeting of the Second International, and its significance is that for the first time a socialist peace conference had recognized that the period of national wars in Europe was over and that all future wars would be imperialist wars.

proletarians of today really nothing but sheep to be led mutely to the slaughter?"

Troelstra spoke in the name of the small nations, in the name of the Belgians as well: "With their blood and with all that they possess the proletariat of the small nations swear their allegiance to the International in everything that it may decide to prevent war. Again we repeat that we expect, when the ruling classes of the large nations call the sons of the proletariat to arms to satiate the lust for power and the greed of their rulers, in the blood and on the lands of the small peoples, we expect that then the sons of the proletariat, under the powerful influence of their proletarian parents and of the proletarian press, will think thrice before they harm us, their friends, in the service of the enemies of culture."

And Jaures closed his speech, after the antiwar manifesto of the International Bureau had been read: "The International represents the moral forces of the world! And when the tragic hour strikes, when we must sacrifice ourselves, this knowledge will support and strengthen us. Not lightly, but from the bottom of our hearts we declare that we are ready for all sacrifices!"

It was like a pledge. The whole world looked toward the Minster of Basel, where the bells, slowly and solemnly, rang to the approaching great fight between the armies of labor and capital.

On the third of December 1912, the social democratic deputy, David, spoke in the German Reichstag: "That was the most beautiful hour of my life. That I here avow. When the chimes of the Minster rang in the long train of international social democrats, when the red flags were planted in the nave of the church about the altar, when the emissaries of the people were greeted by the peals of the organ that resounded the message of peace, that was an impression that I can never forget. . . .

"You must realize what it was that happened here. The masses have ceased to be will-less, thoughtless herds. That is new in the history of the world. Hitherto the masses have always blindly followed the leader of those who were interested in war, who drove the peoples at each other's throats to mass murder. That will stop. The masses have ceased to be the instruments, the yeomen of war profiteers."

A week before the war broke out, on the twenty-sixth of July

1914, the German party papers wrote: "We are no marionettes; we are fighting with all our might, against a system that makes men the powerless tools of blind circumstances, against this capitalism that is preparing to change Europe, thirsty for peace, into a smoking battlefield. If destruction takes its course, if the determined will for peace of the German, of the international proletariat, that will find expression in the next few days in mighty demonstrations, should not be able to prevent the world war, then it must be at least, the last war, it must be the *Götterdämmerung* of capitalism." . . .

And then came the awful, the incredible fourth of August 1914.

Did it *have* to come? An event of such importance cannot be a mere accident. It must have its deep, significant, objective causes. But perhaps these causes may be found in the errors of the leader of the proletariat, the social democracy itself, in the fact that our readiness to fight has flagged, that our courage and our convictions have forsaken us. Scientific socialism has taught us to reccognize the objective laws of historical development. Man does not make history of his own volition, but he makes history nevertheless. . . . And though we can no more skip a period in our historical development than a man can jump over his shadow, it lies within our power to accelerate or to retard it.

Socialism is the first popular movement in the world that has set itself a goal and has established in the social life of man a conscious thought, a definite plan, the free will of mankind. For this reason Friedrich Engels calls the final victory of the socialist proletariat a stride by humankind from the animal kingdom into the kingdom of liberty. . . . Socialism will not fall as manna from heaven. It can only be won by a long chain of powerful struggles, in which the proletariat, under the leadership of the social democracy, will learn to take hold of the rudder of society to become instead of the powerless victim of history, its conscious guide. . . .

We stand today, as Friedrich Engels prophesied more than a generation ago, before the awful proposition: either the triumph of imperialism and the destruction of all culture, and, as in ancient Rome, depopulation, desolation, degeneration, a vast cemetery; or, the victory of socialism, that is, the conscious struggle of the international proletariat against imperialism, against its methods, against war. This is the dilemma of world history, its inevitable choice, whose scales are trembling in the balance awaiting the decision of the proletariat. Upon it depends the future of culture and humanity. In this war imperialism has been victorious. Its brutal sword of murder has dashed the scales, with overbearing brutality, down into the abyss of shame and misery. If the proletariat learns *from* this war and in this war to exert itself, to cast off its serfdom to the ruling classes, to become the lord of its own destiny, the shame and misery will not have been in vain.

The modern working class must pay dearly for each realization of its historic mission. The road to the Golgotha of its class liberation is strewn with awful sacrifices. The June combatants, the victims of the Commune, the martyrs of the Russian Revolution*—an endless line of bloody shadows. They have fallen on the field of honor, as Marx wrote of the heroes of the Commune, to be enshrined forever in the great heart of the working class. Now millions of proletarians are falling on the field of dishonor, of fratricide, of self-destruction, the slave-song on their lips. And that too has not been spared us. We are like the Jews whom Moses led through the desert. But we are not lost, and we will be victorious if we have not forgotten how to learn. And if the modern leaders of the proletariat do not know how to learn, they will go down "to make room for those who will be more able to cope with the problems of a new world."

"We are now facing the irrevocable fact of war. We are threatened by the horrors of invasion. The decision, today, is not for or against war; for us there can be but one question: By what means is this war to be conducted? Much, aye everything, is at stake for our people and its future, if Russian despotism, stained with the blood of its own people, should be the victor. This danger must be averted, the civilization and the independence of our people must be safeguarded. Therefore we will carry out what we have always promised: in the hour of danger we will not desert our fatherland. In this we feel that we stand in harmony with the International, which has always recognized the right of every

* Of 1905.

people to its national independence, as we stand in agreement with the International in emphatically denouncing every war of conquest. Actuated by these motives, we vote in favor of the war credits demanded by the Government."

With these words the Reichstag group issued the countersign that determined and controlled the position of the German working class during the war. Fatherland in danger, national defense, people's war for existence, *Kultur* [national German culture], liberty—these were the slogans proclaimed by the parliamentary representatives of social democracy. What followed was but the logical sequence. The position of the party and the labor union press, the patriotic frenzy of the masses, the civil peace, the disintegration of the International, all these things were the inevitable consequence of that momentous orientation in the Reichstag.

If it is true that this war is really a fight for national existence, for freedom, if it is true that these priceless possessions can be defended only by the iron tools of murder, if this war is the holy cause of the people, then everything else follows as a matter of course, we must take everything that the war may bring as a part of the bargain. He who desires the purpose must be satisfied with the means. War is methodical, organized, gigantic murder. But in normal human beings this systematic murder is possible only when a state of intoxication has been previously created. This has always been the tried and proven method of those who make war. Bestiality of action must find a commensurate bestiality of thought and senses; the latter must prepare and accompany the former. Thus the *Wahre Jacob* of August 28, 1914, with its brutal picture of the German thresher, the party papers of Chemnitz, Hamburg, Kiel, Frankfurt, Koburg and others, with their patriotic drive in poetry and prose, were the necessary narcotic for a proletariat that could rescue its existence and its liberty only by plunging the deadly steel into its French and English brothers. These chauvinistic papers are after all a great deal more logical and consistent than those others who attempted to unite hill and valley, war with humanity, murder with brotherly love, the voting for war credits with socialist internationalism.

If the stand taken by the German Reichstag group on the fourth of August was correct, then the death sentence of the proletarian International has been spoken, not only for this war, but forever. . . . Up to this time we have cherished the belief that the interests of the peoples of all nations, that the class interests of the proletariat are a harmonious unit, that they are identical, that they cannot possibly come into conflict with one another. That was the basis of our theory and practice, the soul of our agitation. Were we mistaken in the cardinal point of our whole world philosophy? We are holding an inquest over international socialism. . . .

The declaration that was read by the social democratic group in the Reichstag on the fourth of August had been agreed upon in advance with representatives of the government and the capitalist parties. It was little more than a patriotic grandstand play, prepared behind the scenes and delivered for the benefit of the people at home and in other nations.

To the leading elements in the labor movement, the vote in favor of the war credits by the Reichstag group was a cue for the immediate settlement of all labor controversies. Nay, more, they announced this to the manufacturers as a patriotic duty incurred by labor when it agreed to observe a civil peace. . . .

In this crisis the social democratic movement has voluntarily relinquished all propaganda and education in the interest of the proletarian class struggle, during Reichstag and Landtag elections. Parliamentary elections have everywhere been reduced to the simple bourgeois formula; the catching of votes for the candidates of the party on the basis of an amicable and peaceful settlement with its capitalist opponents. . . .

The social democratic press, with a few exceptions, proclaimed the principle of national unity as the highest duty of the German people. . . .

Briefly, therefore, beginning with the fourth of August until the day when peace shall be declared, social democracy has declared the class struggle extinct. The first thunder of Krupp cannons in Belgium welded Germany into a wonderland of class solidarity and social harmony.

How is this miracle to be understood? The class struggle is known to be not a social democratic invention that can be arbitrarily set aside for a period of time whenever it may seem convenient to do so. The proletarian class struggle is older than social democracy, is an elementary product of class society. It flamed up all over Europe when capitalism first came into power. The modern proletariat was not led by social democracy into the class struggle. On the contrary the international social democratic movement was called into being by the class struggle to bring a conscious aim and unity into the various local and scattered fragments of the class struggle.

What then has changed in this respect when the war broke out? Have private property, capitalist exploitation, and class rule ceased to exist? Or have the propertied classes in a spell of patriotic fervor declared: In view of the needs of the war we hereby turn over the means of production, the earth, the factories and the mills therein, into the possession of the people? Have they relinquished the right to make profits out of these possessions? Have they set aside all political privileges, will they sacrifice them upon the altar of the fatherland, now that it is in danger? . . .

The cessation of the class struggle was, therefore, a deplorably one-sided affair. While capitalist oppression and exploitation, the worst enemies of the working class, remain, socialist and labor union leaders have generously delivered the working class, without a struggle, into the hands of the enemy for the duration of the war. While the ruling classes are fully armed with the property and supremacy rights, the working class, at the advice of social democracy, has laid down its arms. . . .

When it voted for civil peace and war credits, social democracy silently gave its consent to military rule as well, and laid itself, bound and gagged, at the feet of the ruling classes. The declaration of military rule was purely an antisocialist measure. From no other side were resistance, protest, action, and difficulties to be expected. . . . Never in the history of the world has a party made itself more ridiculous.

But, more! In refuting the existence of the class struggle, social democracy has denied the very basis of its own existence. . . . What role could it expect to play in the war, once having sacrificed the class struggle, the fundamental principle of its existence? Social democracy has destroyed its mission, for the period of the war, as an active political party, as a representative of working-class politics. It has thrown aside the most important weapon it possessed, the power of criticism of the war from the peculiar point of view of the working class. Its only mission now is to play the role of the gendarme over the working class under a state of military rule. . . .

Social democracy has not assured the extension of liberty in Germany. It has sacrificed those liberties that the working class possessed before the war broke out.

The indifference with which the German people have allowed themselves to be deprived of the freedom of the press, of the right of assembly and of public life, the fact that they not only calmly bore, but even applauded, the state of siege is unexampled in the history of modern society. In England the freedom of the press has nowhere been violated, in France there is incomparably more freedom of public opinion than in Germany. In no country has public opinion so completely vanished, nowhere has it been so completely superseded by official opinion, by the order of the government, as in Germany. . . .

By sacrificing the class struggle, our party has moreover, once and for all, given up the possibility of making its influence effectively felt in determining the extent of the war and the terms of peace. . . .

Thus the social democracy has added another crime to the heavy burden it already has to bear, namely the lengthening of the war. . . .

In the present imperialistic milieu there can be no wars of national self-defense. Every socialist policy that depends upon this determining historic milieu, that is willing to fix its policies in the world whirlpool from the point of view of a single nation, is built upon a foundation of sand. . . .

Imperialism is not the creation of any one or of any group of states. It is the product of a particular stage of ripeness in the world development of capital, an innately international condition, an indivisible whole, . . . from which no nation can hold aloof at will. From this point of view only is it possible to understand correctly the question of "national defense" in the present war.

The national state, national unity, and independence were the ideological shield under which the capitalist nations of central Europe constituted themselves in the past century. Capitalism is incompatible with economic and political divisions, with the accompanying splitting up into small states. It needs for its development large, united territories, and a state of mental and intellectual development in the nation that will lift the demands and needs of society to a plane corresponding to the prevailing stage of capitalist production, and to the mechanism of modern capitalist class rule. Before capitalism could develop, it sought to create for itself a territory sharply defined by national limitations. . . . The national program could play a historic role only so long as it represented the ideological expression of a growing bourgeoisie. . . . Since then, imperialism has buried the old bourgeois democratic program completely by substituting expansionist activity irrespective of national relationships for the original program of the bourgeoisie in all nations. . . . Today the nation is but a cloak that covers imperialistic desires, a battle cry for imperialistic rivalries, the last ideological measure with which the masses can be persuaded to play the role of cannon fodder in imperialistic wars. . . .

In view of all these considerations, what shall be the practical attitude of social democracy in the present war? Shall it declare: Since this is an imperialist war, since we do not enjoy in our country any socialist self-determination, its existence or nonexistence is of no consequence to us, and we will surrender it to the enemy? Passive fatalism can never be the role of a revolutionary party like social democracy. It must neither place itself at the disposal of the existing class state, under the command of the ruling classes, nor can it stand silently by to wait until the storm is past. It must adopt a policy of active class politics, a policy that will whip the ruling classes forward in every great social crisis and that will drive the crisis itself far beyond its original extent. . . . Instead of covering this imperialist war with a lying mantle of national self-defense, social democracy should have demanded the right of national self-determination seriously, should have used it as a lever against the imperialist war.

The highest duty of social democracy toward its fatherland demanded that it expose the real background of this imperialist war, that it rend the net of imperialist and diplomatic lies that covers the eyes of the people. It was their duty to speak loudly and clearly, to proclaim to the people of Germany that in this war victory and defeat would be equally fatal, to oppose the gagging of the fatherland by a state of siege, to demand that the people alone decide on war and peace, to demand a permanent session of parliament for the period of the war, to assume a watchful control over the government by parliament, and over parliament by the people, to demand the immediate removal of all political inequalities, since only a free people can adequately govern its country, and finally, to oppose the imperialist war. . . .

Social democracy did not adopt the wrong policy—it had no policy whatsoever. It has wiped itself out completely as a class party with a world conception of its own, has delivered the country, without a word of protest, to the fate of imperialist war without, to the dictatorship of the sword within. Nay, more, it has taken the responsibility for the war upon its own shoulders. The declaration of the "Reichstag group" says: "We have voted only the means for our country's defense. We decline all responsibility for the war." But as a matter of fact, the truth lies in exactly the opposite direction. The means for "national defense," i.e., for imperialistic mass butchery by the armed forces of the military monarchy, were not voted by social democracy. For the availability of the war credits did not in the least depend upon social democracy. They, as a minority, stood against a compact three-quarters majority of the capitalist Reichstag. The social democratic group accomplished only one thing by voting in favor of the war credits. It placed upon the war the stamp of democratic fatherland defense, and supported and sustained the fictions that were propagated by the government concerning the actual conditions and problems of the war. . . .

At first we would perhaps have accomplished nothing but to save the honor of the proletariat, and thousands upon thousands of proletarians who are dying in the trenches would not have died in spiritual confusion, but with the one certainty that that which has been everything in their lives, the international, liberating social democracy is more than the figment of a dream.

The voice of our party would have acted as a wet blanket upon the chauvinistic intoxication of the masses. It would have preserved the intelligent proletariat from delirium, would have [made] it more difficult for imperialism to poison and to stupefy the minds of the people. The crusade against social democracy would have awakened the masses in an incredibly short time.

And as the war went on, as the horror of endless massacre and bloodshed in all countries grew and grew, as its imperialistic hoof became more and more evident, as the exploitation by bloodthirsty speculators became more and more shameless, every live, honest, progressive and humane element in the masses would have rallied to the standard of social democracy. German social democracy would have stood in the midst of this mad whirlpool of collapse and decay, like a rock in a stormy sea, would have been the lighthouse of the whole International, building and leading the labor movements of every country of the earth. The unparalleled moral prestige that lay in the hands of the German socialists would have reacted upon the socialists of all nations in a very short time. Peace sentiments would have spread like wildfire and the popular demand for peace in all countries would have hastened the end of the slaughter, would have decreased the number of its victims.

The German proletariat would have remained the lighthouse keeper of socialism and of human emancipation. . . .

In spite of military dictatorship and press censorship, in spite of the downfall of the social democracy, in spite of fratricidal war, the class struggle arises from civil peace with elemental force: from the blood and smoke of the battlefields the solidarity of international labor arises. Not in weak attempts to artifically galvanize the old International, not in pledges rendered now here, now there, to stand together after the war is over. No, here, in the war, out of the war, arises, with a new might and intensity, the recognition that the proletarians of all lands have one and the same interest. . . .

A return to the old Europe that existed before August 4, 1914, is impossible. . . . The proletariat knows no going back. . . . In this sense, alone, is it possible for the proletariat to oppose, with its policy, both camps in the imperialist world war. . . .

The real problem that the world war has placed before the socialist parties, upon whose solution the future of the working-class movement depends, *is the readiness of the proletarian masses to act in the fight against imperialism.* The international proletariat suffers, not from a dearth of postulates, programs, and slogans, but from a lack of deeds, of effective resistance, of the power to attack imperialism at the decisive moment, just in times of war. It has been unable to put its old slogan, war against war, into actual practice. Here is the Gordian knot of the proletarian movement and of its future. . . .

Capitalist desire for imperialist expansion, as the expression of its highest maturity in the last period of its life, has the economic tendency to change the whole world into capitalistically producing nations, to sweep away all superannuated, precapitalistic methods of production and society, to subjugate all the riches of the earth and all means of production to capital, to turn the laboring masses of the peoples of all zones into wage slaves. In Africa and in Asia, from the most northern regions to the southernmost point of South America and in the South Seas, the remnants of old communistic social groups, of feudal society, of patriarchal systems, and of ancient handicraft production are destroyed and stamped out by capitalism. Whole peoples are destroyed, ancient civilizations are leveled to the ground, and in their place profiteering in its most modern forms is being established.

This brutal triumphant procession of capitalism through the world, accompanied by all the means of force, of robbery, and of infamy, has one bright phase: it has created the premises for its own final overthrow, it has established the capitalist world rule upon which, alone, the socialist world revolution can follow. This is the only cultural and progressive aspect of the great so-called works of culture that were brought to the primitive countries. To capitalist economists and politicians, railroads, matches, sewerage systems and warehouses are progress and culture. Of themselves such works, grafted upon primitive conditions, are neither culture nor progress, for they are too dearly paid for with the sudden economic and cultural ruin of the peoples who must drink down the bitter cup of misery and horror of two social orders, of traditional agricultural landlordism, of supermodern, superrefined capitalist exploitation, at one and the same time. Only as the material conditions for the destruction of capitalism and the abolition of class society can the effects of the capitalist triumphal march through the world bear the stamp of progress in a historical sense. In this sense imperialism, too, is working in our interest.

The present world war is a turning point in the course of

imperialism. For the first time the destructive beasts that have been loosed by capitalist Europe over all other parts of the world have sprung with one awful leap, into the midst of the European nations. . . . this civilized world has just begun to know that the fangs of the imperialist beast are deadly, that its breath is frightfulness, that its tearing claws have sunk deeper into the breasts of its own mother, European culture. . . . They speak of German barbarism, as if every people that goes out for organized murder did not change into a horde of barbarians! They speak of Cossack horrors, as if war itself were not the greatest of all horrors, as if the praise of human slaughter in a socialist periodical were not mental Cossackdom in its very essence. . . .

[The war] is the mass destruction of the European proletariat. Never has a war killed off whole nations; never, within the past century, has it swept over all of the great and established lands of civilized Europe. . . . But nine-tenths of these millions come from the ranks of the working class of the cities and the farms. It is our strength, our hope that was mowed down there, day after day, before the scythe of death. They were the best, the most intelligent, the most thoroughly schooled forces of international socialism, the bearers of the holiest traditions, of the highest heroism, the modern labor movement, the vanguard of the whole world proletariat, the workers of England, France, Belgium, Germany, and Russia who are being gassed and butchered in masses.

Only from Europe, only from the oldest capitalist nations, when the hour is ripe, can the signal come for the social revolution that will free the nations. Only the English, the French, the Belgian, the German, the Russian, the Italian workers together can lead the army of the exploited and oppressed. And when the time comes they alone can call capitalism to account for centuries of crime committed against primitive peoples; they alone can avenge its work of destruction over a whole world. But for the advance and victory of socialism we need a strong, educated, ready proletariat, masses whose strength lies in knowledge as well as in numbers. And these very masses are being decimated all over the world. The flower of our youthful strength, hundreds of thousands whose socialist education in England, in France, in Belgium, in Germany and in Russia was the product of decades of education and propaganda, other hundreds of thousands who were ready to receive the lessons of socialism have fallen, and are rotting upon the battlefields. The fruit of the sacrifices and toil of generations is destroyed in a few short weeks, the choicest troops of the international proletariat are torn out by the life roots. . . .

But . . . the war is not only a grandiose murder, but the suicide of the European working class. The soldiers of socialism, the workers of England, of France, of Germany, of Italy, of Belgium are murdering each other at the bidding of capitalism, are thrusting cold, murderous irons into each other's breasts, are tottering over their graves, grappling in each other's death-bringing arms.

"*Deutschland, Deutschland über alles*" [Germany, Germany above everything], "long live democracy," "long live the czar and slavery," "ten thousand tent cloths, guaranteed according to specifications," "hundred thousand pounds of bacon," "coffee substitute, immediate delivery" . . . dividends are rising—proletarians falling; and with each one there sinks a fighter of the future, a soldier of the revolution, a savior of humanity from the yoke of capitalism, into the grave.

This madness will not stop, and this bloody nightmare of hell will not cease until the workers of Germany, of France, of Russia and of England will wake up out of their drunken sleep; will clasp each others' hands in brotherhood and will drown the bestial chorus of war agitators and the hoarse cry of capitalist hyenas with the mighty cry of labor, "Proletarians of all countries, unite!"

Theses on the Tasks of International Social Democracy

A large number of comrades from different parts of Germany have adopted the following theses, which constitute an application of the Erfurt Program to the contemporary problems of international socialism.

1. The world war has annihilated the work of forty years of European socialism: by destroying the revolutionary proletariat as a political force; by destroying the moral prestige of socialism; by scattering the workers' International; by setting its sections

one against the other in fratricidal massacre; and by tying the aspirations and hopes of the masses of the people of the main countries in which capitalism has developed to the destinies of imperialism.

2. By their vote for war credits and by their proclamation of national unity, the official leaderships of the socialist parties in Germany, France, and England (with the exception of the Independent Labor party) have reinforced imperialism, induced the masses of the people to suffer patiently the misery and horrors of the war, contributed to the unleashing, without restraint, of imperialist frenzy, to the prolongation of the massacre and the increase in the number of its victims, and assumed their share in the responsibility for the war itself and for its consequences.

3. This tactic of the official leaderships of the parties in the belligerent countries, and in the first place in Germany, until recently at the head of the International, constitutes a betrayal of the elementary principles of international socialism, of the vital interests of the working class, and of all the democratic interests of the peoples. By this alone socialist policy is condemned to impotence even in those countries where the leaders have remained faithful to their principles: Russia, Serbia, Italy and—with hardly an exception—Bulgaria.

4. By this alone official social democracy in the principal countries has repudiated the class struggle in wartime and adjourned it until after the war; it has guaranteed to the ruling classes of all countries a delay in which to strengthen, at the proletariat's expense, and in a monstrous fashion, their economic, political, and moral positions.

5. The world war serves neither the national defense nor the economic or political interests of the masses of the people whatever they may be. It is but the product of the imperialist rivalries between the capitalist classes of the different countries for world hegemony and for the monopoly in the exploitation and oppression of areas still not under the heel of capital. In the era of the unleashing of this imperialism, national wars are no longer possible. National interests serve only as the pretext for putting the laboring masses of the people under the domination of their mortal enemy, imperialism.

6. The policy of the imperialist states and the imperialist war

cannot give to a single oppressed nation its liberty and its independence. The small nations, the ruling classes of which are the accomplices of their partners in the big states, constitute only the pawns on the imperialist chessboard of the great powers, and are used by them, just like their own working masses, in wartime, as instruments, to be sacrificed to capitalist interests after the war.

7. The present world war signifies, under these conditions, either in the case of "defeat" or of "victory," a defeat for socialism and democracy. It increases, whatever the outcome—excepting the revolutionary intervention of the international proletariat—and strengthens militarism, national antagonisms, and economic rivalries in the world market. It accentuates capitalist exploitation and reaction in the domain of internal policy, renders the influence of public opinion precarious and derisory, and reduces parliaments to tools more and more obedient to imperialism. The present world war carries within itself the seeds of new conflicts.

8. World peace cannot be assured by projects utopian or, at bottom, reactionary, such as tribunals of arbitration by capitalist diplomats, diplomatic "disarmament" conventions, "the freedom of the seas," abolition of the right of maritime arrest, "the United States of Europe," a "customs union for central Europe," buffer states, and other illusions. Imperialism, militarism and war can never be abolished nor attenuated so long as the capitalist class exercises, uncontested, its class hegemony. The sole means of successful resistance, and the only guarantee of the peace of the world, is the capacity for action and the revolutionary will of the international proletariat to hurl its full weight into the balance.

9. Imperialism, as the last phase in the life, and the highest point in the expansion of the world hegemony, of capital, is the mortal enemy of the proletariat of all countries. But under its rule, just as in the preceding stages of capitalism, the forces of its mortal enemy have increased in pace with its development. It accelerates the concentration of capital, the pauperization of the middle classes, the numerical reinforcement of the proletariat, arouses more and more resistance from the masses; and leads thereby to an intensified sharpening of class antagonisms. In peacetime as in war, the struggle of the proletariat as a class has

to be concentrated first of all against imperialism. For the international proletariat, the struggle against imperialism is at the same time the struggle for power, the decisive settling of accounts between socialism and capitalism. The final goal of socialism will be realized by the international proletariat only if it opposes imperialism all along the line, and if it makes the issue "war against war" the guiding line of its practical policy; and on condition that it deploys all its forces and shows itself ready, by its courage to the point of extreme sacrifice, to do this.

10. In this framework, socialism's principal mission today is to regroup the proletariat of all countries into a living revolutionary force; to make it, through a powerful international organization which has only one conception of its tasks and interests, and only one universal tactic appropriate to political action in peace and war alike, the decisive factor in political life: so that it may fulfill its historic mission.

11. The war has smashed the Second International. Its inadequacy has been demonstrated by its incapacity to place an effective obstacle in the way of the segmentation of its forces behind national boundaries in time of war, and to carry through a common tactic and action by the proletariat in all countries.

12. In view of the betrayal, by the official representatives of the socialist parties in the principal countries, of the aims and interests of the working class; in view of their passage from the camp of the working-class International to the political camp of the imperialist bourgeoisie; it is vitally necessary for socialism to build a new workers' International, which will take into its own hands the leadership and coordination of the revolutionary class struggle against world imperialism.

To accomplish its historic mission, socialism must be guided by the following principles:

1. The class struggle against the ruling classes within the boundaries of the bourgeois states, and international solidarity of the workers of all countries, are the two rules of life, inherent in the working class in struggle and of world-historic importance to it for its emancipation. There is no socialism without international proletarian solidarity, and there is no socialism without class struggle. The renunciation by the socialist proletariat, in

time of peace as in time of war, of the class struggle and of international solidarity, is equivalent to suicide.

2. The activity of the proletariat of all countries as a class, in peacetime as in wartime, must be geared to the fight against imperialism and war as its supreme goal. Parliamentary and trade-union action, like every activity of the workers' movement, must be subordinated to this aim, so that the proletariat in each country is opposed in the sharpest fashion to its national bourgeoisie, so that the political and spiritual opposition between the two becomes at each moment the main issue, and international solidarity between the workers of all countries is underlined and practiced.

3. The center of gravity of the organization of the proletariat as a class is the International. The International decides in time of peace the tactics to be adopted by the national sections on the questions of militarism, colonial policy, commerical policy, the celebration of May Day, and finally, the collective tactic to be followed in the event of war.

4. The obligation to carry out the decisions of the International takes precedence over all else. National sections which do not conform with this place themselves outside the International.

5. The setting in motion of the massed ranks of the proletariat of all countries is alone decisive in the course of struggles against imperialism and against war.

Thus the principal tactic of the national sections aims to render the masses capable of political action and resolute initiative; to ensure the international cohesion of the masses in action; to build the political and trade union organizations in such a way that, through their mediation, prompt and effective collaboration of all the sections is at all times guaranteed, and so that the will of the International materializes in action by the majority of the working-class masses all over the world.

6. The immediate mission of socialism is the spiritual liberation of the proletariat from the tutelage of the bourgeoisie, which expresses itself through the influence of nationalist ideology. The national sections must agitate in the parliaments and the press, denouncing the empty wordiness of nationalism as an instrument

of bourgeois domination. The sole defense of all real national independence is at present the revolutionary class struggle against imperialism. The workers' fatherland, to the defense of which all else must be subordinated, is the socialist International.

PART III
THE THEORETICAL FOUNDATIONS OF LENINISM

Lenin, born Vladimir Ilych Ulyanov (1870–1924), is the single individual responsible for creating the Bolshevik faction of the Russian Social Democratic Labor party and molding it into a "party of a new type" capable of decisive revolutionary action and authoritarian control over Russia. Although (having been in exile at the time) he played no direct role in deposing the czar, Lenin shortly thereafter returned to Russia and rapidly took advantage of the chaos to almost single-handedly lead the Bolsheviks to power. In the difficult months following the Bolshevik Revolution (November 7, 1917[1]), it was again Lenin's political acumen and indomitable will which enabled them to retain and consolidate their power. Thus, more than any other individual, it is Lenin who created Russian Communism in both theory and practice. In so doing, he applied Marxist theory to conditions quite alien to those envisaged as necessary for revolution by Marx, and when he found theory wanting, he improvised. Since Lenin's death, his reinterpretations of Marx, as well as his many improvisations, have become enshrined in the U.S.S.R. as "Marxism-Leninism," which has replaced "Marxism" as the doctrine of Soviet-dominated communist parties. In this chapter we shall examine some of the distinctive aspects of Leninist theory, and in the next we shall follow the course of the Bolshevik Revolution

1. This and all subsequent dates are given according to the Gregorian calendar, adopted in Russia in February 1918.

and the birth of the authoritarian Soviet state under Lenin's direction.

There are essentially five major aspects of "Marxism-Leninism." These are: (1) the conception of the party of the proletariat as a small, tightly disciplined band of professional revolutionaries, whose role is that of "vanguard" of the proletariat rather than that of its parliamentary representative or its economic (i.e., trade union) organization; (2) the emphasis on the supremacy of the political "factor" in analyzing any potentially revolutionary situation, i.e., on the minimization of the role of the theory of economic stages which had for so many years been the excuse for the Western European Social Democrats' passively awaiting the "inevitable" collapse of the capitalist economic system; (3) the formation of an alliance of the vast poor peasantry and the small proletariat as the primary means of effecting revolution in Russia and, by implication, in backward agricultural countries everywhere; (4) the utilization of the theory of imperialism to revise Marxist political strategy on a worldwide, not merely national or exclusively European, scale; and (5) the dogmatic interpretation of the "philosophy" of "Marx and Engels," whose views on every question are assumed to be identical and the dogmatic assertion of an ontological materialism, combined with the utter disregard of Marxian humanism. These salient characteristics of Marxism-Leninism are illustrated in the selections which follow.

12.
THE CONCEPTION
OF THE PARTY

Lenin's characteristic criticism and rejection of the "Orthodox" Social Democratic conception of the party as a mass organization functioning legally within the framework of bourgeois democracy is to be found clearly expressed in his early work What Is to Be Done?, *written in the winter of 1901–1902 and published in March 1902. The arguments presented in this critique form the basis of Lenin's subsequent factional tactics throughout the period prior to the Revolution of 1917. Lenin never wavered from his conception of the Party as comprised of a small, tightly disciplined band of professional revolutionaries, for whom the Revolution encompasses their entire existence. In this respect, it is important to trace the influence upon Lenin of S. G. Nechayev (1847– 1882), the anarchist revolutionary whose ideal of the revolutionary ascetic electrified an earlier generation of Russian youth, including Lenin's elder brother Alexander, executed in 1887 for his part in a plot to assassinate Czar Alexander II. Outlining the character of the true revolutionary, Nechayev, in his* Revolutionary Catechism, *stated:*

1. The revolutionary is a doomed man. He has no personal interests, no business affairs, no emotions, no attachments, no property and no name. Everything in him is wholly absorbed in the single thought and the single passion for revolution.
2. The revolutionary knows that in the very depth of his being, not only in words but also in deeds, he has broken all the bonds which tie him to the social order and the civilized world with all its laws, moralities and customs and with all its generally accepted conventions. He is their implacable enemy, and if he continues to live with them it is only in order to destroy them more speedily. . . .
4. The revolutionary despises public opinion. He despises and hates the existing social morality in all its manifestations. For him, morality is everything which contributes to the triumph of the revolution. Immoral and criminal is everything that stands in its way.
5. The revolutionary is a dedicated man, merciless toward the State and toward the educated classes; and he can expect no mercy from them. Between him and them there exists, declared or undeclared, a relentless and irreconcilable war to the death. He must accustom himself to torture.

SOURCE: From V. I. Lenin, *What Is to Be Done?* (1902), in *Collected Works,* Vol. V (Moscow: Progress Publishers, 1964) .

6. Tyrannical toward himself, he must be tyrannical toward others. All the gentle and ennervating sentiments of kinship, love, friendship, gratitude, and even honor must be suppressed in him and give place to the cold and single-minded passion for revolution. For him there exists only one pleasure, one consolation, one reward, one satisfaction —the success of the revolution. Night and day he must have but one thought, one aim—merciless destruction. Striving cold-bloodedly and indefatigably toward this end, he must be prepared to destroy himself and to destroy with his own hands everything that stands in the path of the revolution. . . .

8. The revolutionary can have no friendship or attachment except for those who have proved by their actions that they, like him, are dedicated to revolution. The degree of friendship, devotion and obligation toward such a comrade is determined solely by the degree of his usefulness to the cause of total revolutionary destruction. . . .

13. The revolutionary enters the world of the state, of the privileged classes, of the so-called civilization, and he lives in this world only for the purpose of bringing about its speedy and total destruction. He is not a revolutionary if he has any sympathy for this world. He should not hesitate to destroy any position, any place or any man in this world. *He must hate everyone and everything in it with an equal hatred. All the worse for him if he has any relations with parents, friends or lovers;* he is no longer a revolutionary if he is swayed by these relationships. . . .

22. The Society has no aim other than the complete liberation and happiness of the masses—i.e. of the people who live by manual labor. Convinced that their emancipation and the achievement of this happiness can only come about as a result of an all-destroying popular revolt, the Society will use all its resources and energy toward increasing and intensifying the evils and miseries of the people until at last their patience is exhausted and they are driven to a general uprising.

23. By a revolution the Society does not mean an orderly revolt according to the classic Western model—a revolt which always stops short of attacking the rights of property and the traditional social systems of so-called civilization and morality. Until now such a revolution has always limited itself to the overthrow of one political form in order to replace it by another, thereby attempting to bring about a so-called revolutionary state. The only form of revolution beneficial to the people is one which destroys the entire state to the roots and exterminates all the state traditions, instructions and classes in Russia. . . .

26. To weld the people into one single unconquerable and all-destructive force—this is our aim, our conspiracy and our task.[1]

Lenin's advocacy of the leading role within Social Democratic politics to be played by professional revolutionaries is equally derived from his disparaging view of orthodox Social Democracy. Beginning with an attack on Bernstein's "Opportunism" and its widespread effect on the

1. Nechayev, *Revolutionary Catechism*, trans. Robert Payne in *The Life and Death of Lenin* (New York: Avon Books, 1967), pp. 26–33. Reprinted by permission of Simon and Schuster, Inc., and Bertha Klausher International Literary Agency.

*Western European Social Democratic parties, Lenin argues that a simi-
lar trend, also closely associated with the trades-union, or purely "economic," struggle for social reform—rather than the political struggle for
socialism—has in fact dominated Russian Social Democracy since its
inception. It is in this alleged bastardization of Marxist revolutionary
theory that Lenin sees the opening wedge in the opportunists' campaign for reform, which must be destroyed by a rigorous subordination
of theory to practice instead of the triumph of pure theory as in the
Western parties. As we shall see below, however, the content of Lenin's
"Marxist" theory is itself a degenerate form of Marxism.*[2]

*The discussion is a "debate" between Lenin and Luxemburg. The
first part of the selection is taken from Lenin's* What Is to Be Done?
*and the second from Rosa Luxemburg's earliest critique of Lenin, en-
titled* Leninism or Marxism?, *in which she exposes the dangers inherent in Lenin's elitism as expressed in his* One Step Forward, Two
Steps Back *(1904) as well as in* What Is to Be Done?

LENIN: THE "PARTY OF A NEW TYPE"

. . . It is no secret for anyone that two trends have taken form
in present-day international Social Democracy. The conflict between these trends now flares up in a bright flame and now dies
down and smolders under the ashes of imposing "truce resolutions." The essence of the "new" trend, which adopts a "critical"
attitude toward "obsolete dogmatic" Marxism, has been clearly
enough *presented* by Bernstein and *demonstrated* by Millerand.

Social Democracy must change from a party of social revolution into a democratic party of social reforms. Bernstein has
surrounded this political demand with a whole battery of well-
attuned "new" arguments and reasonings. Denied was the possibility of putting socialism on a scientific basis and of demonstrating its necessity and inevitability from the point of view of the
materialist conception of history. Denied was the fact of growing
impoverishment, the process of proletarization, and the intensification of capitalist contradictions; the very concept, *"ultimate
aim,"* was declared to be unsound, and the idea of the dictatorship of the proletariat was completely rejected. Denied was the
antithesis in principle between liberalism and socialism. Denied
was *the theory of the class struggle,* on the alleged grounds that it

2. Cf. especially Selections 14, 15, and 17, below.

could not be applied to a strictly democratic society governed according to the will of the majority, etc.

Thus, the demand for a decisive turn from revolutionary Social Democracy to bourgeois social reformism was accompanied by a no less decisive turn toward bourgeois criticism of all the fundamental ideas of Marxism. . . .

He who does not deliberately close his eyes cannot fail to see that the new "critical" trend in socialism is nothing more or less than a new variety of *opportunism*. And if we judge people, not by the glittering uniforms they don or by the high-sounding appellations they give themselves, but by their actions and by what they actually advocate, it will be clear that "freedom of criticism" means freedom for an opportunist trend in Social Democracy, freedom to convert Social Democracy into a democratic party of reform, freedom to introduce bourgeois ideas and bourgeois elements into socialism. . . .

The positions of the opportunists in relation to the revolutionary Social Democrats in Russia are diametrically opposed to those in Germany. In that country, as we know, the revolutionary Social Democrats are in favor of preserving that which exists—the old program and the tactics, which are universally known and have been elucidated in all their details by many decades of experience. But the "Critics" desire to introduce changes, and since these Critics represent an insignificant minority, and since they are very timid in their revisionist efforts, one can understand the motives of the majority in confining themselves to the dry rejection of "innovations." In Russia, however, it is the Critics and the Economists who are in favor of preserving that which exists. . . .

We revolutionary Social Democrats, on the contrary, are dissatisfied with worship of spontaneity, i.e., of that which exists "at the present moment." We demand that the tactics that have prevailed in recent years be changed; we declare that "before we can unite, and in order that we may unite, we must first of all draw firm and definite lines of demarcation." In a word, the Germans stand for that which exists and reject changes; we demand a change of that which exists, and reject subservience thereto and reconciliation to it. . . .

The much vaunted freedom of criticism does not imply substitution of one theory for another, but freedom from all integral and pondered theory; it implies eclecticism and lack of principle. Those who have the slightest acquaintance with the actual state of our movement cannot but see that the wide spread of Marxism was accompanied by a certain lowering of the theoretical level. . . .

Without revolutionary theory there can be no revolutionary movement. This idea cannot be insisted upon too strongly at a time when the fashionable preaching of opportunism goes hand in hand with an infatuation for the narrowest forms of practical activity. Yet, for Russian Social Democrats the importance of theory is enhanced by three other circumstances, which are often forgotten: first, by the fact that our Party is only in process of formation, its features are only just becoming defined, and it has as yet far from settled accounts with the other trends of revolutionary thought that threaten to divert the movement from the correct path. . . . Under these circumstances . . . only short-sighted people can consider factional disputes and a strict differentiation between shades of opinion inopportune or superfluous. The fate of Russian Social Democracy for very many years to come may depend on the strengthening of one or the other "shade."

Second, the Social Democratic movement is in its very essence an international movement. This means not only that we must combat national chauvinism, but that an incipient movement in a young country can be successful only if it makes use of the experiences of other countries. In order to make use of these experiences it is not enough merely to be acquainted with them, or simply to copy out the latest resolutions. What is required is the ability to treat these experiences critically and to test them independently. . . .

Third, the national tasks of Russian Social Democracy are such as have never confronted any other socialist party in the world. . . . At this point, we wish to state only that the *role of vanguard fighter can be fulfilled only by a party that is guided by the most advanced theory.* . . .

History has now confronted us with an immediate task which is the *most revolutionary* of all the *immediate* tasks confronting the proletariat of any country. The fulfillment of this task, the destruction of the most powerful bulwark, not only of European, but (it may now be said) of Asiatic reaction, would make the Russian proletariat the vanguard of the international revolutionary proletariat. . . .

The strength of the present-day movement lies in the awakening of the masses (principally, the industrial proletariat) and its weakness lies in the lack of consciousness and initiative among the revolutionary leaders. . . .

We have said that *there could not have been* Social Democratic consciousness among the workers. It would have to be brought to them from without. The history of all countries shows that the working class, exclusively by its own effort, is able to develop only trade union consciousness, i.e., the conviction that it is necessary to combine in unions, fight the employers, and strive to compel the government to pass necessary labor legislation, etc. The theory of socialism, however, grew out of the philosophic, historical, and economic theories elaborated by educated representatives of the propertied classes, by intellectuals. By their social status the founders of modern scientific socialism, Marx and Engels, themselves belonged to the bourgeois intelligentsia. In the very same way, in Russia, the theoretical doctrine of Social Democracy arose altogether independently of the spontaneous growth of the working-class movement; it arose as a natural and inevitable outcome of the development of thought among the revolutionary socialist intelligentsia. . . .

Hence, we had both the spontaneous awakening of the working masses, their awakening to conscious life and conscious struggle, and a revolutionary youth, armed with Social Democratic theory and straining toward the workers. In this connection it is particularly important to state the oft-forgotten (and comparatively little known) fact that, although the *early* Social Democrats of that period *zealously carried on economic agitation* . . . they did not regard this as their sole task. On the contrary, *from the very beginning* they set for Russian Social Democracy the most far reaching historical tasks, in general, and the task of overthrowing the autocracy, in particular. . . .

All worship of the spontaneity of the working-class movement, all belittling of the role of "the conscious element," of the role of Social Democracy, *means, quite independently of whether he who belittles that role desires it or not, a strengthening of the influence of bourgeois ideology upon the workers.* All those who talk about "overrating the importance of ideology," about exaggerating the role of the conscious element, etc., imagine that the labor movement pure and simple can elaborate, and will elaborate, an independent ideology for itself, if only the workers "wrest their fate from the hands of the leaders." But this is a profound mistake. . . .

Since there can be no talk of an independent ideology formulated by the working masses themselves in the process of their movement, the *only* choice is—either bourgeois or socialist ideology. There is no middle course (for mankind has not created a "third" ideology, and, moreover, in a society torn by class antagonisms there can never be a nonclass or an above-class ideology) . Hence, to belittle the socialist ideology *in any way, to turn aside from it in the slightest degree* means to strengthen bourgeois ideology. There is much talk of spontaneity. But the *spontaneous* development of the working-class movement leads to its subordination to bourgeois ideology, *to its development along the lines of the Credo program;** for the spontaneous working-class movement is trade unionism, and trade unionism means the ideological enslavement of the workers by the bourgeoisie. Hence, our task, the task of Social Democracy, is *to combat spontaneity, to divert* the working-class movement from this spontaneous, trade-unionist striving to come under the wing of the bourgeoisie, and to bring it under the wing of revolutionary Social Democracy. . . .

But why, the reader will ask, does the spontaneous movement, the movement along the line of least resistance, lead to the domination of bourgeois ideology? For the simple reason that bourgeois ideology is far older in origin than socialist ideology, that it is more fully developed, and that it has at its disposal *immeasurably* more means of dissemination. . . .

And so, we have become convinced that the fundamental error committed by the "new trend" in Russian Social Democracy is its bowing to spontaneity and its failure to understand that the

---

* The reference is to Ekaterina Kuskova's *Credo of the Young* (1899) , a cutting attack on the extreme revolutionary wing of the *RSDLP* from a viewpoint approximating Bernstein's.

spontaneity of the masses demands a high degree of consciousness from us Social Democrats. The greater the spontaneous upsurge of the masses and the more widespread the movement, the more rapid, incomparably so, the demand for greater consciousness in the theoretical, political, and organizational work of Social Democracy. . . .

The overwhelming majority of Russian Social Democrats have of late been almost entirely absorbed by this work of organizing the exposure of factory conditions . . . so much so, indeed that they have lost sight of the fact that this, *taken by itself*, is in essence still not Social Democratic work, but merely trade union work. As a matter of fact, the exposures merely dealt with the relations between the workers *in a given trade* and their employers, and all they achieved was that the sellers of labor power learned to sell their "commodity" on better terms and to fight the purchasers over a purely commercial deal. . . . Social Democracy leads the struggle of the working class, not only for better terms for the sale of labor power, but for the abolition of the social system that compels the propertyless to sell themselves to the rich. Social Democracy represents the working class, not in its relation to a given group of employers alone, but in its relation to all classes of modern society and to the state as an organized political force. Hence, it follows that not only must Social Democrats not confine themselves exclusively to the economic struggle, but that they must not allow the organization of economic exposures to become the predominant part of their activities. We must take up actively the political education of the working class and the development of its political consciousness. . . .

It is possible to "raise the activity of the working masses" *only* when this activity *is not restricted* to "political agitation on an economic basis." A basic condition for the necessary expansion of political agitation is the organization of *comprehensive* political exposure. *In no way* except by means of such exposures *can* the masses be trained in political consciousness and revolutionary activity. . . . Working-class consciousness cannot be genuine political consciousness unless the workers are trained to respond to *all* cases of tyranny, oppression, violence, and abuse, no matter *what class* is affected—unless they are trained, moreover, to respond from a Social Democratic point of view and no other. The consciousness of the working masses cannot be genuine class consciousness, unless the workers learn, from concrete, and above all from topical, political facts and events to observe *every* other social class in *all* the manifestations of its intellectual, ethical, and political life. . . . Those who concentrate the attention, observation, and consciousness of the working class . . . upon itself alone are not Social Democrats; for the self-knowledge of the working class is indissolubly bound up . . . with the practical understanding of the relationships between *all* the various classes of modern society, acquired through the experience of political life. For this reason the conception of the economic struggle as the most widely applicable means of drawing the masses into the political movement, which our Economists preach, is so extremely harmful and reactionary in its practical significance. In order to become a Social Democrat, the worker must have a clear picture in his mind of the economic nature and the social and political features of the landlord and the priest, the high state official and the peasant, the student and the vagabond; he must know their strong and weak points; he must grasp the meaning of all the catchwords and sophisms by which each class and each stratum *camouflages* its selfish strivings and its real "inner workings"; he must understand what interests are reflected by certain institutions and certain laws and how they are reflected. . . .

However much we may try to "lend the economic struggle itself a political character," we *shall never be able* to develop the political consciousness of the workers (to the level of Social Democratic political consciousness) by keeping within the framework of the economic struggle, for *that framework is too narrow.* . . .

Class political consciousness can be brought to the workers *only from without,* that is, only from outside the economic struggle, from outside the sphere of relations between workers and employers. The sphere from which alone it is possible to obtain this knowledge is the sphere of relationships of *all* classes and strata to the state and the government, the sphere of the interrelations between *all* classes. For that reason, the reply to the question as to what must be done to bring political knowledge to the workers cannot be merely the answer with which, in the majority of cases, the practical workers, especially those inclined toward Economism, mostly content themselves, namely: "To go among the workers." . . .

In order to be able to provide the workers with real, comprehensive, and live political knowledge, we must have "our own people," Social Democrats, everywhere, among all social strata, and in all positions from which we can learn the inner springs of our state mechanism. Such people are required, not only for propaganda and agitation, but in a still larger measure for organization. . . .

It cannot be too strongly maintained that the Social Democrat's ideal should not be the trade union secretary, but *the tribune of the people,* who is able to react to every manifestation of tyranny and oppression, no matter where it appears, no matter what stratum or class of the people it affects; who is able to generalize all these manifestations and produce a single picture of police violence and capitalist exploitation; who is able to take advantage of every event, however small, in order to set forth *before all* his socialist convictions and his democratic demands, in order to clarify for *all* and everyone the world-historic significance of the struggle for the emancipation of the proletariat. . .

Political exposures are as much a declaration of war against the *government* as economic exposures are a declaration of war against the factory owners. The moral significance of this declaration of war will be all the greater, the wider and more powerful the campaign of exposure will be, and the more numerous and determined the social *class* that has *declared war in order to begin the war.* Hence, political exposures in themselves serve as a powerful instrument for *disintegrating* the system we oppose, as a means for diverting from the enemy his casual or temporary allies, as a means for spreading hostility and distrust among the permanent partners of the autocracy.

In our time only a party that will *organize* really *nationwide* exposures can become the vanguard of the revolutionary forces. . . .

But if we have to undertake the organization of a really nationwide exposure of the government, in what way will then the class character of our movement be expressed?—the over-zealous advocate of "close organic contact with the proletarian struggle" will ask us. The reply is manifold: We Social Democrats will organize these nationwide exposures; all questions raised by the agitation will be explained in a consistently Social Democratic spirit, without any concessions to distortions of Marxism; the all-round political agitation will be conducted by a party which unites into one inseparable whole the assault on the government in the name of the entire people, the revolutionary training of the proletariat, and the safeguarding of its political independence, the guidance of the economic struggle of the working class, and the utilization of all its spontaneous conflicts with its exploiters which rouse and bring into our camp increasing numbers of the proletariat. . . .

It is particularly necessary to arouse in all who participate in practical work, or are preparing to take up that work, discontent with the *amateurism* prevailing among us and an unshakable determination to rid ourselves of it.

. . . The struggle against the *political* police requires special qualities; it requires *professional* revolutionaries. And we must see to it, not only that the masses "advance" concrete demands, but that the masses of the workers "advance" an increasing number of such professional revolutionaries. Thus, we have reached the question of the relation between an organization of professional revolutionaries and the labor movement pure and simple. . . .

The political struggle of Social Democracy is far more extensive and complex than the economic struggle of the workers against the employers and the government. Similarly (indeed for that reason), the organization of the revolutionary Social Democratic party must inevitably be of *a kind different* from the organization of the workers designed for this struggle. The workers' organization must in the first place be a trade union organization; second, it must be as broad as possible; and third, it must be as public as conditions will allow. . . . On the other hand, the organization of the revolutionaries must consist first and foremost of people who make revolutionary activity their profession. . . . In view of this common characteristic of the members of such an organization, *all distinctions as between workers and intellectuals,* not to speak of distinctions of trade and profession, in both categories, *must be effaced*. Such an organization must perforce not be very extensive and must be as secret as possible. . . .

The workers' organizations for the economic struggle should be trade union organizations. Every Social Democratic worker should as far as possible assist and actively work in these organizations. But, while this is true, it is certainly not in our interest to demand that only Social Democrats should be eligible for membership in the "trade" unions, since that would only narrow the scope of our influence upon the masses. Let every worker who understands the need to unite for the struggle against the employers and the government join the trade unions. . . . The broader these organizations, the broader will be our influence over them—an influence due not only to the "spontaneous" development of the economic struggle, but to the direct and conscious effort of the socialist trade union members to influence their comrades. But a broad organization cannot apply methods of strict secrecy (since this demands far greater training than is required for the economic struggle). . . .

A small, compact core of the most reliable, experienced, and hardened workers, with responsible representatives in the principal districts and connected by all the rules of strict secrecy with the organization of revolutionaries, can, with the widest support of the masses and without any formal organization, perform *all* the functions of a trade union organization, in a manner, moreover, desirable to Social Democracy. Only in this way can we secure the *consolidation* and development of a *Social Democratic* trade union movement, despite all the gendarmes. . . .

The moral to be drawn from this is simple. If we begin with the solid foundation of a strong organization of revolutionaries, we can ensure the stability of the movement as a whole and carry out the aims both of Social Democracy and of trade unions proper. If, however, we begin with a broad workers' organization, which is supposedly most "accessible" to the masses (but which is actually most accessible to the gendarmes and makes revolutionaries most accessible to the police), we shall achieve neither the one aim nor the other. . . .

Without tried and talented leaders (and talented men are not born by the hundreds), professionally trained, schooled by long experience, and working in perfect harmony, no class in modern society can wage a determined struggle. . . .

I assert that it is far more difficult to unearth a dozen wise men than a hundred fools. This position I will defend, no matter how much you instigate the masses against me for my "antidemocratic" views, etc. As I have stated repeatedly, by "wise men," in connection with organization, I mean *professional revolutionaries,* irrespective of whether they have developed from among students or working men. I assert: (1) that no revolutionary movement can endure without a stable organization of leaders maintaining continuity; (2) that the broader the popular mass drawn spontaneously into the struggle, which forms the basis of the movement and participates in it, the more urgent the need for such an organization, and the more solid this organization must be . . . ; (3) that such an organization must consist chiefly of people professionally engaged in revolutionary activity; (4) that in an autocratic state, the more we *confine* the membership of such an organization to people who are professionally engaged in revolutionary activity and who have been professionally trained in the art of combating the political police, the more difficult will it be to unearth the organization; and (5) the *greater* will be the number of people from the working class and from the other social classes who will be able to join the movement and perform active work in it. . . .

We can never give a mass organization that degree of secrecy without which there can be no question of persistent and continuous struggle against the government. To concentrate all secret functions in the hands of as small a number of professional revolutionaries as possible does not mean that the latter will "do the thinking for all" and that the rank and file will not take an active part in the *movement.* On the contrary, the membership will promote increasing numbers of the professional revolutionaries from its ranks; . . . and the rank and file will "think," not only of amateurish methods, but of such training. . . .

We must have such circles, trade unions, and organizations everywhere in *as large a number as possible* and with the widest variety of functions; but it would be absurd and harmful *to confound* them with the organization of *revolutionaries.* . . .

Our very first and most pressing duty is to help to train

working-class revolutionaries who will be on the same level *in regard to Party activity* as the revolutionaries from among the intellectuals. . . . Attention, therefore, must be devoted *principally* to *raising* the workers to the level of revolutionaries; it is not at all our task *to descend* to the level of the "working masses" . . . or to the level of the "average worker." . . . The only serious organizational principle for the active workers of our movement should be the strictest secrecy, the strictest selection of members, and the training of professional revolutionaries. Given these qualities, something even more than "democratism" would be guaranteed to us, namely, complete, comradely, mutual confidence among revolutionaries. This is absolutely essential for us, because there can be no question of replacing it by general democratic control in Russia. It would be a great mistake to believe that the impossibility of establishing real "democratic" control renders the members of the revolutionary organization beyond control altogether. They have not the time to think about toy forms of democratism . . . but they have a lively sense of their *responsibility,* knowing as they do from experience that an organization of real revolutionaries will stop at nothing to rid itself of an unworthy member. . . .

LUXEMBURG: LENINISM OR MARXISM?—ROUND ONE

Social Democratic centralism cannot be based on the mechanical subordination and blind obedience of the party membership to the leading party center. . . . The Social Democratic movement cannot allow the erection of an airtight partition between the class-conscious nucleus of the proletariat already in the party and its immediate popular environment, the nonparty sections of the proletariat.

Now the two principles on which Lenin's centralism rests are precisely these: 1. The blind subordination, in the smallest detail, of all party organs, to the party center, which alone thinks, guides, and decides for all. 2. The rigorous separation of the organized nucleus of revolutionaries from its social-revolutionary surroundings.

SOURCE: From Rosa Luxemburg, *Leninism or Marxism?* (Ann Arbor: University of Michigan Press, 1967) .

Such centralism is a mechanical transposition of the organizational principles of Blanquism into the mass movement of the socialist working class.

In accordance with this view, Lenin defines his "revolutionary Social Democrat" as a "Jacobin joined to the organization of the proletariat, which has become conscious of its class interests."

The fact is that Social Democracy is not *joined* to the organization of the proletariat. It is itself the proletariat. . . . It can only be the concentrated will of the individuals and groups representative of the most class-conscious, militant, advanced sections of the working class. It is, so to speak, the "self-centralism" of the advanced sectors of the proletariat. It is the rule of the majority within its own party.

The indispensable conditions for the realization of Social Democratic centralism are: 1. The existence of a large contingent of workers educated in the political struggle. 2. The possibility for the workers to develop their own political activity through direct influence on public life, in a party press, and public congresses, etc.

These conditions are not yet fully formed in Russia. The first—a proletarian vanguard, conscious of its class interests and capable of self-direction in political activity—is only now emerging. . . . The second condition can be had only under a regime of political liberty.

With these conclusions, Lenin disagrees violently. He is convinced that all the conditions necessary for the formation of a powerful and centralized party already exist in Russia. He declares that "it is no longer the proletarians but certain intellectuals in our party who need to be educated in the matters of organization and discipline." He glorifies the educative influence of the factory, which, he says, accustoms the proletariat to "discipline and organization."

Saying all this, Lenin seems to demonstrate again that his conception of socialist organization is quite mechanistic. The discipline Lenin has in mind is being implanted in the working class not only by the factory but also by the military and the existing state bureaucracy—by the entire mechanism of the centralized bourgeois state. . . .

What is there in common between the regulated docility of an oppressed class and the self-discipline and organization of a class struggling for its emancipation?

The self-discipline of Social Democracy is not merely the replacement of the authority of the bourgeois rulers with the authority of a socialist central committee. The working class will acquire the sense of the new discipline, the freely assumed self-discipline of Social Democracy, not as a result of the discipline imposed on it by the capitalist state, but by extirpating, to the last root, its old habits of obedience and servility. . . .

Granting, as Lenin wants, such absolute powers . . . to the top organ of the party, we strengthen, to a dangerous extent, the conservatism inherent in such an organ. If the tactics of the socialist party are not to be the creation of a Central Committee but of the whole party, or, still better, of the whole labor movement, then it is clear that the party sections and federations need the liberty of action which alone will permit them to develop their revolutionary initiative and to utilize all the resources of a situation. The ultracentralism asked by Lenin is full of the sterile spirit of the overseer. It is not a positive and creative spirit. *Lenin's concern is not so much to make the activity of the party more fruitful as to control the party—to narrow the movement rather than to develop it, to bind rather than to unify it.* . . .

The military ultracentralism cried up by Lenin and his friends is not the product of accidental differences of opinion. It is said to be related to a campaign against opportunism which Lenin has carried to the smallest organizational detail. . . .

If instead of mechanically applying to Russia formulas elaborated in Western Europe, we approach the problem of organization from the angle of conditions specific to Russia, we arrive at conclusions that are diametrically opposed to Lenin's.

To attribute to opportunism an invariable preference for a definite form of organization, that is, decentralization, is to miss the essence of opportunism.

On the question of organization, or any other question, opportunism knows only one principle: the absence of principle. Opportunism chooses its means of action with the aim of suiting the given circumstances at hand, provided these means appear to lead toward the ends in view. . . .

If we assume the viewpoint claimed as his own by Lenin and we fear the influence of intellectuals in the proletarian movement, we can conceive of no greater danger to the Russian party than Lenin's plan of organization. *Nothing will more surely enslave a young labor movement to an intellectual elite hungry for power than this bureaucratic strait jacket, which will immobilize the movement and turn it into an automaton manipulated by a Central Committee.* On the other hand, there is no more effective guarantee against opportunist intrigue and personal ambition than the independent revolutionary action of the proletariat, as a result of which the workers acquire the sense of political responsibility and self-reliance. . . .

More important is the fundamental falseness of the idea underlying the plan of unqualified centralism—the idea that the road to opportunism can be barred by means of clauses in a party constitution. . . .

The afflux of nonproletarian recruits to the party of the proletariat is the effect of profound social causes, such as the economic collapse of the petit bourgeoisie, the bankruptcy of bourgeois liberalism, and the degeneration of bourgeois democracy. It is naïve to hope to stop this current by means of a formula written down in a constitution. . . .

Social Democracy has always contended that it represents not only the class interests of the proletariat but also the progressive aspirations of the whole of contemporary society. It represents the interests of all who are oppressed by bourgeois domination. . . . In its capacity as a political party, Social Democracy becomes the haven of all discontented elements in our society and thus of the entire people, as contrasted to the tiny minority of the capitalist masters. . . .

Social Democracy must enclose the tumult of the nonproletarian protestants against existing society within the bounds of the revolutionary action of the proletariat. It must assimilate the elements that come to it.

This is only possible if Social Democracy already contains a strong, politically educated proletarian nucleus class conscious enough to be able, as up to now in Germany, to pull along in its tow the declassed and petit bourgeois elements that join the party. . . .

On the one hand, we have the mass; on the other, its historic goal, located outside of existing society. On one hand, we have the day-to-day struggle; on the other, the social revolution. Such are the terms of the dialectical contradiction through which the socialist movement makes its way.

It follows that this movement can best advance by tacking betwixt and between the two dangers by which it is constantly being threatened. One is the loss of its mass character; the other, the abandonment of its goal. One is the danger of sinking back to the condition of a sect; the other, the danger of becoming a movement of bourgeois social reform.

That is why it is illusory, and contrary to historic experience, to hope to fix, once for always, the direction of the revolutionary socialist struggle with the aid of formal means, which are expected to secure the labor movement against all possibilities of opportunist digression. . . .

Let us speak plainly. Historically, the errors committed by a truly revolutionary movement are infinitely more fruitful than the infallibility of the cleverest Central Committee.

13. LENIN:
TWO TACTICS OF
SOCIAL DEMOCRACY

Lenin, in exile in Geneva, wrote Two Tactics of Social Democracy in the Democratic Revolution *early in 1905 in response to the news of the outbreak of revolution in Russia, which began on January 21, 1905. The book was then illegally distributed in Russia. In it Lenin excoriates the Menshevik (i.e., "Orthodox" majority) faction of the Russian Social Democrats for their "tail-endism"—their advocating cooperation with the bourgeoisie in the anticipated democratic revolution (which did not in fact occur until March 1917). The Mensheviks argued for a policy of nonparticipation in the bourgeois government that it seemed in 1905 would soon be established, confining themselves instead to electoral activity, propaganda, and parliamentary opposition to all bourgeois parties and governments.*

Lenin, on the contrary, argues that the Social Democrats should (1) seize upon the available revolutionary discontent among the peasantry (who had been largely responsible for the events of 1905, without any leadership from the Social Democrats) [1] *and utilize it to overthrow the czarist autocracy, and (2) then immediately participate in the expected provisional revolutionary government so as to utilize real power to attempt the transformation of the bourgeois revolution into a socialist one. Along the way, naturally, the Social Democrats would abandon the peasantry as an ally, but could expect to pick up support among the poorest strata of the so-called rural proletariat. Needless to say, this notion of the proletariat allying itself with the peasantry is a fundamentally new point of tactical departure for Social Democrats, Russian or European. This argument of 1905 thus establishes the characteristically "Leninist" revolutionary strategy, applicable to industrially undeveloped, semifeudal countries, if there is sufficient mass discontent among a nonproletarian class.*

Especially characteristic of Lenin is his remark that "in the final analysis force alone settles the great problems of political liberty and

SOURCE: From V. I. Lenin, *Two Tactics of Social Democracy in the Democratic Revolution, Collected Works,* Vol. IX (Moscow: Foreign Language Publishing House, 1961).

1. The Mensheviks had, however, played a leading role in the uprisings in the cities.

the class struggle"[1] *coupled with his repeated critique of the doctrine of passively awaiting the bourgeoisie's development of capitalism according to the "laws" of the materialist interpretation of history and Marxist economics. That is, Lenin substitutes purely political activity and political force for the economic determinism of Orthodox Social Democracy as the underlying cause of social change, hence arguing that the revolution in Russia must be made without awaiting the supposedly "necessary" development of advanced capitalism.*

Although it is not mentioned by Lenin at this time, he is in fact drawing upon a line of argument used by Marx and Engels in their long-forgotten "Address of the Central Council to the Communist League" (March 1850), in which they admonished the scattered remnants of the Communist League in Germany to work first for the success of the bourgeois-democratic revolution and then to embarrass the bourgeois parties in succession and to endeavor to transform the democratic revolution into a socialist one.[2]

Because of its polemical nature Two Tactics *continually refers to events, journals, and individuals with whom Lenin disagreed. Frequent reference is made to* Iskra *(The Spark), the first all-Russian illegal Marxist newspaper, which was founded in 1900 by Lenin, other Social Democrats (the most important among them being Plekhanov), and the so-called "Legal Marxists" and published abroad. Under Lenin's editorship, the newspaper soon became a rallying point and eventually its control and direction became a matter of dispute among the factions of the RSDLP. On November 1, 1903 (new style) Lenin resigned from the editorial board upon Plekhanov's demand that the board become controlled by Mensheviks. From that time* Iskra *became a Menshevik organ, until its closing in October 1905. In the current selection Lenin's reference to the "New" and "Old"* Iskra *refers to this change in control and orientation of the paper.*

Shortly before the Second Congress of the RSDLP (July–August 1903), the editorial board of the "Old" Iskra, *at Lenin's insistence, drew up a revolutionary program, which was defeated at the congress. The Second Congress, in an attempt to find a compromise between the two main factions, adopted two programs, known as the "maximum" and "minimum" programs. The maximum program, taking the longer view, called for a socialist revolution, the establishment of a proletarian dictatorship, and the building of a socialist society. The minimum program, on the other hand, contained the Party's immediate demands,*

1. Cf. p. 209, below.
2. Cf. *Karl Marx: The Essential Writings,* pp. 264–272.

such as the destruction of the czarist autocracy and its replacement by
a democratic republic (i.e., a bourgeois revolution), the complete
elimination of serfdom, steps to speed industrialization, and the intro-
duction of the eight-hour working day.

Lenin's Two Tactics *was written in June–July 1905, following the*
Third Congress of the Bolshevik faction of the RSDLP, held in Lon-
don at the same time the Mensheviks were holding their Third Congress
in Geneva, which was called the Third Conference. Hence the distinc-
tion in the text between the "Congress," which Lenin praises and de-
fends, and the "Conference," which he bitterly attacks. Insofar as Lenin
draws this distinction, Two Tactics *is, in essence, a statement of the*
differences between the Bolsheviks and the Mensehviks, who are con-
trasted from the Bolshevik point of view. The reader should also note
that the "Legal Marxists," led by Peter Struve, were at that time pub-
lishing a journal called Osvobozhdeniye *(Emancipation), which advo-*
cated a reformist position. This journal, not unexpectedly, is also an ob-
ject of Lenin's scorn, to which he often compares the Mensheviks'
program and positions. In all, what Lenin was doing was sharpening
the intraparty disputes so as to mold the Bolsheviks into a disciplined
monolithic organization, free of all factional division and, thereby,
the strongest faction within the RSDLP.

The resolution [of the Third Congress] clearly defines the
nature and the purpose of a provisional revolutionary government. In origin and basic character such a government must be
the organ of a popular uprising. Its formal purpose must be to
serve as an instrument for convening a national constituent
assembly. The content of its activities must be the implementation of the minimum program of proletarian democracy, the only
program capable of safeguarding the interests of a people that
has risen in revolt against the autocracy. . . .

We note that the resolution, by making implementation of the
minimum program the provisional revolutionary government's
task, eliminates the absurd and semianarchist ideas of giving
immediate effect to the maximum program, and the conquest of
power for a socialist revolution. The degree of Russia's economic
development (an objective condition), and the degree of class
consciousness and organization of the broad masses of the proletariat (a subjective condition inseparably bound up with the

objective condition) make the immediate and complete emancipation of the working class impossible. Only the most ignorant people can close their eyes to the bourgeois nature of the democratic revolution which is now taking place; only the most naïve optimists can forget how little as yet the masses of the workers are informed about the aims of socialism and the methods of achieving it. We are all convinced that the emancipation of the working classes must be won by the working classes themselves; a socialist revolution is out of the question unless the masses become class-conscious and organized, trained, and educated in an open class struggle against the entire bourgeoisie. Replying to the anarchists' objections that we are putting off the socialist revolution, we say: we are not putting it off, but are taking the first step toward it in the only possible way, along the only correct path, namely, the path of a democratic republic. Whoever wants to reach socialism by any other path than that of political democracy will inevitably arrive at conclusions that are absurd and reactionary in both the economic and the political sense. If any workers ask us at the appropriate moment why we should not go ahead and carry out our maximum program we shall answer by pointing out how far from socialism the masses of the democratically-minded people still are, how undeveloped class antagonisms still are, and how unorganized the proletarians still are. Organize hundreds of thousands of workers all over Russia; get the millions to sympathize with our program! Try to do this without confining yourselves to high sounding but hollow anarchist phrases—and you will see at once that achievement of this organization and the spread of this socialist enlightenment depend on the fullest possible achievement of democratic transformations.

Once the significance of a provisional revolutionary government and the attitude of the proletariat toward it have been made clear, the following question arises: Is it permissible for us to participate in such a government (action from above) and, if so, under what conditions? What should be our action from below? The resolution . . . emphatically declares that it is *permissible* in principle for Social Democrats to participate in a provisional revolutionary government (during the period of a democratic revolution, the period of struggle for a republic) . By this we once and for all dissociate ourselves both from the anarchists . . . who answer this question in the negative in principle, and from the tail-enders in Social Democracy (like Martynov and the new *Iskra* supporters), who have *tried to frighten* us with the prospect of a situation in which it might prove necessary for us to participate in such a government. The resolution points to the two purposes for which we participate: (1) a relentless struggle against counterrevolutionary attempts, and (2) the defense of the independent interests of the working class. . . . It is particularly appropriate for the party of the proletariat to call attention to the task of waging a real war against counterrevolution. In the final analysis force alone settles the great problems of political liberty and the class struggle, and it is our business to prepare and organize this force and to employ it actively, not only for defense but also for attack. The long reign of political reaction in Europe, which has lasted almost uninterruptedly since the days of the Paris Commune, has made us too greatly accustomed to the idea that action can proceed only "from below," has too greatly inured us to seeing only defensive struggles. We have now undoubtedly entered a new era—a period of political upheavals and revolutions has begun. . . . We must propagate the idea of action from above. . . . We must in any case exercise pressure on the provisional revolutionary government from below. To be able to exercise this pressure from below, the proletariat must be armed—for in a revolutionary situation matters develop with exceptional rapidity to the stage of open civil war—and must be led by the Social Democratic party. The object of its armed pressure is "to defend, consolidate, and extend the gains of the revolution." . . .

The resolution of the "Conference" is devoted to the question: *"The conquest of power and participation in a provisional government."* As we have already pointed out, there is confusion in the very manner in which the question is presented. On the one hand, the question is presented in a narrow way: it deals only with our participation in a provisional government and not with the Party's tasks in regard to a provisional revolutionary government in general. On the other hand, two totally different questions are confused, viz., the question of our participation in one of the stages of the *democratic* revolution and the question of the *socialist* revolution. Indeed, the "conquest of power" by Social Democracy is precisely a socialist revolution, nor can it be anything else if we use these words in their direct and usual meaning. If, however, we are to understand these words to mean the conquest of power for a democratic revolution and not for a socialist revolution, then what is the point in talking not only about participation in a provisional revolutionary government but also about the "conquest of power" *in general?* Obviously our "conferees" were themselves not very certain as to what they should talk about—the democratic or the socialist revolution. . . .

But enough about the title of the resolution. Its contents reveal errors incomparably more serious and profound. Here is the first part:

"A decisive victory of the revolution over czarism may be marked either by the establishment of a provisional government, which will emerge from a victorious popular insurrection, or by the revolutionary initiative of a representative institution of one kind or another, which, under direct revolutionary pressure from the people, decides to set up a popular constituent assembly."

Thus, we are told that a decisive victory of the revolution over czarism may be marked either by a victorious insurrecton, or . . . by a representative institution's decision to set up a constituent assembly! What does that mean? How are we to understand it? A decisive victory may be marked by a "decision" to set up a constituent assembly?? And such a "victory" is put side by side with the establishment of a provisional government which will "emerge from a victorious popular insurrection"!! The Conference failed to note that a *victorious* popular insurrection and the *establishment* of a provisional government would signify the victory of the revolution *in actual fact,* whereas a "decision" to set up a constituent assembly would signify a victory of the revolution *in words* only.

The Conference of the new-*Iskra* Mensheviks fell into the very error that the liberals, the *Osvobozhdeniye* group, are constantly making. The *Osvobozhdeniye* group prattle about a "constituent" assembly, bashfully shutting their eyes to the fact that power and authority remain in the hands of the czar and forgetting that to "constitute" one must possess the *power* to do so. The Conference also forgot that it is a far cry from a "decision" adopted by representatives—no matter who they are—to the fulfillment of that decision. The Conference also forgot that while power remains in the hands of the czar all decisions of any representatives whatsoever will remain empty and miserable prattle, as was the case with the "decisions" of the Frankfurt Parliament, famous in the history of the German Revolution of 1848. In his *Neue Rheinische Zeitung* Marx, the representative of the revolutionary proletariat, castigated the Frankfurt *Osvobozhdeniye*-type liberals with merciless sarcasm, precisely because they uttered fine words, adopted all sorts of democratic "decisions," "constituted" all kinds of liberties, while in fact they left power in the hands of the king and failed to organize an armed struggle against the military forces at the king's disposal. And while the Frankfurt-*Osvobozhdeniye* liberals were prattling, the king bided his time and consolidated his military forces, and the counterrevolution relying on real force utterly routed the democrats, with all their fine "decisions."

The Conference put on a par with a decisive victory the very thing that lacks the essential condition for victory. How was it possible for Social Democrats, who recognize the republican program of our Party, to commit such an error? . . . Our "conferees" talk of the revolution in exactly the same way as the Economists [i.e. economic determinists] talked of the political struggle or the eight-hour day. The Economists immediately brought forward the "theory of stages": (1) the struggle for rights, (2) political agitation, (3) political struggle; or, (1) a ten-hour day, (2) a nine-hour day, (3) an eight-hour day. The results of this "tactics-as-process" are sufficiently well known to all. Now we are invited to make a preliminary and neat division of the revolution as well into the following stages: (1) the czar convenes a representative institution; (2) this institution "decides" under pressure of the "people" to set up a constituent assembly; (3) . . . the Mensheviks have not yet agreed among themselves as to the third stage; they have forgotten that the revolutionary pressure of the people will meet with the counterrevolutionary pressure of czarism and that therefore either the "decision" will remain unfulfilled or the issue will be decided after all by the victory or the defeat of a popular insurrection. . . .

The objection may be made to us that the authors of the resolution did not mean *to place on a par* the victory of an insurrection and the "decision" of a representative institution convened by the czar, and that they only wanted to provide for the Party's tactics in either case. To this we shall answer: the text of the resolution plainly and unambiguously describes the *decision* of a representative institution as "a decisive victory of the revolution over czarism." Perhaps that is the result of careless wording; perhaps it could be corrected after consulting the minutes, but, until corrected, the present wording can have only one meaning, and that meaning is entirely in keeping with the *Osvobozhdeniye* line of reasoning. . . . The point is that it is impermissible for a Social Democrat to cause confusion in workers' minds as to which is the genuinely revolutionary path; that it is impermissible to describe as a decisive victory, as *Osvobozhdeniye* does, something which lacks the *main* condition for victory. . . .

Of course, the new-Iskrists have not as yet gone so far. . . . But the degree to which the revolutionary spirit has abandoned them, the degree to which lifeless pedantry has blinded them to the militant tasks of the moment, is most vividly shown by the fact that in their resolution they, of all things, *forgot* to say a word about the republic. This is incredible but it is a fact. All the slogans of Social Democracy were endorsed, repeated, explained, and presented in detail in the various resolutions of the Conference—even the election of shop-stewards and deputies by the workers was not forgotten, but they simply found no occasion to mention the republic in a resolution on a provisional revolutionary government. To talk of the "victory" of the people's insurrection, of the establishment of a provisional government without indicating what these "steps" and acts have to do with winning a republic amounts to writing a resolution with the intention of crawling along in the wake of the proletarian movement, and not of giving guidance to the proletariat's struggle.

To sum up: the first part of the resolution (1) gave no explanation whatever of the significance of a provisional revolutionary government from the standpoint of the struggle for a republic and of securing a genuinely popular and genuinely constituent assembly; (2) quite confused the democratic consciousness of the proletariat by placing on a par with revolution's decisive victory over czarism a state of affairs in which precisely the main condition for a real victory is lacking.

Let us go over to the next section of the [Conference] resolution: ". . . in either case such a victory will inaugurate a new phase in the revolutionary epoch.

"The final abolition of the entire regime of the monarchy and social estates in the process of mutual struggle between the elements of politically emancipated bourgeois society for the satisfaction of their social interests and for the direct acquisition of power—such is the task in this new phase which the objective conditions of social development spontaneously evoke.

"Therefore, a provisional government that would undertake to carry out the tasks of this revolution, bourgeois in its historical nature, would, in regulating the mutual struggle between antagonistic classes of a nation in the process of emancipation, not only have to advance revolutionary development, but also to combat factors in that development threatening the foundations of the capitalist system."

Let us examine this section which forms an independent part of the resolution. The basic idea in the arguments quoted above coincides with the one set forth in the third clause of the Congress resolution. However, collation of these parts of the two resolutions will at once reveal the following radical difference between them. The Congress resolution, which briefly describes the social and economic basis of the revolution, concentrates attention entirely on the clear-cut struggle of classes for definite gains, and places in the forefront the militant tasks of the proletariat. The resolution of the Conference, which carries a long, nebulous, and confused description of the socioeconomic basis of the revolution, speaks very vaguely about a struggle for definite gains, and leaves the militant tasks of the proletariat completely in the background. The resolution of the Conference speaks of the old order in the process of mutual struggle among the various elements of society. The Congress resolution says that we, the party of the proletariat, must effect this abolition; that only

establishment of a democratic republic signifies genuine abolition of the old order; that we must win that republic, that we
shall fight for it and for complete liberty, not only against the
autocracy, but also against the bourgeoisie, when it attempts
(and it will surely do so) to wrest our gains from us. The Congress resolution calls on a definite class to wage a struggle for a
precisely defined immediate aim. The Conference resolution
discourses on the mutual struggle of various forces. One resolution expresses the psychology of active struggle, the other that of
the passive onlooker; one resounds with the call for live action,
the other is steeped in lifeless pedantry. Both resolutions state
that the present revolution is only our first step, which will be
followed by a second; but from this, one resolution draws the
conclusion that we must take this first step all the sooner, get it
over all the sooner, win a republic, mercilessly crush the counterrevolution, and prepare the ground for the second step. The
other resolution, however, oozes, so to speak, with verbose descriptions of the first step and (excuse the crude expression)
simply masticates it. . . .

This is the very distinction which has long divided the Russian
Marxists into two wings. . . . From the correct Marxist premise
concerning the deep economic roots of the class struggle in
general and of the political struggle in particular, the Economists
have drawn the singular conclusion that we must turn our backs
on the political struggle and retard its development, narrow its
scope, and reduce its aims. The political wing, on the contrary,
has drawn a different conclusion from these same premises,
namely, that the deeper the roots of our present struggle, the
more widely, the more boldly, the more resolutely, and with
greater initiative must we wage this struggle. . . . From the
premises that a democratic revolution is far from being a socialist
revolution . . . the advanced class must formulate its democratic aims all the more boldly, express them all the more sharply
and completely, put forward the immediate slogan of a republic,
and popularize the idea of the need to establish a provisional
revolutionary government and to crush the counterrevolution
ruthlessly. . . . Good marchers but poor leaders, they disparage
the materialist conception of history by ignoring the active,
leading, and guiding part which can and must be played in

history by parties that have realized the material prerequisites of a revolution and have placed themselves at the head of the progressive classes. . . .

Our reply to our opponents is—a Social Democratic party which operates in a bourgeois society cannot take part in politics without marching, in certain cases, *side by side* with bourgeois democracy. . . .

We intend to guide (if the Great Russian revolution makes progress) not only the proletariat, organized by the Social Democratic party, but also the petit bourgeoisie, which is capable of marching side by side with us. . . .

Such elements are mostly to be found among the peasants. In classifying the big social groups according to their political tendencies we can, without danger of serious error, identify revolutionary and republican democracy with the mass of the peasants. . . . Through its countrywide political slogans, the Party Congress *raises the mass of the peasants to a revolutionary level.* . . .

Marxists are absolutely convinced of the bourgeois character of the Russian revolution. What does that mean? It means that the democratic reforms in the political system, and the social and economic reforms that have become a necessity for Russia, do not in themselves imply the undermining of capitalism, the undermining of bourgeois rule; on the contrary, they will, for the first time, really clear the ground for a wide and rapid, European, and not Asiatic, development of capitalism; they will, for the first time, make it possible for the bourgeoisie to rule as a class. . . .

But it does not by any means follow that a *democratic* revolution (bourgeois in its social and economic essence) would not be of *enormous* interest to the proletariat. It does not follow that the democratic revolution could not take place both in a form advantageous mainly to the big capitalist, the financial magnate, and the "enlightened" landlord, and in a form advantageous to the peasant and the worker. . . .

It is quite absurd to think that a bourgeois revolution does not at all express proletarian interests. This absurd idea boils down either to the hoary Narodnik theory that a bourgeois revolution runs counter to the interests of the proletariat, and that, therefore, we do not need bourgeois political liberty; or to anarchism which denies any participation of the proletariat in bourgeois politics, in a bourgeois revolution and in bourgeois parliamentarism. From the standpoint of theory this idea disregards the elementary propositions of Marxism concerning the inevitability of capitalist development on the basis of commodity production. Marxism teaches us that at a certain stage of its development a society which is based on commodity production and has commercial intercourse with civilized capitalist nations must inevitably take the road of capitalism. Marxism has irrevocably broken with the Narodnik and anarchist gibberish that Russia, for instance, can by-pass capitalist development, escape from capitalism, or skip it in some way other than that of the class struggle, on the basis and within the framework of this same capitalism. . . .

And from these principles it follows that the idea of seeking salvation for the working class in anything save the further development of capitalism is *reactionary*. In countries like Russia the working class suffers not so much from capitalism as from the insufficient development of capitalism. The working class is, therefore, *most certainly interested* in the broadest, freest, and most rapid development of capitalism. The removal of all the remnants of the old order which hamper the broad, free, and rapid development of capitalism is of absolute *advantage* to the working class. . . .

On the other hand, it is more advantageous to the working class for the necessary changes in the direction of bourgeois democracy to take place by way of revolution and not by way of reform, because the way of reform is one of delay, procrastination, the painfully slow decomposition of the putrid parts of the national organism. It is the proletariat and the peasantry that suffer first of all and most of all from that putrefaction. The revolutionary path is one of rapid amputation, which is the least painful to the proletariat, the path of the immediate removal of what is putrescent. . . .

The more consistent the bourgeois revolution, the more does it guarantee the proletariat and the peasantry the benefits accruing from the democratic revolution. . . . We cannot get out of the bourgeois-democratic boundaries of the Russian revolution, but we can vastly extend these boundaries, and within these boundaries we can and must fight for the interests of the proletariat, for its immediate needs and for conditions that will make it possible to prepare its forces for the future complete victory. . . .

We must be perfectly certain in our minds as to what real social forces are opposed to "czarism" . . . and are capable of gaining a "decisive victory" over it. The big bourgeoisie, the landlords, the factory owners, and "society" . . . do not even want a decisive victory . . . owing to their class position they are incapable of waging a decisive struggle against czarism; they are too heavily fettered by private property, by capital and land to enter into a decisive struggle. They stand in too great need of czarism, with its bureaucratic, police, and military forces for use against the proletariat and the peasantry, to want it to be destroyed. No, the only force capable of gaining "a decisive victory over czarism," is the *people,* i.e., the proletariat and the peasantry. . . . "The revolution's decisive victory over czarism" means the establishment of the *revolutionary-democratic dictatorship of the proletariat and the peasantry.* . . . No other force is capable of gaining a decisive victory over czarism.

And such a victory will be precisely a dictatorship, i.e., it must inevitably rely on military force, on the arming of the masses, on an insurrection, and not on institutions of one kind or another established in a "lawful" or "peaceful" way. It can be only a dictatorship, for realization of the changes urgently and absolutely indispensable to the proletariat and the peasantry will evoke desperate resistance from the landlords, the big bourgeoisie, and czarism. Without a dictatorship it is impossible to break down that resistance and repel counterrevolutionary attempts. But of course it will be a democratic, not a socialist dictatorship. It will be unable (without a series of intermediary stages of revolutionary development) to affect the foundations of capitalism. At best, it may bring about a radical redistribution of landed property in favor of the peasantry, establish consistent and full democracy, including the formation of a republic, eradicate all the oppressive features of Asiatic bondage, not only in rural but also in factory life, lay the foundation for a thorough improvement in the conditions of the workers and for a rise in their standard of living, and—last but not least—carry the revolutionary conflagration into Europe. Such a victory will not yet by any means transform our bourgeois revolution into a socialist revolution; the democratic revolution will not immediately overstep the bounds of bourgeois social and economic relationships; nevertheless, the significance of such a victory for the future development of Russia and of the whole world will be immense. Nothing will raise the revolutionary energy of the world proletariat so much, nothing will shorten the path leading to its complete victory to such an extent, as this decisive victory of the revolution that has now started in Russia. . . .

In a word, to avoid finding itself with its hands tied in the struggle against the inconsistent bourgeois democracy the proletariat must be class-conscious and strong enough to rouse the peasantry to revolutionary consciousness, guide its assault, and thereby independently pursue the line of consistent proletarian democratism. . . .

Only the proletariat can be a consistent fighter for democracy. It can become a victorious fighter for democracy only if the peasant masses join its revolutionary struggle. If the proletariat is not strong enough for this the bourgeoisie will be at the head of the democratic revolution and will impart an inconsistent and self-seeking nature to it. Nothing but a revolutionary-democratic dictatorship of the proletariat and the peasantry can prevent this.

We have shown that new-Iskrist tactics do not push the revolution forward—the possibility of which they would like to ensure by their resolution—but pull it back. We have shown that it is precisely these tactics that *tie the hands* of Social Democracy in the struggle against the inconsistent bourgeoisie and does not prevent its being dissolved in bourgeois democracy. The false premises of the resolution naturally lead to the following false conclusion: "Therefore, Social Democracy must not set itself the aim of seizing or sharing power in the provisional government, but must remain the party of extreme revolutionary opposition." . . .

How nicely this hangs together, does it not? We set ourselves the *aim* of subordinating the insurrection of both the proletarian and *nonproletarian* masses to our influence and our leadership, and of using it in our interests. Hence, we set ourselves the aim of leading, in the insurrection, both the proletariat and the revolutionary bourgeoisie and petit bourgeoisie ("the nonprole-tarian groups"), i.e., of *"sharing"* the leadership of the insurrec-tion between the Social Democracy and the revolutionary bourgeoisie. We set ourselves the aim of securing *victory* for the insurrection, which is to lead to the establishment of a provi-sional government . . . therefore we must not set ourselves the aim of seizing power or of sharing it in a provisional revolution-ary government! . . .

The new-Iskra group confuses a deal with czarism and a vic-tory over the latter. They want to take part in a bourgeois revolution. . . . They even consent to lead an insurrection of the people—in order to renounce that leadership immediately after victory is won (or, perhaps, immediately before the victory?), i.e., *in order not to avail themselves of the fruits of victory,* but to turn all these fruits over *entirely to the bourgeoisie.* . . .

The desire to *"remain"* with the old methods, i.e., action only "from below," is voiced with pomp and clamor *precisely at a time* when the revolution has confronted us with the necessity, in the event of a victorious insurrection, of acting *from above.* . . .

Are you not beginning to understand, gentlemen, that the term "extreme opposition" expresses only negative actions—exposing, voting against, refusing? Why is that so? Because this term applies only to the parliamentary struggle and, moreover, in a period when no one makes "decisive victory" the immediate object of the struggle. . . .

One of the objections raised to the slogan of "the revolutionary-democratic dictatorship of the proletariat and the peasantry" is that dictatorship presupposes a "single will" (*Iskra,* No. 95), and that there can be no single will of the proletariat and the petit bourgeoisie. . . . There may be a single will in one respect and not in another. The absence of unity on questions of socialism and in the struggle for socialism does not preclude singleness of will on questions of democracy and in the struggle for a repub-lic. . . . To forget this would be tantamount to forgetting the character of the democratic revolution as one *of the whole people:* if it is "of the whole people," that means that there *is* "singleness of will" precisely insofar as this revolution meets the needs and requirements of the whole people. Beyond the bounds of democratism there can be no question of the proletariat and the peasant bourgeoisie having a single will. Class struggle between them is inevitable, but it is in a democratic republic that this struggle will be the most thoroughgoing and widespread struggle of the people *for socialism*. . . .

Its future is the struggle against private property, the struggle of the wage worker against the employer, the struggle for socialism. Here singleness of will is impossible. Here the path before us lies not from autocracy to a republic, but from a petit-bourgeois democratic republic to socialism. . . .

A Social Democrat must never for a moment forget that the proletariat will inevitably have to wage a class struggle for socialism even against the most democratic and republican bourgeoisie and petit bourgeoisie. This is beyond doubt. Hence, the absolute necessity of a separate, independent, strictly class party of Social Democracy. Hence, the temporary nature of our tactics of "striking a joint blow" with the bourgeoisie and the duty of keeping a strict watch "over our ally, as over an enemy." . . . The revolutionary-democratic dictatorship of the proletariat and the peasantry is unquestionably only a transient, temporary socialist aim, but to ignore this aim in the period of a democratic revolution would be downright reactionary. . . .

The bourgeoisie is inconsistent, self-seeking, and cowardly in its support of the revolution. The bourgeoisie, in the mass, will inevitably turn toward counterrevolution, toward the autocracy, against the revolution, and against the people, as soon as its narrow, selfish interests are met, as soon as it "recoils" from consistent democracy (*and it is already recoiling from it!*). There remains the "people," that is, the proletariat and the peasantry: the proletariat alone can be relied on to march on to the end, for it goes far beyond the democratic revolution. That is why the proletariat fights in the forefront for a republic. . . . The peasantry includes a great number of semiproletarian as well as petit-bourgeois elements. This makes it also unstable, compelling the proletariat to rally in a strictly class party. However, the instability of the peasantry differs radically from that of the bourgeoisie, for at present the peasantry is interested not so much in the absolute preservation of private property as in the confiscation of the landed estates, one of the principal forms of private property. Without thereby becoming socialist, or ceasing to be petit-bourgeois, the peasantry is capable of becoming a wholehearted and most radical adherent of the democratic revolution. . . .

The peasantry stands in need of democracy, for only a democratic system is capable of accurately expressing its interests and ensuring its predominance as a mass, as the majority. . . . A democratic republic will become the peasantry's ideal as soon as it begins to throw off its naïve monarchism. . . .

The proletariat must carry the democratic revolution to completion, allying to itself the mass of the peasantry in order to crush the autocracy's resistance by force and paralyze the bourgeoisie's instability. The proletariat must accomplish the socialist revolution, allying to itself the mass of the semiproletarian elements of the population, so as to crush the bourgeoisie's resistance by force and paralyze the instability of the peasantry and the petit bourgeoisie. . . .

14.
LENIN ON THE THEORY
OF KNOWLEDGE

The locus classicus *of Lenin's epistemology is his* Materialism and Empiriocriticism, *written in 1906 in response to various philosophical trends emerging within Russian Social Democracy. Foremost among these was "empiriocriticism," influenced by the Swiss philosopher Richard Avenarius (1843–1896) and the Austrian physicist Ernst Mach (1838–1916), which attempted to recognize (Lenin would say introduce) the importance of subjective factors in explaining the perception of the objects of the external world. Empiriocriticism is somewhat akin to the Kantianism, and as such represented to Lenin the same threat to Russian Social Democracy as did the neo-Kantianism of Bernstein to Social Democracy in Western Europe. Thus, from Lenin's perspective, empiriocriticism had to be fought not in the name of the "truth" of its theory of knowledge, in which Lenin was hardly interested, but rather in the name of his conception of the Party as the unified and disciplined revolutionary vanguard of the proletariat.*

A. A. Bogdanov (1873–1928) had been, since his joining the Bolsheviks in 1903, one of Lenin's ablest followers and a recognized leader of the faction. His philosophical ideas and his "ultraleftist" political views in the wake of the events of 1905, however, aroused Lenin's wrath and were mercilessly excoriated. The main issue between Lenin and Bogdanov is that of the social relativism (Bogdanov) or the dialectical relativity (Lenin) of truth. In this conflict Lenin is willing to grant the relativity of scientific truth at any given time, but not to abandon the notion that science tends toward an absolute truth, i.e., that it transcends its bourgeois sociopolitical roots and can become a weapon of the soon to be victorious proletariat. From the viewpoint of positivism, in contrast, Lenin is quite mistaken, for it is not even the intention of science to seek such absolute truth, but only to expand knowledge indefinitely by means of the hypothetical-deductive method. Thus, it is meaningless to speak of truth as the ultimate goal of science. But this positivistic reply is not a part of Bogdanov's position and therefore cannot be imputed to him, for from his viewpoint, the chief thing is that cognition is a form of "social adaptation," and since the latter is continually changing (i.e., is historical), so too will be the former; thus all "truths" are to be taken as historically (and socially) relative. The consequences of Bogdanov's position, clearly perceived by Lenin, are the undermining of the claim that dialectical materialism is a "true" ontology, and thus that its "application" to the "laws" of social evolution can provide demonstrable grounds for revolutionary practice. To say that these are "proletarian truths" would be to rob Marxism of its dogmatic content and thus of much of its propaganda value, especially among the uneducated and unsophisticated masses. Thus, empiriocriticism in Marxism becomes, for Lenin, a trend which must be combated as a philosophy incapable of distinguishing Marxist truth from religious nonsense (which Lenin habitually calls "fideism") and for aiding the bourgeoisie by robbing Marxism of its major philosophical weapons. Despite all of Lenin's protestations about "the way things are," the real question for him here (as everywhere in philosophy) is power: *the proletariat (or at least its vanguard party)* needs *a simplified philosophical credo (for that is precisely what dialectical materialism is) from which to "derive" its apparently "scientific" predictions for political practice.*

As far as Lenin's own philosophical assumptions are concerned, it is obvious that he departs radically from Marx's antiphilosophy.[1] Perhaps most interesting is Lenin's tenacious adherence to the thoroughly undialectical "copy" theory of perception, in the name of a "materialism" which differs not at all from the mechanistic French materialism of the eighteenth century which Marx had bitterly criticized.[2] All this, for both Engels and Lenin, is held in the name of "dialectics," but their so-called dialectical epistemology is nothing but a crude form of causal determinism wherein the sensation is allegedly an "image" or "copy" of the material thing which is induced in the brain via *causal action upon our sense organs and further causal action within the nervous system. This is an utterly naïve "realism" which, incidentally, is embraced by Lenin by that name. The reader is referred to Marx's famous "Theses on Feuerbach," in which he is warned of the pitfalls which a dialectical epistemology (i.e., Marx's "modern materialism") should avoid, foremost among these being the undialectical assumption of the passivity of the perceiver.[3] A truly dialectical epistemology could be expected to develop equally the role of the active social subject in perception, which can be equated with neither the giving of form to pure sensation (as in Kant, Avenarius, and Bogdanov) nor with industrial production as in Engels's famous*

1. Cf. pp. 14–29, above.
2. Cf. pp. 19–29, above.
3. Cf. pp. 25–27, above.

"alizarin argument."[4] *The active role—for Marx—is played by* revolutionary *practice, in which a class (currently the proletariat) creates its truth*[5] *by its victories in the class struggle. "Knowledge" which is irrelevant to that class's revolutionary struggle (e.g., classical political economy or speculative metaphysics) is unacceptably "ideological" to Marx, and thus not "knowledge" at all, for it fails to contribute to the transition of humanity from the realm of necessity to that of freedom. This transition, not the production of "images" in the brain (Lenin) or the reproduction of natural products by industry (Engels) is what Marx means by the criterion of practice. That Engels and Lenin failed to grasp this is hardly a surprise, given their failure to distinguish the Hegelian (and Marxian) concept of man as self-creative from man naturalistically conceived as the "product" of the motion of matter.*[6]

The selection begins with short excerpts from Bogdanov's Empiriomonism *(1905), which was the main target of Lenin in* Materialism and Empiriocriticism, *excerpts from which then follow.*

BOGDANOV: MARXISM AND RELATIVISM

Cognition is not merely adaptation in general; it is also *social* adaptation. The social genesis of cognition, its dependence on social experience, the principled difference of value in the thinking of different people, and its constant social interaction, clearly emerge. . . .

We arrive at this conclusion: the characteristics of "objectivity" in general cannot have as their basis individual experience. . . . The basis of "objectivity" must lie in the sphere of *collective* experience. . . .

The agreement in collective experience which is expressed in this "objectivity" can only appear as the result of the progressive concordance of the experience of different people as they express themselves to each other. The objectivity of the physical bodies which we encounter in our experience is established in the last analysis on the basis of mutual verification and the concordance

SOURCE: From A. A. Bogdanov, *Empiriomonism* (St. Petersburg: Dorovatovsky and Charushnikov), Book I, 2d ed., 1905, and Book III, 1906. Trans. by Robert V. Daniels in *A Documentary History of Communism*, Vol. I (New York: Random House, 1960). Reprinted by permission.

4. Cf. pp. 73–74, above.
5. As for Bogdanov.
6. Cf. pp. 95–96, above.

in what different people express. In general the physical world is this: socially agreed upon, socially harmonized, in a word, *socially organized* experience. . . .

Laws do not belong at all to the sphere of immediate experience; laws are the result of conscious reworking of experience; they are not facts in themselves, but are created by thought, as a means of organizing experience, of harmoniously bringing it into agreement as an ordered unity. Laws are *abstract cognition*, and physical laws possess physical qualities just as little as psychological laws possess psychic qualities. . . . The antithesis between the physical and psychic aspects of experience reduces to the distinction between socially organized and individually organized experience. . . .

. . . The social materialism of Marx presented demands to my world view which the old materialism could not satisfy. . . . It was necessary *to know one's knowledge,* to explain one's world view, and according to the idea of Marxism this could and had to be done on the basis of research on its social genesis. It was obvious that the basic concepts of the old materialism—both "matter" and "immutable laws"—were worked out in the course of the *social* development of mankind, and inasmuch as they were "ideological forms," it was necessary to find their "material base." But since the "material base" has the property of changing as society develops, it becomes clear that any given ideological form can have only a historically transitory meaning, not an objectively suprahistorical meaning, that it can be a "truth of the time" (*"objective"* truth, but only within the limits of a given epoch) —but in no case can it be a "truth for all time" ("objective" in the absolute meaning of the word) . . . . For me Marxism includes the denial of the unconditional objectivity of any truth whatsoever, the denial of every eternal truth. . . .

Truth is an ideological form—the organizing form of human experience; and if we know this without doubt, and know that the material basis of ideology changes, that the content of experience expands—do we have any right whatsoever to assert that this given ideological form will never be transformed by the development of its social basis, that this given form of experience will not be burst apart by its growing contents? Consistent Marxism does not allow such dogmatic and static notions. . . .

Marxist philosophy must above all be one of natural science. Of course, natural science is the *ideology of the productive forces of society,* because it serves as the basis for technical experience and the technical sciences; in concordance with the basic idea of historical materialism, the productive forces of society represent the base of its development in general. But it is also clear that Marxist philosophy must reflect the *social form* of the productive forces, relying obviously on the "social" sciences proper. . . .

Ideological forms are the *organizational adaptation of social life,* and in the last analysis (directly or indirectly), of the *technical process.* Therefore the development of ideology is determined by *necessities* in the organizational adaptations of the social process and by the *material present* for them. The viability of ideological forms depends, consequently, on the harmony and order with which they really organize the social content of labor. . . .

The world of experience has been crystalized and continues to be crystallized out of chaos. The force which determines the forms of this crystallization is the intercourse of people. Outside of these forms there is really no *experience,* because a disorganized mass of occurrences is not experience. Thus, experience is social in its very basis, and its progress is the *social-psychological process of organizing it.* The individual psychical organizing process is completely adapted to this. . . .

Summarizing the connection and dependence between "ideology" and "technology" in the process of social development, we arrive at the following formulations:

1. The technical process is the area of the direct struggle of society with nature; ideology is the area of the organizing forms of social life. In the last analysis the technical process represents just that content which is organized by the ideological forms.

2. Corresponding to this relationship, the technical process represents the basic and ideology the derivative area of social life and social development. . . .

In a class society any world view is either the ideology of one definite class or a definite combination of different class ideologies. Even the most individual of them can only be a particular combination of elements of collective, class thinking. For the individual is created and defined by the social milieu—in a class society, by the class milieu. . . .

LENIN: THE BASIC PRINCIPLES OF EPISTEMOLOGY

[There are] two fundamental lines of philosophical outlook. . . . Materialism is the recognition of "objects in themselves," or outside the mind; ideas and sensations are copies or images of those objects. The opposite doctrine (idealism) claims that objects do not exist "without the mind"; objects are "combinations of sensations." . . .

For every scientist who has not been led astray by professorial philosophy, as well as for every materialist, sensation is indeed the direct connection between consciousness and the external world; it is the transformation of the energy of external excitation into the fact of consciousness. This transformation has been, and is, observed by each of us a million times on every hand. The sophism of idealist philosophy consists in the fact that it regards sensation as being not the connection between consciousness and the external world, but a fence, a wall, separating consciousness from the external world—not an image of the external phenomenon corresponding to the sensation, but as the "sole entity." . . . Outside us, independently of us and of our minds, there exists a movement of matter, let us say of ether waves of a definite length and of a definite velocity, which, acting upon the retina, produce in man the sensation of a particular color. This is precisely how natural science regards it. It explains the sensations of various colors by the various lengths of light waves existing outside the human retina, outside man and independently of him. This is materialism: matter acting upon our sense organs produces sensation. Sensation depends on the brain, nerves, retina, etc., i.e., on matter organized in a definite way. The existence of matter does not depend on sensation. Matter is primary. Sensation, thought, consciousness are the supreme product of matter organized in a particular way. Such are the views of materialism in general, and of Marx and Engels in particular. . . .

SOURCE: From V. I. Lenin, *Materialism and Empiriocriticism* (1908), in *Collected Works*, Vol. XIV (Moscow: Progress Publishers, 1968).

The "naïve realism" of any healthy person who has not been an inmate of a lunatic asylum or a pupil of the idealist philosophers consists in the view that things, the environment, the world, exist *independently* of our sensation, of our consciousness, of our *self* and of man in general. . . . The firm conviction that *independently* of us there exist other people, and not mere complexes of my sensations of high, short, yellow, hard, etc. . . . produces in us the conviction that things, the world, the environment exist independently of us. Our sensation, our consciousness is only *an image* of the external world, and it is obvious that an image cannot exist without the thing imaged, and that the latter exists independently of that which images it. Materialism *deliberately* makes the "naïve" belief of mankind the foundation of its theory of knowledge. . . .

Thus, the materialist theory, the theory of the reflection of objects by our mind, is here presented with absolute clarity: things exist outside us. Our perceptions and ideas are their images. Verification of these images, differentiation between true and false images, is given by practice. . . .

For the materialist the "factually given" is the outer world, the image of which is our sensations. For the idealist the "factually given" is sensation, and the outer world is declared to be a "complex of sensations." For the agnostic the "immediately given" is also sensation, but the agnostic *does not go on* either to the materialist recognition of the reality of the outer world, or to the idealist recognition of the world as our sensation. . . .

But Engels says explicitly and clearly that what distinguishes him from the agnostic is not only the agnostic's doubt as to whether our images are "correct," but also the agnostic's doubt as to whether we may speak of the *things themselves,* as to whether we may have "certain" knowledge of their existence. . . . The *basic* question for materialism (and for Engels, as a materialist), [is] the question of the existence of things outside our mind, which by acting on our sense organs evoke sensations. . . .

There is definitely no difference in principle between the phenomenon and the thing-in-itself, and there cannot be any such difference. The only difference is between what is known and what is not yet known. And philosophical inventions of specific boundaries between the one and the other, inventions to the effect that the thing-in-itself is "beyond" phenomena (Kant), or that we can and must fence ourselves off by some philosophical partition from the problem of a world which in one part or another is still unknown but which exists outside us (Hume) — all this is the sheerest nonsense. . . .

In the theory of knowledge, as in every other sphere of science, we must think dialectically, that is, we must not regard our knowledge as ready-made and unalterable, but must determine how *knowledge* emerges from *ignorance,* how incomplete, inexact knowledge becomes more complete and more exact. . . .

Our Machist . . . arrives safely and soundly at pure Kantian idealism: it is man who dictates laws to nature and not nature that dictates laws to man! The important thing is not the repetition of Kant's doctrine of apriorism—which does not define the idealist line in philosophy as such, but only a particular formulation of this line—but the fact that reason, mind, consciousness are here primary, and nature secondary. It is not reason that is a part of nature, one of its highest products, the reflection of its processes, but nature that is a part of reason, which thereby is stretched from the ordinary, simple human reason known to us all to . . . mysterious, divine reason. The Kantian-Machist formula, that "man gives laws to nature," is a fideist formula. . . .

A philosophy which teaches that physical nature itself is a product is a philosophy of clericalism pure and simple. And its character is in no wise altered by the fact that Bogdanov himself emphatically repudiates all religion. . . . If nature is a product, it is obvious that it can be a product only of something that is greater, richer, broader, mightier than nature, of something that exists; for in order to "produce" nature, it must exist independently of nature. That means that something exists *outside* nature, something which moreover *produces* nature. In plain language this is called God. The idealist philosophers have always sought to change this latter name, to make it more abstract, more vague and at the same time (for the sake of plausibility) to bring it nearer to the "psychical," as an "immediate complex," as the immediately given which requires no proof. Absolute Idea, Universal Spirit, World Will, *"general substitu-*

tion" of the psychical for the physical, are different formulations of one and the same idea. Every man knows, and science investigates, idea, mind, will, the psychical, as a function of the normally operating human brain. To divorce this function from matter organized in a definite way, to convert this function into a universal, general abstraction, to "substitute" this abstraction for the whole of physical nature, this is the raving of philosophical idealism and a mockery of science. . . .

Engels says very clearly that Büchner and Co.* "by no means overcame the limitations of their teachers," i.e., the materialists of the eighteenth century, that they had not made a single *step forward.* And it is for this, and *this alone,* that Engels took Büchner and Co. to task; not for their materialism, as the ignoramuses think, but because they did not *advance* materialism, because *"they did not in the least make it their business to develop the theory* [of materialism] *any further."* It was for *this alone* that Engels took Büchner and Co. to task. And thereupon *point by point* Engels enumerates *three* fundamental "limitations" of the French materialists of the eighteenth century, from which Marx and Engels had emancipated themselves, but from which Büchner and Co. were unable to emancipate themselves. The first limitation was that the views of the old materialists were "mechanical," *in the sense* that they believed in "the exclusive application of the standards of mechanics to processes of a chemical and organic nature." . . . The secònd limitation was the metaphysical character of the views of the old materialists, meaning the *"antidialectical character of their philosophy."* . . . The third limitation was the preservation of idealism "up above," in the realm of the social sciences, a nonunderstanding of historical materialism. . . .

Exclusively for these three things and *exclusively* within these limits, does Engels refute both the materialism of the eighteenth century and the doctrines of Büchner and Co.! On all other, more elementary, questions of materialism (questions distorted by the Machists) *there is and can be no difference* between Marx and Engels on the one hand and all these old materialists on the other. . . .

* The reference is to Ludwig Büchner (1824–1899), a leading materialist and popularizer of science.

LENIN: THE "MARXIST" CONCEPTION OF TRUTH

For Bogdanov (as for all the Machists) recognition of the relativity of our knowledge *excludes* even the least admission of absolute truth. For Engels absolute truth is compounded from relative truths. Bogdanov is a relativist: Engels is a dialectician. . . .

Human thought then by its nature is capable of giving, and does give, absolute truth, which is compounded of a sum total of relative truths. Each step in the development of science adds new grains to the sum of absolute truth, but the limits of the truth of each scientific proposition are relative, now expanding, now shrinking with the growth of knowledge. . . .

For dialectical materialism there is no impassable boundary between relative and absolute truth. Bogdanov entirely failed to grasp this if he could write: "It [the world outlook of the old materialism] sets itself up as the absolute *objective knowledge of the essence of things* [Bogdanov's italics] and is incompatible with the historically conditional nature of all ideologies." From the standpoint of modern materialism, i.e., Marxism, the *limits* of approximation of our knowledge to objective, absolute truth are historically conditional, but the existence of such truth is *unconditional,* and the fact that we are approaching nearer to it is also unconditional. . . .

Relativism as a basis of the theory of knowledge is not only recognition of the relativity of our knowledge, but also a denial of any objective measure or model existing independently of mankind to which our relative knowledge approximates. . . .

Dialectics—as Hegel in his time explained—*contains* an element of relativism, of negation, of skepticism, but *is not reducible* to relativism. The materialist dialectics of Marx and Engels certainly does contain relativism, but is not reducible to relativism, that is, it recognizes the relativity of all our knowledge, not in the sense of denying objective truth, but in the sense that the limits of approximation of our knowledge to this truth are historically conditional.

SOURCE: From V. I. Lenin, *Materialism and Empiriocriticism* (1908) , in *Collected Works,* Vol. XIV (Moscow: Progress Publishers, 1968) .

Bogdanov writes in italics: *"Consistent Marxism does not admit such dogmatism and such static concepts"* as eternal truths. This is a muddle. If the world is eternally moving and developing matter (as the Marxists think), reflected by the developing human consciousness, what is there "static" here? The point at issue is not the immutable essence of things, or an immutable consciousness, but the *correspondence* between the consciousness which reflects nature and the nature which is reflected by consciousness. . . .

The development of consciousness in each human individual and the development of the collective knowledge of humanity as a whole presents us at every step with examples of the transformation of the unknown "thing-in-itself" into the known "thing-for-us," of the transformation of blind, unknown necessity, "necessity-in-itself," into the known "necessity-for-us." Epistemologically, there is no difference whatever between these two transformations, for the basic point of view in both cases is the same, viz., materialistic, the recognition of the objective reality of the external world and of the laws of external nature, and of the fact that both this world and these laws are fully knowable to man but can never be known to him *with finality*. . . .

For Engels all living human practice permeates the theory of knowledge itself and provides an *objective* criterion of truth. For until we know a law of nature, it, existing and acting independently of and outside our mind, makes us slaves of "blind necessity." But once we come to know this law, which acts (as Marx repeated a thousand times) *independently* of our will and our mind, we become the masters of nature. The mastery of nature manifested in human practice is a result of an objectively correct reflection within the human head of the phenomena and processes of nature, and is proof of the fact that this reflection (within the limits of what is revealed by practice) is objective, absolute, eternal truth. . . .

LENIN: CRITIQUE OF BOGDANOV

. . . Bogdanov's denial of objective truth is agnosticism and subjectivism. The absurdity of this denial is evident from . . .

SOURCE: From V. I. Lenin, *Materialism and Empiriocriticism* (1908), in *Collected Works*, Vol. XIV (Moscow: Progress Publishers, 1968).

scientific truth. Natural science leaves no room for doubt that its assertion that the earth existed prior to man is a truth. This is entirely compatible with the materialist theory of knowledge: the existence of the thing reflected independent of the reflector (the independence of the external world from the mind) is the fundamental tenet of materialism. . . . This proposition of natural science is incompatible with the philosophy of the Machists and with their doctrine of truth: if truth is an organizing form of human experience, then the assertion that the earth exists *outside* any human experience cannot be true.

But that is not all. If truth is only an organizing form of human experience, then the teachings, say, of Catholicism are also true. For there is not the slightest doubt that Catholicism is an "organizing form of human experience." . . .

[Bogdanov says that] the objective character of the physical world consists in the fact that it exists not for me personally, but for everybody (that is not true! It exists *independently* of "everybody"!) . . . . [And further:] "The objectivity of the physical bodies we encounter in our experience is in the last analysis established by the mutual verification and coordination of the utterances of various people. In general, the physical world is socially coordinated, socially harmonized, in a word, *socially organized experience*." . . .

We shall not repeat that this is a fundamentally untrue, idealist definition, that the physical world exists independently of humanity and of human experience, that the physical world existed at a time when no "sociality" and no "organization" of human experience was possible, and so forth. . . .

The immanentists, the empiriocriticists, and the empiriomonists all argue over particulars, over details, over the formulation of *idealism*, whereas we *from the very outset* reject all the principles of their philosophy common to this trinity. Let Bogdanov, accepting in the best sense and with the best of intentions *all the conclusions* of Marx, preach the "identity" of social being and social consciousness. . . . For this theory of the identity of social being and social consciousness is *sheer nonsense* and an *absolutely reactionary* theory. If certain people reconcile it with Marxism . . . we must not justify outrageous theoretical distortions of Marxism. . . .

Materialism in general recognizes objectively real being (matter) as independent of the consciousness, sensation, experience, etc., of humanity. Historical materialism recognizes social being as independent of the social consciousness of humanity. In both cases consciousness is only the reflection of being, at best an approximately true (adequate, perfectly exact) reflection of it. From this Marxist philosophy, which is cast from a single piece of steel, you cannot eliminate one basic premise, one essential part, without departing from objective truth, without falling a prey to bourgeois-reactionary falsehood. . . .

Once you deny objective reality, given us in sensation, you have already lost every weapon against fideism, for you have slipped into agnosticism or subjectivism—and that is all that fideism requires. If the perceptual world is objective reality, then the door is closed to every other "reality" or quasi-reality. . . . If the world is matter in motion, matter can and must be infinitely studied in the infinitely complex and detailed manifestations and ramifications of *this* motion, the motion of *this* matter; but beyond it, beyond the "physical," external world, with which everyone is familiar, there can be nothing. . . .

There are four standpoints from which a Marxist should proceed to form a judgment of empiriocriticism.

First and foremost, the theoretical foundations of this philosophy must be compared with those of dialectical materialism. Such a comparison . . . reveals, *along the whole line* of epistemological problems, the *thoroughly reactionary* character of empiriocriticism, which uses new artifices, terms, and subtleties to disguise the old errors of *idealism and agnosticism*. Only sheer ignorance of the nature of philosophical materialism generally and of the nature of Marx's and Engels's dialectical method can lead one to speak of "combining" empiriocriticism and Marxism.

Second, the place of empiriocriticism, as one very small school of specialists in philosophy, in relation to the other modern schools of philosophy must be determined. Both Mach and Avenarius started with Kant and, leaving him, proceeded not toward materialism, but in the opposite direction, toward Hume and Berkeley. Imagining that he was "purifying experience" generally, Avenarius was in fact only purifying agnosticism of Kantianism. The whole school of Mach and Avenarius is moving more and more definitely toward idealism, hand in hand with one of the most reactionary of the idealist schools, viz., the so-called immanentists.

Third, the indubitable connection between Machism and one school in one branch of modern natural science must be borne in mind. The vast majority of scientists, both generally and in the special branch of science in question, viz., physics, are invariably on the side of materialism. A minority of new physicists, however, influenced by the breakdown of old theories brought about by the great discoveries of recent years, influenced by the crisis in the new physics, which has very clearly revealed the relativity of our knowledge, have, owing to their ignorance of dialectics, slipped into idealism by way of relativism. The physical idealism in vogue today is as reactionary and transitory an infatuation as was the fashionable physiological idealism of the recent past.

Fourth, behind the epistemological scholasticism of empirio-criticism one must not fail to see the struggle of parties in philosophy, a struggle which in the last analysis reflects the tendencies and ideology of the antagonistic classes in modern society. Recent philosophy is as partisan as was philosophy two thousand years ago. The contending parties are essentially— although this is concealed by a pseudoerudite quackery of new terms or by a weak-minded nonpartisanship—materialism and idealism. The latter is merely a subtle, refined form of fideism, which stands fully armed, commands vast organizations, and steadily continues to exercise influence on the masses, turning the slightest vacillation in philosophical thought to its own advantage. The objective, class role of empiriocriticism consists entirely in rendering faithful service to the fideists in their struggle against materialism in general and historical materialism in particular.

15. LENIN:
THE REINTERPRETATION
OF MARX

Lenin's article "Karl Marx" was written in 1913 and published in part in the Granat Encyclopaedia *in 1915 over the signature of V. Ilyin. It is perhaps his clearest exposition of what he takes Marx to have meant by his "teaching" and is thus ideally suited for evaluating Lenin's misreadings of Marx.*

Lenin's assessment of the three main "components" of Marxism is superficially correct, but his allusion to the "unity of conception" of these ideas fails to divulge the precise nature of this unity, which is precisely what is needed to understand Marx. This is predominantly due to Lenin's inability to grasp the relationship of Marx's thought to that of Hegel—especially significant because many of the writings of the formative period of Marx's thinking, as it evolved from a radical Young Hegelian critical philosophy to communism based upon the concept of the alienation of labor, were unavailable to Lenin and thus played no part in his conception of "Marxism." Yet, owing to the particular circumstances surrounding Soviet hagiography, this and similar fundamental misconceptions of Marx have since become dogmas for Soviet Marxism.

Lenin's most important misinterpretation of Marx concerns the type and extent of Marx's materialism. In noting that Marx "was a materialist" who saw Feuerbach's materialism as "not sufficiently consistent and comprehensive," Lenin of course is reading Engels's materialist ontology and epistemology into Marx; that is, he is simply equating the views of Marx and Engels on this question, as on all others, and selecting passages from either writer which suit his needs of the moment. In fact, Marx's chief criticism of Feuerbach's materialism was not as Lenin would have it, but rather was directed against the abstract (hence "bourgeois") character of Feuerbach's assumption of a passive sensationism.[1] Lenin, on the one hand, attributes the

SOURCE: From V. I. Lenin, "Karl Marx," in Karl Marx and Friedrich Engels, *Selected Works,* Vol. I (Moscow: Co-operative Publishing Society of Foreign Workers in the U.S.S.R., 1935).

1. Cf. pp. 25–26, above.

same passive epistemology to Marx and, on the other, attempts to interpret Marx as a Hegelian! This latter is accomplished by quoting the famous retrospective passage in the afterword to the second edition of Capital *(1873), in which Marx was concerned to account for his ties to the Hegelian tradition against the anti-Hegelianizing materialism which was even then threatening to vulgarize Marxism. Marx's avowal in 1873 that he had once been "a pupil of that mighty thinker" (Hegel) is the basis of much of the subsequent crude re-Hegelianizing of Marxism and of Engels's developing a materialist ontology in the image of Hegel's Philosophy of Nature. Thus, Lenin follows in the footsteps of the Marx of 1873 and the later Engels by abstractly conceiving perception in a way rejected by Hegel as early as the* Phenomenology *of 1807 and fully recognized by Marx.*

This is especially apparent in Lenin's extracts and comments (1914) upon Hegel's Science of Logic, *in which he confronts the source of modern dialectical philosophy with the passion of a beginner, i.e., for the first time reading Hegel's* Logic *without the mediation of Engels. Time and again Lenin's comments reveal his "discovery" of the great importance of Hegel, who must of course be read "materialistically."[2] Incidentally, in the course of making these notes Lenin outlined an epistemology considerably more sophisticated than the naïve "copy" theory, which in his published writings he uncritically adopted from Engels.[3] Whereas previously a "materialist" epistemology had been for Lenin the undialectical copy theory of perception, he here argued that to be "dialectical" the original "copy" or "image" must be "deepened" by a series of abstractions which are necessary in order to grasp the laws which underlie "eternally moving and developing nature." That is, Lenin was able at this point to see some of the limitations of the "copy" theory, although it is questionable indeed how he can account for such processes of abstraction and conceptualization. Importantly, however, Lenin now saw that these concepts intervene between nature and the brain to provide "the form of reflection of nature in human cognition."[4] That is, it is these "concepts, laws, categories, etc."—i.e., human ideas—which structure and bestow the "lawful"*

2. Cf. Lenin's "Philosophical Notebooks," *Collected Works,* Vol. 38 (Moscow: Progress Publishers, 1961), pp. 85–363, in which he correctly notes, among other things, that "it is impossible to completely understand Marx's *Capital* . . . without having studied and understood the *whole* of Hegel's *Logic.* Consequently, half a century later none of the Marxists understood Marx!" (p. 180).

3. Cf. Selection 14, above.

4. Lenin, "Philosophical Notebooks," p. 182, with no reference (of course) to Kant, Mach, Avenarius, Bogdanov, or Plekhanov.

character upon natural events. Despite these concessions to the "active side" of perception, from the standpoint of Marx's "Theses on Feuerbach" Lenin's epistemology remained abstract, ignoring the class character or concreteness of such concepts, categories, and laws which it divorces from the revolutionary practice of the proletariat.[5]

Further, in his encyclopedia article, Lenin uncritically accepts from Engels the "two great camps" interpretation of philosophy,[6] *blissfully unaware that Marx had valid grounds to disdain such idle speculations, given his decisive supersession of all of philosophy in the materialist interpretation of history. There then follows a good deal more of Lenin's paraphrasing of* Engels *in an article purporting to discuss* Marx. *Especially interesting in this regard is Lenin's statement that "dialectics, according to Marx, is 'the science of the general laws of motion—both of the external world and of human thought.'" This argument, designed to prove that the latter is a copy of the former, is in fact a passage written by* Engels *and is even footnoted as such by* Lenin. *There then follows the absurdity that for both Marx and Hegel, "dialectics . . . include . . . the theory of cognition," by which Lenin hypostatizes dialectical thinking into a comprehensive philosophical method.*

Lenin then argues that the materialist interpretation of history is nothing but an "application to social life" of the "copy" theory of perception. He attributes this to Marx!

It should be enough to say that this article provides abundant evidence of Lenin's identification of the ideas of Marx and Engels on all philosophical questions, thereby greatly distorting Marx and turning him into a systematizing philosopher (i.e., a "dialectical materialist") and thus demonstrating a total lack of comprehension of Marx's conception of his own work as an antiphilosophy, inherently critical of both bourgeois social reality and that philosophy which reflects and sustains it.

Marx's Teaching

Marxism is the system of the views and teachings of Marx. Marx was the genius who continued and completed the three chief ideological currents of the nineteenth century, represented respectively by the three most advanced countries of humanity: classical German philosophy, classical English political economy,

5. Cf. Bogdanov's argument, pp. 224–227, above.
6. Cf. pp. 71–72, above and p. 240, below.

and French socialism combined with French revolutionary doctrines. The remarkable consistency and unity of conception of Marx's views, acknowledged even by his opponents, which in their totality constitute modern materialism and modern scientific socialism as the theory and program of the labor movement in all the civilized countries of the world. . . .

Philosophic Materialism

Beginning with the years 1844–1845, when his views were definitely formed, Marx was a materialist, and especially a follower of Feuerbach; even in later times, he saw Feuerbach's weak side only in this, that his materialism was not sufficiently consistent and comprehensive. For Marx, Feuerbach's world-historic and "epochmaking" significance consisted in his having decisively broken away from the idealism of Hegel, and [as Marx put it in *The Holy Family*] in his proclamation of materialism, which even in "the eighteenth century, especially in France, had been a struggle not only against the existing political institutions, and along with it against . . . religion and theology, but also . . . against every form of metaphysics" (in the sense of "intoxicated speculation" as distinguished from "sober philosophy").

To Hegel [wrote Marx, in the preface to the second edition of the first volume of *Capital*] the life process of the human brain, *i.e.*, the process of thinking, which, under the name of "the idea", he even transforms into an independent subject, is the *demiurgos* of the real world, and the real world is only the external, phenomenal form of "the idea." With me, on the contrary, the idea is nothing else than the material world reflected by the human mind, and translated into forms of thought.

In full conformity with Marx's materialist philosophy, and expounding it, Engels wrote in *Anti-Dühring* (which Marx read in manuscript) :

The unity of the world does not consist in its being. . . . The real unity of the world consists in its materiality and this is proved . . . by a long and protracted development of philosophy and natural science. . . . *Motion is the mode of existence of matter.* Never anywhere has there been matter without motion, nor can there be. . . . Matter without motion is just as unthinkable as motion without matter. . . . But if the . . . question is raised: what then are thought and consciousness, and whence they come, it becomes apparent that they are products of the human brain, and that man himself is a product of nature, which has been developed in and along with its environment; whence it is self-evident that the products of the human brain, being in the last analysis also products of nature, do not contradict the rest of nature, but are in correspondence with it. . . . Hegel was an idealist, that is to say, the thoughts within his mind were to him not the more or less abstract images [*Abbilder*, images, copies; sometimes Engels speaks of "imprints"] of real things and processes, but, on the contrary, things and their development were to him only the images made real of the "Idea" existing somewhere or other already before the world existed.

In his *Ludwig Feuerbach*—in which Engels expounds his own and Marx's views on Feuerbach's philosophy, and which Engels sent to the press after rereading an old manuscript, written by Marx and himself in 1844–1845, on Hegel, Feuerbach, and the materialist conception of history*—Engels writes:

The great basic question of all philosophy, especially of modern philosophy, is that concerning the relation of thinking and being . . . spirit to nature . . . which is primary, spirit or nature. . . . The answers which the philosophers gave to this question split them into two great camps. Those who asserted the primacy of spirit to nature and, therefore, in the last instance, assumed world creation in some form or other . . . comprised the camp of idealism. The others, who regarded nature as primary, belong to the various schools of materialism.

Any other use (in a philosophic sense) of the terms "idealism" and "materialism" leads only to confusion. Marx decidedly rejected not only idealism, always connected in one way or another with religion, but also the views of Hume and Kant, which are especially widespread in our day, along with agnosticism, criticism, positivism in their various forms; he considered such philosophy as a "reactionary" concession to idealism, at best as a "shamefaced way of surreptitiously accepting materialism, while denying it before the world." (Engels, *Ludwig Feuerbach*) . . . It is especially important that we should note Marx's opinion concerning the relation between freedom and necessity: "Freedom is the realization of necessity. 'Necessity is *blind* only *insofar as it is not understood*' " (Engels, *Anti-Dühring*). This means the recognition of the objective reign of law in nature and of the

* Engels refers there to *The German Ideology*, written by Marx and himself in 1845–1846. The vast difference between the earliest presentation therein of the materialist interpretation of history, and the remarks Lenin cites here from Engels's *Ludwig Feuerbach* can be seen by comparing *Karl Marx: The Essential Writings*, pp. 155–158 and 164–207. Cf. also pp. 11–14, above.

dialectical transformation of necessity into freedom (at the same time, an acknowledgment of the transformation of the unknown but knowable "thing-in-itself" into the "thing-for-us," of the "essence of things" into "phenomena"). Marx and Engels pointed out the following major shortcomings of the "old" materialism, including Feuerbach's (and, *a fortiori*, the "vulgar" materialism of Büchner, Vogt, and Moleschott). (1) it was "predominantly mechanistic," and took no account of the latest developments of chemistry and biology (in our day it would be necessary to add the electric theory of matter); (2) it was non-historical, nondialectical (metaphysical, in the sense of being antidialectical), and did not apply the standpoint of evolution consistently and all-sidedly; (3) it regarded "human beings" abstractly, and not as a "synthesis" of "all social relationships" (definite, concretely historical)—and thus only "interpreted" the world, whereas it was a question of "changing" it, that is, it did not grasp the significance of "practical revolutionary activity."

Dialectics

Marx and Engels regarded Hegelian dialectics, the theory of evolution which is most comprehensive, rich in content and profound, as the greatest achievement of classical German philosophy. All other formulations of the principle of development, of evolution, they regarded as one-sided, poor in content, as distorting and mutilating the actual course of development in nature and society (which often proceeded by leaps, catastrophes, revolutions).

Marx and I were pretty well the only people to rescue conscious dialectics [from the collapse of idealism including Hegelianism] and apply it in the materialist conception of nature. . . . Nature is the test of dialectics, and it must be said for modern natural science that it has furnished extremely rich and daily increasing materials for this test [written before the discovery of radium, electrons, the transmutation of elements], and has thus proved that in the last analysis nature's process is dialectical and not metaphysical [Engels, *Anti-Dühring*].

Again Engels writes [in *Ludwig Feuerbach*]:

The great basic thought that the world is not to be comprehended as a complex of ready-made *things*, but as a complex of *processes*, in which the things apparently stable no less than their mind images in our heads, the concepts, go through an uninterrupted change of coming into being and passing away, in which, in spite of all seeming accidents and of all temporary retrogression, a progressive development asserts itself in the end—this great fundamental thought has, especially since the time of Hegel, so thoroughly permeated ordinary consciousness that in this generality it is scarcely ever contradicted. But to acknowledge this fundamental thought in words and to apply it in reality in detail to each domain of investigation are two different things.

For dialectical philosophy nothing is final, absolute, sacred. It reveals the transitory character of everything and in everything; nothing can endure before it except the uninterrupted process of becoming and of passing away, of endless ascendency from the lower to the higher. And dialectical philosophy itself is nothing more than the mere reflection of this process in the thinking brain.

Thus dialectics, according to Marx, is "the science of the general laws of motion—both of the external world and of human thought" [Engels, *Ludwig Feuerbach*].

This revolutionary side of Hegel's philosophy was adopted and developed by Marx. Dialectical materialism "no longer needs any philosophy standing above the other sciences" [Engels, *Anti-Dühring*].

Of former philosophies there remains "the science of thought and its laws—formal logic and dialectics" [Engels, *Anti-Dühring*]. Dialectics, as the term is understood by Marx in conformity with Hegel, includes what is now called the theory of cognition, or gnoseology, a science that must contemplate its subject matter in the same way—historically, studying and generalizing the origin and development of cognition, the transition from ignorance to knowledge.

In our times, the idea of development, of evolution, has almost fully penetrated social consciousness, but it has done so in other ways, not through Hegel's philosophy. But the same idea, as formulated by Marx and Engels on the basis of Hegel's philosophy, is much more comprehensive, much more abundant in content than the current theory of evolution. A development that repeats, as it were, the stages already passed but repeats them in a different way, on a higher plane ("negation of negation"); a development, so to speak, in spirals, not in a straight line; a spasmodic, catastrophic, revolutionary development; "breaks of gradualness"; transformation of quantity into quality; inner impulses for development, imparted by the contradiction, the conflict of different forces and tendencies reacting on a given body or inside a given phenomenon or within a given society; interdependence, and the closest, indissoluble connection between all sides of every phenomenon (history disclosing ever newer and newer sides); a connection that provides the one world process of motion proceeding according to law—such are some of the features of dialectics as a doctrine of evolution more full of meaning than the current one. . . .

Materialist Conception of History

Realizing the inconsistency, the incompleteness, and the one-sidedness of the old materialism, Marx became convinced of the necessity of bringing "the science of society . . . into harmony with the materialist foundation, and of reconstructing it there-upon" [Engels, *Ludwig Feuerbach*].

If materialism in general explains consciousness as the outcome of existence, and not conversely, then materialism as applied to the social life of mankind must explain *social* consciousness as the outcome of *social* existence.

"Technology," writes Marx in the first volume of *Capital,* "discloses man's mode of dealing with nature, the process of production by which he sustains his life, and thereby also lays bare the mode of formation of his social relations, and of the mental conceptions that flow from them. In the preface to *A Contribution to the Critique of Political Economy* Marx gives an integral formulation of the fundamental principles of materialism as applied to human society and its history, in the following words:

In the social production which men carry on they enter into definite relations that are indispensable and independent of their will; these relations of production correspond to a definite stage of development of their material forces of production. The sum total of these relations of production constitutes the economic structure of society—the real foundation on which rises a legal and political superstrucure and to which correspond definite forms of social consciousness. The mode of production in material life determines the social, political, and intellectual life processes in general. It is not the consciousness of men that determines their being but, on the contrary, their social being determines their consciousness. At a certain stage of their development, the material forces of production in society come in conflict with the existing relations of productions, or—what is but a legal expression for the same thing—with the property relations within which they had been at work before. From forms of development of the forces of production these relations turn into their fetters. Then begins an epoch of social revolution. With the change of the economic foundation the entire immense superstructure is more or less rapidly transformed. In considering such transformations the distinction should always be made between the material transformation of the economic conditions of production which can be determined with the precision of natural science, and the legal, political, religious, aesthetic or philosophic—in short, ideological forms in which men become conscious of this conflict and fight it out. Just as our opinion of an individual is not based on what he thinks of himself, so can we not judge of such a period of transformation by its own consciousness; on the contrary, this consciousness must be explained rather from the contradictions of material life, from the existing conflict between the social forces of production and the relations of production. . . . In broad outlines we can designate the Asiatic, the ancient, the feudal, and the modern bourgeois modes of production as so many epochs in the progress of the economic formation of society. . . . [Compare Marx's brief formulation in a letter to Engels, dated July 7, 1866: "Our theory that the *organization of labor is determined by the means of production.*"]

The discovery of the materialist conception of history, or, more correctly, the consistent extension of materialism to the domain of social phenomena, obviated the two chief defects in earlier historical theories. For, in the first place, those theories, at best, examined only the ideological motives of the historical activity of human beings without investigating the origin of these ideological motives, without grasping the objective conformity to law in the development of the system of social relationships, and without discerning the roots of these social relationships in the degree of development of material production. In the second place, the earlier historical theories did not cover precisely the activities of the *masses,* whereas historical materialism first made it possible to study with scientific accuracy the social conditions of the life of the masses and the changes in these conditions. *At best,* pre-Marxist "sociology" and historiography gave an accumulation of raw facts collected at random, and a description of separate sides of the historic process. Examining the *totality* of all the opposing tendencies, reducing them to precisely definable conditions in the mode of life and the method of production of the various *classes* of society, discarding subjectivism and arbitrariness in the choice of various "leading" ideas or in their interpretation, showing how all the ideas and all the various tendencies, without exception, have their roots in the condition of the material forces of production, Marxism pointed the way to a comprehensive, an all-embracing study of the rise, development, and decay of social economic structures. People make their own history; but what determines their motives, namely, the motives of people in the mass; what gives rise to the clash of conflicting ideas and endeavors; what is the sum total of all these clashes among the whole mass of human societies; what are the objective conditions of production of material life that form the basis of all the historical activity of man; what is the law of the development of these conditions—to all these matters Marx directed attention, pointing out the way to a scientific study of history as a unified and true-to-law process despite its being extremely variegated and contradictory.

Class Struggle

That in any given society the strivings of some of the members conflict with the strivings of others; that social life is full of contradictions; that history discloses to us a struggle among nations and societies, and also within each nation and each society, manifesting in addition an alternation between periods of revolution and reaction, peace and war, stagnation and rapid progress or decline—these facts are generally known. Marxism provides a clue which enables us to discover the reign of law in this seeming labyrinth and chaos; the theory of the class struggle. Nothing but the study of the totality of the strivings of all the members of a given society, or group of societies, can lead to the scientific definition of the result of these strivings. Now, the conflict of strivings arises from differences in the situation and modes of life of the *classes* into which society is divided.

"The history of all hitherto existing society [wrote Marx in *The Communist Manifesto*] is the history of class struggles" [except the history of the primitive community—Engels added].

Freeman and slave, patrician and plebeian, lord and serf, guild master and journeyman, in a word, oppressor and oppressed, stood in constant opposition to one another, carried on an uninterrupted, now hidden, now open fight, a fight that each time ended either in a revolutionary reconstitution of society at large, or in the common ruin of the contending classes. . . .

The modern bourgeois society that has sprouted from the ruins of feudal society has not done away with class antagonisms. It has but established new classes, new conditions of oppression, new forms of struggle in place of the old ones.

Our epoch, the epoch of the bourgeoisie, possesses, however, this distinctive feature: it has simplified the class antagonisms. Society as a whole is more and more splitting up into two great hostile camps, into two great classes directly facing each other—bourgeoisie and proletariat.

Since the time of the Great French Revolution, the class struggle as the real motive force of events has been most clearly manifest in all European history. During the Restoration period in France, there were already a number of historians (Thierry, Guizot, Mignet, Thiers) who, generalizing events, could not but recognize in the class struggle the key to the understanding of all the history of France. In the modern age—the period of the complete victory of the bourgeoisie, of representative institutions, of extended (if not universal) suffrage, of a cheap daily press reaching the masses, etc., of powerful and ever expanding organizations of workers and employers, etc.—the class struggle (though sometimes in a highly one-sided, "peaceful," "constitutional" form) has shown itself still more obviously to be the mainspring of events. The following passage from Marx's *Communist Manifesto* will show us what Marx demanded of social sciences as regards an objective analysis of the situation of every class in modern society as well as an analysis of the condition of development of every class.

Of all the classes that stand face to face with the bourgeoisie today, the proletariat alone is a really revolutionary class. The other classes decay and finally disappear in the face of modern industry; the proletariat is its special and essential product. The lower middle class, the small manufacturer, the shopkeeper, the artisan, the peasant, all these fight against the bourgeoisie, to save from extinction their existence as fractions of the middle class. They are therefore not revolutionary, but conservative. Nay, more, they are reactionary, for they try to roll back the wheel of history. If by chance they are revolutionary, they are so only in view of their impending transfer into the proletariat; they thus defend not their present, but their future interests; they desert their own standpoint to place themselves at that of the proletariat.

In a number of historical works Marx gave brilliant and profound examples of materialist historiography, an analysis of the position of *each* separate class, and sometimes of that of various groups or strata within a class, showing plainly why and how "every class struggle is a political struggle." The above-quoted passage is an illustration of what a complex network of social relations and *transitional stages* between one class and another, between the past and the future, Marx analyzes in order to determine the resultant of the whole historical development.

Marx's economic doctrine is the most profound, the most many-sided, and the most detailed confirmation and application of his teaching.

16. LENIN:
IMPERIALISM

Lenin's pamphlet "Imperialism: The Highest Stage of Capitalism" was written in Zürich in 1916 and was first published in Russia in mid-1917. Apparently, Lenin first conceived doing a volume on the subject of capitalist imperialism shortly following the outbreak of the war, and intended his argument to demonstrate (1) that that conflict was fundamentally an imperialist war, growing out of four decades of global expansion and rivalry for unrestricted markets and raw materials among the major European powers; (2) that imperialism was a unique characteristic of the final stage of capitalist development, in which the need for such markets and supplies becomes acute owing to the declining average social rate of profit in the "home" country; and (3) that the proletariat should prepare itself for the seizure of power in the collapse which the war would bring in its wake.

Lenin takes most of his arguments from two sources: the anti-imperialist British Liberal J. A. Hobson, whose Imperialism *Lenin had begun to translate into Russian as early as 1904, and the vast amount of material associated with the debate over imperialism which had been current in Western European Social Democracy since about 1907. Lenin is especially critical, as might be expected, of Kautsky's contributions to the debate, but he does remark favorably on Hilferding's Das* Finanzkapital, *which was, indeed, the outstanding socialist work on the subject. Thus, although Lenin's* Imperialism *is hardly an "original" work of scholarship, in its clear and concise analyses it effectively provides the theoretical grounds for what was later to become the "Marxist-Leninist" championing of peasant-led nationalist revolution in colonial and semicolonial countries.*

. . . Capitalism only became capitalist imperialism at a definite and very high stage of its development, when certain of its fundamental characteristics began to change into their opposites, when the features of the epoch of transition from capitalism to a higher social and economic system had taken shape and revealed

SOURCE: From V. I. Lenin, "Imperialism: The Highest Stage of Capitalism" (1916), in *Collected Works,* Vol. XXII (Moscow: Progress Publishers, 1964).

themselves in all spheres. Economically, the main thing in this process is the displacement of capitalist free competition by capitalist monopoly. Free competition is the basic feature of capitalism, and of commodity production generally; monopoly is the exact opposite of free competition, but we have seen the latter being transformed into monopoly before our eyes, creating large-scale industry and forcing out small industry, replacing large-scale by still larger-scale industry, and carrying concentration of production and capital to the point where out of it has grown and is growing monopoly: cartels, syndicates and trusts, and merging with them, the capital of a dozen or so banks, which manipulate thousands of millions. At the same time the monopolies, which have grown out of free competition, do not eliminate the latter, but exist above it and alongside it, and thereby give rise to a number of very acute, intense antagonisms, frictions, and conflicts. Monopoly is the transition from capitalism to a higher system.

If it were necessary to give the briefest possible definition of imperialism we should have to say that imperialism is the monopoly stage of capitalism. Such a definition would include what is most important, for, on the one hand, finance capital is the bank capital of a few very big monopolist banks, merged with the capital of the monopolist associations of industrialists; and, on the other hand, the division of the world is the transition from a colonial policy which has extended without hindrance to territories unseized by any capitalist power, to a colonial policy of monopolist possession of the territory of the world, which has been completely divided up. . . .

We must give a definition of imperialism that will include the following five of its basic features: (1) the concentration of production and capital has developed to such a high stage that it has created monopolies which play a decisive role in economic life; (2) the merging of bank capital with industrial capital, and the creation, on the basis of this "finance capital," of a financial oligarchy; (3) the export of capital as distinguished from the export of commodities acquires exceptional importance; (4) the formation of international monopolist capitalist associations which share the world among themselves, and (5) the territorial division of the whole world among the biggest capitalist powers is completed. Imperialism is capitalism at that stage of development at which the dominance of monopolies and finance capital is established; in which the export of capital has acquired pronounced importance; in which the division of the world among the international trusts has begun, in which the division of all territories of the globe among the biggest capitalist powers has been completed. . . .

The characteristic feature of imperialism is *not* industrial *but* finance capital. . . .

We clearly see from these figures how "complete" was the partition of the world at the turn of the twentieth century. After 1876 colonial possessions increased to enormous dimensions, by more than 50 percent, from 40,000,000 to 65,000,000 square kilometers for the six biggest powers; the increase amounts to 25,000,000 square kilometers, 50 percent more than the area of the metropolitan countries (16,500,000 square kilometers). In 1876 three powers had no colonies, and a fourth, France, had scarcely any. By 1914 these four powers had acquired colonies with an area of 14,100,000 square kilometers, i.e., about half as much again as the area of Europe, with a population of nearly 100,000,000. The unevenness in the rate of expansion of colonial

COLONIAL POSSESSIONS OF THE GREAT POWERS
(1,000,000 square kilometers and 1,000,000 inhabitants)

	Colonies				Metropolitan countries		Total	
	1876		1914		1914		1914	
	Area	Pop.	Area	Pop.	Area	Pop.	Area	Pop.
Great Britain . .	22.5	251.9	33.5	393.5	0.3	46.5	33.8	440.0
Russia	17.0	15.9	17.4	33.2	5.4	136.2	22.8	169.4
France	0.9	6.0	10.6	55.5	0.5	39.6	11.1	95.1
Germany . . .	—	—	2.9	12.3	0.5	64.9	3.4	77.2
United States . .	—	—	0.3	9.7	9.4	97.0	9.7	106.7
Japan	—	—	0.3	19.2	0.4	53.0	0.7	72.2
Total for 6 Great Powers	40.4	273.8	65.0	523.4	16.5	437.2	81.5	960.6
Colonies of other powers (Belgium, Holland, etc.) . . .							9.9	45.3
Semicolonial countries (Persia, China, Turkey)							14.5	361.2
Other countries							28.0	289.9
Total for the world							133.9	1,657.0

possessions is very great. If, for instance, we compare France, Germany, and Japan, which do not differ very much in area and population, we see that the first has acquired almost three times as much colonial territory as the other two combined. In regard to finance capital, France, at the beginning of the period we are considering, was also, perhaps, several times richer than Germany and Japan put together. . . .

Alongside the colonial possessions of the Great Powers, we have placed the small colonies of the small states, which are, so to speak, the next objects of a possible and probable "redivision" of colonies. These small states mostly retain their colonies only because the big powers are torn by conflicting interests, friction, etc., which prevent them from coming to an agreement on the division of the spoils. As to the "semicolonial" states, they provide an example of the transitional forms which are to be found in all spheres of nature and society. Finance capital is such a great, such a decisive, you might say, force in all economic and in all international relations, that it is capable of subjecting, and actually does subject, to itself even states enjoying the fullest political independence. . . . Of course, finance capital finds most "convenient," and derives the greatest profit from, a *form* of subjection which involves the loss of the political independence of the subjected countries and peoples. . . . It is natural that the struggle for these semidependent countries should have become particularly bitter in the epoch of finance capital, when the rest of the world has already been divided up. . . .

The principal feature of the latest stage of capitalism is the domination of monopolist associations of big employers. These monopolies are most firmly established when *all* the sources of raw materials are captured by one group, and we have seen with what zeal the international capitalist associations exert every effort to deprive their rivals of all opportunity of competing, to buy up, for example, iron fields, oil fields, etc. Colonial possession alone gives the monopolies complete guarantee against all contingencies in the struggle against competitors, including the case of the adversary wanting to be protected by a law establishing a state monopoly. The more capitalism is developed, the more strongly the shortage of raw materials is felt, the more intense the competition and the hunt for sources of raw materials throughout the whole world, the more desperate the struggle for the acquisition of colonies. . . .

Finance capital is interested not only in the already discovered sources of raw materials but also in potential sources, because present-day technical development is extremely rapid, and land which is useless today may be improved tomorrow if new methods are devised . . . and if large amounts of capital are invested. This also applies to prospecting for minerals, to new methods of processing up and utilizing raw materials, etc., etc. Hence the inevitable striving of finance capital to enlarge its spheres of influence and even its actual territory. . . . Finance capital in general strives to seize the largest possible amount of land of all kinds in all places, and by every means, taking into account potential sources of raw materials and fearing to be left behind in the fierce struggle for the last remnants of independent territory, or for the repartition of those territories that have been already divided. . . .

The interests pursued in exporting capital also give an impetus to the conquest of colonies, for in the colonial market it is easier to employ monopoly methods (and sometimes they are the only methods that can be employed) to eliminate competition, to ensure supplies, to secure the necessary "connections," etc. . . .

In the following table we see three areas of highly developed capitalism (high development of means of transport, of trade and of industry) : the Central Europeans, the British, and the American areas. Among these are three states which dominate the world: Germany, Great Britain, and the United States. Imperialist rivalry and the struggle between these countries have become extremely keen because Germany has only an insignificant area and few colonies; the creation of "Central Europe" is still a matter for the future; it is being born in the midst of a desperate struggle. For the moment the distinctive feature of the whole of Europe is political disunity. In the British and American areas, on the other hand, political concentration is very highly developed, but there is a vast disparity between the immense colonies of the one and the insignificant colonies of the other. In the colonies, however, capitalism is only beginning to develop. The struggle for South America is becoming more and more acute.

ECONOMIC DEVELOPMENT
IN 1900

Principal economic areas	Area Million Square Kilometers	Population Millions	Transport		Trade	Industry		
			Railways (thousand kilometers)	Mercantile fleet (million tons)	Imports, exports (thousand million marks)	Output		
						Of coal (million tons)	Of pig iron (million tons)	Number of cotton spindles (millions)
Central Europe	27.6 (23.6)*	388 (146)*	204	8	41	251	15	26
Britain	28.9 (23.6)*	398 (355)*	140	11	25	249	9	51
Russia	22	131	63	1	3	16	3	7
Eastern Asia	12	389	8	1	2	8	0.02	2
America	30	148	379	6	14	245	14	19

* The figures in parentheses show the area and population of their colonies.

There are two areas where capitalism is little developed: Russia and Eastern Asia. In the former, the population is extremely sparse, in the latter it is extremely dense; in the former political concentration is high, in the latter it does not exist. The partitioning of China is only just beginning, and the struggle for it between Japan, the U.S., etc., is continually gaining in intensity. . . .

The deepest economic foundation of imperialism is capitalist monopoly, i.e., monopoly which has grown out of capitalism and which exists in the general environment of capitalism. . . . Like all monopoly, it inevitably engenders a tendency of stagnation and decay. Since monopoly prices are established, even temporarily, the motive cause of technical and, consequently, of all other progress disappears to a certain extent and, further, the *economic* possibility arises of deliberately retarding technical progress. . . .

The monopoly ownership of very extensive, rich, or well-situated colonies, operates in the same direction.

Further, imperialism is an immense accumulation of money capital in a few countries. . . . Hence the extraordinary growth of a class or, rather, of a stratum of rentiers, i.e., people who live by "clipping coupons," who take no part in any enterprise whatever, whose profession is idleness. The export of capital, one of the most essential economic bases of imperialism, still more completely isolates the rentiers from production and sets the seal of parasitism on the whole country that lives by exploiting the labor of several overseas countries and colonies. . . .

For that reason the term "rentier state," or usurer state, is coming into common use in the economic literature that deals with imperialism. The world has become divided into a handful of usurer states and a vast majority of debtor states. . . . The rentier state is a state of parasitic, decaying capitalism, and this circumstance cannot fail to influence all the sociopolitical conditions of the countries concerned, in general, and the two fundamental trends in the working class movement, in particular. . . .

Imperialism, which means the partitioning of the world, which means high monopoly profits for a handful of very rich countries, makes it economically possible to bribe the upper strata of the ·proletariat, and thereby fosters, gives shape to, and strengthens opportunism. . . .

An increasing proportion of land in England is being taken out of cultivation and used for sport, for the diversion of the rich. . . . The percentage of the productively employed population to the total population is declining.

[We are] obliged to distinguish systematically between the *"upper stratum"* of the workers and the *"lower stratum of the proletariat proper."* The upper stratum furnishes the bulk of the membership of cooperatives, of trade unions, of sporting clubs and of numerous religious sects. To this level is adapted the electoral system, which in Great Britain is still *"sufficiently restricted to exclude the lower stratum of the proletariat proper"!* . . .

Imperialism has the tendency to create privileged sections also among the workers, and to detach them from the broad masses of the proletariat. . . .

. . . In its economic essence imperialism is monopoly capitalism. This in itself determines its place in history, for monopoly that grows out of the soil of free competition, and precisely out of free competition, is the transition from the capitalist system to a higher socioeconomic order. We must take special note of the four principal types of monopoly, or principal manifestations of monopoly capitalism, which are characteristic of the epoch we are examining.

First, monopoly arose out of the concentration of production at a very high stage. This refers to the monopolist capitalist associations, cartels, syndicates, and trusts. We have seen the important part these play in present-day economic life. At the beginning of the twentieth century, monopolies had acquired complete supremacy in the advanced countries, and although the first steps toward the formation of the cartels were taken by countries enjoying the protection of high tariffs (Germany, America), Great Britain, with her system of free trade, revealed the same basic phenomenon, only a little later, namely, the birth of monopoly out of the concentration of production.

Second, monopolies have stimulated the seizure of the most important sources of raw materials, especially for the basic and most highly cartelized industries in capitalist society: the coal and iron industries. The monopoly of the most important sources of raw materials has enormously increased the power of big capital, and has sharpened the antagonism between cartelized and noncartelized industry.

Third, monopoly has sprung from the banks. The banks have developed from modest middleman enterprises into the monopolists of finance capital. Some three to five of the biggest banks in each of the foremost capitalist countries have achieved the "personal link-up" between industrial and bank capital, and have concentrated in their hands the control of thousands upon thousands of millions which form the greater part of the capital and income of entire countries. A financial oligarchy, which throws a close network of dependence relationships over all the economic and political institutions of present-day bourgeois society without exception—such is the most striking manifestation of this monopoly.

Fourth, monopoly has grown out of colonial policy. To the numerous "old" motives of colonial policy, finance capital has added the struggle for the sources of raw materials, for the export of capital, for spheres of influence, i.e., for spheres for profitable deals, concessions, monopoly profits and so on, economic territory in general. When the colonies of the European powers, for instance, comprised only one-tenth of the territory of Africa (as was the case in 1876), colonial policy was able to develop by methods other than those of monopoly—by the "free grabbing" of territories, so to speak. But when nine-tenths of Africa had been seized (by 1900), when the whole world had been divided up, there was inevitably ushered in the era of monopoly possession of colonies and, consequently, of particularly intense struggle for the division and the redivision of the world.

The extent to which monopolist capital has intensified all the contradictions of capitalism is generally known. It is sufficient to mention the high cost of living and the tyranny of the cartels. This intensification of contradictions constitutes the most powerful driving force of the transitional period of history, which began from the time of the final victory of world finance capital.

Monopolies, oligarchy, the striving for domination and not for freedom, the exploitation of an increasing number of small or weak nations by a handful of the richest or most powerful nations—all these have given birth to those distinctive characteristics of imperialism which compel us to define it as parasitic or decaying capitalism. More and more prominently there emerges, as one of the tendencies of imperialism, the creation of the "rentier state," the usurer state, in which the bourgeoisie to an ever-increasing degree lives on the proceeds of capital exports and by "clipping coupons." It would be a mistake to believe that this tendency to decay precludes the rapid growth of capitalism. It does not. In the epoch of imperialism, certain branches of industry, certain strata of the bourgeoisie, and certain countries betray, to a greater or lesser degree, now one and now another of these tendencies. On the whole, capitalism is growing far more rapidly than before; but this growth is not only becoming more and more uneven in general, its unevenness also manifests itself, in particular, in the decay of the countries which are richest in capital (Britain). . . .

The receipt of high monopoly profits by the capitalists in one of the numerous branches of industry, in one of the numerous countries, etc., makes it economically possible for them to bribe certain sections of the workers, and for a time a fairly considerable minority of them, and win them to the side of the bourgeoisie of a given industry or given nation against all the others. The intensification of antagonisms between imperialist nations for the division of the world increases this urge. And so there is created that bond between imperialism and opportunism, which revealed itself first and most clearly in Great Britain, owing to the fact that certain features of imperialist development were observable there much earlier than in other countries. . . .

From all that has been said in this book on the economic essence of imperialism, it follows that we must define it as capitalism in transition, or, more precisely, as moribund capitalism. It is very instructive in this respect to note that bourgeois economists, in describing modern capitalism, frequently employ catchwords and phrases like "interlocking." . . .

What does this catchword "interlocking" express? It merely expresses the most striking feature of the process going on before our eyes. . . . Ownership of shares, the relations between owners of private property "interlock in a haphazard way." But underlying this interlocking, its very base, are the changing social relations of production. When a big enterprise assumes gigantic proportions, and on the basis of an exact computation of mass data, organizes according to plan the supply of primary raw materials to the extent of two-thirds, or three-fourths, of all that is necessary for tens of millions of people; when the raw materials are transported in a systematic and organized manner to the most suitable places of production, sometimes situated hundreds or thousands of miles from each other; when a single center directs all the consecutive stages of processing the material right up to the manufacture of numerous varieties of finished articles; when these products are distributed according to a single plan among tens and hundreds of millions of consumers (the marketing of oil in America and Germany by the American oil trust) —then it becomes evident that we have socialization of production, and not mere "interlocking"; that private economic and private property relations constitute a shell which no longer fits its contents, a shell which must inevitably decay if its removal is artificially delayed, a shell which may remain in a state of decay for a fairly long period (if, at the worst, the cure of the opportunist abscess is protracted), but which will inevitably be removed. . . .

17.
THE LEGITIMIZATION OF
THE ONE-PARTY STATE

It is generally acknowledged that State and Revolution *is Lenin's greatest single contribution to political theory. Subtitled "The Marxist Theory of the State and the Tasks of the Proletariat in the Revolution," it was written in August–September 1917 while Lenin was in hiding in Finland following the Bolsheviks' abortive July coup d'état. In this work Lenin considers in detail the nature of the dictatorship of the proletariat as a transition stage from capitalism to communism, for as is well known, Marx dealt with this subject only briefly in* The Civil War in France *(1871) and the* Critique of the Gotha Program *(1875).[1] Lenin's argument is more dependent upon Engels's remarks on the subject in* The Origin of the Family, Private Property and the State *(1884), which was the most influential exposition of the Marxist theory of the state prior to* State and Revolution. *This latter work is noteworthy for its emphasis on the transitory nature of the dictatorship of the proletariat, and for the theory of the self-eliminating role to be played therein by the state. The reader might find it interesting to follow the history of the U.S.S.R. in the light of these fundamentals of Lenin's political philosophy and his "predictions" of the course of the Revolution in Russia.*

In State and Revolution, *Lenin resurrected elements of a revolutionary Marxism which had been pronounced dead more than two decades earlier by Engels himself.[2] In so doing, Lenin recognized both the failure of parliamentary Social Democracy in Western Europe and the collapse of the czarist regime in Russia. Although his remarks on the nature of the dictatorship of the proletariat were prophetic of much of what was to occur just weeks after his writing, the description of the highest stage of communism and the transition thereto retains, in the light of fifty-six years of Soviet history, an almost utopian tone. It can, of course, be argued that although the "transition period" is unfortunately a great deal longer than anyone, including Lenin, expected, nonetheless it continues to move in the proper direction. Yet, as we shall see in Parts IV and V, there is perhaps better reason to believe*

---

1. Cf. *Karl Marx: The Essential Writings*, pp. 273–300.
2. Cf. Selection 8, above.

that the course of the evolution of the U.S.S.R. is set in the direction opposed to the overcoming of alienation rather than toward it.

In this regard, it is instructive to return to Bukharin's description of "state capitalism" (in his article "On the Theory of the Imperialist State," written in 1916 and partly the occasion for Lenin's conceiving a book on "Marxism and the State" which later became State and Revolution), *in which he reminds us that "there is no power on earth which can compare with" such a system. The main difference between Lenin and Bukharin is not merely that the latter "verges on anarchism" whereas the former "realistically" assesses the needs of the proletarian dictatorship to defend its successes (as Lenin's apologists might put it), but rather that the central historical problem revolves around Lenin's decision to embrace excessive short-term means and the willingness—or eagerness—of his successors perpetually to turn the machinery of the state against the revolutionary elements among the Russian people as well as among the Bolsheviks themselves. By the height of the Stalin era, the Soviet state, like Bukharin's imperialist state, could "do no wrong"; any suspected criticism of the state (or of the party which dominated it or of the man—Stalin—who dominated the party) was simply declared to be treason.*

But merely to raise the question of the state's having become a dictatorship over, not of, the proletariat is to overlook the dialectical relation between the state and the people. That is, it is in Lenin's conception of the party as the "vanguard" of the proletariat that is to be found the basis of the party's subsequently acting in the name of the ideal proletariat, i.e., of the proletariat of the ideal future, and often against the real, i.e., present, proletariat. In the name of its ontology and comprehensive "scientific" theories of society and history, the Party, and hence the state which it controlled, claimed infallibility. It is precisely in this party authoritarianism and elitism that are sown the seeds of the later totalitarian horrors of Stalin, yet Lenin failed to perceive the danger.[3]

The first part of the selection which follows is taken from Bukharin's "On the Theory of the Imperialist State" (1916) and the second from Lenin's critical reply, State and Revolution *(1917).*

3. But cf. Selection 22, below, where we see that Lenin did perceive this, but not until a time when he was powerless to prevent it.

BUKHARIN: THE IMPERIALIST STATE

. . . From the point of view of Marxism the state is nothing but *the most general organization of the dominant classes, the basic function of which is to maintain and extend the exploitation of the suppressed classes.* . . . Insofar as there is an organization of state power set up according to a plan and consciously regulated (and this appears only at a certain stage in the development of the state), to that extent one can speak of the posing of *goals*, but these goals are defined by the interests of the *dominant* classes and *only by them.* This is not in the least contradicted by the circumstance that the state performs and has performed a whole series of functions for the common good. The latter merely provides the necessary *condition*, the *conditio sine qua non*, for the existence of the state power. The state's "activities for the common good" are thus the *conditions for maximally protracted and maximally successful exploitation of the enslaved classes* in contemporary society, above all the proletariat. . . .

In this connection it is possible to distinguish two types of relationships: either the state organization is the *direct* organization of exploitation—in which case the state stands forth as the union of the capitalists, having its own enterprises (e.g., railroads, monopoly production of certain products, etc.) ; or the state organization participates in an *indirect* manner in the process of exploitation, as a service mechanism to sustain and extend the most profitable conditions for the process of exploitation. In the first case—insofar as we are speaking of productive labor—the state absorbs the surplus value which is created in the sphere of its direct activity; in the second—it appropriates part of the surplus value which is produced in the branches of production that lie outside the sphere of direct state control, by means of taxes, etc. Usually the state extracts not only a part of the surplus value, but also a certain part of wages. . . . In concrete

SOURCE: From N. Bukharin, "On the Theory of the Imperialistic State" (1916), published in *The Revolution of Law*, Collection I (Moscow: Communist Academy, 1952) ; trans. Robert V. Daniels, in *A Documentary History of Communism*, Vol. I (New York. Random House, 1960). Reprinted by permission.

actuality both these types exist simultaneously, although their proportions are subject to change and depend on the stage of historical development which has been attained. . . .

The *foreign* policy of the state organization expresses its struggle to share the surplus value which is produced on a worldwide scale (insofar as there is a noncapitalist world, the struggle for the surplus product), the struggle which is enacted between the various politically organized groups of the dominant classes.

The *internal* policy of the state organization reflects the struggle of the dominant classes for a share of the value (i.e., product) created by way of the systematic suppression of all attempts at liberation on the part of the suppressed classes. . . .

Even the most superficial glance at social-economic life shows us the colossal growth of the economic significance of the state. This is reflected above all in the growth of the *state budget*. The complicated apparatus of the contemporary state organization requires enormous expenses, which increase with astonishing swiftness. . . .

A vast role in such an increase of the budget is undoubtedly played by militarism, one of the aspects of *imperialist* politics, which in turn stems necessarily from the structure of *finance capitalism*. . . . If the preimperialist period—the period of liberalism, which was the political expression of industrial capitalism—was characterized by the noninterference of the state power, and the formula laissez-faire was a symbol of the faith of the ruling circles of the bourgeoisie, who all permitted the "free play of economic forces," our time is characterized by a directly opposite tendency, which has as its logical conclusion *state capitalism*, sucking everything into the area of state regulation. . . .

The *state power thus sucks in almost all branches of production; it not only preserves the general conditions of the process of exploitation; the state becomes more and more a direct exploiter, which organizes and directs production as a collective, composite capitalist.* . . . The anarchistic commodity market is to a significant degree replaced by the organized distribution of the product, in which the supreme authority is again the state power. . .

Socialism is the regulation of production directed by *society*, not by the state; it is the annihilation of class contradictions, not their intensification. The regulation of production by itself does not mean socialism at all; it exists in any sort of economy, in any slave-owning group with a natural economy. What awaits us in the immediate future is in fact *state capitalism.* . . .

The necessities of imperialist development compel bourgeois society to mobilize all its forces, to become organized on the broadest scale: the state draws into itself the whole series of bourgeois organizations.

Here war gives an enormous impetus. Philosophy and medicine, religion and ethics, chemistry and bacteriology—all are "mobilized" and "militarized" just like industry and finance. The whole grand-scale technical, economic, and ideological machine operates more planfully as soon as the conscious organized adaptation to the "whole" has appeared—i.e., when the state in one way or another has drawn these innumerable groups into its overall organization. . . .

We must now raise the fully natural question of the role of the workers, of proletarian organizations.

Theoretically there can be two possibilities here: *Either the workers' organizations, like all the organizations of the bourgeoisie, will grow into the statewide organization and be transformed into a simple appendage of the state apparatus, or they will outgrow the framework of the state and burst it from within,* as they organize their own state power (the dictatorship) . . . .

The immediate development of state organisms—as long as the socialist overturn does not occur—is possible only in the form of *militaristic state capitalism.* Centralization becomes barrack centralization; the intensification of the most hateful militarism among the upper groups, of bestial drilling of the proletariat, of bloody repressions, is inevitable. On the other hand, as we have already noted above, any move by the proletariat is inevitably transformed under these circumstances into a move against the state power. Hence the definite tactical demand—Social Democracy must vigorously underscore its hostility in principle to the state power. . . . To support the contemporary state means to support militarism. The historical task of the day is not to worry about the further development of the forces of production (they are quite sufficient for the realization of socialism), but the preparation of a general attack on the ruling bandits. . . .

LENIN: "STATE AND REVOLUTION"

. . . Let us begin with the most popular of Engels's works, *The Origin of the Family, Private Property, and the State.* . . . Summing up his historical analysis, Engels says:

> The state is, therefore, by no means a power forced on society from without; just as little is it "the reality of the ethical idea," "the image and reality of reason," as Hegel maintains. Rather, it is a product of society at a certain stage of development; it is the admission that this society has become entangled in an insoluble contradiction with itself, that it has split into irreconcilable antagonisms which it is powerless to dispel. But in order that these antagonisms, these classes with conflicting economic interests might not consume themselves and society in fruitless struggle, it became necessary to have a power, seemingly standing above society, that would alleviate the conflict and keep it within the bounds of "order"; and this power, arisen out of society but placing itself above it, and alienating itself more and more from it, is the state.

This expresses with perfect clarity the basic idea of Marxism . . . [that the] state is a product and a manifestation of the *irreconcilability* of class antagonisms. The state arises where, when, and insofar as class antagonisms objectively *cannot* be reconciled. And, conversely, the existence of the state proves that the class antagonisms are irreconcilable. . . .

On the other hand, the "Kautskyite" distortion of Marxism is far more subtle. "Theoretically," it is not denied that the state is an organ of class rule, or that class antagonisms are irreconcilable. But what is overlooked or glossed over is this: if the state is the product of the irreconcilability of class antagonisms, if it is a power standing *above* society and *"alienating* itself *more and more* from it," it is clear that the liberation of the oppressed class is impossible not only without a violent revolution, *but also without the destruction* of the apparatus of state power which was created by the ruling class and which is the embodiment of this "alienation." . . .

[Engels continues:]

SOURCE: From V. I. Lenin, *State and Revolution* (1917), in *Collected Works*, Vol. XXV (Moscow: Progress Publishers, 1964).

Because the state arose from the need to hold class antagonisms in check, but because it arose, at the same time, in the midst of the conflict of these classes, it is, as a rule, the state of the most powerful, economically dominant class, which, through the medium of the state, becomes also the politically dominant class, and thus acquires new means of holding down and exploiting the oppressed class. . . . The ancient and feudal states were organs for the exploitation of the slaves and serfs; likewise, the modern representative state is an instrument of exploitation of wage labor by capital. By way of exception, however, periods occur in which the warring classes balance each other so nearly that the state power as ostensible mediator acquires, for the moment, a certain degree of independence of both. . . .

In a democratic republic, Engels continues, "wealth exercises its power indirectly, but all the more surely," first, by means of the "direct corruption of officials" (America) ; second, by means of an "alliance of the government and the stock exchange" (France and America).

At present, imperialism and the domination of the banks have "developed" into an exceptional art both these methods of upholding and giving effect to the omnipotence of wealth in democratic republics of all descriptions. . . .

Another reason why the omnipotence of "wealth" is more *certain* in a democratic republic is that it does not depend on defects in the political machinery or on the faulty political shell of capitalism. A democratic republic is the best possible political shell for capitalism, and, therefore, once capital has gained possession of this very best shell . . . it establishes its power so securely, so firmly, that *no* change of persons, institutions or parties in the bourgeois-democratic republic can shake it. . . .

Engels gives a general summary of his views in the following words:

The state, then, has not existed from all eternity. There have been societies that did without it, that had no idea of the state and state power. At a certain stage of economic development, which necessarily bound up with the split of society into classes, the state became a necessity owing to this split. We are now rapidly approaching a stage in the development of production at which the existence of these classes not only will have ceased to be a necessity, but will become a positive hindrance to production. They will fall as inevitably as they arose at an earlier stage. Along with them the state will inevitably fall. Society, which will reorganize production on the basis of a free and equal association of the producers, will put the whole machinery of state where it will then belong: into a museum of antiquities, by the side of the spinning wheel and the bronze axe. . . .

Engels's words regarding the "withering away" of the state are so widely known, they are so often quoted, and so clearly reveal the essence of the customary adaptation of Marxism to opportunism that we must deal with them in detail. We shall quote the whole argument from which they are taken.

The proletariat seizes state power and turns the means of production into state property to begin with. But thereby it abolishes itself as the proletariat, abolishes all class distinctions and class antagonisms, and abolishes also the state as state. Society thus far, operating amid class antagonisms, needed the state, that is, an organization of the particular exploiting class, for the maintenance of its external conditions of production, and, therefore, especially, for the purpose of forcibly keeping the exploited class in the conditions of oppression determined by the given mode of production (slavery, serfdom or bondage, wage labor). The state was the official representative of society as a whole, its concentration in a visible corporation. But it was this only insofar as it was the state of that class which itself represented, for its own time, society as a whole: in ancient times, the state of slave-owning citizens; in the Middle Ages, of the feudal nobility; in our own time, of the bourgeoisie. When at last it becomes the real representative of the whole of society, it renders itself unnecessary. As soon as there is no longer any social class to be held in subjection, as soon as class rule, and the individual struggle for existence based upon the present anarchy in production, with the collisions and excesses arising from this struggle, are removed, nothing more remains to be held in subjection—nothing necessitating a special coercive force, a state. The first act by which the state really comes forward as the representative of the whole of society—the taking possession of the means of production in the name of society—is also its last independent act as a state. State interference in social relations becomes, in one domain after another, superfluous, and then dies down of itself. The government of persons is replaced by the administration of things, and by the conduct of processes of production. The state is not "abolished." *It withers away.* This gives the measure of the value of the phrase "a free people's state," both as to its justifiable use for a time from an agitational point of view, and as to its ultimate scientific insufficiency; and also of the so-called anarchists' demand that the state be abolished overnight. (*Herr Eugen Dühring's Revolution in Science.*) . . .

In the first place, Engels speaks of the proletarian revolution "abolishing" the *bourgeois* state, while the words about the state withering away refer to the remnants of the *proletarian* state *after* the socialist revolution. According to Engels, the bourgeois state does not "wither away," but is *"abolished"* by the proletariat in the course of the revolution. What withers away after this revolution is the proletarian state or semistate.

Second, the state is a "special coercive force." . . . And from it follows that the "special coercive force" for the suppression of the proletariat by the bourgeoisie, of millions of working people by handfuls of the rich, must be replaced by a "special coercive force" for the suppression of the bourgeoisie by the proletariat (the dictatorship of the proletariat). This is precisely what is meant by "abolition of the state as state." This is precisely the "act" of taking possession of the means of production in the name of society. And it is self-evident that *such* a replacement of one (bourgeois) "special force" by another (proletarian) "special force" cannot possibly take place in the form of "withering away."

Third, in speaking of the state "withering away," and . . . "dying down of itself," Engels refers quite clearly and definitely to the period *after* "the state has taken possession of the means of production in the name of the whole of society," that is, *after* the socialist revolution. . . .

Engels's historical analysis of its role becomes a veritable panegyric on violent revolution. This "no one remembers."* It is not done in modern socialist parties to talk or even think about the significance of this idea, and it plays no part whatever in their daily propaganda and agitation among the people. . . .

The theory of Marx and Engels of the inevitability of a violent revolution refers to the bourgeois state. The latter *cannot* be superseded by the proletarian state (the dictatorship of the proletariat) through the process of "withering away," but, as a general rule, only through a violent revolution. . . .

The overthrow of bourgeois rule can be accomplished only by the proletariat, the particular class whose economic conditions of existence prepare it for this task and provide it with the possibility and the power to perform it. While the bourgeoisie break up and disintegrate the peasantry and all the petit-bourgeois groups, they weld together, unite, and organize the proletariat. Only the proletariat—by virtue of the economic role it plays in large-scale production—is capable of being the leader of *all* the working and exploited people, whom the bourgeoisie exploit, oppress, and crush, often not less but more than they do the proletarians, but who are incapable of waging an *independent* struggle for their emancipation. . . .

* Least of all Engels! Cf. Selection 8, above.

The overthrow of the bourgeoisie can be achieved only by the proletariat becoming the *ruling class,* capable of crushing the inevitable and desperate resistance of the bourgeoisie, and of organizing *all* the working and exploited people for the new economic system. . . .

By educating the workers' party, Marxism educates the vanguard of the proletariat, capable of assuming power and *leading the whole people* to socialism, of directing and organizing the new system, of being the teacher, the guide, the leader of all the working and exploited people in organizing their social life without the bourgeoisie and against the bourgeoisie. By contrast, the opportunism now prevailing trains the members of the workers' party to be the representatives of the better-paid workers, who lose touch with the masses, "get along" fairly well under capitalism, and . . . renounce their role as revolutionary leaders of the people against the bourgeoisie. . . .

Only he is a Marxist who *extends* the recognition of the class struggle to the recognition of the *dictatorship of the proletariat.* . . .

Further. The essence of Marx's theory of the state has been mastered only by those who realize that the dictatorship of a *single* class is necessary not only for every class society in general, not only for the *proletariat* which has overthrown the bourgeoisie, but also for the entire *historical period* which separates capitalism from "classless society," from communism. Bourgeois states are most varied in form, but their essence is the same: all these states, whatever their form, in the final analysis are inevitably the *dictatorship of the bourgeoisie.* The transition from capitalism to communism is certainly bound to yield a tremendous abundance and variety of political forms, but the essence will inevitably be the same: *the dictatorship of the proletariat.* . . .

Democracy is of enormous importance to the working class in its struggle against the capitalists for its emancipation. But democracy is by no means a boundary not to be overstepped; it is only one of the stages on the road from feudalism to capitalism, and from capitalism to communism.

Democracy means equality. The great significance of the proletariat's struggle for equality and of equality as a slogan will be clear if we correctly interpret it as meaning the abolition of *classes*. But democracy means only *formal* equality. And as soon as equality is achieved for all members of society *in relation* to ownership of the means of production, that is, equality of labor and wages, humanity will inevitably be confronted with the question of advancing further, from formal equality to actual equality, i.e., to the operation of the rule "from each according to his ability, to each according to his needs." By what stages, by means of what practical measures humanity will proceed to this supreme aim we do not and cannot know. . . .

Here "quantity turns into quality": *such* a degree of democracy implies overstepping the boundaries of bourgeois society and beginning its socialist reorganization. If really *all* take part in the administration of the state, capitalism cannot retain its hold. The development of capitalism, in turn, creates the *preconditions* that *enable* really "all" to take part in the administration of the state. . . .

Capitalist culture has *created* large-scale production, factories, railways, the postal service, telephones, etc., and *on this basis* the great majority of the functions of the old "state power" have become so simplified and can be reduced to such exceedingly simple operations of registration, filing, and checking that they can be easily performed by every literate person, can quite easily be performed for ordinary "workmen's wages," and that these functions can (and must) be stripped of every shadow of privilege, of every semblance of "official grandeur."

All officials, without exception, elected and subject to recall *at any time,* their salaries reduced to the level of ordinary "workmen's wages"—these simple and "self-evident" democratic measures, while completely uniting the interests of the workers and the majority of the peasants, at the same time serve as a bridge leading from capitalism to socialism. . . .

Representative institutions remain, but there is *no* parliamentarism here as a special system, as the division of labor between the legislative and the executive, as a privileged position for the deputies. We cannot imagine democracy, even proletarian democracy, without representative institutions, but we can and *must* imagine democracy without parliamentarism. . . .

Abolishing the bureaucracy at once, everywhere and completely, is out of the question. It is a utopia. But to *smash* the old bureaucratic machine at once and to begin immediately to construct a new one that will make possible the gradual abolition of all bureaucracy—this is *not* a utopia, it is the experience of the Commune, the direct and immediate task of the revolutionary proletariat. . . .

We are not utopians, we do not "dream" of dispensing *at once* with all administration, with all subordination. These anarchist dreams, based upon incomprehension of the tasks of the proletarian dictatorship, are totally alien to Marxism, and, as a matter of fact, serve only to postpone the socialist revolution until people are different. No, we want the socialist revolution with people as they are now, with people who cannot dispense with subordination, control, and "foremen and accountants."

The subordination, however, must be to the armed vanguard of all the exploited and working people, i.e., to the proletariat. . . .

We, the workers, shall organize large-scale production on the basis of what capitalism has already created, relying on our own experience as workers, establishing strict, iron discipline backed up by the state power of the armed workers. We shall reduce the role of state officials to that of simply carrying out our instructions as responsible, revocable, modestly paid "foremen and accountants" (of course, with the aid of technicians of all sorts, types and degrees) . . . . Such a beginning, on the basis of large-scale production, will of itself lead to the gradual "withering away" of all bureaucracy, to the gradual creation of an order . . . under which the functions of control and accounting, becoming more and more simple, will be performed by each in turn, will then become a habit and will finally die out as the *special* functions of a special section of the population. . . .

Given these *economic* preconditions, it is quite possible, after the overthrow of the capitalists and the bureaucrats, to proceed immediately, overnight, to replace them in the *control* over production and distribution, in the work of *keeping account* of labor and products, by the armed workers, by the whole of the armed population. (The question of control and accounting should not be confused with the question of the scientifically trained staff of engineers, agronomists, and so on. These gentlemen are working today in obedience to the wishes of the capitalists, and will work even better tomorrow in obedience to the wishes of the armed workers.)

Accounting and control—that is *mainly* what is needed for the "smooth working," for the proper functioning, of the *first phase* of communist society. *All* citizens are transformed into hired employees of the state, which consists of the armed workers. *All* citizens become employees and workers of a *single* countrywide state "syndicate." All that is required is that they should work equally, do their proper share of work, and get equal pay. The accounting and control necessary for this have been *simplified* by capitalism to the utmost and reduced to the extraordinarily simple operations—which any literate person can perform—of supervising and recording, knowledge of the rules of arithmetic, and issuing appropriate receipts.

The whole of society will have become a single office and a single factory, with equality of labor and pay.

But this "factory" discipline, which the proletariat, after defeating the capitalists, after overthrowing the exploiters, will extend to the whole of society, is by no means our ideal, or our ultimate goal. It is only a necessary *step* for thoroughly cleaning society of all the infamies and abominations of capitalist exploitation, *and for further* progress.

From the moment all members of society, or at least the vast majority, have learned to administer the state *themselves,* have taken this work into their own hands, have organized control over the insignificant capitalist minority, over the gentry who wish to preserve their capitalist habits and over the workers who have been thoroughly corrupted by capitalism—from this moment the need for government of any kind begins to disappear altogether. . . .

For when *all* have learned to administer and actually do independently administer social production, independently keep accounts, and exercise control over the parasites, the sons of the wealthy, the swindlers and other "guardians of capitalist traditions," the escape from this popular accounting and control will inevitably become so incredibly difficult, such a rare exception, and will probably be accompanied by such swift and severe punishment (for the armed workers are practical men and not sentimental intellectuals, and they will scarcely allow anyone to trifle with them), that the *necessity* of observing the simple, fundamental rules of the community will very soon become a *habit*.

Then the door will be thrown wide open for the transition from the first phase of communist society to its higher phase, and with it to the complete withering away of the state.

Forward development does not proceed simply, directly and smoothly, toward "greater and greater democracy," as the liberal professors and petit-bourgeois opportunists would have us believe. No, forward development, i.e., development toward communism, proceeds through the dictatorship of the proletariat, and cannot do otherwise, for the *resistance* of the capitalist exploiters cannot be *broken* by anyone else or in any other way. . . .

Simultaneously with an immense expansion of democracy, which *for the first time* becomes democracy for the poor, democracy for the people, and not democracy for the moneybags, the dictatorship of the proletariat imposes a series of restrictions on the freedom of the oppressors, the exploiters, the capitalists. We must suppress them in order to free humanity from wage slavery, their resistance must be crushed by force; it is clear that there is no freedom and no democracy where there is suppression and where there is violence. . . .

Only in communist society, when the resistance of the capitalists has been completely crushed, when the capitalists have disappeared, when there are no classes (i.e., when there is no distinction between the members of society as regards their relation to the social means of production), *only* then "the state . . . ceases to exist," and *"it becomes possible to speak of freedom."* Only then will a truly complete democracy become possible and be realized, a democracy without any exceptions whatever. And only then will democracy begin to *wither away*, owing to the simple fact that, freed from capitalist slavery, from the untold horrors, savagery, absurdities, and infamies of capitalist exploitation, people will gradually *become accustomed* to observing the elementary rules of social intercourse that have been known for centuries and repeated for thousands of years in all copybook maxims. They will become accustomed to observing them without force, without coercion, without subordination, *without the special apparatus* for coercion called the state. . . .

Furthermore, during the *transition* from capitalism to communism suppression is *still* necessary, but it is now the suppression of the exploiting minority by the exploited majority. A special apparatus, a special machine for suppression, the "state," is *still* necessary, but this is now a transitional state. It is no longer a state in the proper sense of the word; for the suppression of the minority of exploiters by the majority of the wage slaves of *yesterday* is comparatively so easy, simple, and natural a task that it will entail far less bloodshed than the suppression of the risings of slaves, serfs, or wage laborers, and it will cost mankind far less. And it is compatible with the extension of democracy to such an overwhelming majority of the population that the need for a *special machine* of suppression will begin to disappear. Naturally, the exploiters are unable to suppress the people without a highly complex machine for performing this task, but *the people* can suppress the exploiters even with a very simple "machine," almost without a "machine," without a special apparatus, by the simple *organization of the armed people* (such as the Soviets of Workers' and Soldiers' Deputies, we would remark, running ahead) .

Lastly, only communism makes the state absolutely unnecessary, for there is *nobody* to be suppressed—"nobody" in the sense of a *class,* of a systematic struggle against a definite section of the population. We are not utopians, and do not in the least deny the possibility and inevitability of excesses on the part of *individual persons,* or the need to stop *such* excesses. In the first place, however, no special machine, no special apparatus of suppression, is needed for this; this will be done by the armed people themselves, as simply and as readily as any crowd of civilized people, even in modern society, interferes to put a stop to a scuffle or to prevent a woman from being assaulted. And, second, we know that the fundamental social cause of excesses, which consist in the violation of the rules of social intercourse, is the exploitation of the people, their want and their poverty. With the removal of this chief cause, excesses will inevitably begin to *"wither away."* We do not know how quickly and in what succession, but we do know they will wither away. With their withering away the state will also *wither away*. . . .

Marx not only most scrupulously takes account of the inevitable inequality of men, but he also takes into account the fact that the mere conversion of the means of production into the common property of the whole of society (commonly called "socialism") *does not remove* the defects of distribution and the inequality of "bourgeois right," which *continues to prevail* so long as products are divided "according to the amount of labor performed." . . .

In the first phase of communist society (usually called socialism) "bourgeois right" is *not* abolished in its entirety, but only in part, only in proportion to the economic revolution so far attained, i.e., only in respect of the means of production. "Bourgeois right" recognizes them as the private property of individuals. Socialism converts them into *common* property. *To that extent*—and to that extent alone—"bourgeois right" disappears.

However, it persists . . . in the capacity of regulator (determining factor) in the distribution of products and the allotment of labor among the members of society. The socialist principle, "He who does not work shall not eat," is *already* realized; the other socialist principle, "An equal amount of products for an equal amount of labor," is also *already* realized. But this is not yet communism, and it does not yet abolish "bourgeois right," which gives unequal individuals, in return for unequal amounts of labor, equal amounts of products.

This is a "defect," says Marx, but it is unavoidable in the first phase of communism; for if we are not to indulge in utopianism, we must not think that having overthrown capitalism people will at once learn to work for society *without any standard of right*. Besides, the abolition of capitalism *does not immediately create* the economic prerequisites for *such* a change.

Now, there is no other standard than that of "bourgeois right." To this extent, therefore, there still remains the need for a state, which, while safeguarding the common ownership of the means of production, would safeguard equality in labor and in the distribution of products.

The state withers away insofar as there are no longer any

capitalists, any classes, and, consequently, no *class* can be *suppressed.*

But the state has not yet completely withered away, since there still remains the safeguarding of "bourgeois right," which sanctifies actual inequality. For the state to wither away completely, complete communism is necessary.

The economic basis for the complete withering away of the state is such a high stage of development of communism at which the antithesis between mental and physical labor disappears, at which there consequently disappears one of the principal sources of modern *social* inequality—a source, moreover, which cannot on any account be removed immediately by the mere conversion of the means of production into public property, by the mere expropriation of the capitalists. . . .

But how rapidly this development will proceed, how soon it will reach the point of breaking away from the division of labor, of doing away with the antithesis between mental and physical labor, of transforming labor into "life's prime want"—we do not and *cannot* know.

That is why we are entitled to speak only of the inevitable withering away of the state, emphasizing the protracted nature of this process and its dependence upon the rapidity of development of the *higher phase* of communism, and leaving the question of the time required for, or the concrete forms of, the withering away quite open, because there is *no* material for answering these questions.

The state will be able to wither away completely when society adopts the rule: "From each according to his ability, to each according to his needs," i.e., when people have become so accustomed to observing the fundamental rules of social intercourse and when their labor has become so productive that they will voluntarily work *according to their ability.* "The narrow horizon of bourgeois right," which compels one to calculate with the heartlessness of a Shylock whether one has not worked half an hour more than somebody else, whether one is not getting less pay than somebody else—this narrow horizon will then be crossed. There will then be no need for society, in distributing products, to regulate the quantity to be received by each; each will take freely "according to his needs."

PART IV
THE BOLSHEVIK REVOLUTION AND THE FIRST "MARXIST" STATE

The Bolshevik Revolution was unquestionably Lenin's revolution —for it was he who planned the Bolsheviks' strategy for gaining power, who called for seizing power at the opportune moment, and who directed the utilizing of that power to maintain Bolshevik—i.e., Communist—domination through five years of economic collapse, foreign invasion, and civil war until he became incapacitated by his first stroke. In the process, much of what Lenin had earlier written concerning the state underwent rapid erosion until, one might say, "quantity turned into quality" and "Marxism-Leninism" became a system of human degradation and enslavement to the totalitarian state rather than the theory and practice of the overcoming of alienation and the liberation from the state. The major turning points of the first months of the revolution can be specified.

Lenin reached St. Petersburg on the night of April 16, 1917, after having traveled with the aid of Germany in a sealed railway car across German lines following the fall of the czar in the previous month. At that time a provisonal government under Prince Lvov was managing to rule, and the Bolsheviks (including Stalin and Trotsky) who had been in Russia during this time were inclined to acquiesce under the new government provided it would end Russian involvement in the war. On the first night following his arrival, Lenin delivered his "Theses on the Tasks of the Proletariat in the Present Revolution," in which he urged the Bolsheviks to revise their strategy and work toward a revolution which would place them in complete control over the destiny of Russia.

On April 22, Lenin's article "The Dual Power" appeared in Pravda; *in it he outlined his strategy for revolution. The basis of this strategy was the existence of two organs of power: on the one hand the Provisional Government (at the time controlled by Lvov and the bourgeoisie) and, on the other hand, the Soviets (i.e. Councils) of Workers' and Soldiers' Deputies. The soviets, which had first emerged as the predominant form of local revolutionary organization in the 1905 revolution, were reactivated in all major cities by the three chief socialist parties: the Bolsheviks, the Mensheviks, and the Socialist Revolutionaries. At the outset the Socialist Revolutionaries were by far the largest of the three parties and the Bolsheviks the smallest. Lenin's general strategy, then, was simply to increase the power of the soviets vis-à-vis the Provisional Government and that of the Bolsheviks vis-à-vis the other parties within the soviets.*

On September 25, Lenin wrote to the Central Committee of the St. Petersburg and Moscow committees of the Bolsheviks calling for an immediate seizure of power from the government, which was by then a coalition of the Socialist Revolutionaries and the Mensheviks and was led by the Socialist Revolutionary Alexander Kerensky. At the same time, Lenin wrote a letter entitled "Marxism and Insurrection" to the Central Committee of the Bolshevik wing of the Russian Social Democratic Labor party outlining both his arguments for the opportuneness of the moment and his tactics for the insurrection. The Central Committee of the Bolshevik faction decided on October 25 to adopt Lenin's resolution to seize power, and henceforth arrangements were made for what was to become known as the October Revolution.[1]

On November 7, 1917, the Bolsheviks ousted Kerensky's government and, with the help of the left-wing Socialist Revolutionaries, seized power in the name of the soviets. Lenin immediately issued decrees calling for peace, land reform, and the declaration of a Workers' and Peasants' (i.e., a soviet) government.

Meanwhile, shortly after the fall of the czar, the Provisional

1. The "October Revolution" occurred on October 25, 1917 (Old Style), or November 7, 1917 (New Style). We shall use New Style, i.e., Gregorian, dates throughout.

Government had announced the convocation of a Constituent Assembly and, after some postponements, the election was set for November 1917. The Bolsheviks agreed to allow the election to be held on schedule, on the basis of lists drawn up and distributed prior to the October Revolution. It is questionable whether, at the time of the election, the bulk of the population in the rural areas was aware of the full significance of the recent events in the main cities. Regardless, the Bolsheviks came in second behind the right-wing Socialist Revolutionaries, who, in fact, commanded an absolute majority of delegates to the Assembly.

The Constituent Assembly was called into session by the Soviet Government and opened in St. Petersburg on January 18, 1918. The opening session witnessed separate walkouts by the Bolsheviks and the left-wing Socialist Revolutionaries. The following day, Lenin drafted a decree dissolving the Assembly and thereby dissolved the only freely elected representative body in Russian history.

Following a relatively quiet year on the Eastern front, at the end of 1917 the Germans and the Bolsheviks agreed to a temporary armistice and began peace negotiations at the town of Brest-Litovsk, Poland. The chief negotiator for the Bolsheviks was Leon Trotsky, who used the talks as a forum for revolutionary propaganda, expecting, along with the majority of Bolsheviks, that the talks would eventually break off and the fighting resume. But on January 20, 1918, Lenin presented his "Theses on the Question of the Immediate Conclusion of a Separate and Annexationist Peace," in which he argued for Russian acceptance of the German conditions, which would include the loss of the Ukraine, the Baltic States, and Poland, in order to give the revolution the time it desperately needed to be able to consolidate its domestic position. Finally, following the signing, the left-wing Socialist Revolutionaries resigned from the cabinet and the government was entirely in the hands of the Bolsheviks, where it has remained ever since.

At the end of April 1918, with the Treaty of Brest-Litovsk ratified, Lenin turned to pressing problems of economic policy, increasing centralization and adopting numerous measures for *increasing industrialization, such as the introduction of piece-work and increasing the authority of the managers. Thus, just six months after the October Revolution, the ideas of workers' control over production and the elimination of alienation were being reduced to little if any importance in Soviet economic policy. The spring of 1918 also saw armed resistance to the authority of the Bolsheviks become widespread, and the first "White" armies were organized, marking the outbreak of the period of civil war, which was to last a full two years. The Bolsheviks reacted to this threat to their control by ousting all other socialist parties, except the left-wing Socialist Revolutionaries, from the soviets. When the latter party attempted a coup against the Bolsheviks that July, owing to their opposition to the peace treaty, they too were outlawed. Thus, not only the government, but now also the soviets, came under the complete control of the Communist party (the name having been changed at the Seventh Party Congress in March 1918), and thence the soviets themselves began their rapid decline in importance vis-à-vis the central government.*

18. LUXEMBURG:
LENINISM OR MARXISM?
—ROUND TWO

While serving a prison sentence, Rosa Luxemburg wrote her pamphlet
The Russian Revolution *(1918) in which she criticized the antidemo-*
cratic policies of the Bolsheviks. That she, along with Karl Liebknecht,
was the only leading Western European Social Democrat whose reputa-
tion was untarnished by the war made it doubly significant that she
should have been the one to speak out against the dictatorship of Lenin
and Trotsky. Yet, at the same time she was even harsher on those
Social Democrats who betrayed the international cause and aided their
governments' war policies. Admitting the great significance of the
Bolshevik Revolution, she exposed in no uncertain terms the Com-
munists' drift toward totalitarianism and criticized their failure to
establish a dialectical relationship between the Party and the working
masses such as had briefly existed in mid-1917.

The Russian Revolution *stands as Rosa Luxemburg's final testament*
to revolutionary and democratic Marxism and the spontaneity of the
working class. Insofar as she recognized the failures of Lenin with
respect to these, she pointed out what within six years would lead to
the triumph of Stalin and the victory of the counterrevolution of the
bureaucracy in Russia.

Fundamental Significance of the Russian Revolution

The Russian Revolution is the mightiest event of the world
war. Its outbreak, its unexampled radicalism, its enduring consequences, constitute the clearest condemnation of the lying
phrases which official Social Democracy so zealously supplied at
the beginning of the war as an ideological cover for German
imperialism's campaign of conquest. . . .

Moreover, for every thinking observer, these developments are
a decisive refutation of the doctrinaire theory which Kautsky
shared with the Government Social Democrats, according to

SOURCE: From **Rosa Luxemburg**, *The Russian Revolution* (Ann Arbor: University of Michigan Press, 1967).

which Russia, as an economically backward and predominantly agrarian land, was supposed not to be ripe for social revolution and proletarian dictatorship. This theory, which regards only a *bourgeois* revolution as feasible in Russia, is also the theory of the opportunist wing of the Russian labor movement, of the so-called Mensheviks. . . . And from this conception follow the tactics of the coalition of the socialists in Russia with bourgeois liberalism. . . . According to this view, if the revolution has set as its task the dictatorship of the proletariat, this is simply a mistake of the radical wing of the Russian labor movement, the Bolsheviks. . . .

Practically, this same doctrine represents an attempt to get rid of any responsibility for the course of the Russian Revolution, so far as that responsibility concerns the international, and especially the German, proletariat, and to deny the international connections of this revolution. It is not Russia's unripeness which has been proved by the events of the war and the Russian Revolution, but the unripeness of the German proletariat for the fulfillment of its historic tasks. And to make this fully clear is the first task of a critical examination of the Russian Revolution.

The fate of the revolution in Russia depended fully upon international events. That the Bolsheviks have based their policy entirely upon the world proletarian revolution is the clearest proof of their political farsightedness and firmness of principle and of the bold scope of their policies. . . .

It would be a crazy idea to think that every last thing done or left undone in an experiment with the dictatorship of the proletariat under such abnormal conditions represented the very pinnacle of perfection. . . .

To make this stand out clearly in all its fundamental aspects and consequences is the elementary duty of the socialists of all countries; for only on the background of this bitter knowledge can we measure the enormous magnitude of the responsibility of the international proletariat itself for the fate of the Russian Revolution. . . .

There is no doubt either that the wise heads at the helm of the Russian Revolution, that Lenin and Trotsky on their thorny path beset by traps of all kinds, have taken many a decisive step only with the greatest inner hesitation and with most violent inner opposition. And surely nothing can be further from their thoughts than to believe that all the things they have done or left undone under the conditions of bitter compulsion and necessity in the midst of the roaring whirlpool of events should be regarded by the International as a shining example of socialist policy toward which only uncritical admiration and zealous imitation are in order.

It would be no less wrong to fear that a critical examination of the road so far taken by the Russian Revolution would serve to weaken the respect for and the attractive power of the example of the Russian Revolution, which alone can overcome the fatal inertia of the German masses. Nothing is further from the truth. An awakening of the revolutionary energy of the working class in Germany can never again be called forth in the spirit of the guardianship methods of the German Social Democracy of late-lamented memory. It can never again be conjured forth by any spotless authority, be it that of our own "higher committees" or that of "the Russian example." Not by the creation of a revolutionary hurrah-spirit, but quite the contrary: only by an insight into all the fearful seriousness, all the complexity of the tasks involved, only as a result of political maturity and independence of spirit, only as a result of a capacity for critical judgment on the part of the masses, which capacity was systematically killed by Social Democracy for decades under various pretexts, only thus can the genuine capacity for historical action be born in the German proletariat. To concern one's self with a critical analysis of the Russian Revolution in all its historical connections is the best training for the German and the international working class for the tasks which confront them as an outgrowth of the present situation. . . .

In this situation, the Bolshevik tendency performs the historic service of having proclaimed from the very beginning, and having followed with iron consistency, those tactics which alone could save democracy and drive the revolution ahead. All power exclusively in the hands of the worker and peasant masses, in the hands of the soviets—this was indeed the only way out of the difficulty into which the revolution had gotten. . . .

The party of Lenin was thus the only one in Russia which grasped the true interest of the revolution in that first period. It was the element that drove the revolution forward, and thus it was the only party which really carried on a socialist policy. . . .

The real situation in which the Russian Revolution found itself narrowed down in a few months to the alternative: victory of the counterrevolution or dictatorship of the proletariat—Kaledin or Lenin. Such was the objective situation, just as it quickly presents itself in every revolution after the first intoxication is over, and as it presented itself in Russia as a result of the concrete, burning questions of peace and land, for which there was no solution within the framework of bourgeois revolution.

In this, the Russian Revolution has but confirmed the basic lesson of every great revolution, the law of its being, which decrees: either the revolution must advance at a rapid, stormy, and resolute tempo, break down all barriers with an iron hand, and place its goals ever further ahead, or it is quite soon thrown backward behind its feeble point of departure and suppressed by counterrevolution. . . .

Thereby the Bolsheviks solved the famous problem of "winning a majority of the people," which problem has ever weighed on the German Social Democracy like a nightmare. As bred-in-the-bone disciples of parliamentary cretinism, these German Social Democrats have sought to apply to revolutions the home-made wisdom of the parliamentary nursery: in order to carry anything, you must first have a majority. The same, they say, applies to revolution: first let's become a "majority." The true dialectic of revolutions, however, stands this wisdom of parliamentary moles on its head: not through a majority to revolutionary tactics, but through revolutionary tactics to a majority—that is the way the road runs. . . .

Only a party which knows how to lead, that is, to advance things, wins support in stormy times. The determination with which, at the decisive moment, Lenin and his comrades offered the only solution which could advance things ("all power in the hands of the proletariat and peasantry"), transformed them almost overnight from a persecuted, slandered, outlawed minority whose leader had to hide like Marat in cellars, into the absolute master of the situation.

Moreover, the Bolsheviks immediately set as the aim of their seizure of power a complete, far-reaching revolutionary program:

not the safeguarding of bourgeois democracy, but a dictatorship of the proletariat for the purpose of realizing socialism. Thereby they won for themselves the imperishable historic distinction of having for the first time proclaimed the final aim of socialism as the direct program of practical politics. . . .

Whatever a party could offer of courage, revolutionary far-sightedness and consistency in an historic hour, Lenin, Trotsky and the other comrades have given in good measure. All the revolutionary honor and capacity which Western Social Democracy lacked was represented by the Bolsheviks. Their October uprising was not only the actual salvation of the Russian Revolution; it was also the salvation of the honor of international socialism.

The Bolshevik Land Policy

. . . Surely the solution of the problem by the direct, immediate seizure and distribution of the land by the peasants was the shortest, simplest, most clean-cut formula to achieve two diverse things: to break down large landownership, and immediately to bind the peasants to the revolutionary government. As a political measure to fortify the proletarian socialist government, it was an excellent tactical move. Unfortunately, however, it had two sides to it; and the reverse side consisted in the fact that the direct seizure of the land by the peasants has in general nothing at all in common with socialist economy. . . .

Only the nationalization of the large landed estates, as the technically most advanced and most concentrated means and methods of agrarian production, can serve as the point of departure for the socialist mode of production on the land. Of course, it is not necessary to take away from the small peasant his parcel of land, and we can with confidence leave him to be won over voluntarily by the superior advantages of social production and to be persuaded of the advantages first of union in cooperatives and then finally of inclusion in the general socialized economy as a whole. Still, every socialist economic reform on the land must obviously begin with large and medium landownership. Here the property right must first of all be turned over to the nation, or to the state, which, with a socialist government, amounts to the same thing, for it is this alone which affords the possibility of organizing agricultural production in accord with the requirements of interrelated, large-scale socialist production. . . .

The nationalization of the large and middle-sized estates and the union of industry and agriculture—these are two fundamental requirements of any socialist economic reform, without which there is no socialism. . . .

Now the slogan launched by the Bolsheviks, immediate seizure and distribution of the land by the peasants, necessarily tended in the opposite direction. Not only is it not a socialist measure; it even cuts off the way to such measures; it piles up insurmountable obstacles to the socialist transformation of agrarian relations.

The seizure of the landed estates by the peasants according to the short and precise slogan of Lenin and his friends—"*Go and take the land for yourselves*"—simply led to the sudden, chaotic conversion of large landownership into peasant landownership. What was created is not social property but a new form of private property, namely, the breaking up of large estates into medium and small estates. . . .

In the course of the distribution of the land, social and economic inequality among the peasants was not eliminated but rather increased, and class antagonisms were further sharpened. This shift of power, however, took place to the *disadvantage* of the interests of the proletariat and of socialism. Formerly, there was only a small caste of noble and capitalist landed proprietors and a small minority of rich village bourgeoisie to oppose a socialist reform on the land. And their expropriation by a revolutionary mass movement of the people is mere child's play. But now, after the "seizure," as an opponent of any attempt at socialization of agrarian production, there is an enormous, newly developed, and powerful mass of owning peasants who will defend their newly won property with tooth and nail against every socialist attack. The question of the future socialization of agrarian economy—that is, any socialization of production in general in Russia—has now become a question of opposition and of struggle between the urban proletariat and the mass of the peasantry. . . .

The Leninist agrarian reform has created a new and powerful

layer of popular enemies of socialism in the countryside, enemies whose resistance will be much more dangerous and stubborn than that of the noble large landowners.

The Constituent Assembly

. . . The well-known dissolution of the Constituent Assembly . . . played an outstanding role in the policy of the Bolsheviks. This measure was decisive for their further position; to a certain extent, it represented a turning point in their tactics.

It is a fact that Lenin and his comrades were stormily demanding the calling of a Constituent Assembly up to the time of their October victory, and that the policy of dragging out this matter on the part of the Kerensky government constituted an article in the indictment of that government by the Bolsheviks and was the basis of some of their most violent attacks upon it. Indeed, Trotsky says in his interesting pamphlet *From October to Brest-Litovsk* that the October Revolution represented "the salvation of the Constituent Assembly" as well as of the revolution as a whole. . . .

And then, after these declarations, Lenin's first step after the October Revolution was . . . the dissolution of this same Constituent Assembly, to which it was supposed to be an entrance. . . . Trotsky [says:]

there was the circumstance that the elections themselves took place in the course of the first weeks after the October Revolution. The news of the change that had taken place spread rather slowly in concentric circles from the capital to the provinces and from the towns to the villages. The peasant masses in many places had little notion of what went on in Petrograd and Moscow. They voted for "Land and Freedom," and elected as their representatives in the land committees those who stood under the banner of the "Narodniki." . . . This state of affairs gives a clear idea of the extent to which the Constituent Assembly had lagged behind the development of the political struggle and the development of party groupings.

All of this is very fine and quite convincing. But one cannot help wondering how such clever people as Lenin and Trotsky failed to arrive at the conclusion which follows immediately from the above facts. Since the Constituent Assembly was elected long before the decisive turning point, the October Revolution, and its composition reflected the picture of the vanished past and not of the new state of affairs, then it follows automatically that the outgrown and therefore stillborn Constituent Assembly should have been annulled, and without delay, new elections to a new Constituent Assembly should have been arranged. They did not want to entrust, nor should they have entrusted, the fate of the revolution to an assemblage which reflected the Kerenskyan Russia of yesterday, of the period of vacillations and coalition with the bourgeoisie. Hence there was nothing left to do except to convoke an assembly that would issue forth out of the renewed Russia that had advanced further.

Instead of this, from the special inadequacy of the Constituent Assembly which came together in October, Trotsky draws a general conclusion concerning the inadequacy of any popular representation whatsoever which might come from universal popular elections during the revolution.

> Thanks to the open and direct struggle for governmental power [he writes], the laboring masses acquire in the shortest time an accumulation of political experience, and they climb rapidly from step to step in their political development. The bigger the country and the more rudimentary its technical apparatus, the less is the cumbersome mechanism of democratic institutions able to keep pace with this development.

Here we find the "mechanism of democratic institutions" as such called in question. . . . According to Trotsky's theory, every elected assembly reflects once and for all only the mental composition, political maturity, and mood of its electorate just at the moment when the latter goes to the polling place. . . . Any living mental connection between the representatives, once they have been elected, and the electorate, any permanent interaction between one and the other, is hereby denied. . . .

Yet . . . experience demonstrates quite the contrary: namely, that the living fluid of the popular mood continuously flows around the representative bodies, penetrates them, guides them. . . .

And is this ever-living influence of the mood and degree of political ripeness of the masses upon the elected bodies to be renounced in favor of a rigid scheme of party emblems and tickets in the very midst of revolution? Quite the contrary! It is precisely the revolution which creates by its glowing heat that delicate, vibrant, sensitive political atmosphere in which the waves of popular feeling, the pulse of popular life, work for the moment on the representative bodies in most wonderful fashion. . . .

"The cumbersome mechanism of democratic institutions" possesses a powerful corrective—namely, the living movement of the masses, their unending pressure. And the more democratic the institutions, the livelier and stronger the pulse beat of the political life of the masses, the more direct and complete is their influence—despite rigid party banners, outgrown tickets (electoral lists), etc. To be sure, every democratic institution has its limits and shortcomings, things which it doubtless shares with all other human institutions. But the remedy which Trotsky and Lenin have found, the elimination of democracy as such, is worse than the disease it is supposed to cure; for it stops up the very living source from which alone can come the correction of all the innate shortcomings of social institutions. That source is the active, untrammeled, energetic political life of the broadest masses of the people.

The Question of Suffrage

The Constituent Assembly and the suffrage law do not exhaust the matter. We did not consider above the destruction of the most important democratic guarantees of a healthy public life and of the political activity of the laboring masses: freedom of the press, the rights of association and assembly, which have been outlawed for all opponents of the Soviet regime. For these attacks (on democratic rights), the arguments of Trotsky cited above, on the cumbersome nature of democratic electoral bodies, are far from satisfactory. On the other hand, it is a well-known and indisputable fact that without a free and untrammeled press, without the unlimited right of association and assemblage, the rule of the broad mass of the people is entirely unthinkable.

The Problem of Dictatorship

Lenin says: the bourgeois state is an instrument of oppression of the working class; the socialist state, of the bourgeoisie. . . . This simplified view misses the most essential thing: bourgeois class rule has no need of the political training and education of the entire mass of the people, at least not beyond certain narrow limits. But for the proletarian dictatorship that is the life element, the very air without which it is not able to exist. . . .

. . . It is the very giant tasks which the Bolsheviks have undertaken with courage and determination that demand the most intensive political training of the masses and the accumulation of experience.

Freedom only for the supporters of the government, only for the members of one party—however numerous they may be—is no freedom at all. Freedom is always and exclusively freedom for the one who thinks differently. Not because of any fanatical concept of "justice" but because all that is instructive, wholesome and purifying in political freedom depends on this essential characteristic, and its effectiveness vanishes when "freedom" becomes a special privilege. . . .

The tacit assumption underlying the Lenin-Trotsky theory of the dictatorship is this: that the socialist transformation is something for which a ready-made formula lies completed in the pocket of the revolutionary party, which needs only to be carried out energetically in practice. This is, unfortunately—or perhaps fortunately—not the case. Far from being a sum of ready-made prescriptions which have only to be applied, the practical realization of socialism as an economic, social, and juridical system is something which lies completely hidden in the mists of the future. What we possess in our program is nothing but a few main signposts which indicate the general direction in which to look for the necessary measures, and the indications are mainly negative in character at that. Thus we know more or less what we must eliminate at the outset in order to free the road for a socialist economy. But when it comes to the nature of the thousand concrete, practical measures, large and small, necessary to introduce socialist principles into economy, law, and all social relationships, there is no key in any socialist party program or textbook. That is not a shortcoming but rather the very thing that makes scientific socialism superior to the utopian varieties.

. . . However, if such is the case, then it is clear that socialism by its very nature cannot be decreed or introduced by ukase. It has as its prerequisite a number of measures of force—against property, etc. The negative, the tearing down, can be decreed; the building up, the positive, cannot. . . . The whole mass of the people must take part in it. Otherwise, socialism will be decreed from behind a few official desks by a dozen intellectuals.

Public control is indispensably necessary. Otherwise the exchange of experiences remains only with the closed circle of the officials of the new regime. Corruption becomes inevitable. Socialism in life demands a complete spiritual transformation in the masses degraded by centuries of bourgeois class rule. Social instincts in place of egotistical ones, mass initiative in place of inertia, idealism which conquers all suffering, etc., etc. No one knows this better, describes it more penetratingly, repeats it more stubbornly than Lenin. But he is completely mistaken in the means he employs. Decree, dictatorial force of the factory overseer, draconic penalties, rule by terror—all these things are but palliatives. The only way to a rebirth is the school of public life itself, the most unlimited, the broadest democracy and public opinion. It is rule by terror which demoralizes.

When all this is eliminated, what really remains? In place of the representative bodies created by general, popular elections, Lenin and Trotsky have laid down the soviets as the only true representation of the laboring masses. But with the repression of political life in the land as a whole, life in the soviets must also become more and more crippled. Without general elections, without unrestricted freedom of press and assembly, without a free struggle of opinion, life dies out in every public institution, becomes a mere semblance of life, in which only the bureaucracy remains as the active element. Public life gradually falls asleep, a few dozen party leaders of inexhaustible energy and boundless experience direct and rule. Among them, in reality only a dozen outstanding heads do the leading and an elite of the working class is invited from time to time to meetings where they are to applaud the speeches of the leaders, and to approve proposed resolutions unanimously—at bottom, then, a clique affair—a dictatorship, to be sure, not the dictatorship of the proletariat, however, but only the dictatorship of a handful of politicians. . . .

The basic error of the Lenin-Trotsky theory is that they too, just like Kautsky, oppose dictatorship to democracy. "Dictatorship or democracy" is the way the question is put by Bolsheviks and Kautsky alike. The latter naturally decides in favor of "democracy," that is, of bourgeois democracy, precisely because he opposes it to the alternative of the socialist revolution. Lenin and Trotsky, on the other hand, decide in favor of dictatorship in contradistinction to democracy, and thereby, in favor of the dictatorship of a handful of persons, that is, in favor of dictatorship on the bourgeois model. They are two opposite poles, both alike being far removed from a genuine socialist policy. The proletariat, when it seizes power, can never follow the good advice of Kautsky, given on the pretext of the "unripeness of the country," the advice being to renounce the socialist revolution and devote itself to democracy. It cannot follow this advice without betraying thereby itself, the International, and the revolution. It should and must at once undertake socialist measures in the most energetic, unyielding and unhesitant fashion, in other words, exercise a dictatorship, but a dictatorship of the *class,* not of a party or of a clique—dictatorship of the class, that means in the broadest public form on the basis of the most active, unlimited participation of the mass of the people, of unlimited democracy.

"As Marxists," writes Trotsky, "we have never been idol worshipers of formal democracy." . . . All that that really means is: We have always distinguished the social kernel from the political form of *bourgeois* democracy; we have always revealed the hard kernel of social inequality and lack of freedom hidden under the sweet shell of formal equality and freedom—not in order to reject the latter but to spur the working class into not being satisfied with the shell, but rather, by conquering political power, to create a socialist democracy to replace bourgeois democracy—not to eliminate democracy altogether.

But socialist democracy is not something which begins only in the promised land after the foundations of socialist economy are created; it does not come as some sort of Christmas present for the worthy people who, in the interim, have loyally supported a handful of socialist dictators. Socialist democracy begins simultaneously with the beginnings of the destruction of class rule and of the construction of socialism. It begins at the very moment of the seizure of power by the socialist party. It is the same thing as the dictatorship of the proletariat.

Yes, dictatorship! But this dictatorship consists in the *manner of applying democracy,* not in its *elimination,* in energetic, resolute attacks upon the well-entrenched rights and economic relationships of bourgeois society, without which a socialist transformation cannot be accomplished. But this dictatorship must be the work of the *class* and not of a little leading minority in the name of the class—that is, it must proceed step by step out of the active participation of the masses; it must be under their direct influence, subjected to the control of complete public activity; it must arise out of the growing political training of the mass of the people.

Doubtless the Bolsheviks would have proceeded in this very way were it not that they suffered under the frightful compulsion of the world war, the German occupation and all the abnormal difficulties connected therewith, things which were inevitably bound to distort any socialist policy, however imbued it might be with the best intentions and the finest principles. . . .

Everything that happens in Russia is comprehensible and represents an inevitable chain of causes and effects, the starting point and end term of which are: the failure of the German proletariat and the occupation of Russia by German imperialism. It would be demanding something superhuman from Lenin and his comrades if we should expect of them that under such circumstances they should conjure forth the finest democracy, the most exemplary dictatorship of the proletariat, and a flourishing socialist economy. By their determined revolutionary stand, their exemplary strength in action, and their unbreakable loyalty to international socialism, they have contributed whatever could possibly be contributed under such devilishly hard conditions. The danger begins only when they make a virtue of necessity and want to freeze into a complete theoretical system all the tactics forced upon them by these fatal circumstances, and want to recommend them to the international proletariat as a model of socialist tactics. . . .*

Let the German Government Socialists cry that the rule of the Bolsheviks in Russia is a distorted expression of the dictatorship of the proletariat. If it was or is such, that is only because it is a

* Cf. Selection 19, below.

product of the behavior of the German proletariat, in itself a distorted expression of the socialist class struggle. All of us are subject to the laws of history, and it is only internationally that the socialist order of society can be realized. The Bolsheviks have shown that they are capable of everything that a genuine revolutionary party can contribute within the limits of the historical possibilities. They are not supposed to perform miracles. For a model and faultless proletarian revolution in an isolated land, exhausted by world war, strangled by imperialism, betrayed by the international proletariat, would be a miracle. . . .

19. LENIN:
THE THIRD INTERNATIONAL

By the end of 1918, the Soviet leadership felt that its successes provided it with the authority to found a third International, for which Lenin had been calling since August 1914. It was expected that the International would prove instrumental in achieving revolutionary successes in Western Europe, but in fact the history of its operations in the 1920s and 1930s testifies to the far more sinister purpose of supervising the successive defeats of the Western Communist parties. Be that as it may, with the appearance of imminent revolutionary successes in the days shortly following the end of the war, a third International was founded under the direction of Lenin and packed with Russian Communists.

The initial meeting, which was postponed a number of times for lack of sufficient non-Russian participation, was a complete tour de force for Lenin and the Russian Communist party, who completely dominated the fledgling organization. The most serious potential threat to their hegemony, the anticipated appearance of Rosa Luxemburg, was eliminated by her assassination by agents of the German government of Philipp Scheidemann, a Social Democrat and follower of Bernstein. Thus, with the only potential rival of stature equal to Lenin's removed, Lenin could organize the Third (or Communist) International with no opposition.

The Communist International was conceived from the outset as a tightly disciplined army of Communist parties, including those from the underdeveloped countries of Asia and Africa as well as from Europe, which would be directed and coordinated by Russia in the battle against bourgeois imperialist governments. That there was never any question concerning the dominance of the Russians, and of the International being organized along Bolshevik lines, is amply attested by Lenin's twenty-one "conditions" for admission to the organization, which were accepted by the International in 1920, excerpts from which follow.

The First, Inaugural Congress of the Communist International did not draw up precise conditions for the admission of parties into the Third International. . . .

SOURCE: From V. I. Lenin, "The Terms of Admission into the Communist International," in *Collected Works*, Vol. XXXI (Moscow: Progress Publishers, 1966) .

Parties and groups only recently affiliated to the Second International are more and more frequently applying for membership in the Third International, though they have not become really Communist. . . . Aware that the Second International is beyond hope, the intermediate parties and groups of the "Center" are trying to lean on the Communist International, which is steadily gaining in strength. At the same time, however, they hope to retain a degree of "autonomy" that will enable them to pursue their previous opportunist or "Centrist" policies. . . .

In certain circumstances, the Communist International may be faced with the danger of dilution by the influx of wavering and irresolute groups that have not as yet broken with their Second International ideology.

Besides, some of the big parties (Italy, Sweden), in which the majority have adopted the Communist standpoint, still contain a strong reformist and social-pacifist wing that is only waiting for an opportune moment to raise its head again, begin active sabotage of the proletarian revolution, and thereby help the bourgeoisie and the Second International. . . .

In view of all this, the Second World Congress deems it necessary to lay down absolutely precise terms for the admission of new parties, and also to set forth the obligations incurred by the parties already affiliated.

The Second Congress of the Communist International resolves that the following are the terms of Comintern membership:

1. Day-by-day propaganda and agitation must be genuinely Communist in character. All press organs belonging to the parties must be edited by reliable Communists who have given proof of their devotion to the cause of the proletarian revolution. . . .

2. Any organization that wishes to join the Communist International must consistently and systematically *dismiss* reformists and "Centrists" from positions of any responsibility in the working-class movement, . . . replacing them by reliable Communists. The fact that in some cases rank-and-file workers may at first have to replace "experienced" leaders should be no deterrent.

3. In countries where a state of siege or emergency legislation makes it impossible for Communists to conduct their activities legally, it is absolutely essential that legal and illegal work

should be combined. In almost all the countries of Europe and America, the class struggle is entering the phase of civil war. In these conditions, Communists can place no trust in bourgeois legality. They must *everywhere* build up a parallel illegal organization, which, at the decisive moment, will be in a position to help the Party fulfill its duty to the revolution.

4. Persistent and systematic propaganda and agitation must be conducted in the armed forces, and Communist cells formed in every military unit. In the main Communists will have to do this work illegally; failure to engage in it would be tantamount to a betrayal of their revolutionary duty and incompatible with membership in the Third International.

5. Regular and systematic agitation is indispensable in the countryside. The working class cannot consolidate its victory without support from at least a section of the farm laborers and poor peasants, and without neutralizing, through its policy, part of the rest of the rural population. . . . Communist activity in the countryside . . . should be conducted, in the main, through revolutionary *worker*-Communists who have contacts with the rural areas. To forgo this work or entrust it to unreliable semi-reformist elements is tantamount to renouncing the proletarian revolution.

6. It is the duty of any party wishing to belong to the Third International to expose not only avowed social-patriotism but also the falsehood and hypocrisy of social-pacifism. It must systematically demonstrate to the workers that without the revolutionary overthrow of capitalism, no international arbitration courts, no talk about a reduction of armaments, no "democratic" reorganization of the League of Nations will save mankind from new imperialist wars.

7. It is the duty of parties wishing to belong to the Communist International to recognize the need for a complete and absolute break with reformism and "Centrist" policy, and to conduct propaganda among the party membership for that break. Without this, a consistent Communist policy is impossible.

The Communist International demands imperatively and uncompromisingly that this break be effected at the earliest possible date. . . .

8. . . . Any party wishing to join the Third International

must ruthlessly expose the colonial machinations of the imperialists of its "own" country, most support—in deed, not merely in word—every colonial liberation movement, demand the expulsion of its compatriot imperialists from the colonies, inculcate in the hearts of the workers of its own country an attitude of true brotherhood with the working population of the colonies and the oppressed nations, and conduct systematic agitation among the armed forces against all oppression of the colonial peoples.

9. It is the duty of any party wishing to join the Communist International to conduct systematic and unflagging Communist work in the trade unions, cooperative societies, and other mass workers' organizations. Communist cells should be formed in the trade unions, and, by their sustained and unflagging work, win the unions over to the Communist cause. . . . The cells must be completely subordinate to the Party as a whole. . . .

13. Parties belonging to the Communist International must be organized on the principle of democratic *centralism*. In this period of acute civil war, the Communist parties can perform their duty only if they are organized in a most centralized manner, are marked by an iron discipline bordering on military discipline, and have strong and authoritative party centers invested with wide powers and enjoying the unanimous confidence of the membership.

14. Communist parties in countries where Communists can conduct their work legally must carry out periodic membership purges (reregistrations) with the aim of systematically ridding the party of petit-bourgeois elements that inevitably percolate into them.

15. It is the duty of any party wishing to join the Communist International selflessly to help any Soviet republic in its struggle against counterrevolutionary forces. Communist parties must conduct incessant propaganda urging the workers to refuse to transport war materials destined for the enemies of the Soviet republics; they must conduct legal or illegal propaganda in the armed forces dispatched to strangle the workers' republics, etc. . . .

17. All decisions of the Communist International's congresses and of its Executive Committee are binding on all affiliated parties. Operating in conditions of acute civil war, the Com-

munist International must be far more centralized than the Second International was. It stands to reason, however, that in every aspect of their work the Communist International and its Executive Committee must take into account the diversity of conditions in which the respective parties have to fight and work, and adopt decisions binding on all parties only on matters in which such decisions are possible.

18. In view of the foregoing, parties wishing to join the Communist International must change their name. Any party seeking affiliation must call itself the *Communist* party of the country in question (Section of the Third, Communist International). The question of a party's name is not merely a formality, but a matter of major political importance. The Communist International has declared a resolute war on the bourgeois world and all yellow Social Democratic parties. The difference between the Communist parties and the old and official "Social Democratic," or "socialist," parties, which have betrayed the banner of the working class, must be made absolutely clear to every rank-and-file worker. . . .

20.
"WAR COMMUNISM"

Through the Civil War period (1918–1920), the Bolsheviks were compelled to organize Russia as a military state. As the fighting neared its end, however, the policies of "War Communism" were not abated, and the militarism and terrorism of the civil wars became permanent aspects of Soviet life.

By 1920, it was recognized that the economy had fallen far below even the underdeveloped levels of the last years of the czarist regime, largely as a result of resistance to the Communist dictatorship by the technical intelligentsia and the former small- and medium-scale proprietors. Bukharin, in his book The Economics of the Transformation Period, *argued that the revitalization of the economy would require the subordination of these elements of society to the state apparatus, thereby inaugurating the rise of both the technical and the political bureaucracies over the working masses.*

At the same time, the Communists deemed it necessary to take the most drastic steps to avoid general economic collapse and thus the possible loss of the civil war. To this end, Trotsky advocated the use of state terrorism against recalcitrant elements in the population, as well as the imposition of military discipline on the working classes.

Also at about the same time, Lenin wrote his polemical Left-Wing Communism: An Infantile Disorder *(April–May 1920), in which he attacked the growing chorus of Marxist critics opposing the centralization of authority, bureaucratization, militarization, and terrorization adopted by the Communists. It is especially significant that most of this criticism emanated from the left, thereby testifying to Lenin's clear turn toward strict authoritarian methods. The "dictatorship" that was to be the means for the liberation of the masses was turning out—as many could already see—to be another state machine for their enslavement.*

The three parts of this selection are taken from the works mentioned of Bukharin and Lenin and from Trotsky's Terrorism and Communism *(1920).*

BUKHARIN: ON ECONOMICS

. . . One cannot simply "take possession" of the old economic apparatus. Anarchy in production, or . . . the "revolutionary disintegration of industry" is a historically inevitable stage. . . . Certainly, from the absolute standpoint it would be fine if the revolution and the breakdown of the old production relationships were not accompanied by any collapse of the technical relations of production. But . . . the scientific analysis of them tells us that the period of this collapse is historically inevitable and historically necessary.

The collapse of the *technical* hierarchy . . . exerts pressure in turn on the condition of the forces of production. The forces of production are fused with the relationships of production in a definite system of the social organization of labor. Consequently, the collapse of the "apparatus" must inevitably be followed by a further decline in the forces of production. In this way the process of further negative reproduction is extraordinarily accelerated. . . .

From the above analysis it follows that the "restoration of industry" which capitalistic utopians dream about is impossible on the basis of the old capitalistic relationships, which are flying apart. The only remedy is for the lower links of the system, the basic productive force of capitalist society, the working class, to assume a dominant position in the organization of social labor. In other words, the establishment of communism is the prerequisite for a rebirth of society. . . .

We have seen that that which for society as a whole constitutes a condition of its further existence represents for the proletariat an organizational problem which it must solve in practice. In this period the proletariat must *actively build* socialism and at the same time, in the process of this building, educate itself anew. This task can be met only with the help of specific methods with

SOURCE: From N. Bukharin. *The Economics of the Transformation Period* (1920), trans. from the German by Robert V. Daniels, in *A Documentary History of Communism,* Vol. I (New York: Random House, 1960). Reprinted by permission.

methods of *organized* labor. But these methods have already been prepared in the development of capitalism. . . .

Socialism as an organized system must be built by the proletariat as the organized collective subject. Whereas the process of the growth of capitalism was elemental nature, the process of building communism is to a high degree a conscious, i.e., organized process. . . . The epoch of building communism will therefore inevitably be the epoch of planned and organized labor; the proletariat will fulfill its tasks as social-technical tasks of building a new society, tasks which are consciously posed and consciously fulfilled. . . .

In this period the proletariat educates itself, closes ranks, and organizes itself as a class with tremendous intensity and swiftness. . . . But the problem of the social organization of production consists of *new combinations of the old elements.* . . .

The ex-bourgeois group of organizers and the *technical* intelligentsia which stands beneath it are material which is obviously necessary for the reconstruction period: it is the social deposit of organizational and technical-scientific experience. It is indeed apparent that both these categories must be regrouped. How and under what circumstances is this possible?

We wish to point out above all that this is the decisive—one could say basic—question for our structure. . . .

We know that earlier types of social ties survive in the heads of the people in these categories, in the form of an ideological and physiological residue. "Healthy capitalism" hovers before them with the persistency of a fixed idea. The prerequisite for the possibility of a new social combination of production is therefore to dissolve the earlier types of associations in the heads of this technical intelligentsia. . . .

Above all: Under the proletarian state power and with the proletarian nationalization of production the process of creating surplus value, a specific feature of bourgeois society, ceases. . . . With the dialectical transformation of the bourgeois dictatorship into the proletarian, the technical function of the intelligentsia changes from a capitalistic to a social function of labor, and the creation of surplus value changes . . . into the creation of surplus product, which is applied to the expansion of the reproduction fund. Paralleling this, the *basic type of association* changes, *although in the hierarchical scheme the intelligentsia occupies the same "middle" place.* For the highest authority in the state economy is the concentrated social power of the proletariat. Here the technical intelligentsia on the one hand stands above the great mass of the working class, but on the other is in the last analysis *subordinated* to its collective will, the expression of which is found in the proletariat's organization of the state economy. . . .

It is indeed clear that formally the same method is necessary for the working class as for the bourgeoisie of the era of state capitalism. This organizational method consists of the coordination of all proletarian organizations by means of the most all-embracing organization possible, i.e., by means of the state organization of the working class, by means of the *proletarian Soviet state.* The "governmentalization" of the trade unions and in practice the governmentalization of all the mass organizations of the proletariat result from the inner logic of the transformation process itself. The smallest germ cell of the labor apparatus must become a support for the general process of organization, which is planfully led and conducted by the collective reason of the working class, which has its material embodiment in the highest, all-embracing organization, its state power. Thus the system of state capitalism is dialectically transformed into its own opposite, into the governmental form of workers' socialism. . . .

TROTSKY: ON TERRORISM

. . . The problem of revolution, as of war, consists in breaking the will of the foe, forcing him to capitulate and to accept the conditions of the conqueror. . . . but in contradistinction to a meeting, a dispute, or a congress, the revolution carries out its object by means of the employment of material resources—though to a less degree than war. The bourgeoisie itself conquered power by means of revolts, and consolidated it by the civil war. In the peaceful period, it retains power by means of a system of repression. As long as class society, founded on the most

SOURCE: From Leon Trotsky, *Terrorism and Communism,* 1920, trans. into English as *Dictatorship vs. Democracy: A Reply to Karl Kautsky* (New York: Workers' Party of America, 1922).

deep-rooted antagonisms, continues to exist, repression remains a necessary means of breaking the will of the opposing side.

Even if, in one country or another, the dictatorship of the proletariat grew up within the external framework of democracy, this would by no means avert the civil war. The question as to who is to rule the country, i.e., of the life or death of the bourgeoisie, will be decided not by references to the paragraphs of the constitution, but by the employment of all forms of violence. . . .

The revolution "logically" does not demand terrorism, just as "logically" it does not demand an armed insurrection. . . . But the revolution does require of the revolutionary class that it should attain its end by all methods at its disposal—if necessary, by an armed rising: if required, by terrorism. A revolutionary class which has conquered power with arms in its hands is bound to, and will, suppress, rifle in hand, all attempts to tear the power out of its hands. . . .

The question of the form of repression, or of its degree, of course, is not one of "principle." It is a question of expediency. . . .

Terror can be very efficient against a reactionary class which does not want to leave the scene of operations. *Intimidation* is a powerful weapon of policy, both internationally and internally. War, like revolution, is founded upon intimidation. A victorious war, generally speaking, destroys only an insignificant part of the conquered army, intimidating the remainder and breaking their will. The revolution works in the same way: it kills individuals, and intimidates thousands. In this sense, the Red Terror is not distinguishable from the armed insurrection, the direct continuation of which it represents. The State terror of a revolutionary class can be condemned "morally" only by a man who, as a principle, rejects (in words) every form of violence whatsoever—consequently, every war and every rising. For this one has to be merely and simply a hypocritical Quaker.

"But, in that case, in what do your tactics differ from the tactics of czarism?" we are asked, by the high priests of Liberalism and Kautskyanism.

You do not understand this, holy men? We shall explain to you. The terror of czarism was directed against the proletariat. The gendarmerie of czarism throttled the workers who were fighting for the Socialist order. Our Extraordinary Commissions shoot landlords, capitalists, and generals who are striving to restore the capitalist order. Do you grasp this—distinction? Yes? For us Communists it is quite sufficient. . . .

The Labor State collects numerous staffs of employees, to a considerable extent from the ranks of the bourgeoisie and the bourgeois educated classes. To the extent that they become disciplined under the Soviet system, they find representation in the Soviet system. . . . With the final triumph of the social revolution, the Soviet system will expand and include the whole population, in order thereby to lose the characteristics of a form of State, and melt away into a mighty system of producing and consuming cooperation. . . .

In the hands of the party is concentrated the general control. It does not immediately administer, since its apparatus is not adapted for this purpose. But it has the final word in all fundamental questions. Further, our practice has led to the result that, in all moot questions, generally—conflicts between departments and personal conflicts within departments—the last word belongs to the Central Committee of the party. This affords extreme economy of time and energy, and in the most difficult and complicated circumstances gives a guarantee for the necessary unity of action. Such a regime is possible only in the presence of the unquestioned authority of the party, and the faultlessness of its discipline. . . .

If the organization of the new society can be reduced fundamentally to the reorganization of labor, the organization of labor signifies in its turn the correct introduction of general labor service. This problem is in no way met by measures of a purely departmental and administrative character. It touches the very foundations of economic life and the social structure. It finds itself in conflict with the most powerful psychological habits and prejudices. . . .

The introduction of compulsory labor service is unthinkable without the application, to a greater or less degree, of the methods of militarization of labor. This term at once brings us into the region of the greatest possible superstitions and outcries from the opposition. . . .

The foundations of the militarization of labor are those forms of State compulsion without which the replacement of capitalist economy by the Socialist will forever remain an empty sound. Why do we speak of *militarization?* Of course, this is only an analogy—but an analogy very rich in content. No social organization except the army has ever considered itself justified in subordinating citizens to itself in such a measure, and to control them by its will on all sides to such a degree, as the State of the proletarian dictatorship considers itself justified in doing, and does. Only the army—just because in its way it used to decide questions of the life or death of nations, States, and ruling classes—was endowed with powers of demanding from each and all complete submission to its problems, aims, regulations, and orders. And it achieved this to the greater degree the more the problems of military organization coincided with the requirements of social development.

The question of the life or death of Soviet Russia is at present being settled on the labor front; our economic, and together with them our professional and productive organizations, have the right to demand from their members all that devotion, discipline, and executive thoroughness, which hitherto only the army required. . . .

We can have no way to Socialism except by the authoritative regulation of the economic forces and resources of the country, and the centralized distribution of labor power in harmony with the general State plan. The Labor State considers itself empowered to send every worker to the place where his work is necessary. And not one serious Socialist will begin to deny to the Labor State the right to lay its hand upon the worker who refuses to execute his labor duty. . . .

The young Socialist State requires trade unions, not for a struggle for better conditions of labor—that is the task of the social and State organizations as a whole—but to organize the working class for the ends of production, to educate, discipline, distribute, group, retain certain categories and certain workers at their posts for fixed periods—in a word, hand in hand with the State to exercise their authority in order to lead the workers into the framework of a single economic plan. To defend, under such conditions, the "freedom" of labor means to defend fruitless, helpless, absolutely unregulated searches for better conditions, unsystematic, chaotic changes from factory to factory, in a hungry country, in conditions of terrible disorganization of the transport and food apparatus. What except the complete collapse of the working class and complete economic anarchy could be the result of the stupid attempt to reconcile bourgeois freedom of labor with proletarian socialization of the means of production? . . .

LENIN: ON "LEFT-COMMUNISM"

It is, I think, almost universally realized at present that the Bolsheviks could not have retained power for two and a half months, let alone two and a half years, without the most rigorous and truly iron discipline in our Party, or without the fullest and unreserved support from the entire mass of the working class, that is, from all thinking, honest, devoted, and influential elements in it, capable of leading the backward strata or carrying the latter along with them.

The dictatorship of the proletariat means a most determined and most ruthless war waged by the new class against a *more powerful* enemy, the bourgeoisie, whose resistance is increased *tenfold* by their overthrow (even if only in a single country), and whose power lies not only in the strength of international capital, the strength and durability of their international connections, but also in the *force of habit,* in the strength of *small-scale production.* . . . Victory over the bourgeoisie is impossible without a long, stubborn, and desperate life-and-death struggle which calls for tenacity, discipline, and a single and inflexible will.

I repeat: the experience of the victorious dictatorship of the proletariat in Russia has clearly shown . . . that absolute centralization and rigorous discipline in the proletariat are an essential condition of victory over the bourgeoisie. . . .

How is the discipline of the proletariat's revolutionary party maintained? How is it tested? How is it reinforced? First, by the class consciousness of the proletarian vanguard and by its devotion to the revolution, by its tenacity, self-sacrifice, and heroism.

SOURCE: From V. I. Lenin, *"Left-Wing" Communism: An Infantile Disorder* (April–May 1920), in *Collected Works,* Vol. XXXI (Moscow: Progress Publishers, 1966).

Second, by its ability to link up, maintain the closest contact, and—if you wish—merge, in certain measure, with the broadest masses of the working people—primarily with the proletariat, *but also with the nonproletarian* masses of working people. Third, by the correctness of the political leadership exercised by this vanguard, by the correctness of its political strategy and tactics, provided the broad masses have seen, *from their own experience,* that they are correct. Without these conditions, discipline in a revolutionary party really capable of being the party of the advanced class, whose mission it is to overthrow the bourgeoisie and transform the whole of society, cannot be achieved. Without these conditions, all attempts to establish discipline inevitably fall flat and end up in phrase-mongering and clowning. On the other hand, these conditions cannot emerge at once. They are created only by prolonged effort and hard-won experience. Their creation is facilitated by a correct revolutionary theory, which, in its turn, is not a dogma, but assumes final shape only in close connection with the practical activity of a truly mass and truly revolutionary movement. . . .

To reject compromises "on principle," to reject the permissibility of compromises in general, no matter of what kind, is childishness, which it is difficult even to consider seriously. . . .

There are different kinds of compromises. One must be able to analyze the situation and the concrete conditions of each compromise, or of each variety of compromise. One must learn to distinguish between a man who has given up his money and firearms to bandits so as to lessen the evil they can do and to facilitate their capture and execution, and a man who gives his money and firearms to bandits so as to share in the loot. In politics this is by no means always as elementary as it is in this childishly simple example. However, anyone who is out to think up for the workers some kind of recipe that will provide them with cut-and-dried solutions for all contingencies, or promises that the policy of the revolutionary proletariat will never come up against difficult or complex situations, is simply a charlatan. . . .

The mere presentation of the question—"dictatorship of the party *or* dictatorship of the class; dictatorship (party) of the leaders, *or* dictatorship (party) of the masses?"—testifies to most incredibly and hopelessly muddled thinking. . . .

Repudiation of the Party principle and of Party discipline—that is what the opposition has *arrived at*. And this is tantamount to completely disarming the proletariat *in the interests of the bourgeoisie*. It all adds up to that petit-bourgeois diffuseness and instability, that incapacity for sustained effort, unity, and organized action, which, if encouraged, must inevitably destroy any proletarian revolutionary movement. From the standpoint of communism, repudiation of the party principle means attempting to leap from the eve of capitalism's collapse (in Germany), not to the lower or the intermediate phase of communism, but to the higher. We in Russia (in the third year since the overthrow of the bourgeoisie) are making the first steps in the transition from capitalism to socialism or the lower stage of communism. Classes still remain, and will remain everywhere *for years after* the proletariat's conquest of power. Perhaps in Britain, where there is no peasantry (but where proprietors exist), this period may be shorter. The abolition of classes means not merely ousting the landowners and the capitalists—that is something we accomplished with comparative ease—it also means *abolishing the small commodity producers,* and they *cannot be ousted,* or crushed; we *must learn to live* with them. They can (and must) be transformed and reeducated only by means of very prolonged, slow, and cautious organizational work. They surround the proletariat on every side with a petit-bourgeois atmosphere, which permeates and corrupts the proletariat, and constantly causes among the proletariat relapses into petit-bourgeois spinelessness, disunity, individualism, and alternating moods of exaltation and dejection. The strictest centralization and discipline are required within the political party of the proletariat in order to counteract this, in order that the *organizational* role of the proletariat (and that is its *principal* role) may be exercised correctly, successfully, and victoriously. The dictatorship of the proletariat means a persistent struggle—bloody and bloodless, violent and peaceful, military and economic, educational and administrative—against the forces and traditions of the old society. The force of habit in millions and tens of millions is a most formidable force. Without a party of iron that has been tempered in the struggle, a party enjoying the confidence of all honest people in the class in question, a party capable of watching and influencing the mood of the masses, such a struggle cannot be waged successfully. It is a thousand times easier to vanquish the centralized big bourgeoisie than to "vanquish" the millions upon millions of petit proprietors; however, through their ordinary, everyday, imperceptible, elusive, and demoralizing activities, they produce the *very* results which the bourgeoisie need and which tend to *restore* the bourgeoisie. Whoever brings about even the slightest weakening of the iron discipline of the party of the proletariat (especially during its dictatorship) is actually aiding the bourgeoisie against the proletariat.

21.
REVOLUTION WITHIN
THE REVOLUTION

The rigors of "War Communism" eventually led to widespread dissatisfaction with Lenin's policies, both within and without the Communist party. By early March 1921, an uprising occurred at the naval base on the island of Kronstadt in the Baltic. The Kronstadt sailors, who had a longstanding reputation for "left-wing Communism," revolted in protest against the repressive policies of the Communist government, thereby offering the first revolutionary, rather than counterrevolutionary, challenge to Lenin's dictatorship. The manifesto of the Kronstadt Commune accused the Communists of having betrayed the "Second" (i.e., the October) Revolution (the "First" Revolution being that of March 1917) and called upon the populace to carry out a "Third" Revolution, this time directed against the Communists, in the name of the general liberation of the laboring classes. When the uprising failed to find sufficient support among the populace it was speedily crushed.

In the wake of the events at Kronstadt, Lenin moved swiftly to end all factional disputes within the Communist party and to require total obedience to the Party leadership. Thus, the last forum of legal dissent was in principle eliminated from the Soviet political system, although intra-Party factions were not in fact entirely eliminated until Stalin's complete triumph in 1929.

With the Party and the populace in his complete control, Lenin then moved to bring an end to the period of "War Communism," in an attempt to ease the widespread discontent, especially among the peasantry, whose interests had been systematically neglected during the Civil War years. In April 1921, Lenin introduced the New Economic Policy (NEP), which began to reemphasize the needs of the countryside versus those of the previously favored urban centers, and which allowed for the limited restoration of capitalism, even allowing foreign investment in Russia on a concessionary basis! The policy was, of course, designed to gain time for further economic development (beginning with the recovery of prewar levels), and thus began a more realistic period of slow recovery, requiring many compromises with the newly legalized capitalists, or "Nepmen."

The selections illustrate these three important events as they led to the solidification of Lenin's dictatorship.

THE KRONSTADT COMMUNE: *WHAT WE ARE FIGHTING FOR*

. . . After carrying out the October Revolution, the working class hoped to achieve emancipation. The result has been to create even greater enslavement of the individual man.

The power of the police-gendarme monarchy has gone into the hands of the Communist usurpers, who instead of freedom offer the toilers the constant fear of falling into the torture chambers of the Cheka, which in their horrors surpass many times the gendarme administration of the czarist regime.

Bayonets, bullets, and the harsh shouts of the *oprichniki*** of the Cheka are what the working man of Soviet Russia has got after a multitude of struggles and sufferings. The glorious arms of labor's state—the sickle and hammer—have actually been replaced by the Communist authorities with the bayonet and the barred window, for the sake of preserving the calm, carefree life of the new bureaucracy of Communist commissars and officials.

But the most hateful and criminal thing which the Communists have created is moral servitude: they laid their hands even on the inner life of the toilers and compelled them to think only in the Communist way.

With the aid of militarized trade unions they have bound the workers to their benches, and have made labor not into a joy but into a new slavery. To the protests of the peasants, expressed in spontaneous uprisings, and of the workers, who are compelled to strike by the circumstances of their life, they answer with mass executions and bloodthirstiness, in which they are not surpassed by the czarist generals.

Labor's Russia, the first country to raise the banner of the liberation of labor, has been continuously covered with the blood

SOURCE: From "What We Are Fighting For," *News* of the Kronstadt Temporary Revolutionary Committee, March 8, 1921, reprinted in *The Truth about Kronstadt* (Prague: Volia Rossii, 1921) ; trans. Robert V. Daniels, in *A Documentary History of Communism* (New York: Random House, 1960). Reprinted by permission.

* *Oprichniki:* originally, members of the sixteenth-century police force of Czar Ivan the Terrible.

of the people who have been tortured for the glory of Communist domination. In this sea of blood the Communists are drowning all the great and glowing pledges and slogans of labor's revolution.

It has been sketched out more and more sharply, and now has become obvious, that the Russian Communist party is not the defender of the toilers which it represents itself to be; the interests of the working nation are alien to it; having attained power, it is afraid only of losing it, and therefore all means are allowed: slander, violence, deceit, murder, vengeance on the families of rebels.

The enduring patience of the toilers has reached its end.

Here and there the glow of insurrection has illuminated the country in its struggle against oppression and violence. Strikes by the workers have flared up, but the Bolshevik *okhrana** has not slept and has taken every measure to forestall and suppress the unavoidable third revolution. . . .

There can be no middle ground. Victory or death!

Red Kronstadt gives this example, threatening the counter-revolutionaries of the right and of the left.

The new revolutionary upheaval has been accomplished here. Here the banner of insurrection has been raised for liberation from the three-year violence and oppression of Communist domination, which has overshadowed the three-century yoke of monarchism. Here at Kronstadt the first stone of the third revolution has been laid, to break off the last fetters on the toiling masses and open a new broad road for socialist creativity.

This new revolution will rouse the laboring masses of the East and of the West, since it shows an example of the new socialist construction as opposed to the Communists' barrackroom "creativity" and directly convinces the laboring masses abroad that everything created here up to now by the will of the workers and peasants was not socialism.

The first step has been completed without a single shot, without a drop of blood. The toilers do not need blood. They will shed it only at a moment of self-defense. Firmness is enough for us, in spite of the outrageous actions of the Communists, to

---

* *Okhrana:* originally, the czarist secret police.

confine ourselves to isolating them from social life, so that their evil false agitation will not interfere with revolutionary work.

The workers and peasants unreservedly go forward, abandoning behind them the Constituent Assembly with its bourgeois stratum and the dictatorship of the party of the Communists with its Cheka men, its state capitalism, its hangman's noose encircling the neck of the masses and threatening to strangle them for good.

The present overturn at last makes it possible for the toilers to have their freely elected soviets, working without any violent party pressure, and remake the state trade unions into free associations of workers, peasants, and the laboring intelligentsia. At last the policeman's club of the Communist autocracy has been broken.

LENIN: DICTATORSHIP WITHIN THE ONE-PARTY DICTATORSHIP

1. The Congress calls the attention of all members of the Party to the fact that the unity and cohesion of the ranks of the Party, the guarantee of complete mutual confidence among Party members and genuine teamwork that really embodies the unanimity of will of the vanguard of the proletariat, are particularly essential at the present time, when a number of circumstances are increasing the vacillation among the petit-bourgeois population of the country.

2. Notwithstanding this . . . certain signs of factionalism had been apparent in the Party—the formation of groups with separate platforms, striving to a certain degree to segregate and create their own group discipline. . . .

All class-conscious workers must clearly realize that factionalism of any kind is harmful and impermissible, for no matter how members of individual groups may desire to safeguard Party unity, factionalism in practice inevitably leads to the weakening of teamwork and to intensified and repeated attempts by the enemies of the governing Party, who have wormed their way into

SOURCE: From V. I. Lenin, "Preliminary Draft Resolution of the Tenth Party Congress of the R.C.P. on Party Unity" (March 1921), in *Collected Works*, Vol. XXXII (Moscow: Progress Publishers, 1965) .

it, to widen the cleavage and to use it for counterrevolutionary purposes.

The way the enemies of the proletariat take advantage of every deviation from a thoroughly consistent communist line was perhaps most strikingly shown in the case of the Kronstadt mutiny, when the bourgeois counterrevolutionaries and whiteguards in all countries of the world immediately expressed their readiness to accept the slogans of the Soviet system, if only they might thereby secure the overthrow of the dictatorship of the proletariat in Russia, and when the Socialist Revolutionaries and the bourgeois counterrevolutionaries in general resorted in Kronstadt to slogans calling for an insurrection against the Soviet Government of Russia ostensibly in the interest of the Soviet power. These facts fully prove that the whiteguards strive, and are able, to disguise themselves as Communists, and even as the most left-wing Communists, solely for the purpose of weakening and destroying the bulwark of the proletarian revolution in Russia. . . .

3. . . . These enemies, having realized the hopelessness of counter-revolution under an openly whiteguard flag, are now doing their utmost to utilize the disagreements within the Russian Communist party and to further the counterrevolution in one way or another by transferring power to a political group which is outwardly closest to recognition of the Soviet power.

Propaganda must also teach the lessons of preceding revolutions, in which the counterrevolution made a point of supporting the opposition to the extreme revolutionary party which stood closest to the latter, in order to undermine and overthrow the revolutionary dictatorship and thus pave the way for the subsequent complete victory of the counterrevolution, of the capitalists and landowners.

4. In the practical struggle against factionalism, every organization of the Party must take strict measures to prevent all factional actions. Criticism of the Party's shortcomings, which is absolutely necessary, must be conducted in such a way that every practical proposal shall be submitted immediately, without any delay, in the most precise form possible, for consideration and decision to the leading local and central bodies of the Party. Moreover, every critic must see to it that the form of his criticism

takes account of the position of the Party, surrounded as it is by a ring of enemies, and that the content of his criticism is such that, by directly participating in Soviet and Party work, he can test the rectification of the errors of the Party or of individual Party members in practice. . . .

6. The Congress, therefore, hereby declares dissolved and orders the immediate dissolution of all groups without exception formed on the basis of one platform or another. . . . Nonobservance of this decision of the Congress shall entail unconditional and instant expulsion from the Party.

7. In order to ensure strict discipline within the Party and in all Soviet work and to secure the maximum unanimity in eliminating all factionalism, the Congress authorizes the Central Committee, in cases of breach of discipline or of a revival or toleration of factionalism, to apply all Party penalties, including expulsion, and in regard to members of the Central Committee, reduction to the status of alternate members and, as an extreme measure, expulsion from the Party. . . .

LENIN: THE NEW ECONOMIC POLICY

. . . The Civil War of 1918–1920 aggravated the havoc in the country, retarded the restoration of its productive forces, and bled the proletariat more than any other class. To this was added the 1920 crop failure, the fodder shortage and the loss of cattle, which still further retarded the rehabilitation of transport and industry, because, among other things, it interfered with the employment of peasants' horses for carting wood, our main type of fuel.

As a result, the political situation in the spring of 1921 was such that immediate, very resolute, and urgent measures had to be taken to improve the condition of the peasants and to increase their productive forces.

Why the peasants and not the workers?

Because you need grain and fuel to improve the condition of the workers. This is the biggest "hitch" at the present time, from

SOURCE: From V. I. Lenin, "The Tax in Kind (The Significance of the New Policy and Its Conditions)" (April 1921), in *Collected Works*, Vol. XXXII (Moscow: Progress Publishers, 1965).

the standpoint of the economy as a whole. For it is impossible to increase the production and collection of grain and the storage and delivery of fuel except by improving the condition of the peasantry, and raising their productive forces. We must start with the peasantry. Those who fail to understand this, and think this putting the peasantry in the forefront is "renunciation" of the dictatorship of the proletariat, or something like that, simply do not stop to think, and allow themselves to be swayed by the power of words. The dictatorship of the proletariat is the direction of policy by the proletariat. The proletariat, as the leading and ruling class, must be able to direct policy in such a way as to solve first the most urgent and "vexed" problem. The most urgent thing at the present time is to take measures that will immediately increase the productive forces of peasant farming. Only *in this way* will it be possible to improve the condition of the workers, strengthen the alliance between the workers and peasants, and consolidate the dictatorship of the proletariat. The proletarian or representative of the proletariat who *refused* to improve the condition of the workers *in this way* would *in fact* prove himself to be an accomplice of the whiteguards and the capitalists; to refuse to do it in this way means putting the craft interests of the workers above their class interests, and sacrificing the interests of the whole of the working class, its dictatorship, its alliance with the peasantry against the landowners and capitalists, and its leading role in the struggle for the emancipation of labor from the yoke of capital, for the sake of an immediate, short-term, and partial advantage for the workers.

Thus, the first thing we need is immediate and serious measures to raise the productive forces of the peasantry.

This cannot be done without making important changes in our food policy. One such change was the replacement of the surplus appropriation system by the tax in kind, which implies a free market, at least in local economic exchange, after the tax has been paid.

What is the essence of this change? . . .

The tax in kind is one of the forms of transition from that peculiar War Communism, which was forced on us by extreme want, ruin, and war, to regular socialist exchange of products. The latter, in its turn, is one of the forms of transition from socialism, with the peculiar features due to the predominantly small-peasant population, to communism.

Under this peculiar War Communism we actually took from the peasant all his surpluses—and sometimes even a part of his necessaries—to meet the requirements of the army and sustain the workers. Most of it we took on loan, for paper money. But for that, we would not have beaten the landowners and capitalists in a ruined small-peasant country. The fact that we did (in spite of the help our exploiters got from the most powerful countries of the world) shows the miracles of herosim the workers and peasants can perform in the struggle for their emancipation. . . .

It was the war and the ruin that forced us into War Communism. It was not, and could not be, a policy that corresponded to the economic tasks of the proletariat. It was a makeshift. The correct policy of the proletariat exercising its dictatorship in a small-peasant country is to obtain grain in exchange for the manufactured goods the peasant needs. That is the only kind of food policy that corresponds to the tasks of the proletariat, and can strengthen the foundations of socialism and lead to its complete victory.

The tax in kind is a transition to this policy. We are still so ruined and crushed by the burden of war (which was on but yesterday and could break out anew tomorrow, owing to the rapacity and malice of the capitalists) that we cannot give the peasant manufactured goods in return for *all* the grain we need. Being aware of this, we are introducing the tax in kind, that is, we shall take the minimum of grain we require (for the army and the workers) in the form of a tax and obtain the rest in exchange for manufactured goods.

There is something else we must not forget. Our poverty and ruin are so great that we cannot restore large-scale socialist state industry *at one stroke*. This can be done with large stocks of grain and fuel in the big industrial centers, replacement of worn-out machinery, and so on. Experience has convinced us that this cannot be done at one stroke, and we know that after the ruinous imperialist war even the wealthiest and most advanced countries will be able to solve this problem only over a fairly long period of years. Hence, it is necessary, to a certain extent, to help to restore *small* industry, which does not demand of the state machines large stocks of raw material, fuel and food, and which can immediately render some assistance to peasant farming and increase its productive forces right away.

What is to be the effect of all this?

It is the revival of the petit bourgeoisie and of capitalism on the basis of some freedom of trade (if only local). That much is certain and it is ridiculous to shut our eyes to it.

Is it necessary? Can it be justified? Is it not dangerous? . . .

Is it to give the small peasant *all* he needs of the goods produced by large-scale socialist industries in exchange for his grain and raw materials? This would be the most desirable and "correct" policy—and we have started on it. But we cannot supply *all* the goods, very far from it; nor shall we be able to do so very soon—at all events not until we complete the first stage of the electrification of the whole country. What is to be done? One way is to try to prohibit entirely, to put the lock on all development of private, nonstate exchange, i.e., trade, i.e., capitalism, which is inevitable with millions of small producers. But such a policy would be foolish and suicidal for the party that tried to apply it. It would be foolish because it is economically impossible. It would be suicidal because the party that tried to apply it would meet with inevitable disater. Let us admit it: some Communists have sinned "in thought, word and deed" by adopting just *such* a policy. We shall try to rectify these mistakes, and this must be done without fail, otherwise things will come to a very sorry state.

The alternative (and this is the only sensible and the last *possible* policy) is not to try to prohibit or put the lock on the development of capitalism, but to channel it into *state capitalism*. This is economically possible, for state capitalism exists—in varying form and degree—wherever there are elements of unrestricted trade and capitalism in general.

Can the Soviet state and the dictatorship of the proletariat be combined with state capitalism? Are they compatible?

Of course they are. This is exactly what I argued in May 1918. I hope I had proved it then. I had also proved that state capitalism is a step forward compared with the small-proprietor (both small patriarchal and petit-bourgeois) element. Those who compare state capitalism only with socialism commit a host of mistakes, for in the present political and economic circumstances it is essential to compare state capitalism also with petit-bourgeois production.

The whole problem—in theoretical and practical terms—is to find the correct methods of directing the development of capitalism (which is to some extent and for some time inevitable) into the channels of state capitalism, and to determine how we are to hedge it about with conditions to ensure its transformation into socialism in the near future. . . .

By "implanting" state capitalism in the form of concessions, the Soviet government strengthens large-scale production as against petit production, advanced production as against backward production, and machine production as against hand production. . . . The moderate and cautious application of the concessions policy will undoubtedly help us quickly to improve (to a modest extent) the state of industry and the condition of the workers and peasants. We shall, of course, have all this at the price of certain sacrifices and the surrender to the capitalist of many millions of poods of very valuable products. The scale and the conditions under which concessions cease to be a danger and are turned to our advantage depend on the relation of forces and are decided in the struggle, for concessions are also a form of struggle, and are a continuation of the class struggle in another form, and in no circumstances are they a substitution of class peace for class war. Practice will determine the methods of struggle.

Compared with other forms of state capitalism within the Soviet system, concessions are perhaps the most simple and clear-cut form of state capitalism. It involves a formal written agreement with the most civilized, advanced, West European capitalism. . . . We pay a certain "tribute" to world capitalism; we "ransom" ourselves under certain arrangements, thereby immediately stabilizing the Soviet power and improving our economic conditions. The whole difficulty with concessions is giving the proper consideration and appraisal of all the circumstances when concluding a concession agreement, and then seeing that it is fulfilled. . . .

Since the tax in kind means the free sale of surplus grain (over and above that taken in the form of the tax), we must exert every effort to direct *this* development of capitalism—for a free market *is* development of capitalism—into the channels of cooperative capitalism. It resembles state capitalism in that it facilitates accounting, control, supervision, and the establishment of contractual relations between the state (in this case the Soviet state) and the capitalist. Cooperative trade is more advantageous and useful than private trade not only for the above-mentioned reasons, but also because it facilitates the association and organization of millions of people, and eventually of the entire population, and this in its turn is an enormous gain from the standpoint of the subsequent transition from state capitalism to socialism.

Let us make a comparison of concessions and cooperatives as forms of state capitalism. Concessions are based on large-scale machine industry; cooperatives are based on small, handicraft, and partly even on patriarchal industry. Each concession agreement affects one capitalist, firm, syndicate, cartel or trust. Cooperative societies embrace many thousands and even millions of small proprietors. Concessions allow and even imply a definite agreement for a specified period. Cooperative societies allow of neither. It is much easier to repeal the law on the cooperatives than to annul a concession agreement, but the annulment of an agreement means a sudden rupture of the practical relations of economic alliance, or economic coexistence, with the capitalist, whereas the repeal of the law on the cooperatives, or any law, for that matter, does not immediately break off the practical coexistence of Soviet power and the small capitalists, nor, in general, is it able to break off the actual economic relations. It is easy to "keep an eye" on a concessionaire but not on the cooperators. The transition from concessions to socialism is a transition from one form of large-scale production to another. The transition from small proprietor cooperatives to socialism is a transition from small to large-scale production, i.e., it is more complicated, but, if successful, is capable of embracing wider masses of the population, and pulling up the deeper and more tenacious roots of the old, presocialist, and even precapitalist relations, which most stubbornly resist all "innovations." The concessions policy, if successful, will give us a few model—compared with our own— large enterprises built on the level of modern advance capitalism. After a few decades these enterprises will revert to us in their entirety. The cooperative policy, if successful, will result in raising the small economy and in facilitating its transition, within an indefinite period, to large-scale production on the basis of voluntary association. . . .

If we are successfully to solve the problem of our immediate transition to socialism, we must understand what *intermediary* paths, methods, means, and instruments are required for the transition from *precapitalist* relations to socialism. That is the whole point. . . .

Inasmuch as we are as yet unable to pass directly from small production to socialism, some capitalism is inevitable as the elemental product of small production and exchange; so that we must utilize capitalism (particularly by directing it into the channels of state capitalism) as the intermediary link between small production and socialism, as a means, a path, and a method of increasing the productive forces. . . .

We must do everything possible to develop trade at all costs, without being afraid of capitalism, because the limits we have put to it (the expropriation of the landowners and of the bourgeoisie in the economy, the rule of the workers and peasants in politics) are sufficiently narrow and "moderate." This is the fundamental idea and economic significance of the tax in kind. . . .

PART V
STALIN AND THE
BETRAYAL OF THE
RUSSIAN REVOLUTION

The period covered by this section includes the years during which Lenin struggled against both his fading health and the Frankenstein (Stalin) he had come to realize he had created; a second period in which, following Lenin's death in 1924, Stalin triumphed over Trotsky, his only serious rival, and assumed the mantle of "Marxist-Leninist" Orthodoxy while turning the dead Lenin into a god and himself into his only prophet; a third period, ending in 1929, in which, one by one, the remaining Bolshevik leaders were eliminated from possible contention; and fourth, the period from 1929 until his death in 1953 in which Stalin drastically remade Soviet society by forcing the development of heavy industry and the collectivization of agriculture, the opposition to both of which was mercilessly crushed; by encouraging the growth of the new class of managers and bureaucrats necessary to the industrialization drive; and by systematically eliminating all vestiges of revolutionary democracy and socialist egalitarianism and replacing these with the ubiquitous terrorism of the secret police apparatus.

Recognizing the enormous difficulty of illustrating briefly the deviation of Stalin's U.S.S.R. from the goals of Marxian Communism and from the "withering away" of the state promised by Engels and Lenin,[1] we would like to mention the following as being the major nodal points in that betrayal of the Revolution.

Lenin's unsuccessful struggle against Stalin was followed, in

1. Cf. Selection 17, above.

*fact even before the former's death, by Stalin's eminently success-
ful drive to eliminate Trotsky from contention for the succession.
As early as the end of 1923, with Lenin incapacitated, a major
split had emerged in the Russian Communist party over the problem of its increasing bureaucratization. By then there was neither
workers' democracy for the masses nor elective democracy for the
Party; nearly all positions had become appointive, with the effect
that the Party apparatus had become increasingly defensive, conservative, and increasingly beholden to Stalin, who had become
the chief spokesman for the apparatus. Although Lenin lay
seriously ill at the time, rumors had spread of a great improvement in his health and of his plans to return to lead the fight
against bureaucratization. With the support of a large number
of respected Bolsheviks, including the secret support of Lenin,
Trotsky initiated the struggle for the adoption of an antibureau-
cratic "New Course," but found himself isolated within the Central Committee, with Zinoviev and Kamenev backing Stalin. Trotsky, nonetheless, had seen to it that the Party Politburo had passed
a resolution proposing major reforms, and he then published an
open letter advocating its support against the expected criticism
by the apparatus. This letter of December 8, 1923, brought the
controversy out into the open, but the New Course proposal was
defeated at the Thirteenth Party Conference, which Stalin was
able to manipulate, just a few days before Lenin's death.[2] This
early defeat in fact virtually ended Trotsky's chances for deposing
the future dictator, although there was to be a protracted struggle
between the two men until Trotsky's exile in 1929 and his murder in 1940.*

*Following Lenin's death on January 21, 1924, Stalin moved
swiftly to assume for himself the mantle of the sole authoritative
interpreter of Lenin's ideas. This became apparent with his
lectures* The Foundations of Leninism, *delivered in April of that
year. From that time on his ascendancy could not be stopped.*

*By the fall of that same year, Stalin stepped up his attack on
Trotsky by attempting to demonstrate an unbridgeable gulf between Trotsky and Lenin concerning the U.S.S.R.'s role with*

2. The Party conferences were held a few months prior to the scheduled
opening of the upcoming Party congresses, so that the top leadership could
decide all important questions in advance.

respect to revolutionary movements in other countries. Textually, his argument proceeds on the basis of views expressed by Trotsky as early as 1906 (and subsequently abandoned in many cases), and the fact of Trotsky's previous affiliation with the Mensheviks (until 1917) was turned by Stalin into an allegation of complete opposition between the two men. More importantly, however, Stalin's argument for "socialism in one country" on the basis of the alleged "law of the uneven development of capitalism" (i.e., the claim that in the West the revolutionary period of 1918–1922 had passed and that the bourgeoisie in those countries had managed to stabilize the situation) served as a pretext to withdraw support from those Western Communists who favored immediate revolution during what was in fact a period of economic stagnation and political chaos. Objectively speaking, no time could have been more propitious for revolution in Germany, with the middle classes ruined by runaway inflation, large-scale unemployment that showed no signs of abating and a government powerless to mobilize the nation's resources or command the respect of the people. But the rigid control exercised by Moscow over the German Communist party made it impossible for the revolutionary elements within that party to become anything more than splinter groups, which were therefore easily defeated. Stalin even audaciously claimed at that time that the "moral support" of the Western European working class was all that the U.S.S.R. needed for the foreseeable future. What was developing in this policy was the self-aggrandizement of Stalin and the U.S.S.R. at the expense of the non-Russian revolutionary movements; for the revolutionary success of a movement as significant as, say, the German, could certainly have been expected to produce a rival claim to Stalin's for control of the world Communist movement.

Between 1924 and 1929, Stalin continued Lenin's New Economic Policy[3] *as he worked toward absolute supremacy within the Party. Having vanquished Trotsky as early as 1924, he turned his attention the following year to the opposition headed by Zinoviev and Kamenev, who by then were also arguing the case against bureaucratization as destructive of the Party and rendering it incapable of relating to the broad masses of the people. At*

---

3. Cf. Selection 21, above, Lenin on the NEP.

this time Bukharin served as Stalin's spokesman against Zinoviev and Kamenev; it was not to be until Stalin's campaign against Bukharin's "Right Opposition" in 1929 that his last potential rival would be eliminated.

Thus, only by 1929 could Stalin finally abandon the NEP and begin forced industrialization under the First Five-Year Plan (made retroactive to October 1928), with a totally subservient Party to work his will on the populace. The major thrust of the Plan was toward intensive industrialization and the collectivization of agriculure, defended on the basis that it had now become essential to develop heavy industry, regardless of the human cost. As one consequence of the new emphasis being placed upon rapid industrialization, it was recognized that trained technicians were of essential importance to the Soviet state, thereby accelerating the growth of the new elite class of technical and political bureaucrats. A second consequence was the immediate order to collectivize the peasantry, which was vehemently resisted by the kulaks, i.e., the moderately well-off peasants, with the eventual starvation of tens of millions of animals and millions of Russians in the early 1930s.

At the same time, recognizing that the Five-Year Plan would produce opposition among the intellectuals, Stalin moved swiftly against those philosophers who he expected might challenge his interpretation of Marxism-Leninism. In April 1929 he had the Second All-Union Congress of Marxist-Leninist Scientific Research Institutions require all intellectuals (including scientists as well as philosophers) to subordinate their views to the official line of Marxist-Leninist interpretation. At the same time, large numbers of intellectuals, from both within and outside the Party, were imprisoned for their alleged failure to accept the official line with the appropriate enthusiasm. Thus began the Party interference in Soviet science that was to cripple scientific progress in the U.S.S.R. for the next two decades.

By 1931, Stalin was prepared to eliminate the last few vestiges of industrial democracy and egalitarianism and replace them with strict managerial control and a broad policy of incentives to reward, and thereby to stratify, the working class. There thus began the fetishism of the Plan. In so doing, Stalin was, of course, responding to a growing need of any technological society for the elimination of egalitarianism. Nonetheless, such bourgeois practices were adopted by Stalin under the smoke screen of the continually repeated avowal that such "Marxist-Leninist" principles would produce the future victory of Communism. It is interesting to note that, in the process, Stalin replaced the Marxian idea that productive relations condition all other social relations with the doctrine that the Party and the Soviet state can achieve any goal they set themselves; i.e., Stalin replaced the leading role of economic relations with the glorification of the state, the Party, and, of course, himself. Thus was begun Stalin's characteristic elevation of the "subjective factors" into a position of preeminence over the "objective factors," such that the Soviet Union was now held to be "invincible."

In July 1934, at the Seventeenth Party Congress, Stalin spoke in glowing terms of the successes of the First Five-Year Plan, attributing them primarily to the leadership of the Party and the discipline it had instilled in the populace. Under the guise of claiming these as successes of "Marxism," Stalin initiated a general attack upon egalitarianism, ending with the telling remark that "it is time it was understood that Marxism is the enemy of equalization." It was also about this time that Stalin and his followers began extolling the Party Line as the foremost weapon of Soviet successes, thereby making any opposition to the line tantamount to sabotage. Thus was laid the groundwork for the Party purges which were to follow within two years.

Having already proclaimed, in the name of "Marxism-Leninism," a stratified society which was to be led by a carefully chosen and docile elite, Stalin next began a campaign to instill in the populace a "socialist patriotism," featuring the extolling of Russian history, which was, wherever possible, interpreted "socialistically." Thus, besides inventing still another way of demanding an increase in the sacrifices of the toiling masses, Stalin added one more foundation stone for the forthcoming purges by making all actions even remotely critical of the Party and its omniscient leader tantamount to treason.

In 1935, still another method was found to ensure the exceeding of the planned production quotas: the extolling of "Heroes of

Labor," the so-called Stakhanovites, named after Alexei Stakhanov, the first worker to be so honored for his extraordinary contributions to the "building of socialism" (he cut 102 tons of coal in a single shift, roughly fourteen times the established quota). There followed a period of intense propaganda directed toward "Stakhanovizing" the Soviet working class. We see in this movement the utter abasement of Marxian humanism and its replacement by the conception of "New Socialist Man" as nothing more than an extremely efficient machine. One is irresistibly reminded of Marx's descriptions of the struggle of the bourgeoisie to increase the exploitation of labor to the maximum level short of destroying the proletariat altogether or of forcing it to revolt. The chief difference, of course, was that in the U.S.S.R. the exploited laborers lived in a "socialist" society.

The assassination in 1934 of Sergei Kirov, Stalin's heir apparent, was the pretext for his inaugurating the purges both of the Party and of foreign Communists living in the U.S.S.R. Beginning in 1936 and lasting until 1939, these purges eventually decimated the Party and then spread far beyond it to permeate every stratum of Soviet society. By the end of the purge period the Party and the country were in abject subservience to Stalin and entirely in the control of his secret police apparatus, the notorious NKVD. In the process, all the leading Bolsheviks—e.g., Zinoviev, Kamenev, and Bukharin—were executed, after having been tortured to the point of "confessing" their—and others'—"crimes" against the U.S.S.R. There followed, by 1939, Stalin's rewriting of history on the basis of these confessions and the raising of Stalin to godlike status. Trotsky was murdered by a Comintern agent in 1940 after having spoken out against Stalin's betrayal of the Revolution and of the Bolsheviks, and thus there was no one left who could even conceivably challenge Stalin.

During the 1930s the most critical question for Soviet foreign policy was the rise of Fascism in Europe. The Soviet relation to Fascism developed in essentially three stages prior to the outbreak of the Second World War. First came the period of the "struggle" between the Nazis and the German Communists during the waning years of the Weimar Republic, ending with the order in late 1932 from Stalin that the Communists prepare to go underground, i.e., that they anticipate and not oppose a Nazi election victory, *above all refusing to cooperate with the Social Democrats to prevent this disaster. Hitler's takeover was then followed by some two years of vicious propaganda attacks against the Social Democrats, who were, of course, blamed for the Nazi victory despite their consistent opposition to Hitler. Secondly, by 1935 it had become rather clear that Nazi Germany was indeed a threat to the existence of the Soviet state, and so Stalin switched course and enjoined the Communist parties of Europe to cooperate with the parties of the non-Communist Left in forming "United (or Popular) Fronts" in parliamentary democracies such as France and Spain. This stage is best typified by Stalin's maneuverings during the Spanish Civil War, in which the Popular Front government was given the choice of either succumbing to Communist control or having Soviet aid withheld, thereby ensuring its defeat by the Fascists. That is, Stalin demanded the liquidation of the non-Communist Left in Spain, primarily the Anarchists and those Marxists not controlled by the Comintern (i.e., the so-called Trotskyites) as the price of limited military and diplomatic assistance. Finally, the third stage was that inaugurated by the signing of the Stalin-Hitler Pact of August 1939, which was the signal for the German and Russian advances into Poland and Hitler's engaging the Western democracies in a war in which Russia had agreed to remain neutral. Stalin, of course, eagerly sought the defeat of the Western democracies, prior to the anticipated future struggle for world domination between the U.S.S.R. and Nazi Germany. Finally, after the German attack on Russia in June 1941 and the ultimate victory of the Allies four years later, Russia gained control over the small states of Eastern Europe and the cold war with the United States began. The last period of Stalin's regime, until his death in 1953, was in no respects less harsh than the earlier ones. The captive peoples of Eastern and Central Europe, as well as the Soviet intelligentsia, suffered repeated hardships under the heel of the Soviet secret police, while Stalin was preparing, at the time of his death, a purge which was reportedly to surpass even that of the late 1930s.*

Admittedly, the selections which comprise this chapter can barely begin to illustrate the salient characteristics of Stalin's betrayal of the Russian Revolution and of Marx's humanism.

22. LENIN:
NOTES ON THE STRUGGLE
WITH STALIN

Lenin's last months, from his first stroke in May 1922 to his death in January 1924, are in many ways the most epochal of his life, for his partial recoveries and subsequent relapses are closely interwined with a growing realization that the Revolution he had made was becoming misguided and possibly even betrayed by his eventual successor.

Recognizing as early as the Eleventh Party Congress (March 1922) that "the essential is not in institutions, not in reorganizations, not in new decrees but in the selection of personnel and in checking performance . . . the gap between the grandeur of the tasks imposed on our poverty, not only material but also cultural,"[1] Lenin began to sense that the forces now emerging were slipping beyond his control. He coupled his criticism of the men around him with uncompromising attacks upon the Mensheviks and Socialist Revolutionaries, but it was beginning to dawn upon him that there was something seriously wrong with the Communists themselves. He excoriated the inadequacies of the Soviet government and especially the bureaucratic inefficiency that was choking the vital breath of the Revolution.

At the same Congress Stalin was appointed to the newly created position of Party General Secretary—a mistake that was to prove fatal to both the Revolution and Lenin himself. A week following the announcement of this appointment, Lenin proposed that Trotsky be made deputy chairman of the Council of People's Commissars, and thus the designated heir apparent, but Trotsky refused.[2]

Two months later (May 26) Lenin had his first stroke. His summerlong convalescence yielded a partial recovery, and he returned to work in Moscow on October 2, but by November 20 he announced that the work he had formerly done would be handled—except in an emergency —by Tsyurupa, Rykov, and Kamenev.[3] This triumvirate, then, was

SOURCE: From V. I. Lenin, *Collected Works*, Vol. XXXVI, and Vol. XLV (Moscow: Progress Publishers) , 1966 and 1970, respectively.

1. V. I. Lenin, *Collected Works*, Vol. XXXVI (Moscow: Progress Publishers, 1966), pp. 573–574.
2. Cf. Robert Payne, *The Life and Death of Lenin* (New York: Avon Books, 1965) , p. 471.
3. V. I. Lenin, *Collected Works*, Vol. XXXIII (Moscow: Progress Publishers, 1966) , p. 435.

Lenin's second choice for the succession. On December 16 he suffered his second stroke, and from that moment he no longer was to possess the power to guide Russia's destiny.

In the weeks following his second stroke, Lenin brooded over the problems he knew he would not be able to solve, and resolved that he would use the time left him to try to effect future policy on the most pressing problems. His first concern was the growing power of the Central Committee, which was devoid of any working class members, Stalin's increasing domination within the Central Committee, and the possibility of an open split between him and Trotsky. Lenin thus proposed drastically increasing the size of the Central Committee to fifty or even a hundred members, and that the bulk of these new members be recruited from the working class rather than from the intelligentsia or from the already existing Party cadres (the lower ranks of which were increasingly beholden to Stalin as the latter's power over the Party visibly grew). This proposal—and the warning against Stalin's ambitions—constitutes the material of Lenin's first dictated letter following his second stroke, dated December 23-25, 1922 (he was allowed by his doctors to dictate for only five minutes a day), which was addressed to the forthcoming Twelfth Party Congress, due to meet the following spring. This first letter deals with the two most important items: his evaluation of the individuals around him (including a decidedly negative one of Stalin) and his plan to end the dictatorship of the leaders over the party as a whole, a dictatorship which had been, of course, of his own making.[4]

Following the "Letter to the Congress," Lenin dictated an endorsement of Trotsky's plan—which he had earlier rejected—to entrust executive power to the State Planning Commission, which need not consist solely of Communists, but which would be made up of individuals picked on the basis of their technical abilities. This, in effect, was a proposal to replace the power of the Soviets (dominated by the Communist party and its Central Committee) with that of a body over which Stalin would have no control.

By the end of December 1922, Lenin turned to the problem of "Great-Russian chauvinism," i.e., the continuation of czarist imperialism under Communist rule, most eagerly pursued by the "Russified non-Russian," i.e., Stalin. The immediate problem concerned events in Georgia, which was at that time officially autonomous. G. K. Orjonikidze had led Soviet troops against the Georgian Soviet government in an action in which hundreds were killed and thousands jailed. Stalin, under

4. Cf. Selection 21, above, on Lenin's dictatorship within the R.C.P.

criticism for his support of Orjonikidze, then sent Secret Police Chief
F. E. Dzerzhinsky to investigate, with instructions to submit a report
exonerating Orjonikidze. In short, Stalin, who was himself a Georgian,
was pursuing a policy of conquest of non-Russian areas, in express violation of Lenin's well-known and longstanding insistence on the strictest
maintenance of the autonomy of weaker areas. Lenin, in his note
of December 30, 1922, admits his prior neglect of the nationalities
question, which he now sees as having been of disservice to the Revolution. His criticisms of Great-Russian chauvinism, and of Stalin, Orjonikidze, and Dzerzhinsky by name, are clear and unambiguous. There
could be no doubt that by then the fate of Stalin's ambitions depended
entirely upon Lenin's health.

By January 4, 1923, Lenin declared his intention of removing Stalin
from the post of Party General Secretary, which was stated in the post-
script added to the "Letter to the Congress."

Lenin's distrust and fear of Stalin was by no means ill-founded, nor
was that of Stalin for Lenin. On December 22, 1922, just six days after
his second stroke, Lenin dictated to his wife (Nadezhda Krupskaya)
a short note to Stalin, the contents of which are unknown. Stalin, upon
receiving the message (which had Krupskaya's initials on it), telephoned
her and coarsely abused her, to the extent that the next day she wrote
the following appeal to Kamenev:

Because I took down a short message by dictation from Vladimir
Ilych by permission of the doctors, Stalin permitted himself yesterday
an unusually coarse outburst directed at me. This was not my first day
in the Party. During all these years no comrade has ever addressed
me with such coarse words.

The business of the party and of Ilych are not less dear to me than to
Stalin. I have to have the greatest self-control. I know better than any
doctor what can and what cannot be discussed with Ilych, because I
know what makes him nervous and what does not, and in any case I
know better than Stalin. I am turning to you and [Zinoviev], as being
much closer comrades of V.I., and I am begging you to protect me
from rude interference in my private life and from those invectives
and threats. I have no doubt what will be the unanimous decision of the
Control Commission, with which Stalin sees fit to threaten me. However I have neither the strength nor the time to waste on this stupid
quarrel. I am a human being and my nerves are strained to the utmost.[5]

Stalin was thus beginning to achieve his goal—a chance to affect Lenin's
health by pressuring his wife (who was, of course, suffering under the
strains of her husband's illness). Stalin, of course, had no fear of
Kamenev and Zinoviev, and presumably wanted only that Krupskaya

5. Payne, Life and Death of Lenin, pp. 596–597.

should break down and reveal all to Lenin. It is thus that Stalin plotted Lenin's death. Krupskaya, for her part, apparently did not seek the help of Trotsky, and was unaware of the ineffectiveness of Kamenev and Zinoviev against Stalin.

As the winter drew on, Lenin's health improved and he secretly planned further steps to remove Stalin, relying upon the upcoming Twelfth Party Congress. His strategy was to attack the People's Commissariat for the Workers' and Peasants' Inspectorate, the institution over which Stalin had presided since 1919, and through which he had earned his reputation as an outstanding administrator. The attack upon Stalin was abundantly clear: Lenin first proposed that the Inspectorate be amalgamated with the enlarged Central Control Commission and thus submerged in it, thereby ceasing to be an independent base of Stalin's power.[6] In what was to prove to be the last article he was to write, Lenin summed up his view of the situation in the following words:

> *Our state apparatus is so deplorable, not to say wretched, that we must first think very carefully how to combat its defects, bearing in mind that these defects are rooted in the past, which, although it has been overthrown, has not yet been overcome, has not yet reached the stage of a culture that has receded into the distant past. I say culture deliberately, because in these matters we can only regard as achieved what has become part and parcel of our culture, of our social life, our habits. We might say that the good in our social system has not been properly studied, understood, and taken to heart; it has been hastily grasped at; it has been verified or tested, corroborated by experience, and not made durable, etc. Of course, it could not be otherwise in a revolutionary epoch, when development proceeded at such breakneck speed that in a matter of five years we passed from czarism to the Soviet system.[7]*

Singling out the source of Stalin's authority, Lenin goes on to note:

> *Let us say frankly that the People's Commissariat of the Workers' and Peasants' Inspectorate does not at present enjoy the slightest authority. Everybody knows that no other institutions are worse organized than those of our Workers' and Peasants' Inspection, and that under present conditions nothing can be expected from this People's Commissariat.[8]*

6. Lenin, "How We Should Reorganize the Workers' and Peasants' Inspectorate: Recommendations to the Twelfth Party Congress" (written January 23, 1923) , *Collected Works*, Vol. XXXIII (Moscow: Progress Publishers, 1966) , pp. 481–486.

7. Lenin: "Better Fewer but Better," *ibid.*, pp. 487–488. This article was written on March 2, 1923.

8. *Ibid.*, p. 490.

Lenin's conclusion, that "we must make the Workers' and Peasants' Inspectorate a really exemplary institution, an instrument to improve our state apparatus," indicated his intention to thoroughly overhaul the Inspectorate.

On March 5, 1923, the day following the appearance of this article in Pravda, Lenin dictated a short note to Trotsky admonishing him to pursue the Georgian question against Stalin as well as a note to Stalin in which he thereatened to break off relations altogether. The following day Lenin dictated a note to the leaders of the Georgian Soviet, promising them his full support for their grievances. These are the last letters Lenin wrote.

On March 9, Lenin suffered his third stroke, but, like a man obsessed with the work that remained, he would not consent to die. By that October, his condition had improved dramatically, and he was regaining his bodily strength and his mental abilities at a pace which astounded his physicians. On October 19 he went out for the first time since the third stroke and was instantly recognized (having long been rumored dead) and walked, followed by numerous admirers, straight into the Kremlin. By early January 1924, he was receiving Zinoviev, Kamenev, and Bukharin, and preparations were being made for the Thirteenth Party Conference, which was to begin on January 16. As mentioned previously, the Party Conferences enabled the leadership to decide all the important issues in advance of the following Party Congress. This was to be the first conference which was attended by neither Lenin nor Trotsky (who was also ill), and it was therefore easily controlled by Stalin, who viciously attacked the absent Trotsky, declaring him to have made "six major errors" which were each tantamount to treason and demanding his expulsion from the Party. Although not expelled, Trotsky was nonetheless seriously discredited, and now only Lenin stood in the way of Stalin's absolute power.

But, at the same time, Lenin's doctors were publicly predicting his complete cure by the following summer. There also exist numerous reports corroborating Lenin's steady recovery from persons who saw him during that January. Nonetheless, on January 21, 1924, Lenin suddenly died. It is to be noted that by that date Lenin's residence was entirely staffed with secret police agents, who were responsible directly to Stalin. Although there will never, presumably, be sufficient proof that Lenin was in fact poisoned, it is clear that Stalin had everything to lose from Lenin's anticipated recovery and everything to gain from his speedy demise.

The selection which follows includes Lenin's "Letter to the Congress" and most of the letters written between late December 1922 and March 1923 documenting his growing mistrust of Stalin and his futile plans to remove him from power.

Letter to the Congress

December 23, 1922

I would urge strongly that at this Congress a number of changes be made in our political structure.

I want to tell you of the considerations to which I attach most importance.

At the head of the list I set an increase in the number of Central Committee members to a few dozen or even a hundred. It is my opinion that without this reform our Central Committee would be in great danger if the course of events were not quite favorable for us (and that is something we cannot count on).

Then, I intend to propose that the Congress should on certain conditions invest the decisions of the State Planning Commission with legislative force, meeting, in this respect, the wishes of Comrade Trotsky—to a certain extent and on certain conditions.

As for the first point, i.e., increasing the number of C.C. members, I think it must be done in order to raise the prestige of the Central Committee, to do a thorough job of improving our administrative machinery and to prevent conflicts between small sections of the C.C. from acquiring excessive importance for the future of the Party.

It seems to me that our Party has every right to demand from the working class fifty to one hundred C.C. members, and that it could get them from it without unduly taxing the resources of that class.

Such a reform would considerably increase the stability of our Party and ease its struggle in the encirclement of hostile states, which, in my opinion, is likely to, and must, become much more acute in the next few years. I think that the stability of our Party would gain a thousandfold by such a measure.

Continuation of the notes
December 24, 1922

By stability of the Central Committee, of which I spoke above, I mean measures against a split, as far as such measures can at all be taken. For, of course, the whiteguard . . . was right when, first, in the whiteguards' game against Soviet Russia he banked on a split in our Party, and when, second, he banked on grave differences in our Party to cause that split.

Our Party relies on two classes, and therefore its instability would be possible and its downfall inevitable if there were no agreement between those two classes. In that event this or that measure, and generally all talk about the stability of our C.C., would be futile. No measures of any kind could prevent a split in such a case. But I hope that this is too remote a future and too improbable an event to talk about.

I have in mind stability as a guarantee against a split in the immediate future, and I intend to deal here with a few ideas concerning personal qualities.

I think that from this standpoint the prime factors in the question of stability are such members of the C.C. as Stalin and Trotsky. I think relations between them make up the greater part of the danger of a split, which could be avoided, and this purpose, in my opinion, would be served, among other things, by increasing the number of C.C. members to fifty or one hundred.

Comrade Stalin, having become Secretary General, has unlimited authority concentrated in his hands, and I am not sure whether he will always be capable of using that authority with sufficient caution. Comrade Trotsky, on the other hand, as his struggle against the C.C. on the question of the People's Commissariat for Communications has already proved, is distinguished not only by outstanding ability. He is personally perhaps the most capable man in the present C.C., but he has displayed excessive self-assurance and shown excessive preoccupation with the purely administrative side of the work.

These two qualities of the two outstanding leaders of the present C.C. can inadvertently lead to a split, and if our Party does not take steps to avert this, the split may come unexpectedly.

I shall not give any further appraisals of the personal qualities of other members of the C.C. I shall just recall that the October episode with Zinoviev and Kamenev* was, of course, no accident,

* Having unsuccessfully opposed the prospective Bolshevik seizure of power, Zinoviev and Kamenev revealed publicly the existence of the plot eight days prior to its execution. Cf. pp. 418–419, below.

but neither can the blame for it be laid upon them personally, any more than non-Bolshevism can upon Trotsky.

Speaking of the young C.C. members, I wish to say a few words about Bukharin and Pyatakov. They are, in my opinion, the most outstanding figures (among the youngest ones), and the following must be borne in mind about them: Bukharin is not only a most valuable and major theorist of the Party; he is also rightly considered the favorite of the whole Party, but his theoretical views can be classified as fully Marxist only with great reserve, for there is something scholastic about him (he has never made a study of dialectics, and, I think, never fully understood it).

December 25

As for Pyatakov, he is unquestionably a man of outstanding will and outstanding ability, but shows too much zeal for administrating and the administrative side of the work to be relied upon in a serious political matter.

Both of these remarks, of course, are made only for the present, on the assumption that both these outstanding and devoted Party workers fail to find an occasion to enhance their knowledge and amend their one-sidedness.

Addition to the letter of December 24, 1922
January 4, 1923

Stalin is too rude, and this defect, although quite tolerable in our midst and in dealings among us Communists, becomes intolerable in a Secretary General. That is why I suggest that the comrades think about a way of removing Stalin from that post and appointing another man in his stead who in all other respects differs from Comrade Stalin in having only one advantage, namely, that of being more tolerant, more loyal, more polite, and more considerate to the comrades, less capricious, etc. This circumstance may appear to be a negligible detail. But I think that from the standpoint of safeguards against a split and from the standpoint of what I wrote above about the relationship between Stalin and Trotsky it is not a detail, or it is a detail which can assume decisive importance.

Continuation of the notes
December 26, 1922

The increase in the number of C.C. members to fifty or even one hundred must, in my opinion, serve a double or even a treble purpose: the more members there are in the C.C., the more men will be trained in C.C. work and the less danger there will be of a split due to some indiscretion. The enlistment of many workers to the C.C. will help the workers to improve our administrative machinery, which is pretty bad. We inherited it, in effect, from the old regime, for it was absolutely impossible to reorganize it in such a short time, especially in conditions of war, famine, etc. That is why those "critics" who point to the defects of our administrative machinery out of mockery or malice may be calmly answered that they do not in the least understand the conditions of the revolution today. It is altogether impossible in five years to reorganize the machinery adequately, especially in the conditions in which our revolution took place. It is enough that in five years we have created a new type of state in which the workers are leading the peasants against the bourgeoisie; and in a hostile international environment this in itself is a gigantic achievement. But knowledge of this must on no account blind us to the fact that, in effect, we took over the old machinery of state from the czar and the bourgeoisie and that now, with the onset of peace and the satisfaction of the minimum requirements against famine, all our work must be directed toward improving the administrative machinery.

I think that a few dozen workers, being members of the C.C., can deal better than anybody else with checking, improving, and remodeling our state apparatus. The Workers' and Peasants' Inspection on whom this function devolved at the beginning proved unable to cope with it and can be used only as an "appendage" or, on certain conditions, as an assistant to these members of the C.C. In my opinion, the workers admitted to the Central Committee should come preferably not from among those who have had long service in Soviet bodies (in this part of my letter the term "workers" everywhere includes peasants), because those workers have already acquired the very traditions and the very prejudices which it is desirable to combat.

The working-class members of the C.C. must be mainly workers of a lower stratum than those promoted in the last five years to work in Soviet bodies; they must be people closer to being rank-and-file workers and peasants, who, however, do not fall into the category of direct or indirect exploiters. I think that by attending all sittings of the C.C. and all sittings of the Political Bureau, and by reading all the documents of the C.C., such workers can form a staff of devoted supporters of the Soviet system, able, first, to give stability to the C.C. itself, and second, to work effectively on the renewal and improvement of the state apparatus.

Continuation of the notes
December 27, 1922

Granting Legislative Functions to the State Planning Commission

This idea was suggested by Comrade Trotsky, it seems, quite a long time ago. I was against it at the time, because I thought that there would then be a fundamental lack of coordination in the system of our legislative institutions. But after closer consideration of the matter I find that in substance there is a sound idea in it, namely: the State Planning Commission stands somewhat apart from our legislative institutions, although, as a body of experienced people, experts, representatives of science and technology, it is actually in a better position to form a correct judgment of affairs. . . .

I think that we must now take a step towards extending the competence of the State Planning Commission. . . .

I think that the State Planning Commission must be headed by a man who, on the one hand, has scientific education, namely, either technical or agronomic, with decades of experience in practical work in the field of technology or of agronomics. I think this man must possess not so much the qualities of an administrator as broad experience and the ability to enlist the services of other men.

Continuation of the letter on the legislative nature of State
Planning Commission decisions
December 28, 1922

I have noticed that some of our comrades who are able to
exercise a decisive influence on the direction of state affairs
exaggerate the administrative side, which, of course, is necessary
in its time and place, but which should not be confused with the
scientific side, with a grasp of the broad facts, the ability to
recruit men, etc. . . .

I think that here it is just as harmful to exaggerate "administrating" as it is to exaggerate anything at all. The chief of a state
institution must possess a high degree of personal appeal and
sufficiently solid scientific and technical knowledge to be able to
check people's work. That much is basic. Without it the work
cannot be done properly. On the other hand, it is very important
that he should be capable of administering and should have a
worthy assistant, or assistants, in the matter. The combination of
these two qualities in one person will hardly be found, and it is
hardly necessary.

Continuation of the notes
December 30, 1922

The Question of Nationalities or "Autonomization"

I suppose I have been very remiss with respect to the workers
of Russia for not having intervened energetically and decisively
enough in the notorious question of autonomization, which, it
appears, is officially called the question of the union of Soviet
socialist republics.

When this question arose last summer, I was ill; and then in
autumn I relied too much on my recovery and on the October
and December plenary meetings giving me an opportunity of
intervening in this question. However, I did not manage to
attend the October Plenary Meeting (when this question came
up) or the one in December, and so the question passed me by
almost completely.

I have only had time for a talk with Comrade Dzerzhinsky,

who came from the Caucasus and told me how this matter stood in Georgia. I have also managed to exchange a few words with Comrade Zinoviev and express my apprehensions on this matter. From what I was told by Comrade Dzerzhinsky, who was at the head of the commission sent by the C.C. to "investigate" the Georgian incident, I could only draw the greatest apprehensions. If matters had come to such a pass that Orjonikidze could go to the extreme of applying physical violence, as Comrade Dzerzhinsky informed me, we can imagine what a mess we have got ourselves into. Obviously the whole business of "autonomization" was radically wrong and badly timed.

It is said that a united apparatus was needed. Where did that assurance come from? Did it not come from that same Russian apparatus which, as I pointed out in one of the preceding sections of my diary, we took over from czarism and slightly anointed with Soviet oil?

There is no doubt that that measure should have been delayed somewhat until we could say that we vouched for our apparatus as our own. But now, we must, in all conscience, admit the contrary; the apparatus we call ours is, in fact, still quite alien to us; it is a bourgeois and czarist hodgepodge, and there has been no possibility of getting rid of it in the course of the past five years without the help of other countries and because we have been "busy" most of the time with military engagements and the fight against famine.

It is quite natural that in such circumstances the "freedom to secede from the union" by which we justify ourselves will be a mere scrap of paper, unable to defend the non-Russians from the onslaught of that really Russian man, the Great-Russian chauvinist, in substance a rascal and a tyrant, such as the typical Russian bureaucrat is. There is no doubt that the infinitesimal percentage of Soviet and sovietized workers will drown in that tide of chauvinistic Great-Russian riffraff like a fly in milk.

It is said in defense of this measure that the People's Commissariats directly concerned with national psychology and national education were set up as separate bodies. But there the question arises: can these People's Commissariats be made quite independent? and second: Were we careful enough to take measures to provide the non-Russians with a real safeguard against the truly Russian bully? I do not think we took such measures, although we could and should have done so.

I think that Stalin's haste and his infatuation with pure administration, together with his spite against the notorious "nationalist-socialism," played a fatal role here. In politics spite generally plays the basest of roles.

I also fear that Comrade Dzerzhinsky, who went to the Caucasus to investigate the "crime" of those "nationalist-socialists," distinguished himself there by his truly Russian frame of mind (it is common knowledge that people of other nationalities who have become Russified overdo this Russian frame of mind) and that the impartiality of his whole commission was typified well enough by Orjonikidze's "manhandling." I think that no provocation or even insult can justify such Russian manhandling and that Comrade Dzerzhinsky was inexcusably guilty in adopting a light-hearted attitude toward it.

For all the citizens in the Caucasus Orjonikidze was the authority. Orojonikidze had no right to display that irritability to which he and Dzerzhinsky referred. On the contrary, Orjonikidze should have behaved with a restraint which cannot be demanded of any ordinary citizen, still less of a man accused of a "political" crime. And, to tell the truth, those nationalist-socialists were citizens who were accused of a political crime, and the terms of the accusation were such that it could not be described otherwise.

Here we have an important question of principle: how is internationalism to be understood?

Continuation of the notes
December 31, 1922

The Question of Nationalities or "Autonomization" (Continued)

In my writings on the national question I have already said that an abstract presentation of the question of nationalism in general is of no use at all. A distinction must necessarily be made between the nationalism of an oppressor nation and that of an oppressed nation, the nationalism of a big nation and that of a small nation.

In respect of the second kind of nationalism we, nationals of a big nation, have nearly always been guilty, in historic practice, of an infinite number of cases of violence; furthermore, we commit violence and insult an infinite number of times without noticing it. . . .

That is why internationalism on the part of oppressors or "great" nations, as they are called (though they are great only in their violence, only great as bullies) , must consist not only in the observance of the formal equality of nations but even in an inequality of the oppressor nation, the great nation, that must make up for the inequality which obtains in actual practice. Anybody who does not understand this has not grasped the real proletarian attitude to the national question; he is still essentially petit-bourgeois in his point of view and is, therefore, sure to descend to the bourgeois point of view.

What is important for the proletarian? For the proletarian it is not only important, it is absolutely essential, that he should be assured that the non-Russians place the greatest possible trust in the proletarian class struggle. What is needed to ensure this? Not merely formal equality. In one way or another, by one's attitude or by concessions, it is necessary to compensate the non-Russians for the lack of trust, for the suspicion and the insults to which the government of the "dominant" nation subjected them in the past.

I think it is unnecessary to explain this to Bolsheviks, to Communists, in greater detail. And I think that in the present instance, as far as the Georgian nation is concerned, we have a typical case in which a genuinely proletarian attitude makes profound caution, thoughtfulness, and a readiness to compromise a matter of necessity for us. The Georgian who is neglectful of this aspect of the question, or who carelessly flings about accusations of "nationalist-socialism" (whereas he himself is a real and true "nationalist-socialist," and even a vulgar Great-Russian bully) , violates, in substance, the interests of proletarian class solidarity, for nothing holds up the development and strengthening of proletarian class solidarity so much as national injustice;

"offended" nationals are not sensitive to anything so much as to the feeling of equality and the violation of this equality, if only through negligence or jest—to the violation of that equality by their proletarian comrades. That is why in this case it is better to overdo rather than underdo the concessions and leniency toward the national minorities. That is why, in this case, the fundamental interest of proletarian solidarity, and consequently of the proletarian class struggle, requires that we never adopt a formal attitude to the national question, but always take into account the specific attitude of the proletarian of the oppressed (or small) nation toward the oppressor (or great) nation.

Continuation of the notes
December 31, 1922

What practical measures must be taken in the present situation?

. . . We must maintain and strengthen the union of socialist republics. Of this there can be no doubt. This measure is necessary for us, and it is necessary for the world communist proletariat in its struggle against the world bourgeoisie and its defense against bourgeois intrigues. . . .

. . . Exemplary punishment must be inflicted on Comrade Orjonikidze (I say this all the more regretfully as I am one of his personal friends and have worked with him abroad) and the investigation of all the material which Dzerzhinsky's commission has collected must be completed or started over again to correct the enormous mass of wrongs and biased judgments which it doubtlessly contains. The political responsibility for all this truly Great-Russian nationalist campaign must, of course, be laid on Stalin and Dzerzhinsky. . . .

It must be borne in mind that the decentralization of the People's Commissariats and the lack of coordination in their work as far as Moscow and other centers are concerned can be compensated sufficiently by Party authority, if it is exercised with sufficient prudence and impartiality; the harm that can result to our state from a lack of unification between the national apparatuses and the Russian apparatus is infinitely less than that which will be done not only to us, but to the whole International, and to the hundreds of millions of the peoples of Asia, which is destined to follow us on to the stage of history in the near future. It would be unpardonable opportunism if, on the eve of the debut of the East, just as it is awakening, we undermined our prestige with its peoples, even if only by the slightest crudity or injustice toward our own non-Russian nationalities. The need to rally against the imperialists of the West, who are defending the capitalist world, is one thing. There can be no doubt about that, and it would be superfluous for me to speak about my unconditional approval of it. It is another thing when we ourselves lapse, even if only in trifles, into imperialist attitudes toward oppressed nationalities, thus undermining all our principled sincerity, all our principled defense of the struggle against imperialism. But the morrow of world history will be a day when the awakening peoples oppressed by imperialism are finally aroused and the decisive long and hard struggle for their liberation begins.

Top secret
Personal

Dear Comrade Trotsky:

It is my earnest request that you should undertake the defense of the Georgian case in the Party C.C. This case is now under "persecution" by Stalin and Dzerzhinsky, and I cannot rely on their impartiality. Quite to the contrary. I would feel at ease if you agreed to undertake its defense. If you should refuse to do so for any reason, return the whole case to me. I shall consider it a sign that you do not accept.

With best comradely greetings
Lenin

March 5, 1923

Top secret
Personal

Copy to Comrades Kamenev and Zinoviev
Dear Comrade Stalin:

You have been so rude as to summon my wife to the telephone and use bad language. Although she had told you that she was prepared to forget this, the fact nevertheless became known through her to Zinoviev and Kamenev. I have no intention of forgetting so easily what has been done against me, and it goes without saying that what has been done against my wife I consider having been done against me as well. I ask you, therefore, to think it over whether you are prepared to withdraw what you have said and to make your apologies, or whether you prefer that relations between us should be broken off.

Respectfully yours,
Lenin

March 5, 1923

Top secret

Comrades Mdivani, Makharadze and others
Copy to Comrades *Trotsky and Kamenev*

Dear Comrades:

I am following your case with all my heart. I am indignant over Orjonikidze's rudeness and the connivance of Stalin and Dzerzhinsky. I am preparing for you notes and a speech.

Respectfully yours,
Lenin

March 6, 1923

23. STALIN:
SEIZING THE MANTLE OF
LENINIST ORTHODOXY

Within three months of Lenin's death, Stalin declared his authority over the Communist party by presenting himself as the sole authoritative interpreter of "Marxism-Leninism" by means of his series of lectures entitled The Foundations of Leninism. *With Lenin's death and the start of the cult of his memory (over the protests of his widow), it was now required that Soviet Marxist "Orthodoxy" be "Leninist" as well. There thus arose the ideology of "Marxism-Leninism," within the boundaries of which all subsequent thought in the U.S.S.R. has been confined. What is particularly important to note is that it thereby became mandatory that Marx be seen only through the mediation of Lenin (and Stalin), and never be studied and interpreted directly. It is this fact which is most largely responsible for the chasm often separating the interpretation of Marx by Communist apologists and of those who approach Marx's ideas in the spirit of critical inquiry.*

In The Foundations of Leninism, *Stalin shows that he has indeed grasped the essential features of Lenin's characteristic ideas. The excerpts that follow are from that work and are chosen to illustrate some nascent ideas of Stalin's which were shortly thereafter to become dogmas themselves. Among these are the notions of the worldwide perspective of Communism (which Lenin had institutionalized in the Comintern), and which Stalin shifts in the direction of the East; the polemical rejection of Trotsky's doctrine of "permanent revolution" and the allegation that he had "underestimated the peasantry"; the doctrine of the uneven development of capitalism in various countries, which was soon to be used in conjunction with the doctrine of the "relative stabilization" of Western capitalism to camouflage Stalin's refusal to aid the revolution in Germany; and the doctrine that the "dictatorship of the proletariat," i.e., the dictatorship of the Communist party over the Russian people and of Stalin over the Party, would require an entire "historical era" of indefinite duration.*

SOURCE: From Joseph Stalin, *The Foundations of Leninism*, in *Works*, Vol. VI (Moscow: Foreign Languages Publishing House, 1953).

. . . Leninism is Marxism of the era of imperialism and the proletarian revolution. To be more exact, Leninism is the theory and tactics of the proletarian revolution in general, the theory and tactics of the dictatorship of the proletariat in particular. Marx and Engels pursued their activities in the pre-revolutionary period . . . when developed imperialism did not yet exist, in the period of the proletarians' preparation for revolution, in the period when the proletarian revolution was not yet an immediate practical inevitability. But Lenin, the disciple of Marx and Engels, pursued his activities in the period of developed imperialism, in the period of the unfolding proletarian revolution, when the proletarian revolution had already triumphed in one country, had smashed bourgeois democracy, and had ushered in the era of proletarian democracy, the era of the soviets. . . .

The exceptionally militant and exceptionally revolutionary character of Leninism . . . is due to two causes: first, to the fact that Leninism emerged from the proletarian revolution, the imprint of which it cannot but bear; second, to the fact that it grew and became strong in clashes with the opportunism of the Second International, the fight against which was and remains an essential preliminary condition for a successful fight against capitalism. . . .

Formerly, the analysis of the prerequisites for the proletarian revolution was usually approached from the point of view of the economic state of individual countries. Now, this approach is no longer adequate. Now the matter must be approached from the point of view of the economic state of all or the majority of countries, from the point of view of the state of world economy; for individual countries and individual national economies have ceased to be self-sufficient units, have become links in a single chain called world economy; for the old "cultured" capitalism has evolved into imperialism, and imperialism is a world system of financial enslavement and colonial oppression of the vast majority of the population of the world by a handful of "advanced" countries.

Formerly it was the accepted thing to speak of the existence or absence of objective conditions for the proletarian revolution in individual countries, or, to be more precise, in one or another developed country. Now this point of view is no longer adequate. Now we must speak of the existence of objective conditions for the revolution in the entire system of world imperialist economy as an integral whole; the existence within this system of some countries that are not sufficiently developed industrially cannot serve as an insuperable obstacle to the revolution, *if* the system as a whole or, more correctly, *because* the system as a whole is already ripe for revolution. . . .

Where will the revolution begin? Where, in what country, can the front of capital be pierced first?

Where industry is more developed, where the proletariat constitutes the majority, where there is more culture, where there is more democracy—that was the reply usually given formerly.

No, objects the Leninist theory of revolution, *not necessarily where industry is more developed,* and so forth. The front of capital will be pierced where the chain of imperialism is weakest, for the proletarian revolution is the result of the breaking of the chain of the world imperialist front at its weakest link. . . .

Very well, we may be told; but if that is the case, why did Lenin combat the idea of "permanent (uninterrupted) revolution"?

Because Lenin proposed that the revolutionary capacities of the peasantry be "exhausted" and that the fullest use be made of their revolutionary energy for the complete liquidation of czarism and for the transition to the proletarian revolution, whereas the adherents of "permanent revolution" [i.e., Trotsky] did not understand the important role of the peasantry in the Russian revolution, underestimated the strength of the revolutionary energy of the peasantry, underestimated the strength and ability of the Russian proletariat to lead the peasantry, and thereby hampered the work of emancipating the peasantry from the influence of the bourgeoisie, the work of rallying the peasantry around the proletariat.

Because Lenin proposed that the revolution *be crowned* with the transfer of power to the proletariat, whereas the adherents of "permanent" revolution wanted *to begin* at once with the establishment of the power of the proletariat, failing to realize that in so doing they were closing their eyes to such a "minor detail" as the survivals of serfdom and . . . failing to understand that such a policy could only retard the winning of the peasantry over to the side of the proletariat. . . .

The idea of "permanent" revolution should not be regarded as a new idea. It was first advanced by Marx at the end of the forties in his well-known *Address to the Communist League* (1850). . . .

Marx did not at all propose *to begin* the revolution in the Germany of the fifties with the immediate establishment of proletarian power—*contrary* to the plans of our Russian "permanentists."

Marx proposed only that the revolution *be crowned* with the establishment of proletarian state power, by hurling, step by step, one section of the bourgeoisie after another from the heights of power, in order, after the attainment of power by the proletariat, to kindle the fire of revolution in every country—and everything that Lenin taught and carried out in the course of our revolution in pursuit of his theory of the proletarian revolution under the conditions of imperialism was *fully in line* with that proposition.

It follows, then, that our Russian "permanentists" have not only underestimated the role of the peasantry in the Russian revolution and the importance of the idea of the hegemony of the proletariat, but have altered (for the worse) Marx's idea of "permanent" revolution and made it unfit for practical use. . . .

Formerly, the victory of the revolution in one country was considered impossible, on the assumption that it would require the combined action of the proletarians of all or at least of a majority of the advanced countries to achieve victory over the bourgeoisie. Now this point of view no longer fits in with the facts. Now we must proceed from the possibility of such a victory, for the uneven and spasmodic character of the development of the various capitalist countries under the conditions of imperialism, the development within imperialism of catastrophic contradictions leading to inevitable wars, the growth of the revolutionary movement in all countries of the world—all this leads, not only to the possibility, but also to the necessity of the victory of the proletariat in individual countries. . . .

"The fundamental question of every revolution is the question of power" (*Lenin*). Does this mean that all that is required is to assume power, to seize it? No, it does not. The seizure of power is only the beginning. For many reasons, the bourgeoisie that is overthrown in one country remains for a long time stronger than the proletariat which has overthrown it. Therefore, the whole point is to retain power, to consolidate it, to make it invincible. What is needed to attain this? To attain this it is necessary to carry out at least three main tasks that confront the dictatorship of the proletariat "on the morrow" of victory:

1. to break the resistance of the landlords and capitalists who have been overthrown and expropriated by the revolution, to liquidate every attempt on their part to restore the power of capital;

2. to organize construction in such a way as to rally all the working people around the proletariat, and to carry on this work along the lines of preparing for the elimination, the abolition of classes;

3. to arm the revolution, to organize the army of the revolution for the struggle against foreign enemies, for the struggle against imperialism. . . .

It scarcely needs proof that there is not the slightest possibility of carrying out these tasks in a short period, of accomplishing all this in a few years. Therefore, the dictatorship of the proletariat, the transition from capitalism to communism, must not be regarded as a fleeting period of "superrevolutionary" acts and decrees, but as an entire historical era, replete with civil wars and external conflicts, with persistent organizational work and economic construction, with advances and retreats, victories and defeats. This historical era is needed not only to create the economic and cultural prerequisites for the complete victory of socialism, but also to enable the proletariat, first, to educate itself and become steeled as a force capable of governing the country, and, second, to reeducate and remold the petit-bourgeois strata along such lines as will assure the organization of socialist production. . . .

Formerly, the national question was usually confined to a narrow circle of questions, concerning, primarily, "civilized" nationalities. The Irish, the Hungarians, the Poles, the Finns, the Serbs, and several other European nationalities—that was the circle of unequal peoples in whose destinies the leaders of the

Second International were interested. The scores and hundreds of millions of Asiatic and African peoples who are suffering national oppression in its most savage and cruel form usually remained outside of their field of vision. . . . Leninism laid bare this crying incongruity, broke down the wall between whites and blacks, between Europeans and Asiatics, between the "civilized" and "uncivilized" slaves of imperialism, and thus linked the national question with the question of the colonies. The national question was thereby transformed from a particular and internal state problem into a general and international problem, into a world problem of emancipating the oppressed peoples in the dependent countries and colonies from the yoke of imperialism. . . .

Leninism broadened the conception of self-determination, interpreting it as the right of the oppressed peoples of the dependent countries and colonies to complete secession, as the right of nations to independent existence as states. . . .

Formerly, the national question was regarded from a reformist point of view, as an independent question having no connection with the general question of the power of capital, of the overthrow of imperialism, of the proletarian revolution. It was tacitly assumed that the victory of the proletariat in Europe was possible without a direct alliance with the liberation movement in the colonies, that the national-colonial question could be solved . . . without a revolutionary struggle against imperialism. Now we can say that this antirevolutionary point of view has been exposed. Leninism has proved, and the imperialist war and the revolution in Russia have confirmed, that the national question can be solved only in connection with and on the basis of the proletarian revolution, and that the road to victory of the revolution in the West lies through the revolutionary alliance with the liberation movement of the colonies and dependent countries against imperialism. . . .

This does not mean, of course, that the proletariat must support *every* national movement, everywhere and always, in every individual concrete case. It means that support must be given to such national movements as tend to weaken, to overthrow imperialism, and not to strengthen and preserve it. Cases occur when the national movements in certain oppressed countries come into conflict with the interests of the development of the proletarian movement. In such cases support is, of course, entirely out of the question. The question of the rights of nations is not an isolated, self-sufficient question; it is a part of the general problem of the proletarian revolution, subordinate to the whole, and must be considered from the point of view of the whole. . . .

Under the dictatorship of the proletariat, under certain conditions, in a certain situation, the proletarian power may find itself compelled temporarily to leave the path of the revolutionary reconstruction of the existing order of things and to take the path of its gradual transformation, the "reformist path," as Lenin says.*. . . But it must be borne in mind that there is a fundamental distinction here, which consists in the fact that in this case the reform emanates from the proletarian power, it strengthens the proletarian power, it procures for it a necessary respite, its purpose is to disintegrate, not the revolution, but the nonproletarian classes.

Under such conditions a reform is thus transformed into its opposite. . . .

The Party is the General Staff of the proletariat.

But the Party cannot be only an *advanced* detachment. It must at the same time be a detachment of the *class,* part of the class, closely bound up with it by all the fibers of its being. The distinction between the advanced detachment and the rest of the working class, between Party members and non-Party people, cannot disappear until classes disappear; it will exist as long as the ranks of the proletariat continue to be replenished with former members of other classes, as long as the working class as a whole is not in a position to rise to the level of the advanced detachment. But the Party would cease to be a party if this distinction developed into a gap, if the Party turned in on itself and became divorced from the non-Party masses. The Party cannot lead the class if it is not connected with the non-Party masses, if there is no bond between the Party and the non-Party masses, if these masses do not accept its leadership, if the Party enjoys no moral and political credit among the masses. . . .

* Cf. pp. 314–320, above.

But the Party can fulfill these tasks only if it is itself the embodiment of discipline and organization, if it is itself the *organized* detachment of the proletariat. . . .

The Party is the organized detachment of the working class. But the Party is not the only organization of the working class. The proletariat has also a number of other organizations, without which it cannot wage a successful struggle against capital: trade unions, cooperatives, factory organizations, parliamentary groups, non-Party women's associations, the press, cultural and educational organizations, youth leagues, revolutionary fighting organizations (in times of open revolutionary action), soviets of deputies as the form of state organization (if the proletariat is in power), etc. The overwhelming majority of these organizations are non-Party. . . . Without them it would be impossible to steel the proletariat as the force whose mission it is to replace the bourgeois order by the socialist order. . . . But it is also true that all these organizations should work in one direction for they serve *one* class, the class of the proletarians. The question then arises: who is to determine the line, the general direction, along which the work of all these organizations is to be conducted? . . .

That organization is the Party of the proletariat. . . .

But from this it follows that the existence of factions is compatible neither with the Party's unity nor with its iron discipline. It scarcely needs proof that the existence of factions leads to the existence of a number of centers, and the existence of a number of centers means the absence of one common center in the Party, the breaking up of unity of will, the weakening and disintegration of discipline, the weakening and disintegration of the dictatorship. . . . But the parties of the Communist International, whose activities are conditioned by the task of achieving and consolidating the dictatorship of the proletariat, cannot afford to be "liberal" or to permit freedom of factions. . . .

The Party becomes strong by purging itself of opportunist elements. The source of factionalism in the Party is its opportunist elements. The proletariat is not an isolated class. It is constantly replenished by the influx of peasants, petit bourgeois, and intellectuals proletarianized by the development of capitalism. . . .

In one way or another, all these petit-bourgeois groups penetrate into the Party and introduce into it the spirit of hesitancy and opportunism, the spirit of demoralization and uncertainty. It is they, principally, that constitute the source of factionalism and disintegration, the source of disorganization and disruption of the Party from within. To fight imperialism with such "allies" in one's rear means to put oneself in the position of being caught between two fires, from the front and from the rear. Therefore, ruthless struggle against such elements, their expulsion from the Party, is a prerequisite for the successful struggle against imperialism.

The theory of "defeating" opportunist elements by ideological struggle within the Party, the theory of "overcoming" these elements within the confines of a single party, is a rotten and dangerous theory, which threatens to condemn the Party to paralysis and chronic infirmity, threatens to make the Party a prey to opportunism, threatens to leave the proletariat without a revolutionary party, threatens to deprive the proletariat of its main weapon in the fight against imperialism. . . . Proletarian parties develop and become strong by purging themselves of opportunists and reformists, social-imperialists and social-chauvinists, social-patriots and social-pacifists. . . .

24. TROTSKY:
THE BETRAYAL OF
THE REVOLUTION

The most penetrating analysis of Stalinism to come from a major Bolshevik leader was Trotsky's book The Revolution Betrayed, *written while he was in exile in 1936. At a time when most Western observers were being duped by the successes of Stalin's industrialization drive, it was Trotsky who pointed out that the reason for this admiration lay in the common bourgeois predilections of Stalin and his Western admirers. Trotsky's argument is an attempt to expose the social, i.e., economic, basis of the victory of Stalin's parvenu bureaucrats over the revolutionary proletariat and the Bolshevik leaders of Lenin's day. In his conclusion, Trotsky calls for a continuation of the October Revolution, the necessary first step of which will be the overthrow of Stalin and his bureaucrats by the clandestine successors of Trotsky's Left Opposition. This was all the pretext Stalin needed to decimate any conceivable (or imaginable) opposition within the Party; and the Great Purge was readied for the following year.*

[*Program and Reality*]

   . . . The process of economic and cultural development in the Soviet Union has already passed through several stages, but has by no means arrived at an inner equilibrium. If you remember that the task of socialism is to create a classless society based upon solidarity and the harmonious satisfaction of all needs, there is not yet, in this fundamental sense, a hint of socialism in the Soviet Union. To be sure, the contradictions of soviet society are deeply different from the contradictions of capitalism. But they are nevertheless very tense. They find their expression in material and cultural inequalities, governmental repressions, political groupings, and the struggle of factions. Police repression hushes

SOURCE: From Leon Trotsky, *The Revolution Betrayed,* trans. Max Eastman (New York: Pathfinder Press, 1972). Reprinted by permission.

up and distorts a political struggle, but does not eliminate it. . . .

However you may interpret the nature of the present Soviet state, one thing is indubitable: at the end of its second decade of existence, it has not only not died away, but not begun to "die away." Worse than that, it has grown into a hitherto unheard-of apparatus of compulsion. The bureaucracy not only has not disappeared, yielding its place to the masses, but has turned into an uncontrolled force dominating the masses. The army not only has not been replaced by an armed people, but has given birth to a privileged officers' caste, crowned with marshals, while the people, "the armed bearers of the dictatorship," are now forbidden in the Soviet Union to carry even nonexplosive weapons. With the utmost stretch of fancy it would be difficult to imagine a contrast more striking than that which exists between the schema of the workers' state according to Marx, Engels and Lenin, and the actual state now headed by Stalin. . . .

The Seventh Congress of the Communist International, in a resolution of August 20, 1935, solemnly affirmed that in the sum total of the successes of the nationalized industries, the achievement of collectivization, the crowding out of capitalist elements, and the liquidation of the kulaks as a class, "the final and irrevocable triumph of socialism and the all-sided reinforcement of the state of the proletarian dictatorship is achieved in the Soviet Union." With all its categorical tone, this testimony of the Communist International is wholly self-contradictory. If socialism has "finally and irrevocably" triumphed, not as a principle but as a living social regime, then a renewed "reinforcement" of the dictatorship is obvious nonsense. And on the contrary, if the reinforcement of the dictatorship is evoked by the real demands of the regime, that means that the triumph of socialism is still remote. Not only a Marxist, but any realistic political thinker, ought to understand that the very necessity of "reinforcing" the dictatorship—that is, governmental repression—testifies not to the triumph of a classless harmony, but to the growth of new social antagonisms. What lies at the bottom of all this? Lack of the means of subsistence resulting from the low productivity of labor. . . .

[*Why Stalin Triumphed*]

. . . It is sufficiently well known that every revolution up to this time has been followed by a reaction, or even a counterrevolution. This, to be sure, has never thrown the nation all the way back to its starting point, but it has always taken from the people the lion's share of their conquests. The victims of the first reactionary wave have been, as a general rule, those pioneers, initiators, and instigators who stood at the head of the masses in the period of the revolutionary offensive. In their stead people of the second line, in league with the former enemies of the revolution, have been advanced to the front. Beneath this dramatic duel . . . on the open political scene, shifts have taken place in the relations between classes, and, no less important, profound changes in the psychology of the recently revolutionary masses.

Answering the bewildered questions of many comrades as to what has become of the activity of the Bolshevik party and the working class—where is its revolutionary initiative, its spirit of self-sacrifice and plebeian pride—why, in place of all this, has appeared so much vileness, cowardice, pusillanimity and careerism—Rakovsky referred to the life story of the French revolution of the eighteenth century, and offered the example of Babeuf, who on emerging from the Abbaye prison likewise wondered what had become of the heroic people of the Parisian suburbs. A revolution is a mighty devourer of human energy, both individual and collective. The nerves give way. Consciousness is shaken and characters are worn out. Events unfold too swiftly for the flow of fresh forces to replace the loss. Hunger, unemployment, the death of the revolutionary cadres, the removal of the masses from administration, all this led to such a physical and moral impoverishment of the Parisian suburbs that they required three decades before they were ready for a new insurrection.

The axiomlike assertions of the Soviet literature, to the effect that the laws of bourgeois revolutions are "inapplicable" to a proletarian revolution, have no scientific content whatever. The proletarian character of the October Revolution was determined by the world situation and by a special correlation of internal forces. But the classes themselves were formed in the barbarous circumstances of czarism and backward capitalism, and were anything but made to order for the demands of a socialist revolution. The exact opposite is true. It is for the very reason that a proletariat still backward in many respects achieved in the space of a few months the unprecedented leap from a semifeudal monarchy to a socialist dictatorship, that the reaction in its ranks was inevitable. This reaction has developed in a series of consecutive waves. External conditions and events have vied with each other in nourishing it. Intervention followed intervention. The revolution got no direct help from the West. Instead of the expected prosperity of the country an ominous destitution reigned for long. Moreover, the outstanding representatives of the working class either died in the civil war or rose a few steps higher and broke away from the masses. And thus after an unexampled tension of forces, hopes, and illusions, there came a long period of weariness, decline, and sheer disappointment in the results of the revolution. The ebb of the "plebeian pride" made room for a flood of pusillanimity and careerism. The new commanding caste rose to its place upon this wave.

The demobilization of the Red army of five million played no small role in the formation of the bureaucracy. The victorious commanders assumed leading posts in the local soviets, in economy, in education, and they persistently introduced everywhere that regime which had ensured success in the civil war. Thus on all sides the masses were pushed away gradually from actual participation in the leadership of the country.

The reaction within the proletariat caused an extraordinary flush of hope and confidence in the petit-bourgeois strata of town and country, aroused as they were to new life by the NEP, and growing bolder and bolder. The young bureaucracy, which had arisen at first as an agent of the proletariat, began now to feel itself a court of arbitration between the classes. Its independence increased from month to month.

The international situation was pushing with mighty forces in the same direction. The Soviet bureaucracy became more self-confident, the heavier the blows dealt to the world working class. Between these two facts there was not only a chronological but a causal connection, and one which worked in two directions. The leaders of the bureaucracy promoted the proletarian defeats; the defeats promoted the rise of the bureaucracy. The crushing of the Bulgarian insurrection and the inglorious retreat of the German workers' party in 1923, the collapse of the Estonian attempt at insurrection in 1924, the treacherous liquidation of the General Strike in England and the unworthy conduct of the Polish workers' party at the installation of Pilsudski in 1926, the terrible massacre of the Chinese revolution in 1927, and, finally, the still more ominous recent defeats in Germany and Austria—these are the historic catastrophes which killed the faith of the Soviet masses in world revolution, and permitted the bureaucracy to rise higher and higher as the sole light of salvation.

The defeat of the world proletariat during the last thirteen years [is due largely to] the ruinous part played by the leadership in the Kremlin, isolated from the masses and profoundly conservative as it is, in the revolutionary movement of all countries. . . . The continual defeats of the revolution in Europe and Asia, while weakening the international position of the Soviet Union, have vastly strengthened the Soviet bureaucracy. Two dates are especially significant in this historic series. In the second half of 1923, the attention of the Soviet workers was passionately fixed upon Germany, where the proletariat, it seemed, had stretched out its hand to power. The panicky retreat of the German Communist party was the heaviest possible disappointment to the working masses of the Soviet Union. The Soviet bureaucracy straightway opened a campaign against the theory of "permanent revolution," and dealt the Left Opposition its first cruel blow. During the years 1926 and 1927 the population of the Soviet Union experienced a new tide of hope. All eyes were now directed to the East where the drama of the Chinese revolution was unfolding. The Left Opposition had recovered from the previous blows and was recruiting a phalanx of new adherents. At the end of 1927 the Chinese revolution was massacred by the hangman, Chiang Kai-shek, into whose hands the Communist International had literally betrayed the Chinese workers and peasants. A cold wave of disappointment swept over the masses of the Soviet Union. After an unbridled baiting in the press and at meetings, the bureaucracy finally, in 1928, ventured upon mass arrests among the Left Opposition.

To be sure, tens of thousands of revolutionary fighters gathered around the banner of the Bolshevik-Leninists. The advanced workers were indubitably sympathetic to the Opposition, but that sympathy remained passive. The masses lacked faith that the situation could be seriously changed by a new struggle. Meantime the bureaucracy asserted: "For the sake of an international revolution, the Opposition proposes to drag us into a revolutionary war. Enough of shake-ups! We have earned the right to rest. We will build the socialist society at home. Rely upon us, your leaders!" This gospel of repose firmly consolidated the *apparatchiki* and the military and state officials and indubitably found an echo among the weary workers, and still more the peasant masses. Can it be, they asked themselves, that the Opposition is actually ready to sacrifice the interests of the Soviet Union for the idea of "permanent revolution"? In reality, the struggle had been about the life interests of the Soviet state. The false policy of the International in Germany resulted ten years later in the victory of Hitler—that is, in a threatening war danger from the West. And the no less false policy in China reinforced Japanese imperialism and brought very much nearer the danger in the East. . . .

The Opposition was isolated. The bureaucracy struck while the iron was hot, exploiting the bewilderment and passivity of the workers, setting their more backward strata against the advanced, and relying more and more boldly upon the kulak and the petit-bourgeois ally in general. In the course of a few years, the bureaucracy thus shattered the revolutionary vanguard of the proletariat.

It would be naïve to imagine that Stalin, previously unknown to the masses, suddenly issued from the wings fully armed with a complete strategical plan. No, indeed. Before he felt out his own course, the bureaucracy felt out Stalin himself. He brought it all the necessary guarantees: the prestige of an old Bolshevik, a strong character, narrow vision, and close bonds with the political machine as the sole source of his influence. The success which fell upon him was a surprise at first to Stalin himself. It was the friendly welcome of the new ruling group, trying to free itself from the old principles and from the control of the masses, and having need of a reliable arbiter in its inner affairs. A secondary figure before the masses and in the events of the revolution,

Stalin revealed himself as the indubitable leader of the Thermidorian bureaucracy. . . .

The new ruling caste soon revealed its own ideas, feelings, and, more important, its interests. The overwhelming majority of the older generation of the present bureaucracy had stood on the other side of the barricades during the October Revolution. . . . Or at best they had stood aside from the struggle. Those of the present bureaucrats who were in the Bolshevik camp in the October days played in the majority of cases no considerable role. As for the young bureaucrats, they have been chosen and educated by the elders, frequently from among their own offspring. These people could not have achieved the October Revolution, but they were perfectly suited to exploit it.

Personal incidents in the interval between these two historic chapters were not, of course, without influence. Thus the sickness and death of Lenin undoubtedly hastened the denouement. Had Lenin lived longer, the pressure of the bureaucratic power would have developed, at least during the first years, more slowly. But as early as 1926 Krupskaya said, in a circle of Left Oppositionists: "If Ilych were alive, he would probably already be in prison." . . .

The bureaucracy conquered something more than the Left Opposition. It conquered the Bolshevik party. It defeated the program of Lenin, who had seen the chief danger in the conversion of the organs of the state "from servants of society to lords over society." It defeated all these enemies, the Opposition, the Party, and Lenin, not with ideas and arguments, but with its own social weight. The leaden rump of the bureaucracy outweighed the head of the revolution. That is the secret of the Soviet's Thermidor.

The Degeneration of the Bolshevik Party

The Bolshevik party prepared and ensured the October victory. It also created the Soviet state, supplying it with a sturdy skeleton. The degeneration of the Party became both cause and consequence of the bureaucratization of the state. . . .

The inner regime of the Bolshevik party was characterized by the method of *democratic centralism*. The combination of these two concepts, democracy and centralism, is not in the least contradictory. The Party took watchful care not only that its boundaries should always be strictly defined, but also that all those who entered these boundaries should enjoy the actual right to define the direction of the party policy. Freedom of criticism and intellectual struggle was an irrevocable content of the Party democracy. The present doctrine that Bolshevism does not tolerate factions is a myth of the epoch of decline. In reality the history of Bolshevism is a history of the struggle of factions. And, indeed, how could a genuinely revolutionary organization, setting itself the task of overthrowing the world and uniting under its banner the most audacious iconoclasts, fighters and insurgents, live and develop without intellectual conflicts, without groupings and temporary factional formations? . . .

The regime of the Bolshevik party, especially before it came to power, stood thus in complete contradiction to the regime of the present sections of the Communist International, with their "leaders" appointed from above, making complete changes of policy at a word of command, with their uncontrolled apparatus, haughty in its attitude to the rank and file, servile in its attitude to the Kremlin. . . .

The very center of Lenin's attention and that of his colleagues was occupied by a continual concern to protect the Bolshevik ranks from the vices of those in power. However, the extraordinary closeness and at times actual merging of the Party with the state apparatus had already in those first years done indubitable harm to the freedom and elasticity of the Party regime. Democracy had been narrowed in proportion as difficulties increased. In the beginning, the Party had wished and hoped to preserve freedom of political struggle within the framework of the soviets. The civil war introduced stern amendments into this calculation. The opposition parties were forbidden one after the other. This measure, obviously in conflict with the spirit of Soviet democracy, the leaders of Bolshevism regarded not as a principle, but as an episodic act of self-defense.

The swift growth of the ruling party, with the novelty and immensity of its tasks, inevitably gave rise to inner disagreements. The underground oppositional currents in the country exerted a pressure through various channels upon the sole legal political organization, increasing the acuteness of the factional struggle. At the moment of completion of the civil war, this struggle took such sharp forms as to threaten to unsettle the state power. In March 1921, in the days of the Kronstadt revolt, which attracted into its ranks no small number of Bolsheviks, the Tenth Congress of the Party thought it necessary to resort to a prohibition of factions—that is, to transfer the political regime prevailing in the state to the inner life of the ruling party. This forbidding of factions was again regarded as an exceptional measure to be abandoned at the first serious improvement in the situation. . . .

However, what was in its original design merely a necessary concession to a difficult situation proved perfectly suited to the taste of the bureaucracy, which had then begun to approach the inner life of the Party exclusively from the viewpoint of convenience in administration. Already in 1922, during a brief improvement in his health, Lenin, horrified at the threatening growth of bureaucratism, was preparing a struggle against the faction of Stalin, which had made itself the axis of the Party machine as a first step toward capturing the machinery of state. A second stroke and then death prevented him from measuring forces with this internal reaction.

The entire effort of Stalin . . . was thenceforth directed to freeing the party machine from the control of the rank-and-file members of the Party. . . . The petit-bourgeois outlook of the new ruling stratum was his own outlook. He profoundly believed that the task of creating socialism was national and administrative in its nature. He looked upon the Communist International as a necessary evil which should be used so far as possible for the purposes of foreign policy. His own party kept a value in his eyes merely as a submissive support for the machine.

Together with the theory of socialism in one country, there was put into circulation by the bureaucracy a theory that in Bolshevism the Central Committee is everything and the Party nothing. . . . Availing itself of the death of Lenin, the ruling group announced a "Leninist levy." The gates of the Party, always carefully guarded, were now thrown wide open. Workers, clerks, petty officials, flocked through in crowds. The political aim of this maneuver was to dissolve the revolutionary vanguard in raw human material, without experience, without independence, and yet with the old habit of submitting to the authorities. The scheme was successful. By freeing the bureaucracy from the control of the proletarian vanguard, the "Leninist levy" dealt a death blow to the party of Lenin. . . . Democratic centralism gave place to bureaucratic centralism. In the party apparatus itself there now took place a radical reshuffling of personnel from top to bottom. The chief merit of a Bolshevik was declared to be obedience. Under the guise of a struggle with the Opposition, there occurred a sweeping replacement of revolutionists with *chinovniks*.* The history of the Bolshevik party became a history of its rapid degeneration. . . .

Of the Politburo of Lenin's epoch there now remains only Stalin. Two of its members, Zinoviev and Kamenev, collaborators of Lenin throughout many years as émigrés, are enduring ten-year prison terms for a crime which they did not commit. Three other members. Rykov, Bukharin, and Tomsky, are completely removed from the leadership, but as a reward for submission occupy secondary posts. And, finally, the author of these lines is in exile.† The widow of Lenin, Krupskaya, is also under the ban, having proved unable with all her efforts to adjust herself completely to the Thermidor.

The members of the present Politburo occupied secondary posts throughout the history of the Bolshevik party. . . . For this very reason, the rule is more stern at present that the Politburo is always right, and in any case that no man can be right against the Politburo. But, moreover, the Politburo cannot be right against Stalin, who is unable to make mistakes. . . .

Of party democracy there remained only recollections in the memory of the older generation. And together with it had disappeared the democracy of the soviets, the trade unions, the cooperatives, the cultural and athletic organizations. Above each and every one of them there reigns an unlimited hierarchy of party secretaries. The regime had become "totalitarian" in character several years before this word arrived from Germany. . . .

* Professional governmental functionaries.

† Zinoviev and Kamenev were executed in August 1936 for alleged complicity in a "terroristic plot" against Stalin; Tomsky committed suicide or was shot in connection with the same case; Rykov and Bukharin were both executed following their trial in 1938; Trotsky was executed at Stalin's order in Mexico in 1940.

If Molotov in March 1936 was able to boast to a French journalist that the ruling party no longer contains any factional struggle, it is only because disagreements are now settled by the automatic intervention of the political police. The old Bolshevik party is dead, and no force will resurrect it.

Parallel with the political degeneration of the party, there occurred a moral decay of the uncontrolled apparatus. The word *sovbour*—soviet bourgeois—as applied to a privileged dignitary appeared very early in the workers' vocabulary. With the transfer to the NEP bourgeois tendencies received a more copious field of action. At the Eleventh Congress of the Party, in March 1922, Lenin gave warning of the danger of a degeneration of the ruling stratum. . . . "Four thousand seven hundred responsible Communists" in Moscow administer the state machine. "Who is leading whom? I doubt very much whether you can say that the Communists are in the lead. . . ." In subsequent Congresses, Lenin could not speak. But all his thoughts in the last months of his active life were of warning and arming the workers against the oppression, caprice, and decay of the bureaucracy. He, however, saw only the first symptoms of the disease.

Christian Rakovsky, former president of the Soviet of People's Commissars of the Ukraine, and later Soviet ambassador in London and Paris, sent to his friends in 1928, when already in [Siberian] exile, a brief inquiry into the Soviet bureaucracy. . . . "In the mind of Lenin, and in all our minds," says Rakovsky,

the task of the party leadership was to protect both the Party and the working class from the corrupting action of privilege, place, and patronage on the part of those in power, from rapprochement with the relics of the old nobility and burgherdom, from the corrupting influence of the NEP, from the temptation of bourgeois morals and ideologies. . . . We must say frankly, definitely and loudly that the party apparatus has not fulfilled this task, that it has revealed a complete incapacity for its double role of protector and educator. It has failed. It is bankrupt. . . .

The Social Roots of Thermidor

We have defined the Soviet Thermidor as a triumph of the bureaucracy over the masses. We have tried to disclose the historic conditions of this triumph. The revolutionary vanguard of the proletariat was in part devoured by the administrative apparatus and gradually demoralized, in part annihilated in the civil war, and in part thrown out and crushed. The tired and disappointed masses were indifferent to what was happening on the summits. These conditions, however, important as they may have been in themselves, are inadequate to explain why the bureaucracy succeeded in raising itself above society and getting its fate firmly into its own hands. . . .

The dying away of the state begins, according to Lenin, on the very day after the expropriation of the expropriators—that is, before the new regime has had time to take up its economic and cultural problems. Every success in the solution of these problems means a further step in the liquidation of the state, its dissolution in the socialist society. The degree of this dissolution is the best index of the depth and efficacy of the socialist structure. We may lay down approximately this sociological theorem: The strength of the compulsion exercised by the masses in a workers' state is directly proportional to the strength of the exploitive tendencies, or the danger of a restoration of capitalism, and inversely proportional to the strength of the social solidarity and the general loyalty to the new regime. Thus the bureaucracy— that is, the "privileged officials and commanders of a standing army"—represents a special kind of compulsion which the masses cannot or do not wish to exercise, and which, one way or another, is directed against the masses themselves. . . .

First of all we must ask ourselves: What social cause stands behind this stubborn virility of the state and especially behind its policification? . . .

Let us now take from the latest number of a Moscow newspaper a stereotyped characterization of the present Soviet regime, one of those which are repeated throughout the country from day to day and which schoolchildren learn by heart: "In the Soviet Union the parasitical classes of capitalists, landlords, and kulaks are completely liquidated, and thus is forever ended the exploitation of man by man. The whole national economy has become socialistic, and the growing Stakhanov movement is preparing the conditions for a transition from socialism to communism" (*Pravda*, April 4, 1936). . . . But if exploitation is "ended forever," if the country is really now on the road from socialism, that is, the lowest stage of communism, to its higher stage, then there remains nothing for society to do but to throw off at last the straitjacket of the state. In place of this . . . the Soviet state has acquired a totalitarian-bureaucratic character.

The same fatal contradiction finds illustration in the fate of the Party. Here the problem may be formulated approximately thus: Why, from 1917 to 1921, when the old ruling classes were still fighting with weapons in their hands, when they were actively supported by the imperialists of the whole world, when the kulaks in arms were sabotaging the army and food supplies of the country—why was it possible to dispute openly and fearlessly in the Party about the most critical questions of policy? Why now, after the cessation of intervention, after the shattering of the exploiting classes, after the indubitable successes of industrialization, after the collectivization of the overwhelming majority of the peasants, is it impossible to permit the slightest word of criticism of the unremovable leaders? Why is it that any Bolshevik who should demand a calling of the congress of the Party in accordance with its constitution would be immediately expelled, any citizen who expressed out loud a doubt of the infallibility of Stalin would be tried and convicted almost as though a participant in a terrorist plot? Whence this terrible, monstrous and unbearable intensity of repression and of the police apparatus? . . .

We must find out those real social forces which have given rise to the contrast between Soviet reality and the traditional Marxian conception. . . .

In a speech at a session of the Central Executive Committee in January 1936, Molotov, the president of the Council of People's Commissars, declared: "The national economy of the country has become socialistic (applause). In that sense [?] we have solved the problem of the liquidation of classes (applause)." However, there still remain from the past "elements in their nature hostile to us," fragments of the former ruling classes. Moreover, among the collectivized farmers, state employees and sometimes also the workers, petty speculators, are discovered, "grafters in relation to the collective and state wealth, anti-Soviet gossips, etc." And hence results the necessity of a further reinforcement of the dictatorship. In opposition to Engels, the workers' state must not "fall asleep," but on the contrary become more and more vigilant. . . .

"We are not Utopians," responded Lenin in 1917 to the bourgeois and reformist theoreticians of the bureaucratic state, and "by no means deny the possibility and inevitability of excesses on the part of *individual persons,* and likewise the necessity for suppressing *such* excesses. But . . . for this there is no need of a special machine, a special apparatus of repression. This will be done by the armed people themselves, with the same simplicity and ease with which any crowd of civilized people even in contemporary society separate a couple of fighters or stop an act of violence against a woman."*. . . The flagrant contradiction between the founder and his epigones is before us! Whereas Lenin judged that even the liquidation of the exploiting classes might be accomplished without a bureaucratic apparatus, Molotov, in explaining why *after* the liquidation of classes the bureaucratic machine has strangled the independence of the people, finds no better pretext than a reference to the "remnants" of the liquidated classes. . . .

The present Soviet society cannot get along without a state, or even—within limits—without a bureaucracy. But the cause of this is by no means the pitiful remnants of the past, but the mighty forces and tendencies of the present. The justification for the existence of a Soviet state as an apparatus of compulsion lies in the fact that the present transitional structure is still full of social contradictions, which in the sphere of *consumption*—most close and sensitively felt by all—are extremely tense, and forever threaten to break over into the sphere of production. The triumph of socialism cannot be called either final or irrevocable.

The basis of bureaucratic rule is the poverty of society in objects of consumption, with the resulting struggle of each against all. When there are enough goods in a store, the purchasers can come whenever they want to. When there are few goods, the purchasers are compelled to stand in line. When the lines are very long, it is necessary to appoint a policeman to keep order. Such is the starting point of the power of the Soviet

* Cf. p. 272, above.

bureaucracy. It "knows" who is to get something and who has to wait. . . . The growth of the productive forces has been so far accompanied by an extreme development of all forms of inequality, privilege, and advantage, and therewith of bureaucratism. That too is not accidental.

In its first period, the Soviet regime was undoubtedly far more equalitarian and less bureaucratic than now. But that was an equality of general poverty. The resources of the country were so scant that there was no opportunity to separate out from the masses of the population any broad privileged strata. At the same time the "equalizing" character of wages, destroying personal interestedness, became a brake upon the development of the productive forces. Soviet economy had to lift itself from its poverty to a somewhat higher level before fat deposits of privilege became possible. The present state of production is still far from guaranteeing all necessities to everybody. But it is already adequate to give significant privileges to a minority, and convert inequality into a whip for the spurring on of the majority. That is the first reason why the growth of production has so far strengthened not the socialist but the bourgeois features of the state.

But that is not the sole reason. Alongside the economic factor dictating capitalistic methods of payment at the present stage, there operates a parallel political factor in the person of the bureaucracy itself. In its very essence it is the planter and protector of inequality. It arose in the beginning as the bourgeois organ of a workers' state. In establishing and defending the advantages of a minority, it of course draws off the cream for its own use. Nobody who has wealth to distribute ever omits himself. Thus out of a social necessity there has developed an organ which has far outgrown its socially necessary function, and become an independent factor and therewith the source of great danger for the whole social organism.

The social meaning of the Soviet Thermidor now begins to take form before us. The poverty and cultural backwardness of the masses has again become incarnate in the malignant figure of the ruler with a great club in his hand. The deposed and abused bureaucracy, from being a servant of society, has again become its lord. On this road it has attained a [huge] degree of social and moral alienation from the popular masses. . . .

Is the Bureaucracy a Ruling Class?

. . . In its intermediary and regulating function, its concern to maintain social ranks, and its exploitation of the state apparatus for personal goals, the Soviet bureaucracy is similar to every other bureaucracy, especially the fascist. But it is also in a vast way different. In no other regime has a bureaucracy ever achieved such a degree of independence from the dominating class. In bourgeois society, the bureaucracy represents the interests of a possessing and educated class, which has at its disposal innumerable means of everyday control over its administration of affairs. The Soviet bureaucracy has risen above a class which is hardly emerging from destitution and darkness, and has no tradition of dominion or command. Whereas the fascists, when they find themselves in power, are united with the big bourgeoisie by bonds of common interest, friendship, marriage, etc., the Soviet bureaucracy takes on bourgeois customs without having beside it a national bourgeoisie. In this sense we cannot deny that it is something more than a bureaucracy. It is in the full sense of the word the sole privileged and commanding stratum in the Soviet society. . . .

But the very fact of its appropriation of political power in a country where the principal means of production are in the hands of the state creates a new and hitherto unknown relation between the bureaucracy and the riches of the nation. The means of production belong to the state. But the state, so to speak, "belongs" to the bureaucracy. If these as yet wholly new relations should solidify, become the norm and be legalized, whether with or without resistance from the workers, they would, in the long run, lead to a complete liquidation of the social conquests of the proletarian revolution. But to speak of that now is at least premature. The proletariat has not yet said its last word. The bureaucracy has not yet created social supports for its dominion in the form of special types of property. It is compelled to defend state property as the source of its power and its income.

In this aspect of its activity it still remains a weapon of proletarian dictatorship. . . .

Since of all the strata of Soviet society the bureaucracy has best solved its own social problem, and is fully content with the existing situation, it has ceased to offer any subjective guarantee whatever of the socialist direction of its policy. It continues to preserve state property only to the extent that it fears the proletariat. This saving fear is nourished and supported by the illegal party of Bolshevik-Leninists, which is the most conscious expression of the socialist tendencies opposing that bourgeois reaction with which the Thermidorian bureaucracy is completely saturated. As a conscious political force the bureaucracy has betrayed the revolution. But a victorious revolution is fortunately not only a program and a banner, not only political institutions, but also a system of social relations. To betray it is not enough. You have to overthrow it. The October Revolution has been betrayed by the ruling stratum, but not yet overthrown. It has a great power of resistance, coinciding with the established property relations, with the living force of the proletariat, the consciousness of its best elements, the impasse of world capitalism, and the inevitability of world revolution.

The Question of the Character of the Soviet Union Not Yet Decided by History

In order better to understand the character of the present Soviet Union, let us make two different hypotheses about its future. Let us assume first that the Soviet bureaucracy is overthrown by a revolutionary party having all the attributes of the old Bolshevism, enriched moreover by the world experience of the recent period. Such a party would begin with the restoration of democracy in the trade unions and the soviets. It would be able to, and would have to, restore freedom of soviet parties. Together with the masses, and at their head, it would carry out a ruthless purgation of the state apparatus. It would abolish ranks and decorations, all kinds of privileges, and would limit inequality in the payment of labor to the life necessities of the economy and the state apparatus. It would give the youth free opportunity to think independently, learn, criticize, and grow. It would introduce profound changes in the distribution of the national income in correspondence with the interests and will of the worker and peasant masses. But so far as concerns property relations, the new power would not have to resort to revolutionary measures. It would retain and further develop the experiment of planned economy. After the political revolution—that is, the deposing of the bureaucracy—the proletariat would have to introduce in the economy a series of very important reforms, but not another social revolution.

If—to adopt a second hypothesis—a bourgeois party were to overthrow the ruling Soviet caste, it would find no small number of ready servants among the present bureaucrats, administrators, technicians, directors, party secretaries, and privileged upper circles in general. A purgation of the state apparatus would, of course, be necessary in this case too. But a bourgeois restoration would probably have to clean out fewer people than a revolutionary party. The chief task of the new power would be to restore private property in the means of production. . . . Notwithstanding that the Soviet bureaucracy has gone far toward preparing a bourgeois restoration, the new regime would have to introduce in the matter of forms of property and methods of industry not a reform, but a social revolution.

Let us assume—to take a third variant—that neither a revolutionary nor a counterrevolutionary party seizes power. The bureaucracy continues at the head of the state. . . . We cannot count upon the bureaucracy's peacefully and voluntarily renouncing itself in behalf of socialist equality. If at the present time, notwithstanding the too obvious inconveniences of such an operation, it has considered it possible to introduce ranks and decorations, it must inevitably in future stages seek supports for itself in property relations. One may argue that the big bureaucrat cares little what are the prevailing forms of property, provided only they guarantee him the necessary income. This argument ignores not only the instability of the bureaucrat's own rights, but also the question of his descendants. The new cult of the family has not fallen out of the clouds. Privileges have only half their worth, if they cannot be transmitted to one's children. But the right of testament is inseparable from the right of property. It is not enough to be the director of a trust; it is necessary to be a stockholder. The victory of the bureaucracy in this decisive sphere would mean its conversion into a new possessing class. On the other hand, the victory of the proletariat over the bureaucracy would insure a revival of the socialist revolution. . . .

To define the Soviet regime as transitional, or intermediate, means to abandon such finished social categories as *capitalism* (and therewith "state capitalism") and also *socialism*. But besides being completely inadequate in itself, such a definition is capable of producing the mistaken idea that from the present Soviet regime *only* a transition to socialism is possible. In reality a backslide to capitalism is wholly possible. . . .

The Soviet Union is a contradictory society halfway between capitalism and socialism, in which: (a) the productive forces are still far from adequate to give the state property a socialist character; (b) the tendency toward primitive accumulation created by want breaks out through innumerable pores of the planned economy; (c) norms of distribution preserving a bourgeois character lie at the basis of a new differentiation of society; (d) the economic growth, while slowly bettering the situation of the toilers, promotes a swift formation of privileged strata; (e) exploiting the social antagonisms, a bureaucracy has converted itself into an uncontrolled caste alien to socialism; (f) the social revolution, betrayed by the ruling party, still exists in property relations and in the consciousness of the toiling masses; (g) a further development of the accumulating contradictions can as well lead to socialism as back to capitalism; (h) on the road to capitalism the counterrevolution would have to break the resistance of the workers; (i) on the road to socialism the workers would have to overthrow the bureaucracy. In the last analysis, the question will be decided by a struggle of living social forces, both on the national and the world arena. . . .

The Soviet bureaucracy is like all ruling classes in that it is ready to shut its eyes to the crudest mistakes of its leaders in the sphere of general politics, provided in return they show an unconditional fidelity in the defense of its privileges. The more alarmed becomes the mood of the new lords of the situation, the higher the value they set upon ruthlessness against the least threat to their so justly earned rights. It is from this point of view that the caste of parvenus selects its leaders. Therein lies the secret of Stalin's success. . . .

The ancient philosopher [Heraclitus] said that strife is the father of all things. No new values can be created where a free conflict of ideas is impossible. To be sure, a revolutionary dictatorship means by its very essence strict limitations of freedom. But for that very reason epochs of revolution have never been directly favorable to cultural creation: they have only cleared the arena for it. The dictatorship of the proletariat opens a wider scope to human genius the more it ceases to be a dictatorship. The socialist culture will flourish only in proportion to the dying away of the state. In that simple and unshakable historic law is contained the death sentence of the present political regime in the Soviet Union. Soviet democracy is not the demand of an abstract policy, still less an abstract moral. It has become a life-and-death need of the country. . . .

The increasingly insistent deification of Stalin is, with all its elements of caricature, a necessary element of the regime. The bureaucracy has need of an inviolable superarbiter, a first consul if not an emperor, and it raises upon its shoulders him who best responds to its claim for lordship. . . . Each one of them at his post is thinking: *l'état—c'est moi*. In Stalin each one easily finds himself. But Stalin also finds in each one a small part of his own spirit. Stalin is the personification of the bureaucracy. That is the substance of his political personality. . . .

In the last analysis, Soviet Bonapartism owes its birth to the belatedness of the world revolution. But in the capitalist countries the same cause gave rise to fascism. We thus arrive at the conclusion, unexpected at first glance, but in reality inevitable, that the crushing of Soviet democracy by an all-powerful bureaucracy and the extermination of bourgeois democracy by fascism were produced by one and the same cause: the dilatoriness of the world proletariat in solving the problems set for it by history. Stalinism and fascism, in spite of a deep difference in social foundations, are symmetrical phenomena. In many of their features they show a deadly similarity. A victorious revolutionary movement in Europe would immediately shake not only fascism, but Soviet Bonapartism. In turning its back to the international revolution, the Stalinist bureaucracy was, from its own point of view, right. It was merely obeying the voice of self-preservation.

The Struggle of the Bureaucracy with the "Class Enemy"

From the first days of the Soviet regime the counterweight to bureaucratism was the Party. If the bureaucracy managed the state, still the Party controlled the bureaucracy. Keenly vigilant lest inequality transcend the limits of what was necessary, the Party was always in a state of open or disguised struggle with the bureaucracy. The historic role of Stalin's faction was to destroy this duplication, subjecting the Party to its own officialdom and merging the latter in the officialdom of the state. Thus was created the present totalitarian regime. It was his doing the bureaucracy this not unimportant service that guaranteed Stalin's victory. . . .

The continual purgations of the Party and the soviet organizations have the object of preventing the discontent of the masses from finding a coherent political expression. But repressions do not kill thought; they merely drive it underground. Wide circles of Communists, as well as nonparty citizens, keep up two systems of thought, one official and one secret. Spying and talebearing are corroding social relations throughout. The bureaucracy unfailingly represents its enemies as the enemies of socialism. With the help of judicial forgeries, which have become the normal thing, it imputes to them any crime it finds convenient. Under threat of the firing squad, it extracts confessions dictated by itself from the weak, and then makes these confessions the basis for accusations against the more sturdy. . . .

The hysteria of the bureaucratic hatred against the Bolshevik opposition acquires an especially sharp political meaning in connection with the removal of limitations upon people of bourgeois origin. The conciliatory decrees in relation to their employment, work, and education are based upon the consideration that the resistance of the former ruling classes dies away in proportion as the stability of the new order becomes clear. . . .

At the same moment, however, it was revealed that the most malicious "class enemies" are recruited from among those who struggled throughout their whole lives for socialism, starting with the closest co-workers of Lenin, such as Zinoviev and Kamenev. In distinction from the bourgeoisie, the "Trotskyists," according to *Pravda,* become more desperate, "the more clearly the features of a nonclass socialist society are drawn." The delirious character of this philosophy, arising from the necessity of covering up new relations with old formulas, cannot, of course, conceal a real shift in the social antagonisms. On the one hand, the creation of a caste of "gentry" opens broad opportunities for careers to the more ambitious offspring of the bourgeoisie: there is no risk in giving them equal rights. On the other hand, the same phenomenon produces a sharp and extremely dangerous discontent in the masses, and especially the worker youths. . . . The sword of the dictatorship, which used to fell those who wanted to restore the privileges of the bourgeoisie, is now directed against those who revolt against the privileges of the bureaucracy. The blows fall not upon the class enemies of the proletariat, but upon the proletarian vanguard. Corresponding to this basic change in its functions, the political police, formerly recruited from especially devoted and self-sacrificing Bolsheviks, is now composed of the most demoralized part of the bureaucracy.

In their persecution of revolutionists, the Thermidorians pour out all their hatred upon those who remind them of the past, and make them dread the future. The prisons, the remote corners of Siberia and Central Asia, the fast multiplying concentration camps, contain the flower of the Bolshevik party, the most sturdy and true. . . .

Within the last twelve years, the authorities have scores of times announced to the world the final rooting out of the Opposition. But during the "purgations" in the last month of 1935 and the first half of 1936, hundreds of thousands of members of the Party were again expelled, among them several tens of thousands of "Trotskyists." The most active were immediately arrested and thrown into prisons and concentration camps. As to the rest, Stalin, through *Pravda,* openly advised the local organs not to give them work. In a country where the sole employer is the state, this means death by slow starvation. The old principle: who does not work shall not eat, has been replaced with a new one: who does not obey shall not eat. . . .

The Inevitability of a New Revolution

Discussing the dying away of the state, Lenin wrote that the custom of observing the rules of social life can lose all need of compulsion "*if* there is nothing which provokes indignation, protest and revolt, and thus creates the necessity for repression." The essence of the matter lies in that *if*. The present regime in the Soviet Union provokes protest at every step, a protest the more burning in that it is repressed. The bureaucracy is not only a machine of compulsion but also a constant source of provocation. The very existence of a greedy, lying, and cynical caste of rulers inevitably creates a hidden indignation. The improvement of the material situation of the workers does not reconcile them with the authorities; on the contrary, by increasing their self-respect and freeing their thought for general problems of politics, it prepares the way for an open conflict with the bureaucracy. . . .

Will the bureaucrat devour the workers' state, or will the working class clean up the bureaucrat? Thus stands the question upon whose decision hangs the fate of the Soviet Union. The vast majority of the Soviet workers are even now hostile to the bureaucracy. The peasant masses hate them with their healthy plebean hatred. . . . [Yet] without a planned economy the Soviet Union would be thrown back for decades. In that sense the bureaucracy continues to fulfill a necessary function. But it fulfills it in such a way as to prepare an explosion of the whole system which may completely sweep out the results of the revolution. . . .

In any case, the bureaucracy can be removed only by a revolutionary force. And, as always, there will be fewer victims the more bold and decisive is the attack. To prepare this and stand at the head of the masses in a favorable historic situation—that is the task of the Soviet section of the Fourth International.*

* Founded by Trotsky in 1933 in protest of the Comintern's apathy over Hitler's victory in Germany and the destruction of the German workers' movement.

Today it is still weak and driven underground. But the illegal existence of a party is not nonexistence. It is only a difficult form of existence. . . .

The revolution which the bureaucracy is preparing against itself will not be social, like the October Revolution of 1917. It is not a question this time of changing the economic foundations of society, of replacing certain forms of property with other forms. History has known elsewhere not only social revolutions which substituted the bourgeois for the feudal regime, but also political revolutions which, without destroying the economic foundations of society, swept out an old ruling upper crust (1830 and 1848 in France, February 1917 in Russia, etc.). The overthrow of the Bonapartist caste will, of course, have deep social consequences, but in itself it will be confined within the limits of political revolution.

This is the first time in history that a state resulting from a workers' revolution has existed. The stages through which it must go are nowhere written down. It is true that the theoreticians and creators of the Soviet Union hoped that the completely transparent and flexible Soviet system would permit the state peacefully to transform itself, dissolve, and die away, in correspondence with the stages of the economic and cultural evolution of society. Here again, however, life proved more complicated than theory anticipated. The proletariat of a backward country was fated to accomplish the first socialist revolution. For this historic privilege, it must, according to all evidence, pay with a second supplementary revolution—against bureaucratic absolutism. . . .

It is not a question of substituting one ruling clique for another, but of changing the very methods of administering the economy and guiding the culture of the country. Bureaucratic autocracy must give place to Soviet democracy. A restoration of the right of criticism and a genuine freedom of elections are necessary conditions for the further development of the country. This assumes a revival of freedom of Soviet parties, beginning with the party of Bolsheviks, and a resurrection of the trade unions. The bringing of democracy into industry means a radical revision of plans in the interests of the toilers. . . .

More than ever the fate of the October Revolution is bound

up now with the fate of Europe and of the whole world. The problems of the Soviet Union are now being decided on the Spanish peninsula, in France, in Belgium. If the Soviet bureaucracy succeeds, with its treacherous policy of "people's fronts," in ensuring the victory of reaction in Spain and France—and the Communist International is doing all it can in that direction—the Soviet Union will find itself on the edge of ruin. A bourgeois counterrevolution rather than an insurrection of the workers against the bureaucracy will be on the order of the day. If, in spite of the united sabotage of reformists and "Communist" leaders, the proletariat of Western Europe finds the road to power, a new chapter will open in the history of the Soviet Union. The first victory of a revolution in Europe would pass like an electric shock through the Soviet masses, straighten them up, raise their spirit of independence, awaken the traditions of 1905 and 1917, undermine the position of the Bonapartist bureaucracy, and acquire for the Fourth International no less significance than the October Revolution possessed for the Third. Only in that way can the first Workers' State be saved for the socialist future.

25. ZHDANOV:
"SOCIALIST REALISM":
THE STALINIST AESTHETIC

Andrei A. Zhdanov (1896–1948) rose from obscurity to occupy numerous important posts in the Soviet Union of Stalin, his father-in-law, among these being those of secretary of the Party Central Committee, member of the Presidium of the Supreme Soviet of the U.S.S.R. and lieutenant general in charge of the defense of Leningrad during the Second World War. At various times Stalin also assigned Zhdanov the task of delivering the official line on matters of theoretical importance, including the status of artists and philosophers in the Soviet Union.

The selection is taken from Zhdanov's official speech of greeting from the Central Committee to the First Congress of Soviet Writers (August 17, 1934), in which he outlined the basic principles of "Socialist Realism," contrasted these with contemporary trends in Western literature, and admonished the Soviet writers to play a leading role in the "building of socialism" in the U.S.S.R., i.e., to do the bidding of the Party. The second part of this selection is taken from Zhdanov's attack, "Report to the Leningrad Branch of the Union of Soviet Writers and the Leningrad City Committee of the Communist Party" (August 21, 1946), upon the alleged failures of Soviet writers to meet the full demands of the Party. We thus witness a subordination of aesthetics to politics unmatched since Plato excoriated the artists in The Republic.

. . . The key to the success of Soviet literature is to be sought in the success of socialist construction. Its growth is an expression of the successes and achievements of our socialist system. Our literature is the youngest of all literatures of all peoples and of all countries. At the same time it is the richest in ideas, the most advanced, and the most revolutionary literature. Never before has there been a literature which has organized the toilers and the oppressed for the struggle to abolish once and for all every kind of exploitation and the yoke of wage slavery. Never before

SOURCE: From *Essays on Literature, Philosophy and Music* by Andrei A. Zhdanov. Reprinted by permission of International Publishers Co., Inc. Copyright © 1950.

has there been a literature which has based the subject matter of its works on the life of the working class and peasantry and their fight for socialism. Nowhere, in no country in the world, has there been a literature which has defended and upheld the principle of equal rights for the toilers of all nations, the principle of equal rights for women. There is not, there cannot be, in bourgeois countries a literature which consistently smashes every kind of obscurantism, every kind of mysticism, bigotry, and superstition, as our literature is doing.

Only Soviet literature, which is one flesh and blood with socialist construction, could become, and has indeed become, a literature so rich in ideas, so advanced, and so revolutionary. . . .

And in the light of our Soviet literature's successes, we see standing out in yet sharper relief the full contrast between our system—the system of victorious socialism—and the system of dying, moldering capitalism.

What can the bourgeois author write about, what can he dream about, what inspiration can animate his thoughts, whence can he borrow his inspiration, when the worker in capitalist countries is uncertain of the morrow, when he does not know whether he will have work the next day, when the peasant does not know whether he will work on his plot of ground tomorrow or whether he will be chased off it by the capitalist crisis, when the intellectual worker is out of work today and does not know whether he will get work tomorrow? . . .

The present state of bourgeois literature is such that it is no longer able to create great works of art. The decadence and disintegration of bourgeois literature, resulting from the collapse and decay of the capitalist system, represent the characteristic trait, the characteristic peculiarity of the state of bourgeois culture and bourgeois literature at the present time. Gone never to return are the times when bourgeois literature, reflecting the victory of bourgeois society over feudalism, was able to create the great works of the period when capitalism was flourishing. Now everything is degenerating—themes, talents, authors, heroes. . . .

Characteristic of that section of bourgeois literature that is trying to conceal the decay of bourgeois society, that is vainly trying to prove that nothing has happened, that all is well in the "state of Denmark," that there is nothing rotten as yet in the system of capitalism. Those representatives of bourgeois literature who feel the state of things more acutely are absorbed in pessimism, doubt of the morrow, the eulogy of darkness; they extol pessimism as the theory and practice of art. And only a small section—the most honest and farsighted writers—are trying to find a way out along other paths, in other directions, to link their destiny with the proletariat and its revolutionary struggle. . . .

In our country the main heroes of works of literature are the active builders of a new life—working men and women, collective farmers, Communist party members, business managers, engineers, members of the Young Communist League, Pioneers. Such are the chief types and the chief heroes of our Soviet literature. Our literature is impregnated with enthusiasm and the spirit of heroic deeds. It is optimistic, but not optimistic in accordance with any "inner" animal instinct. It is optimistic in essence, because it is the literature of the rising class of the proletariat, the only progressive and advanced class. Our Soviet literature is strong by virtue of the fact that it is serving a new cause— the cause of building socialism.

Comrade Stalin has called our writers engineers of human souls. What does this mean? What duties does the title confer upon you?

In the first place, it means knowing life so as to be able to depict it truthfully in works of art, to depict it not in a dead, scholastic way, not simply as "objective reality," but to depict reality in its revolutionary development.

In addition to this, the truthfulness and historical concreteness of the artistic portrayal should be combined with the ideological remolding and education of the working people in the spirit of socialism. This method in literature and literary criticism is what we call the method of socialist realism.

Our Soviet literature is not afraid of the charge of being "tendentious." Yes, Soviet literature is tendentious, for in an epoch of class struggle there is not and cannot be a literature which is not class literature, is not tendentious, is allegedly nonpolitical. . . .

We say that socialist realism is the basic method of Soviet literature and literary criticism, and this presupposes that revolutionary romanticism should enter into literary creation as a component part, for the whole life of our party, the whole life of the working class and its struggle, consist in a combination of the most stern and sober practical work with a supreme spirit of heroic deeds and magnificent future prospects. . . . Soviet literature should be able to portray our heroes; it should be able to glimpse our tomorrow. This will be no utopian dream, for our tomorrow is already being prepared today by conscious, planned work. . . .

To be engineers of human souls means to fight actively for a rich language, for works of a high quality. Our literature does not as yet come up to the requirements of our era. The weaknesses of our literature are a reflection of the fact that people's consciousness lags behind economic life—a defect from which our writers are not, of course, free. That is why untiring work at educating themselves and at improving their ideological equipment in the spirit of socialism is an indispensable condition without which Soviet writers cannot remold the consciousness of their readers and thereby become engineers of human souls. . . .

. . . . A great shortcoming in the work of our writers is also withdrawal from contemporary Soviet themes, a one-sided infatuation with historical themes, on the one hand, and, on the other, an attempt to utilize only vacuous subjects of a purely diverting nature. Some writers, in justification of their neglect of great contemporary Soviet themes, say that the time has come when one must give the people empty, diverting literature, when one cannot pay heed to the ideological content of works. This is a profoundly untrue notion of our people, their demands and interests. Our people are waiting for Soviet writers to comprehend and generalize the tremendous experience gained by the people in the Great Patriotic War, for them to portray and generalize the heroism with which the people now work on the restoration of the national economy of the country after the expulsion of the enemy. . . .

What is the root of these errors and shortcomings? It lies in the fact that the editors of the journals named . . . have forgotten some fundamental postulates of Leninism on literature. Many writers . . . think that politics is the business of the government and the Central Committee. As for writers, it is not their business to occupy themselves with politics. A work is written well, artistically, beautifully—give it a start, regardless of the fact that it has rotten passages that disorient our youth and poison them. We demand that our comrades, both those who give leadership in the literary field and those who write, be guided by that without which the Soviet order cannot live, i.e., by politics, so that our youth may be brought up not in a devil-may-care, nonideological spirit, but in a vigorous and revolutionary spirit. . . .

V. I. Lenin was the first to formulate with utmost precision the attitude of advanced social thought to literature and art. I remind you of Lenin's well-known article, "Party Organization and Party Literature," written at the end of 1905, in which he showed with characteristic force that literature cannot be nonpartisan, that it must be an important component part of the general proletarian cause. In this article by Lenin are laid all the foundations on which the development of our Soviet literature is based. Lenin wrote:

> Literature must become Party literature. In contrast to bourgeois customs, in contrast to the privately owned and commercialized press, in contrast to bourgeois literary careerism and individualism, "aristocratic anarchism" and rapacity—the socialist proletariat must advance the principle of *Party literature,* must develop this principle and put it into effect as fully and completely as possible.
> What is this principle of Party literature? It is not only that for the socialist proletariat literary activity cannot be a means of gain for individuals or groups of individuals, but that in general it cannot be the private affair of individuals, independent of the general interests of the proletariat. Down with non-Party publicists! Down with literary supermen! Literary activity must become *part* of the general proletarian cause.

And further on in the same article: "You cannot live in a society and be free from society. The freedom of a bourgeois author, artist, or actress is nothing but masked (or hypocritically camouflaged) dependence on the moneybag, on corruption, on prostitution."

The Leninist point of departure is that our literature cannot be apolitical, cannot be "art for art's sake," but is called upon to fill an important vanguard role in social life. Hence the Leninist principle of partisanship in literature—a most important contribution of V. I. Lenin to the science of literature. . . .

To some it seems strange that the Central Committee of the

Communist party adopted such severe measures on a literary question. . . . By its decision the Central Committee has in view the bringing of the ideological front into line with all the other sectors of our work. . . .

The level of the demands and tastes of our people has risen very high, and he who does not want to rise, or is incapable of rising to this level, will be left behind. Literature is called upon not only to keep abreast of the demands of the people, but more than that—it is obligated to develop the people's tastes, to raise higher their demands, to enrich them with new ideas, to carry the people forward. He who is incapable of marching in step with the people, of satisfying their growing demands, of keeping up with the tasks of development of Soviet culture, will inevitably be retired. . . .

26.

STALINISM AND PHILOSOPHY

Stalin's craving for a position as a great Marxist theoretician led to the publication of his Dialectical and Historical Materialism *in 1938, for which he was immediately acclaimed a philosophical genius. In this work he outlined dialectical materialism as a comprehensive ontology which is allegedly corroborated in the progress of the natural and social sciences. Stalin's version of dialectical materialism subordinates historical materialism (which is itself a dogmatic version of the Marxian materialist interpretation of history) and allows for no direct relationship between historical materialism and the natural sciences. Stalin's conception of science and philosophy might be seen in this diagram:*

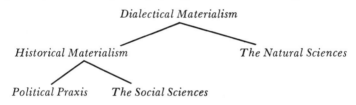

Such a philosophical scheme carries the Engels-Lenin misinterpretations of Marx to an extreme, and Stalin regurgitates many of the arguments of his predecessors in an attempt to "derive" historical materialism from his dialectical materialist ontology. In so doing, Stalin finally ends all philosophical inquiry among Communists, who were henceforth required to parrot the official line in philosophy; to disagree with "the great philosophical genius" was not only to be wrong but also to be counterrevolutionary! The net effect of Dialectical and Historical Materialism *was, of course, to underpin the antihumanist "Marxism" of Stalin, his Bolshevik predecessors, and his successors to this day.[1]*

In June 1947 the Party Central Committee called a congress of Soviet philosophers to discuss (i.e., to condemn) G. F. Alexandrov's recently published textbook The History of Western Philosophy, *the first such text published in the U.S.S.R. The task of officially reprimanding Alexandrov fell to Zhdanov, whose "arguments" are merely a rehashing of* Dialectical and Historical Materialism, *presented in a thoroughly political spirit. Alexandrov's "failings" are simply that he deviated from, or in places ignored, Engels's, Lenin's, or Stalin's pronounce-*

---

1. Cf. the Introduction and Selections 1, 2, 3, 4, 5, and 14, above.

ments on various thinkers in the Western tradition. Following Zhdanov's criticisms, which were not unexpectedly echoed by the entire chorus of assembled Soviet philosophers, Alexandrov withdrew the controversial text and submitted a self-criticism, the contents of which provide instructive insight into the status of philosophy in the U.S.S.R.

The selection which follows contains excerpts from (a) Stalin's philosophical "classic," (b) Zhdanov's speech condemning Alexandrov's book, and (c) Alexandrov's "self-criticism."

STALIN: DIALECTICAL AND HISTORICAL MATERIALISM

Dialectical materialism is the world outlook of the Marxist-Leninist party. It is called dialectical materialism because its approach to the phenomena of nature, its method of studying and apprehending them, is *dialectical,* while its interpretation of the phenomena of nature, its conception of these phenomena, its theory, is *materialistic.*

Historical materialism is the extension of the principles of dialectical materialism to the study of social life, an application of the principles of dialectical materialism to the phenomena of the life of society, to the study of society and its history.

When describing their dialectical method, Marx and Engels usually refer to Hegel as the philosopher who formulated the main features of dialectics. This, however, does not mean that the dialectics of Marx and Engels is identical with the dialectics of Hegel. As a matter of fact, Marx and Engels took from the Hegelian dialectics only its "rational kernel," casting aside its idealistic shell, and developed it further so as to lend it a modern scientific form.

My dialectic method [says Marx] is fundamentally not only different from the Hegelian, but is its direct opposite. To Hegel, the process of thinking, which, under the name of "the Idea," he even transforms into an independent subject, is the demiurge (creator) of the real world, and the real world is only the external, phenomenal form of "the Idea." With me, on the contrary, the ideal is nothing else than the material world reflected by the human mind, and translated into forms of thought. (*Capital,* Vol. I.)

When describing their materialism, Marx and Engels usually refer to Feuerbach as the philosopher who restored materialism

SOURCE: From Joseph Stalin, *Problems of Leninism* (Moscow: Foreign Languages Publishing House, 1947).

to its rights. This, however, does not mean that the materialism of Marx and Engels is identical with Feuerbach's materialism. As a matter of fact, Marx and Engels took from Feuerbach's materialism its "inner kernel," developed it into a scientific-philosophical theory of materialism and cast aside its idealistic and religious-ethical encumbrances. We know that Feuerbach, although he was fundamentally a materialist, objected to the name materialism. Engels more than once declared that "in spite of the materialist foundation, Feuerbach remained bound by the traditional idealist fetters," and that "the real idealism of Feuerbach becomes evident as soon as we come to his philosophy of religion and ethics" (*Ludwig Feuerbach*).

Dialectics comes from the Greek *dialego,* to discourse, to debate. In ancient times dialectics was the art of arriving at the truth by disclosing the contradictions in the argument of an opponent and overcoming these contradictions. There were philosophers in ancient times who believed that the disclosure of contradictions in thought and the clash of opposite opinions was the best method of arriving at the truth. This dialectical method of thought, later extended to the phenomena of nature, developed into the dialectical method of apprehending nature, which regards the phenomena of nature as being in constant movement and undergoing constant change, and the development of nature as the result of the development of the contradictions in nature, as the result of the interaction of opposed forces in nature.

In its essence, dialectics is the direct opposite of metaphysics.

The principal features of the Marxist *dialectical method* are as follows:

1. Contrary to metaphysics, dialectics does not regard nature as an accidental agglomeration of things, of phenomena, unconnected with, isolated from, and independent of, each other, but as a connected and integral whole, in which things, phenomena, are organically connected with, dependent on, and determined by, each other.

The dialectical method therefore holds that no phenomenon in nature can be understood if taken by itself, isolated from surrounding phenomena, inasmuch as any phenomenon in any realm of nature may become meaningless to us if it is not considered in connection with the surrounding conditions, but divorced from them; and that, vice versa, any phenomenon can be understood and explained if considered in its inseparable connection with surrounding phenomena, as one conditioned by surrounding phenomena.

2. Contrary to metaphysics, dialectics holds that nature is not a state of rest and immobility, stagnation and immutability, but a state of continuous movement and change, of continuous renewal and development, where something is always arising and developing, and something always disintegrating and dying away.

The dialectical method therefore requires that phenomena should be considered not only from the standpoint of their interconnection and interdependence, but also from the standpoint of their movement, their change, their development, their coming into being and going out of being.

The dialectical method regards as important primarily not that which at the given moment seems to be durable and yet is already beginning to die away, but that which is arising and developing, even though at the given moment it may appear to be not durable, for the dialectical method considers invincible only that which is arising and developing.

"All nature," says Engels, "from the smallest thing to the biggest, from a grain of sand to the sun, from the protista [the primary living cell] to man, is in a constant state of coming into being and going out of being, in a constant flux, in a ceaseless state of movement and change" (*Dialectics of Nature*).

Therefore, dialectics, Engels says, "takes things and their perceptual images essentially in their interconnection, in their concatenation, in their movement, in their rise and disappearance" (*ibid.*).

3. Contrary to metaphysics, dialectics does not regard the process of development as a simple process of growth, where quantitative changes do not lead to qualitative changes, but as a development which passes from insignificant and imperceptible quantitative changes to open, fundamental changes, to qualitative changes; a development in which the qualitative changes occur not gradually, but rapidly and abruptly, taking the form of a leap from one state to another; they occur not accidentally but

as the natural result of an accumulation of imperceptible and gradual quantitative changes.

The dialectical method therefore holds that the process of development should be understood not as movement in a circle, not as a simple repetition of what has already occurred, but as an onward and upward movement, as a transition from an old qualitative state to a new qualitative state, as a development from the simple to the complex, from the lower to the higher:

> Nature [says Engels] is the test of dialectics, and it must be said for modern natural science that it has furnished extremely rich and daily increasing materials for this test, and has thus proved that in the last analysis nature's process is dialectical and not metaphysical, that it does not move in an eternally uniform and constantly repeated circle, but passes through a real history. Here prime mention should be made of Darwin, who dealt a severe blow to the metaphysical conception of nature by proving that the organic world of today, plants and animals, and consequently man too, is all a product of a process of development that has been in progress for millions of years. (*Socialism, Utopian and Scientific.*)

Describing dialectical development as a transition from quantitative changes to qualitative changes, Engels says:

> In physics . . . every change is a passing of quantity into quality, as a result of quantitative change of some form of movement either inherent in a body or imparted to it. For example, the temperature of water has at first no effect on its liquid state; but as the temperature of liquid water rises or falls, a moment arrives when this state of cohesion changes and the water is converted in one case into steam and in the other into ice. . . . A definite minimum current is required to make a platinum wire glow; every metal has its melting temperature; every liquid has a definite freezing point and boiling point at a given pressure, as far as we are able with the means at our disposal to attain the required temperatures; finally, every gas has its critical point at which, by proper pressure and cooling, it can be converted into a liquid state. . . . What are known as the constants of physics [the point at which one state passes into another] are in most cases nothing but designations for the nodal points at which a quantitative (change) increase or decrease of movement causes a qualitative change in the state of the given body, and at which, consequently, quantity is transformed into quality. (*Dialectics of Nature.*)

Passing to chemistry and physics Engels continues:

> Chemistry may be called the science of the qualitative changes which take place in bodies as the effect of changes of quantitative composition. This was already known to Hegel. . . . Take oxygen: if the molecule contains three atoms instead of the customary two, we get ozone, a

body definitely distinct in odor and reaction from ordinary oxygen. And what shall we say of the different proportions in which oxygen combines with nitrogen or sulphur, and each of which produces a body qualitatively different from all other bodies! (*Ibid.*) . . .

. . . at certain definite nodal points, the purely quantitative increase or decrease gives rise to a *qualitative leap;* for example, in the case of water which is heated or cooled, where boiling point and freezing point are the nodes at which—under normal pressure—the leap to a new aggregate state takes place, and where consequently quantity is transformed into quality. (*Anti-Dühring.*)

4. Contrary to metaphysics, dialectics holds that internal contradictions are inherent in all things and phenomena of nature, for they all have their negative and positive sides, a past and a future, something dying away and something developing; and that the struggle between these opposites, the struggle between the old and the new, between that which is dying away and that which is being born, between that which is disappearing and that which is developing, constitutes the internal content of the process of development, the internal content of the transformation of quantitative changes into qualitative changes.

The dialectical method therefore holds that the process of development from the lower to the higher takes place not as a harmonious unfolding of phenomena, but as a disclosure of the contradictions inherent in things and phenomena, as a "struggle" of opposite tendencies which operate on the basis of these contradictions.

"In its proper meaning," Lenin says, "dialectics is the study of the contradiction *within the very essence of things*" (*Philosophical Notebooks*) .

And further: "Development is the 'struggle' of opposites" (*Materialism and Empiriocriticism*) .

Such, in brief, are the principal features of the Marxist dialectical method.

It is easy to understand how immensely important is the extension of the principles of the dialectical method to the study of social life and the history of society, and how immensely important is the application of these principles to the history of society and to the practical activities of the party of the proletariat.

If there are no isolated phenomena in the world, if all phenomena are interconnected and interdependent, then it is clear that every social system and every social movement in history must be evaluated not from the standpoint of "eternal justice" or some other preconceived idea, as is not infrequently done by historians, but from the standpoint of the conditions which gave rise to that system or that social movement and with which they are connected. . . .

Everything depends on the conditions, time, and place.

It is clear that without such a *historical* approach to social phenomena, the existence and development of the science of history is impossible, for only such an approach saves the science of history from becoming a jumble of accidents and an agglomeration of most absurd mistakes.

Further, if the world is in a state of constant movement and development, if the dying away of the old and the upgrowth of the new is a law of development, then it is clear that there can be no "immutable" social systems, no "eternal principles" of private property and exploitation, no "eternal ideas" of the subjugation of the peasant to the landlord, of the worker to the capitalist.

Hence the capitalist system can be replaced by the socialist system, just as at one time the feudal system was replaced by the capitalist system.

Hence we must not base our orientation on the strata of society which are no longer developing, even though they at present constitute the predominant force, but on those strata which are developing and have a future before them, even though they at present do not constitute the predominant force. . . .

Hence, in order not to err in policy, one must look forward, not backward.

Further, if the passing of slow quantitative changes into rapid and abrupt qualitative changes is a law of development, then it is clear that revolutions made by oppressed classes are a quite natural and inevitable phenomenon.

Hence the transition from capitalism to socialism and the liberation of the working class from the yoke of capitalism cannot be effected by slow changes, by reforms, but only by a qualitative change of the capitalist system, by revolution.

Hence, in order not to err in policy, one must be a revolutionary, not a reformist.

Further, if development proceeds by way of the disclosure of internal contradictions, by way of collisions between opposite forces on the basis of these contradictions and so as to overcome these contradictions, then it is clear that the class struggle of the proletariat is a quite natural and inevitable phenomenon.

Hence we must not cover up the contradictions of the capitalist system, but disclose and unravel them; we must not try to check the class struggle but carry it to its conclusion.

Hence, in order not to err in policy, one must pursue an uncompromising proletarian class policy, not a reformist policy of harmony of the interests of the proletariat and the bourgeoisie, not a compromisers' policy of "the growing of capitalism into socialism."

Such is the Marxist dialectical method when applied to social life, to the history of society.

As to Marxist philosophical materialism, it is fundamentally the direct opposite of philosophical idealism.

The principal features of Marxist philosophical *materialism* are as follows:

1. Contrary to idealism, which regards the world as the embodiment of an "absolute idea," a "universal spirit," "consciousness," Marx's philosophical materialism holds that the world is by its very nature *material,* that the multifold phenomena of the world constitute different forms of matter in motion, that interconnection and interdependence of phenomena, as established by the dialectical method, are a law of the development of moving matter, and that the world develops in accordance with the laws of movement of matter and stands in no need of a "universal spirit."

"The materialist world outlook," says Engels, "is simply the conception of nature as it is, without any reservations" (MS of *Ludwig Feuerbach*).

Speaking of the materialist views of the ancient philosopher Heraclitus, who held that "the world, the all in one, was not created by any god or any man, but was, is and ever will be a living flame, systematically flaring up and systematically dying down," Lenin comments: "A very good exposition of the rudiments of dialectical materialism" (*Philosophical Notebooks*).

2. Contrary to idealism, which asserts that only our mind really exists, and that the material world, being, nature, exists only in our mind, in our sensations, ideas, and perceptions, the

Marxist materialist philosophy holds that matter, nature, being, is an objective reality existing outside and independent of our mind; that matter is primary, since it is the source of sensations, ideas, mind, and that mind is secondary, derivative, since it is a reflection of matter, a reflection of being; that thought is a product of matter which in its development has reached a high degree of perfection, namely, of the brain, and the brain is the organ of thought; and that therefore one cannot separate thought from matter without committing a grave error. Engels says:

The question of the relation of thinking to being, the relation of spirit to nature is the paramount question of the whole of philosophy. . . . The answers which the philosophers gave to this question split them into two great camps. Those who asserted the primacy of spirit to nature . . . comprised the camp of *idealism*. The others, who regarded nature as primary, belong to the various schools of *materialism*. (*Ludwig Feuerbach*.)

And further:

The material, sensuously perceptible world to which we ourselves belong is the only reality. . . . Our consciousness and thinking, however suprasensuous they may seem, are the product of a material, bodily organ, the brain. Matter is not a product of mind, but mind itself is merely the highest product of matter. (*Ibid.*)

Concerning the question of matter and thought, Engels says: "*It is impossible to separate thought from matter that thinks.* Matter is the subject of all changes" (*Socialism, Utopian and Scientific*).

Describing the Marxist philosophy of materialism, Lenin says:

Materialism in general recognizes objectively real being (matter) as independent of consciousness, sensation, experience. . . . Consciousness is only the reflection of being, at best, an approximately true (adequate, ideally exact) reflection of it. (*Materialism and Empiriocriticism.*)

And further:

Matter is that which, acting upon our sense organs, produces sensation; matter is the objective reality given to us in sensation. . . . Matter, nature, being, the physical—is primary, and spirit, consciousness, sensation, the psychical—is secondary. (*Ibid.*)

The world picture is a picture of how matter moves and of how "*matter thinks.*" (*Ibid.*)

The brain is the organ of thought. (*Ibid.*)

3. Contrary to idealism, which denies the possibility of knowing the world and its laws, which does not believe in the authenticity of our knowledge, does not recognize objective truth, and holds that the world is full of "things-in-themselves" that can never be known to science, Marxist philosophical materialism holds that the world and its laws are fully knowable, that our knowledge of the laws of nature, tested by experiment and practice, is authentic knowledge having the validity of objective truth, and that there are no things in the world which are unknowable, but only things which are still not known, but which will be disclosed and made known by the efforts of science and practice.

Criticizing the thesis of Kant and other idealists that the world is unknowable and that there are "things-in-themselves" which are unknowable, and defending the well-known materialist thesis that our knowledge is authentic knowledge, Engels writes:

> The most telling refutation of this as of all other philosophical fancies is practice, viz., experiment and industry. If we are able to prove the correctness of our conception of a natural process by making it ourselves, bringing it into being out of its conditions and using it for our own purposes in the bargain, then there is an end of the Kantian "thing-in-itself." The chemical substances produced in the bodies of plants and animals remained such "things-in-themselves" until organic chemistry began to produce them one after another, whereupon the "thing-in-itself" became a thing for us, as for instance, alizarin, the coloring matter of the madder, which we no longer trouble to grow in the madder roots in the field, but produce much more cheaply and simply from coal tar. For three hundred years the Copernican solar system was a hypothesis, with a hundred, a thousand, or ten thousand chances to one in its favor, but still always a hypothesis. But when Leverrier, by means of the data provided by this system, not only deduced the necessity of the existence of an unknown planet, but also calculated the position in the heavens which this planet must necessarily occupy, and when Galle really found this planet, the Copernican system was proved. (*Ludwig Feuerbach.*) . . .
>
> [Lenin says:] If objective truth exists (as the materialists think), if natural science, reflecting the outer world in human "experience," is alone capable of giving us objective truth, then all fideism is absolutely refuted. (*Materialism and Empiriocriticism.*)

Such, in brief, are the characteristic features of the Marxist philosophical materialism.

It is easy to understand how immensely important is the extension of the principles of philosophical materialism to the study of social life, of the history of society, and how immensely important is the application of these principles to the history of society and to the practical activities of the party of the proletariat.

If the connection between the phenomena of nature and their interdependence are laws of the development of nature, it follows, too, that the connection and interdependence of the phenomena of social life are laws of the development of society, and not something accidental.

Hence social life, the history of society, ceases to be an agglomeration of "accidents," and becomes the history of the development of society according to regular laws, and the study of the history of society becomes a science.

Hence the practical activity of the party of the proletariat must not be based on the good wishes of "outstanding individuals," not on the dictates of "reason," "universal morals," etc., but on the laws of development of society and on the study of these laws.

Further, if the world is knowable and our knowledge of the laws of development of nature is authentic knowledge, having the validity of objective truth, it follows that social life, the development of society, is also knowable, and that the data of science regarding the laws of development of society are authentic data having the validity of objective truths.

Hence the science of the history of society, despite all the complexity of the phenomena of social life, can become as precise a science as, let us say, biology, and capable of making use of the laws of development of society for practical purposes.

Hence the party of the proletariat should not guide itself in its practical activity by casual motives, but by the laws of development of society, and by practical deductions from these laws.

Hence socialism is converted from a dream of a better future for humanity into a science.

Hence the bond between science and practical activity, between theory and practice, their unity, should be the guiding star of the party of the proletariat.

Further, if nature, being the material world, is primary, and mind, thought, is secondary, derivative; if the material world represents objective reality existing independently of the mind of men, while the mind is a reflection of this objective reality, it follows that the material life of society, its being, is also primary, and its spiritual life secondary, derivative, and that the material life of society is an objective reality existing independently of the will of men, while the spiritual life of society is a reflection of this objective reality, a reflection of being.

Hence the source of formation of the spiritual life of society, the origin of social ideas, social theories, political views, and political institutions, should not be sought for in the ideas, theories, views, and political institutions themselves, but in the conditions of the material life of society, in social being, of which these ideas, theories, views, etc., are the reflection.

Hence, if in different periods of the history of society different social ideas, theories, views, and political institutions are to be observed; if under the slave system we encounter certain social ideas, theories, views, and political institutions, under feudalism others, and under capitalism others still, this is not to be explained by the "nature," the "properties" of the ideas, theories, views, and political institutions themselves but by the different conditions of the material life of society at different periods of social development.

Whatever is the being of a society, whatever are the conditions of material life of a society, such are the ideas, theories, political views and political institutions of that society.

In this connection, Marx says: "It is not the consciousness of men that determines their being, but, on the contrary, their social being that determines their consciousness" (*A Contribution to the Critique of Political Economy*).

Hence, in order not to err in policy, in order not to find itself in the position of idle dreamers, the party of the proletariat must not base its activities on abstract "principles of human reason," but on the concrete conditions of the material life of society, as the determining force of social development; not on the good wishes of "great men," but on the real needs of development of the material life of society. . . .

It does not follow from Marx's words, however, that social ideas, theories, political views, and political institutions are of no significance in the life of society, that they do not reciprocally affect social being, the development of the material conditions of the life of society. We have been speaking so far of the *origin* of social ideas, theories, views, and political institutions, of *the way they arise,* of the fact that the spiritual life of society is a reflection of the conditions of its material life. As regards the *significance* of social ideas, theories, views, and political institutions, as regards their *role* in history, historical materialism, far from denying them, stresses the role and importance of these factors in the life of society, in its history. . . .

New social ideas and theories arise only after the development of the material life of society has set new tasks before society. But once they have arisen they become a most potent force which facilitates the carrying out of the new tasks set by the development of the material life of society, a force which facilitates the progress of society. It is precisely here that the tremendous organizing, mobilizing, and transforming value of new ideas, new theories, new political views, and new political institutions manifests itself. New social ideas and theories arise precisely because they are necessary to society, because it is *impossible* to carry out the urgent tasks of development of the material life of society without their organizing, mobilizing, and transforming action. Arising out of the new tasks set by the development of the material life of society, the new social ideas and theories force their way through, become the possession of the masses, mobilize, and organize them against the moribund forces of society, and thus facilitate the overthrow of these forces which hamper the development of the material life of society.

Thus social ideas, theories and political institutions, having arisen on the basis of the urgent tasks of the development of the material life of society, the development of social being, themselves then react upon social being, upon the material life of society, creating the conditions necessary for completely carrying out the urgent tasks of the material life of society, and for rendering its further development possible.

In this connection, Marx says: "Theory becomes a material force as soon as it has gripped the masses" (*Zur Kritik der Hegelschen Rechtsphilosophie*). Hence, in order to be able to influence the conditions of material life of society and to accelerate their development and their improvement, the party of the proletariat must rely upon such a social theory, such a social idea as correctly reflects the needs of development of the material life of society, and which is therefore capable of setting into motion broad masses of the people and of mobilizing them and organizing them into a great army of the proletarian party, prepared to smash the reactionary forces and to clear the way for the advanced forces of society. . . .

It now remains to elucidate the following question: What, from the viewpoint of historical materialism, is meant by the "conditions of material life of society" which in the final analysis determine the physiognomy of society, its ideas, views, political institutions, etc.? . . .

There can be no doubt that the concept "conditions of material life of society" includes, first of all, nature which surrounds society, geographical environment, which is one of the indispensable and constant conditions of material life of society and which, of course, influences the development of society. What role does geographical environment play in the development of society? Is geographical environment the chief force determining the physiognomy of society, the character of the social system of men, the transition from one system to another?

Historical materialism answers this question in the negative.

Geographical environment is unquestionably one of the constant and indispensable conditions of development of society and, of course, influences the development of society, accelerates or retards its development. But its influence is not the *determining* influence, inasmuch as the changes and development of society proceed at an incomparably faster rate than the changes and development of geographical environment. . . .

It follows from this that geographical environment cannot be the chief cause, the *determining* cause of social development, for that which remains almost unchanged in the course of tens of thousands of years cannot be the chief cause of development of that which undergoes fundamental changes in the course of a few hundred years.

Further, there can be no doubt that the concept "conditions of material life of society" also includes growth of population, density of population of one degree or another, for people are an essential element of the conditions of material life of society, and without a definite minimum number of people there can be no material life of society. Is not growth of population the chief force that determines the character of the social system of man?

Historical materialism answers this question too in the negative.

Of course, growth of population does influence the development of society, does facilitate or retard the development of society, but it cannot be the chief force of development of society, and its influence on the development of society cannot be the *determining* influence because, by itself, growth of population does not furnish the clue to the question why a given social system is replaced precisely by such and such a new system and not by another, why the primitive communal system is succeeded precisely by the slave system, the slave system by the feudal system, and the feudal system by the bourgeois system, and not by some other. . . .

It follows from this that growth of population is not, and cannot be, the chief force of development of society, the force which *determines* the character of the social system, the physiognomy of society.

What, then, is the chief force in the complex of conditions of material life of society which determines the physiognomy of society, the character of the social system, the development of society from one system to another?

This force, historical materialism holds, is the *method of procuring the means of life* necessary for human existence, the *mode of production of material values*—food, clothing, footwear, houses, fuel, instruments of production, etc.—which are indispensable for the life and development of society.

In order to live, people must have food, clothing, footwear, shelter, fuel, etc.; in order to have these material values, people must produce them; and in order to produce them, people must have the instruments of production with which food, clothing, footwear, shelter, fuel, etc., are produced; they must be able to produce these instruments and to use them.

The *instruments of production* wherewith material values are produced, the *people* who operate the instruments of production and carry on the production of material values thanks to a certain *production experience* and *labor skill*—all these elements jointly constitute the *production forces* of society.

But the productive forces are only one aspect of production, only one aspect of the mode of production, an aspect that expresses the relation of men to the objects and forces of nature which they make use of for the production of material values. Another aspect of production, another aspect of the mode of production, is the relation of men to each other in the process of production, men's *relations of production.* Men carry on a struggle against nature and utilize nature for the production of material values not in isolation from each other, not as separate individuals, but in common, in groups, in societies. Production, therefore, is at all times and under all conditions *social* production. In the production of material values men enter into mutual relations of one kind or another within production, into relations of production of one kind or another. These may be relations of cooperation and mutual help between people who are free from exploitation; they may be relations of domination and subordination; and, lastly, they may be transitional from one form of relations of production to another. But whatever the character of the relations of production may be, always and in every system, they constitute just as essential an element of production as the productive forces of society.

In production [Marx says] men not only act on nature but also on one another. They produce only by cooperating in a certain way and mutually exchanging their activities. In order to produce, they enter into definite connections and relations with one another and only within these social connections and relations does their action on nature, does production, take place. (*Wage Labor and Capital.*)

Consequently, production, the mode of production, embraces both the productive forces of society and men's relations of production, and is thus the embodiment of their unity in the process of production of material values.

One of the features of production is that it never stays at one point for a long time and is always in a state of change and development, and that, furthermore, changes in the mode of production inevitably call forth changes in the whole social system, social ideas, political views and political institutions— they call forth a reconstruction of the whole social and political order. At different stages of development people make use of different modes of production, or, to put it more crudely, lead different manners of life. In the primitive commune there is one mode of production, under slavery there is another mode of production, under feudalism a third mode of production, and so on. And, correspondingly, men's social system, the spiritual life of men, their views and political institutions also vary.

Whatever is the mode of production of a society, such in the main is the society itself, its ideas and theories, its political views and institutions.

Or, to put it more crudely, whatever is man's manner of life, such is his manner of thought.

This means that the history of development of society is above all the history of the development of production, the history of the modes of production which succeed each other in the course of centuries, the history of the development of productive forces and people's relations of production.

Hence the history of social development is at the same time the history of the producers of material values themselves, the history of the laboring masses who are the chief force in the process of production and who carry on the production of material values necessary for the existence of society.

Hence, if historical science is to be a real science, it can no longer reduce the history of social development to the actions of kings and generals, to the actions of "conquerors" and "subjugators" of states, but must above all devote itself to the history of the producers of material values, the history of the laboring masses, the history of peoples.

Hence the clue to the study of the laws of history of society must not be sought in men's minds, in the views and ideas of society, but in the mode of production practiced by society in any given historical period; it must be sought in the economic life of society.

Hence the prime task of historical science is to study and disclose the laws of production, the laws of development of the productive forces and of the relations of production, the laws of economic development of society. . . .

Hence, if it is not to err in policy, the party of the proletariat must both in drafting its program and in its practical activities proceed primarily from the laws of development of production, from the laws of economic development of society.

A second feature of production is that its changes and development always begin with changes and development of the productive forces, and, in the first place, with changes and development of the instruments of production. Productive forces are therefore the most mobile and revolutionary element of production. First the productive forces of society change and develop, and then, *depending* on these changes and *in conformity with them,* men's relations of production, their economic relations, change. This, however, does not mean that the relations of production do not influence the development of the productive forces and that the latter are not dependent on the former. While their development is dependent on the development of the productive forces, the relations of production in their turn react upon the development of the productive forces, accelerating or retarding it. In this connection it should be noted that the relations of production cannot for too long a time lag behind and be in a state of contradiction to the growth of the productive forces, inasmuch as the productive forces can develop in full measure only when the relations of production correspond to the character, the state of the productive forces, and allow full scope for their development. Therefore, however much the relations of production may lag behind the development of the productive forces, they must, sooner or later, come into correspondence with—and actually do come into correspondence with—the level of development of the productive forces, the character of the productive forces. Otherwise we would have a fundamental violation of the unity of the productive forces and the relations of production within the system of production, a disruption of production as a whole, a crisis of production, a destruction of productive forces.

An instance in which the relations of production do not correspond to the character of the productive forces, conflict with them, is the economic crises in capitalist countries, where private capitalist ownership of the means of production is in glaring incongruity with the social character of the process of production, with the character of the productive forces. This results in economic crises, which lead to the destruction of productive forces. Furthermore, this incongruity itself constitutes the economic basis of social revolution, the purpose of which is to destroy the existing relations of production and to create new relations of production corresponding to the character of the productive forces.

In contrast, an instance in which the relations of production completely correspond to the character of the productive forces is the socialist national economy of the U.S.S.R., where the social ownership of the means of production fully corresponds to the social character of the process of production, and where, because of this, economic crises and the destruction of productive forces are unknown.

Consequently, the productive forces are not only the most mobile and revolutionary element in production, but are also the determining element in the development of production. . . .

The basis of the relations of production under the socialist system, which so far has been established only in the U.S.S.R., is the social ownership of the means of production. Here there are no longer exploiters and exploited. The goods produced are distributed according to labor performed, on the principle: "He who does not work, neither shall he eat." Here the mutual relations of people in the process of production are marked by comradely cooperation and the socialist mutual assistance of workers who are free from exploitation. Here the relations of production fully correspond to the state of productive forces, for the social character of the process of production is reinforced by the social ownership of the means of production.

For this reason socialist production in the U.S.S.R. knows no periodical crises of overproduction and their accompanying absurdities.

For this reason, the productive forces here develop at an accelerated pace, for the relations of production that correspond to them offer full scope for such development. . . .

ZHDANOV: PHILOSOPHY AND THE DEMANDS OF THE PARTY

Comrade Alexandrov does not present a clear idea of the subject of this science, and although the book contains a large number of definitions having individual importance, in that they illuminate only individual aspects of the question, one does not

SOURCE: From A. A. Zhdanov, "Speech to the Philosophers' Congress" (June 1947), in *Essays on Literature, Philosophy and Music* (New York: International Publishers, 1950). Reprinted by permission.

find in the work an exhaustive general definition. . . . The subject of the history of philosophy as a science is not defined. . . .

In defining the subject of the history of philosophy it is necessary to proceed from the definition of philosophical science, given by Marx, Engels, Lenin, and Stalin. [Lenin says:]

This revolutionary side of Hegel's philosophy was adopted and developed by Marx. Dialectical materialism no longer needs any philosophy standing above the other sciences. Of former philosophy there remains the science of thought and its laws—formal logic and dialectics. And dialectics, as understood by Marx, and in conformity with Hegel, includes what is now called the theory of knowledge, or epistemology, which, too, must regard its subject matter historically, studying and generalizing the origin and development of knowledge, the transition from *non*knowledge to knowledge.

Consequently, a scientific history of philosophy is the history of the origin, rise, and development of the scientific materialist world outlook and its laws. Inasmuch as materialism grew and developed in the struggle with idealist currents, the history of philosophy is also the history of the struggle of materialism against idealism. . . .

The author describes the history of philosophy and the development of philosophical ideas and systems as a smooth, evolutionary process through the accumulation of quantitative changes. He creates the impression that Marxism arose simply as the successor to preceding progressive teachings—primarily the teachings of the French materialists, of English political economy, and the idealist school of Hegel. . . .

As you see, it is a question here only of quantitative changes. But that is metaphysics. The rise of Marxism was a genuine discovery, a revolution in philosophy. Like every discovery, like every leap, like every break in continuity, like every transition into a new condition, the rise of Marxism could not have occurred without the previous accumulation of quantitative changes—in this case, the development of philosophy before Marx and Engels. But the author evidently does not understand that Marx and Engels created a new philosophy, differing qualitatively from all antecedent philosophies, however progressive they were. The relationship of Marxist philosophy to all preceding philosophies and the basic change which Marxism effected in philosophy, in transforming it into a science, is well known. All the more strange, therefore, is the fact that the author focuses his attention not on that which is new and revolutionary in Marxism but on that which unites it with the development of pre-Marxist philosophy. This, notwithstanding the statement of Marx and Engels that their discovery meant the end of the old philosophy.

Evidently the author does not understand the concrete historical process of the development of philosophy. . . .

The creators of the philosophical systems of the past, who laid claim to the knowledge of absolute truth in the ultimate sense, were unable to further the development of the natural sciences, since aspiring to stand above the sciences, they mummified them with their schemes, imposing on living human understanding conclusions dictated not by real life but by the requirements of their philosophic system. And so philosophy was transformed into a museum in which were piled the most diverse facts, conclusions, hypotheses, and outright fantasies. If philosophy was nonetheless able to serve as a means of surveying phenomena, of contemplation, it still was not suitable as an instrument for practical action on the world, as an instrument for understanding the world.

The last system of this kind was the system of Hegel, who attempted to erect a philosophical structure subordinating all other sciences, pressing them into the Procrustean bed of its own categories. . . .

But [as noted by Engels in *Ludwig Feuerbach*]:

. . . As soon as we have once realized . . . that the task of philosophy thus stated means nothing but the task that a single philosopher should accomplish that which can only be accomplished by the entire human race in its progressive development—as soon as we realize that, there is an end of all philosophy in the hitherto accepted sense of the word. One leaves alone "absolute truth," which is unattainable along this path or by any single individual; instead, one pursues attainable, relative truths along the path of the positive sciences, and the summation of their results by means of dialectical thinking.

The discovery of Marx and Engels represents the end of the old philosophy, i.e., the end of that philosophy which claimed to give a universal explanation of the world.

Comrade Alexandrov's vague formulations blur the great revolutionary significance of the philosophical discovery of Marx and Engels, since he emphasizes that which connected Marx with the antecedent philosophers, but fails to show that with Marx there begins a completely new period in the history of philosophy—philosophy which for the first time has become science.

Closely connected with this error, we find in Alexandrov's book a non-Marxist treatment of the history of philosophy as the gradual change from one philosophical school to another. The appearance of Marxism as the scientific world outlook of the proletariat ends the old period in the history of philosophy, when philosophy was the occupation of isolated individuals, the possession of philosophical schools consisting of a small number of philosophers and their disciples, detached from life and the people, and alien to the people.

Marxism is not that kind of philosophical school. On the contrary, it supersedes the old philosophy that was the property of a small elite, the aristocracy of the intellect. . . .

Marxist philosophy, as distinguished from preceding philosophical systems, is not a science dominating the other sciences; rather, it is an instrument of scientific investigation, a method, penetrating all natural and social sciences, enriching itself with their attainments in the course of their development. In this sense Marxist philosophy is the most complete and decisive negation of all preceding philosophy. But to negate, as Engels emphasized, does not mean merely to say "no." Negation includes continuity, signifies absorption, the critical reforming and unification in a new and higher synthesis of everything advanced and progressive that has been achieved in the history of human thought. . . .

The author actually takes the position of denying the principle of the party character of philosophy, inherent in Marxism-Leninism. It is well known with what passion and irreconcilability Marxism-Leninism has always conducted the sharpest struggle against all enemies of materialism. In this struggle Marxist-Leninists subject their opponents to ruthless criticism. . . .

How then after that could Comrade Alexandrov appear in his book like a preacher of toothless vegetarianism in relation to philosophical opponents, presenting unqualified tribute to professorial pseudo-objectivism, when Marxism arose, developed, and triumphed in a merciless struggle against all representatives of the idealist tendency? . . .

Comrade Alexandrov finds it possible to say something good about almost every philosopher of the past. The more eminent the bourgeois philosopher, the greater the flattery that is offered him. All of this shows that Comrade Alexandrov, perhaps without being aware of it, is himself a captive of bourgeois historians, who proceed from the assumption that every philosopher is first of all an associate in the profession, and only secondarily an opponent. Such conceptions . . . would mean departure from the basic principle of materialism—its principle of direction, its partisanship. Well did Lenin teach us that "materialism includes, so to speak, partisanship, i.e., the obligation when estimating any event to adopt directly and frankly the viewpoint of a definite social group." . . .

It is incomprehensible why Comrade Alexandrov chose to pay tribute to the academic scientific traditions of the old bourgeois schools, forgetting the fundamental principle of materialism which demands irreconcilability in the struggle against one's opponents.

A critical study of philosophical systems must have an orientation. Philosophical views and ideas long slain and buried should not attract much attention. On the other hand, philosophical systems and ideas still current, which, notwithstanding their reactionary character, are being utilized today by the enemies of Marxism, demand especially sharp criticism. This includes particularly neo-Kantianism, theology, old and new editions of agnosticism, the attempts to smuggle God into modern natural science, and every other cookery that has for its aim the freshening up of stale idealist merchandise for the market. That is the arsenal which the philosopher lackeys of imperialism make use of at the present time in order to bolster their masters in defeat. . . .

While the author correctly notes that the development of philosophical thought in the final analysis is determined by the material conditions of social life and that the development of philosophical thought has only relative independence, he repeatedly violates that basic position of scientific materialism. Time and again he presents the various philosophical systems without relating them to their actual historical environment, and without showing the social class roots of this or that philosopher. . . . Such a method is, clearly, not scientific; it justifies the assumption that the author has slipped into the course of treating the development of philosophical ideas as independent of history, a distinguishing characteristic of idealist philosophy. . . .

The conclusion is that the textbook is bad, that it must be basically revised. . . .

The fact that the book did not evoke any considerable protest, that it required the intervention of the Central Committee of the Communist party, and particularly Comrade Stalin, to expose its inadequacies, shows the absence of developed Bolshevik criticism and self-criticism on the philosophical front. The lack of creative discussions, of criticism and self-criticism, could not but have a harmful effect upon our scientific work in philosophy. . . .

Philosophical studies, including works submitted for university degrees, turn for their themes toward the past, toward quiet and less responsible historical subjects of the type of: "The Copernican Heresy—Past and Present." This leads toward a certain revival of scholasticism. From this point of view the dispute about Hegel which took place here appears strange. The participants in that dispute forced an open door. The question of Hegel was settled long ago. There is no reason whatsoever to post it anew. No material was presented here beyond that which has already been analyzed and evaluated. The discussion itself was irritating in its scholasticism and as unproductive as the probings at one time in certain circles into such questions as whether one should cross oneself with two or with three fingers, or whether God can create a stone which he cannot lift, or whether the mother of God was a virgin. Problems of present-day actuality are hardly dealt with at all. All this taken together is pregnant with great dangers, much greater than you imagine. The gravest danger is the fact that some of you have already fallen into the habit of accepting these weaknesses.

Our philosophical work does not show either a militant spirit or a Bolshevik tempo. Considered in that light, some of the erroneous theses of Alexandrov's textbook reflect the lag on the whole philosophical front, thus constituting not an isolated accidental factor but a general phenomenon. We have often used in our discussion the term "philosophical front." But where, in actuality, is this front? When we speak of the philosophical front, it immediately suggests an organized detachment of militant philosophers, perfectly equipped with Marxist theory, waging a determined offensive against hostile ideology abroad and against the survivals of bourgeois ideology in the consciousness of Soviet people within our country—a detachment ceaselessly advancing our science, arming the toilers of our socialist society with the consciousness of the correctness of our path, and with confidence, scientifically grounded, in the ultimate victory of our cause. . . .

It is clear that the creation of such a work as a textbook on the history of philosophy is beyond the capacity of one man and that Comrade Alexandrov from the very beginning should have drawn upon a wide circle of authors—dialectical materialists, historical materialists, historians, natural scientists, and economists. . . .

This fault must be corrected. Philosophical knowledge, naturally, is the property of the collective body of Soviet philosophers. The method of drawing in a large number of authors is now being applied to the editing of the textbook on political economy which should be ready in the near future. Into this work there have been drawn wide circles not only of economists but also of historians and philosophers. Such a method of creative work is the most reliable. This implies also another idea—that of uniting the efforts of ideological workers in various fields, who at present have insufficient contact with each other, for the solution of large problems of general scientific significance. . . .

In our Soviet society, where antagonistic classes have been liquidated, the struggle between the old and the new, and consequently the development from the lower to the higher, proceeds not in the form of struggle between antagonistic classes and of cataclysms, as is the case under capitalism, but in the form of criticism and self-criticism, which is the real motive force of our development, a powerful instrument in the hands of the Communist party. This is incontestably a new aspect of movement, a new type of development, a new dialectical law. . . .

ALEXANDROV: THE "CONFESSION" OF A
SOVIET PHILOSOPHER

. . . Comrade Zhdanov and the other comrades, who have spoken, have pointed out a number of gross mistakes, errors, and imperfections in my book *The History of Western European Philosophy*. . . . I do not want to conceal from the comrades the fact that I—and, apparently, not I alone—have undergone a rigorous examination in Marxist-Leninist philosophy which, I must admit, we needed as much as we need sunshine and air. . . . This discussion would not have taken place had not the Central Committee and Comrade Stalin taken us in hand, and it is impossible to say where this crisis would have led if they hadn't. Whatever I myself may feel as the author of this thoroughly unsatisfactory book which has shown me up as a bad scholar, yet I find some consolation in the fact that our philosophic workers have rapidly followed comrade Zhdanov's directives with regard to the unsatisfactory nature of my book and its philosophical imperfections. . . .

Comrade Zhdanov! Comrade Secretary of the Central Committee! The Party has educated and instructed us. We want to be worthy of our Party, which has entrusted such great tasks to us. I believe that I express the thought of all the comrades here present when I say: we want to assure the Party through you, Comrade Zhdanov, and we give to our beloved Comrade Stalin our firm and honest word as Bolsheviks that we, as a team, are resolved to apply all our passionate enthusiasm to the task of raising the level of philosophical work in our country and of spreading, far and wide, propaganda for Marxism-Leninism. . .

SOURCE: From Alexandrov's recantations, in J. M. Bochenski, *Soviet Russian Dialectical Materialism*, trans. Nicholas Sollohub (Dordrecht, Netherlands: D. Reidel, 1963). Reprinted by permission.

27. KHRUSHCHEV:
THE CRIMES OF
THE STALIN ERA

The following selection, comprising excerpts from Nikita S. Khrush-
chev's Special Report to the Twentieth Congress of the CPSU (closed
session, February 24–25, 1956), is the major document of the secret
reassessment of Stalin undertaken by his successors. Stopping quite a bit
short of a full condemnation, Khrushchev nonetheless condemned many
of the most flagrant abuses of the "cult of personality," thereby initiating
what at the time appeared to be a new era in the history of Com-
munism. The speech was followed by a "thaw" in central control over
the Party until, eight months later, the Hungarian Communists went so
far as to attempt to install a regime, headed by the reformer Imre Nagy,
which would be genuinely responsive to the aspirations of the Hun-
garian people. This threat of democracy within a Communist party
forced the Soviet leaders to resort to armed intervention in order to
crush the Hungarian reform movement (October 1956), and thus the
true extent of Khrushchev's "liberalization" soon became apparent.

. . . After Stalin's death the Central Committee of the Party
began to implement a policy of explaining concisely and consistently that it is impermissible and foreign to the spirit of
Marxism-Leninism to elevate one person, to transform him into a
superman possessing supernatural characteristics akin to those of
a god. Such a man supposedly knows everything, sees everything,
thinks for everyone, can do anything, is infallible in his behavior.

Such a belief about a man, and specifically about Stalin, was
cultivated among us for many years.

The objective of the present report is not a thorough evaluation of Stalin's life and activity. Concerning Stalin's merits an
entirely sufficient number of books, pamphlets, and studies had
already been written in his lifetime. The role of Stalin in the
preparation and execution of the Socialist Revolution, in the

SOURCE: From *Khrushchev and Stalin's Ghost*, trans. by Bertram D. Wolfe
(New York: Frederick A. Praeger, 1957). Reprinted by permission.

Civil War, and in the fight for the construction of Socialism in our country is universally known. Everyone knows this well. At present we are concerned with a question which has immense importance for the Party now and for the future—[we are concerned] with how the cult of the person of Stalin has been gradually growing, the cult which became at a certain specific stage the source of a whole series of exceedingly serious and grave perversions of Party principles, of Party democracy, of revolutionary legality. . . .

Allow me first of all to remind you how severely the classics of Marxism-Leninism denounced every manifestation of the cult of the individual. In a letter to the German political worker Wilhelm Bloss, Marx stated:

From my antipathy to any cult of the individual, I never made public during the existence of the International the numerous addresses from various countries which recognized my merits and which annoyed me. I did not even reply to them, except sometimes to rebuke their authors. Engels and I first joined the secret society of Communists on the condition that everything making for superstitious worship of authority would be deleted from its statute. Lasalle subsequently did quite the opposite.

Some time later Engels wrote: "Both Marx and I have always been against any public manifestation with regard to individuals, with the exception of cases when it had an important purpose; and we most strongly opposed such manifestations which during our lifetime concerned us personally."

The great modesty of the genius of the Revolution, Vladimir Ilych Lenin, is known. Lenin had always stressed the role of the people as the creator of history, the directing and organizational role of the Party as a living and creative organism, and also the role of the Central Committee. . . .

While ascribing great importance to the role of the leaders and organizers of the masses, Lenin at the same time mercilessly condemned every manifestation of the cult of the individual, inexorably combated the views, alien to Marxism, about the "hero" and the "crowd," and countered all efforts to oppose a "hero" to the masses and to the people.

Lenin taught that the Party's strength depends on its indissoluble unity with the masses, on the fact that behind the Party follow the people—workers, peasants, and intelligentsia. "Only he will win and retain the power," said Lenin, "who believes in the people, who submerges himself in the fountain of the living creativeness of the people."

Lenin spoke with pride about the Bolshevik Communist party as the leader and teacher of the people; he called for the presentation of all the most important questions before the opinion of the conscious workers, before the opinion of their party. He said (of the Party), "We believe in it, we see in it the wisdom, the honor, and the conscience of our epoch."

Lenin resolutely stood against every attempt aimed at belittling or weakening the directing role of the Party in the structure of the Soviet state. He worked out Bolshevik principles of party leadership and norms of Party life, stressing that the guiding principle of Party leadership is its collegiality [leadership by a group]. Already during the prerevolutionary years Lenin called the Central Committee of the Party a collective of leaders and the guardian and interpreter of Party principles. "During the period between congresses," pointed out Lenin, "the Central Committee guards and interprets the principles of the Party." . . .

During Lenin's life the Central Committee of the Party was a real expression of collective leadership of the Party and of the nation. Being a militant Marxist-revolutionist, always unyielding in matters of principle, Lenin never imposed by force his views on his co-workers. He tried to convince; he patiently explained his opinions to others. Lenin always diligently observed that the norms of Party life were realized, that the Party statute was enforced, that the Party congresses and the plenary sessions of the Central Committee took place at the proper intervals.

In addition to the great accomplishments of V. I. Lenin for the victory of the working class and of the working peasants, for the victory of our Party and for the application of the ideas of scientific Communism to life, his acute mind expressed itself also in this—that he detected in Stalin in time those negative characteristics which resulted later in grave consequences. Fearing the future fate of the Party and of the Soviet nation, V. I. Lenin made a completely correct characterization of Stalin, pointing out that it was necessary to consider the question of transferring Stalin from the position of the Secretary General because of the fact that Stalin is excessively rude, that he does not have a proper attitude toward his comrades, that he is capricious and abuses his power.

In December 1922, in a letter to the Party Congress [see Selection 22, above], Vladimir Ilych wrote: "After taking over the position of Secretary General, Comrade Stalin accumulated in his hands immeasurable power, and I am not certain whether he will be always able to use this power with the required care."

This letter—a political document of tremendous importance, known in the Party history as Lenin's "Testament"—was distributed among the delegates to the Twentieth Party Congress. You have read it and will undoubtedly read it again more than once. You might reflect on Lenin's plain words, in which expression is given to Vladimir Ilych's anxiety concerning the Party, the people, the state, and the future direction of Party policy.

Vladimir Ilych said:

Stalin is excessively rude, and this defect, which can be freely tolerated in our midst and in contacts among us Communists, becomes a defect which cannot be tolerated in one holding the position of the Secretary General. Because of this, I propose that the comrades consider the method by which Stalin would be removed from this position and by which another man would be selected for it, a man who, above all, would differ from Stalin in only one quality, namely, greater tolerance, greater loyalty, greater kindness and a more considerate attitude toward the comrades, a less capricious temper, etc.

This document of Lenin's was made known to the delegates at the Thirteenth Party Congress, who discussed the question of transferring Stalin from the position of Secretary General. The delegates declared themselves in favor of retaining Stalin in this post, hoping that he would heed the critical remarks of Vladimir Ilych and would be able to overcome the defects which caused Lenin serious anxiety.

Comrades! The Party Congress should become acquainted with two new documents, which confirm Stalin's character as already outlined by Vladimir Ilych Lenin in his "testament." These documents are a letter from Nadezhda Konstantinovna Krupskaya to Kamenev, who was at that time head of the Political Bureau, and a personal letter from Vladimir Ilych Lenin to Stalin.

I will now read these documents. . . .

[Khrushchev then read Krupskaya's letter to Kamenev of December 23, 1922 (see p. 330, above), and Lenin's letter to Stalin of March 5, 1923 (see pp. 343–344, above)].

(*Commotion in the hall.*)

Comrades! I will not comment on these documents. They speak eloquently for themselves. Since Stalin could behave in this manner during Lenin's life, could behave thus toward Nadezhda Konstantinovna Krupskaya—whom the Party knows well and values highly as a loyal friend of Lenin and as an active fighter for the cause of the Party since its creation—we can easily imagine how Stalin treated other people. These negative characteristics of his developed steadily and during the last years acquired an absolutely insufferable character.

As later events have proven, Lenin's anxiety was justified: in the first period after Lenin's death Stalin still paid attention to his (i.e., Lenin's) advice, but later he began to disregard the serious admonitions of Vladimir Ilych.

When we analyze the practice of Stalin in regard to the direction of the Party and of the country, when we pause to consider everything which Stalin perpetrated, we must be convinced that Lenin's fears were justified. The negative characteristics of Stalin, which, in Lenin's time, were only incipient, transformed themselves during the last years into a grave abuse of power by Stalin, which caused untold harm to our Party.

We have to consider seriously and analyze correctly this matter in order that we may preclude any possibility of a repetition in any form whatever of what took place during the life of Stalin, who absolutely did not tolerate collegiality in leadership and in work, and who practiced brutal violence, not only toward everything which opposed him, but also toward that which seemed, to his capricious and despotic character, contrary to his concepts.

Stalin acted not through persuasion, explanation, and patient cooperation with people, but by imposing his concepts and demanding absolute submission to his opinion. Whoever opposed this concept or tried to prove his viewpoint and the correctness of his position was doomed to removal from the leading collective and to subsequent moral and physical annihilation. . . .

We must affirm that the Party fought a serious fight against the Trotskyites, the Rightists, and Bourgeois Nationalists, and that it disarmed ideologically all the enemies of Leninism. This ideological fight was carried on successfully, as a result of which the Party became strengthened and tempered. Here Stalin played a positive role.

The Party led a great political-ideological struggle against those in its own ranks who proposed anti-Leninist theses, who represented a political line hostile to the Party and to the cause of socialism. This was a stubborn and a difficult fight but a necessary one, because the political line of both the Trotskyite-Zinovievite bloc and of the Bukharinites led actually toward the restoration of capitalism and capitulation to the world bourgeoisie. Let us consider for a moment what would have happened if in 1928–1929 the political line of right deviation had prevailed among us, or orientation toward "cotton-dress industrialization," or toward the kulak, etc. We would not now have a powerful heavy industry, we would not have the *kolkhozes,** we would find ourselves disarmed and weak in a capitalist encirclement.

It was for this reason that the Party led an inexorable ideological fight and explained to all Party members and to the non-Party masses the harm and the danger of the anti-Leninist proposals of the Trotskyite opposition and the rightist opportunists. And this great work of explaining the Party line bore fruit; both the Trotskyites and the rightist opportunists were politically isolated; the overwhelming Party majority supported the Leninist line, and the Party was able to awaken and organize the working masses to apply the Leninist Party line and to build socialism.

Worth noting is the fact that, even during the progress of the furious ideological fight against the Trotskyites, the Zinovievites, the Bukharinites and others, extreme repressive measures were not used against them. The fight was on ideological grounds. But some years later, when socialism in our country was fundamentally constructed, when the exploiting classes were generally liquidated, when the Soviet social structure had radically changed, when the social basis for political movements and groups hostile to the party had violently contracted, when the ideological opponents of the Party had long since been defeated politically—then the repression directed against them began.

* Collective farms.

It was precisely during this period (1935–1937–1938) that the practice of mass repression through the Government apparatus was born, first against the enemies of Leninism—Trotskyites, Zinovievites, Bukharinites, long since politically defeated by the Party—and subsequently also against many honest Communists, against those Party cadres who had borne the heavy load of the civil war and the first and most difficult years of industrialization and collectivization, who actively fought against the Trotskyites and the rightists for the Leninist Party line.

Stalin originated the concept "enemy of the people." This term automatically rendered it unnecessary that the ideological errors of a man or men engaged in a controversy be proved; this term made possible the usage of the most cruel repression, violating all norms of revolutionary legality, against anyone who in any way disagreed with Stalin, against those who were only suspected of hostile intent, against those who had bad reputations. This concept "enemy of the people" actually eliminated the possibility of any kind of ideological fight or the making of one's views known on this or that issue, even those of a practical character. In the main, and in actuality, the only proof of guilt used, against all norms of current legal science, was the "confession" of the accused himself; and, as subsequent investigation proved, "confessions" were secured through physical pressures against the accused. This led to glaring violations of revolutionary legality and to the fact that many entirely innocent persons, who in the past had defended the Party line, became victims.

We must assert that, in regard to those persons who in their time had opposed the Party line, there were often no sufficiently serious reasons for their physical annihilation. The formula "enemy of the people" was specifically introduced for the purpose of physically annihilating such individuals.

It is a sad fact that many persons who were later annihilated as enemies of the Party and people had worked with Lenin during his life. Some of these persons had made errors during Lenin's life, but despite this, Lenin benefited by their work; he corrected them and he did everything possible to retain them in the ranks of the Party; he induced them to follow him. . . .

An entirely different relationship with people characterized

Stalin. Lenin's traits—patient work with people, stubborn and painstaking education of them, the ability to induce people to follow him without using compulsion, but rather through the ideological influence on them of the whole collective—were entirely foreign to Stalin. He discarded the Leninist method of convincing and educating, he abandoned the method of ideological struggle for that of administrative violence, mass repressions, and terror. He acted on an increasingly larger scale and more stubbornly through punitive organs, at the same time often violating all existing norms of morality and of Soviet laws.

Arbitrary behavior by one person encouraged and permitted arbitrariness in others. Mass arrests and deportations of many thousands of people, execution without trial and without normal investigation, created conditions of insecurity, fear, and even despair.

This, of course, did not contribute toward unity of the Party ranks and of all strata of working people, but, on the contrary, brought about annihilation and the expulsion from the Party of workers who were loyal but inconvenient to Stalin.

Our Party fought for the implementation of Lenin's plans for the construction of socialism. This was an ideological fight. Had Leninist principles been observed during the course of this fight, had the Party's devotion to principles been skillfully combined with a keen and solicitous concern for people, had they not been repelled and wasted but rather drawn to our side, we certainly would not have had such a brutal violation of revolutionary legality and many thousands of people would not have fallen victim to the method of terror. Extraordinary methods would then have been resorted to only against those people who had in fact committed criminal acts against the Soviet system.

Let us recall some historical facts.

In the days before the October Revolution, two members of the Central Committee of the Bolshevik party—Kamenev and Zinoviev—declared themselves against Lenin's plan for an armed uprising. In addition, on October 18 they published in the Menshevik newspaper, *Novaya Zhizn,* a statement declaring that the Bolsheviks were making preparations for an uprising and that they considered it adventuristic. Kamenev and Zinoviev thus disclosed to the enemy the decision of the Central Committee to stage the uprising, and that the uprising had been organized to take place within the very near future.*

This was treason against the Party and against the Revolution. In this connection, V. I. Lenin wrote: "Kamenev and Zinoviev revealed the decision of the Central Committee of their Party on the armed uprising to Rodzyanko and Kerensky . . ." He put before the Central Committee the question of Zinoviev's and Kamenev's expulsion from the party.

However, after the Great Socialist October Revolution, as is known, Zinoviev and Kamenev were given leading positions. Lenin put them in positions in which they carried out most responsible Party tasks and participated actively in the work of the leading Party and Soviet organs. It is known that Zinoviev and Kamenev committed a number of other serious errors during Lenin's life. In his "Testament" Lenin warned that "Zinoviev's and Kamenev's October episode was of course not an accident." But Lenin did not pose the question of their arrest and certainly not their shooting.

Let us take the example of the Trotskyites. At present, after a sufficiently long historical period, we can speak about the fight with the Trotskyites with complete calm and can analyze this matter with sufficient objectivity. After all, around Trotsky were people whose origin cannot by any means be traced to bourgeois society. Part of them belonged to the Party intelligentsia and a certain part were recruited from among the workers. We can name many individuals who, in their time, joined the Trotsky-ites; however, these same individuals took an active part in the workers' movement before the Revolution, during the Socialist October Revolution itself, and also in the consolidation of the victory of this greatest of revolutions. Many of them broke with Trotskyism and returned to Leninist positions. Was it necessary to annihilate such people? We are deeply convinced that, had Lenin lived, such an extreme method would not have been used against any of them. . . .

But can it be said that Lenin did not decide to use even the most severe means against enemies of the Revolution when this was actually necessary? No; no one can say this. Vladimir Ilych

---

* Cf. p. 334, above.

demanded uncompromising dealings with the enemies of the Revolution and of the working class and when necessary resorted ruthlessly to such methods. You will recall only V. I. Lenin's fight with the Socialist Revolutionary organizers of the anti-Soviet uprising, with the counterrevolutionary kulaks in 1918 and with others, when Lenin without hesitation used the most extreme methods against the enemies. Lenin used such methods, however, only against actual class enemies and not against those who blunder, who err, and whom it was possible to lead through ideological influence and even retain in the leadership. Lenin used severe methods only in the most necessary cases, when the exploiting classes were still in existence and were vigorously opposing the Revolution, when the struggle for survival was decidedly assuming the sharpest forms, even including a civil war.

Stalin, on the other hand, used extreme methods and mass repressions at a time when the Revolution was already victorious, when the Soviet state was strengthened, when the exploiting classes were already liquidated and socialist relations were rooted solidly in all phases of national economy, when our Party was politically consolidated and had strengthened itself both numerically and ideologically.

It is clear that here Stalin showed in a whole series of cases his intolerance, his brutality and his abuse of power. Instead of proving his political correctness and mobilizing the masses, he often chose the path of repression and physical annihilation, not only against actual enemies, but also against individuals who had not committed any crimes against the Party and the Soviet government. . . .

Mass repressions grew tremendously from the end of 1936 after a telegram from Stalin and Zhdanov, dated September 25, 1936, was addressed to Kaganovich, Molotov, and other members of the Political Bureau. The content of the telegram was as follows:

We deem it absolutely necessary and urgent that Comrade Yezhov be nominated to the post of People's Commissar for Internal Affairs. Yagoda has definitely proved himself to be incapable of unmasking the Trotskyite-Zinovievite bloc. The OGPU [secret police] is four years behind in this matter. This is noted by all party workers and by the majority of the representatives of the NKVD.

Strictly speaking, we should stress that Stalin did not meet with and, therefore, could not know the opinion of Party workers.

This Stalinist formulation that the "NKVD (term used interchangeably with 'OGPU') is four years behind" in applying mass repression and that there is need of "catching up" with the neglected work directly pushed the NKVD workers on the path of mass arrests and executions. . . .

The mass repressions at this time were made under the slogan of a fight against the Trotskyites. Did the Trotskyites at this time actually constitute such a danger to our party and to the Soviet state? We should recall that in 1927, on the eve of the Fifteenth Party Congress, only some 4,000 votes were cast for the Trotskyite-Zinovievite opposition while there were 724,000 for the Party line. During the ten years which passed between the Fifteenth Party Congress and the February–March Central Committee plenum, Trotskyism was completely disarmed; many former Trotskyites had changed their former views and worked in the various sectors building socialism. It is clear that in the situation of socialist victory there was no basis for mass terror in the country.

Stalin's report at the February–March Central Committee plenum in 1937, "Deficiencies of Party Work and Methods for the Liquidation of the Trotskyites and of Other Two-facers," contained an attempt at theoretical justification of the mass terror policy under the pretext that as we march forward toward socialism class war must allegedly sharpen. Stalin asserted that both history and Lenin taught him this.

Actually Lenin taught that the application of revolutionary violence is necessitated by the resistance of the exploiting classes, and this referred to the era when the exploiting classes existed and were powerful. As soon as the nation's political situation had improved, when in January 1920, the Red Army took Rostov and thus won a most important victory over Denikin, Lenin instructed Dzherzhinsky to stop mass terror and to abolish the death penalty. Lenin justified this important political move of the Soviet state in the following manner in his report at the session of the All-Union Central Executive Committee on February 2, 1920:

"We were forced to use terror because of the terror practiced by the entente, when strong world powers threw their hordes against us, not avoiding any type of conduct. We would not have lasted two days had we not answered these attempts of officers and White Guardists in a merciless fashion; this meant the use of terror, but this was forced upon us by the terrorist methods of the entente.

"But as soon as we attained a decisive victory, even before the end of the war, immediately after taking Rostov, we gave up the use of the death penalty and thus proved that we intend to execute our own program in the manner that we promised. We say that the application of violence flows out of the decision to crush the capitalists; as soon as this was accomplished we gave up the use of all extraordinary methods. We have proved this in practice."

Using Stalin's formulation, namely, that the closer we are to Socialism the more enemies we will have, and using the resolution of the February–March Central Committee plenum passed on the basis of Yezhov's report—the provocateurs who had infiltrated the organs of state security, together with conscienceless careerists, began to cover with the Party name the mass terror against Party cadres, cadres of the Soviet state, and ordinary Soviet citizens. It should suffice to say that the number of arrests based on charges of counterrevolutionary crimes grew ten times between 1936 and 1937.

It is known that brutal willfulness was practiced against leading Party workers. The Party Statutes, approved at the Seventeenth Party Congress, were based on Leninist principles expressed at the Tenth Party Congress. They stated that, in order to apply an extreme method such as exclusion from the Party against a Central Committee member, against a Central Committee candidate, and against a member of the Party Control Commission, "it is necessary to call a Central Committee plenum and to invite to the plenum all Central Committee candidate members and all members of the Party Control Commission"; only if two-thirds of the members of such a general assembly of responsible Party leaders find it necessary, only then can a Central Committee member or candidate be expelled.

The majority of the Central Committee members and candidates elected at the Seventeenth Congress and arrested in 1937–1938 were expelled from the Party illegally through the brutal abuse of the Party Statutes, because the question of their expulsion was never studied at the Central Committee plenum.

Now, when the cases of some of these so-called spies and saboteurs were examined, it was found that all their cases were fabricated. Confessions of guilt of many arrested and charged with enemy activity were gained with the help of cruel and inhuman tortures. . . .

[Khrushchev then presented numerous examples.]

In those years repressions on a mass scale were applied which were based on nothing tangible and which resulted in heavy cadre losses to the Party.

The vicious practice was condoned of having the NKVD prepare lists of persons whose cases were under the jurisdiction of the Military Collegium and whose sentences were prepared in advance. Yezhov would send these lists to Stalin personally for his approval of the proposed punishment. In 1937–1938, 383 such lists containing the names of many thousands of Party, Soviet, Komsomol,* army, and economic workers were sent to Stalin. He approved these lists.

A large part of these cases are being reviewed now, and a great part of them are being voided because they were baseless and falsified. Suffice it to say that from 1954 to the present time the Military Collegium of the Supreme Court has rehabilitated 7,679 persons, many of whom were rehabilitated posthumously.

Mass arrests of Party, Soviet, economic, and military workers caused tremendous harm to our country and to the cause of socialist advancement.

Mass repressions had a negative influence on the moral-political condition of the Party, created a situation of uncertainty, contributed to the spreading of unhealthy suspicion, and sowed distrust among Communists. All sorts of slanderers and careerists were active. . . .

In such a situation, there is no need for any approval, for what sort of an approval could there be when Stalin decided everything? He was the chief prosecutor in these cases. Stalin not only agreed to but on his own initiative issued arrest orders. . . .

And what proofs were offered? The confessions of the arrested. And the investigative judges accepted these "confessions."

And how is it possible that a person confesses to crimes which

* Communist Youth League.

he has not committed? Only in one way—because of application of physical methods of pressuring him, tortures, bringing him to a state of unconsciousness, deprivation of his judgment, taking away of his human dignity. In this manner were "confessions" secured.

When the wave of mass arrests began to recede in 1939, and the leaders of territorial party organizations began to accuse the NKVD workers of using methods of physical pressure on the arrested, Stalin dispatched a coded telegram on January 20, 1939, to the committee secretaries of *oblasts* and *krais,* to the Central Committees of republic Communist parties, to the People's Commissars of Internal Affairs, and to the heads of NKVD organizations. The telegram stated:

> The Central Committee of the All-Union Communist party (Bolsheviks) explains that the application of methods of physical pressure in NKVD practice is permissible from 1937 on in accordance with permission of the Central Committee of the All-Union Communist party (Bolsheviks). . . . It is known that all bourgeois intelligence services use methods of physical influence against representatives of the socialist proletariat and that they use them in their most scandalous forms.
>
> The question arises as to why the socialist intelligence service should be more humanitarian against the mad agents of the bourgeoisie, against the deadly enemies of the working class and of the *kolkhoz* workers. The Central Committee of the All-Union Communist party (Bolsheviks) considers that physical pressure should still be used obligatorily, as an exception applicable to known and obstinate enemies of the people, as a method both justifiable and appropriate.

Thus, Stalin sanctioned in the name of the Central Committee of the All-Union Communist party (Bolsheviks) the most brutal violation of socialist legality, torture and oppression, which led as we have seen to the slandering and self-accusation of innocent people. . . .

These and many other facts show that all norms of correct party solution of problems were invalidated and everything was dependent upon the willfullness of one man. . . .

Comrades!

If we sharply criticize today the cult of the individual which was so widespread during Stalin's life and if we speak about the so many negative phenomena generated by this cult which is so alien to the spirit of Marxism-Leninism, various persons may ask: How could it be? Stalin headed the Party and the country for thirty years and many victories were gained during his lifetime. Can we deny this? In my opinion, the question can be asked in this manner only by those who are blinded and hopelessly hypnotized by the cult of the individual, only by those who do not understand the essence of the Revolution and of the Soviet state, only by those who do not understand, in a Leninist manner, the role of the Party and of the people in the development of Soviet society.

The Socialist Revolution was attained by the working class and by the poor peasantry with the partial support of middle class peasants. It was attained by the people under the leadership of the Bolshevik party. Lenin's great service consisted in the fact that he created a militant party of the working class, but he was armed with Marxist understanding of the laws of social development and with the science of proletarian victory in the fight with capitalism, and he steeled this party in the crucible of revolutionary struggle of the masses of the people.

During this fight the Party consistently defended the interests of the people, became its experienced leader, and led the working masses to power, to the creation of the first socialist state. . .

Our historical victories were attained thanks to the organizational work of the Party, to the many provincial organizations, and to the self-sacrificing work of our great nation. These victories are the result of the great drive and activity of the nation and of the Party as a whole; they are not at all the fruit of the leadership of Stalin, as the situation was pictured during the period of the cult of the individual.

If we are to consider this matter as Marxists and as Leninists, then we have to state unequivocally that the leadership practice which came into being during the last years of Stalin's life became a serious obstacle in the path of Soviet social development. . . .

Some comrades may ask us: Where were the members of the Political Bureau of the Central Committee? Why did they not assert themselves against the cult of the individual in time? And why is this being done only now?

First of all, we have to consider the fact that the members of the Political Bureau viewed these matters in a different way at different times. Initially, many of them backed Stalin actively because Stalin was one of the strongest Marxists, and his logic, his strength, and his will greatly influenced the cadres and Party work.

It is known that Stalin, after Lenin's death, especially during the first years, actively fought for Leninism against the enemies of Leninist theory and against those who deviated. Beginning with Leninist theory, the Party, with its Central Committee at the head, started on a great scale the work of socialist industrialization of the country, agricultural collectivization, and the cultural revolution.

At that time Stalin gained great popularity, sympathy, and support. The party had to fight those who attempted to lead the country away from the correct Leninist path; it had to fight Trotskyites, Zinovievites, and Rightists, and Bourgeois Nationalists. This fight was indispensable.

Later, however, Stalin, abusing his power more and more, began to fight eminent party and government leaders and to use terroristic methods against honest Soviet people. . . .

Attempts to oppose groundless suspicions and charges resulted in the opponent falling victim of the repression. . . .

In the situation which then prevailed I talked often with Nikolai Aleksandrovich Bulganin; once when we two were traveling in a car, he said, "It has happened sometimes that a man goes to Stalin on his invitation as a friend. And when he sits with Stalin, he does not know where he will be sent next—home or to jail."

It is clear that such conditions put every member of the Political Bureau in a very difficult situation. And, when we also consider the fact that in the last years Central Committee plenary sessions were not convened and that sessions of the Political Bureau occurred only occasionally, from time to time, then we will understand how difficult it was for any member of the Political Bureau to take a stand against one or another unjust or improper procedure, against serious errors and shortcomings in the practices of leadership. . . .

Stalin evidently had plans to finish off the old members of the Political Bureau. He often stated that Political Bureau members should be replaced by new ones.

His proposal, after the Nineteenth Congress, concerning the

selection of twenty-five persons to the Central Committee Presidium, was aimed at the removal of the old Political Bureau members and the bringing in of less experienced persons so that these would extol him in all sorts of ways.

We can assume that this was also a design for the future annihilation of the old Political Bureau members and, in this way, a cover for all the shameful acts of Stalin, acts which we are now considering.

Comrades! In order not to repeat the errors of the past, the Central Committee has declared itself resolutely against the cult of the individual.

We consider that Stalin was excessively extolled. However, in the past, Stalin doubtlessly performed great services to the Party, to the working class, and to the international workers' movement.

The question is complicated by the fact that all this which we have just discussed was done during Stalin's life under his leadership and with his concurrence; here Stalin was convinced that this was necessary for the defense of the interests of the working classes against the plotting of enemies and against the attack of the imperialist camp.

He saw this from the position of the interest of the working class, of the interest of the laboring people, of the interest of the victory of Socialism and Communism. We cannot say that these were the deeds of a giddy despot. He considered that this should be done in the interest of the Party: of the working masses, in the name of the defense of the Revolution's gains. In this lies the whole tragedy! . . .

We should, in all seriousness, consider the question of the cult of the individual. We cannot let this matter get out of the party, especially not to the press. It is for this reason that we are considering it here at a closed Congress session. We should know the limits; we should not give ammunition to the enemy; we should not wash our dirty linen before their eyes. I think that the delegates to the Congress will understand and assess properly all these proposals.

(*Tumultuous applause.*)

Comrades! We must abolish the cult of the individual decisively, once and for all. . . .

Comrades! The Twentieth Congress of the Communist party of the Soviet Union has manifested with a new strength the unshakable unity of our Party, its cohesiveness around the Central Committee, its resolute will to accomplish the great task of building Communism.

(*Tumultuous applause.*)

And the fact that we present in all their ramifications the basic problems of overcoming the cult of the individual which is alien to Marxism-Leninism, as well as the problem of liquidating its burdensome consequences, is an evidence of the great moral and political strength of our party.

(*Prolonged applause.*)

We are absolutely certain that our party, armed with the historical resolutions of the Twentieth Congress, will lead the Soviet people along the Leninist path to new successes, to new victories.

(*Tumultuous, prolonged applause.*)

Long live the victorious banner of our party—Leninism!

(*Tumultuous, prolonged applause ending in ovation. All rise.*)

1818	May 5	Birth of Karl Marx
1820	November 28	Birth of Friedrich Engels
1844	Spring–Summer	Marx develops concepts of alienated labor and communism
1844	Autumn	Marx and Engels begin collaboration on *The Holy Family*
1847	September 20	Birth of Sergei Gennadevitch Nechayev
1848	January	Marx writes *Communist Manifesto*
1848–1849		Year of revolution throughout Europe
1850	January 6	Birth of Eduard Bernstein
1850	March	Marx and Engels's "Address of the Central Council to the Communist League"
1854	October 16	Birth of Karl Kautsky
1856	December 11	Birth of Georgi Valentinovitch Plekhanov
1859		Charles Darwin publishes *The Origin of Species*
1864	September 28	Inauguration of First International
1867	September 14	Marx publishes first volume of *Capital*
1870	April 22	Birth of Vladimir Ilych Ulyanov (Lenin)
1871	March 5	Birth of Rosa Luxemburg
1871	March 18–May 28	The Paris Commune
1871	June–July	Marx publishes *The Civil War in France*
1872		Publication of Russian translation of *Capital*
1872	September	The Hague Conference and the split of the First International (final dissolution occurs in 1876)
1873		Engels begins work on *Dialectics of Nature*
1873	January 20	Nechayev condemned to 20 years' hard labor
1875	May	Founding Congress of the SPD at Gotha
1875	May	Marx writes *Critique of the Gotha Program*
1877		Engels publishes *Anti-Dühring*
1878	October	Antisocialist laws take effect in Germany
1879	November 7	Birth of Lev Davidovitch Bronstein (Trotsky)

1879	December 21	Birth of Yosif Vissarionovitch Djugashvili (Stalin)
1880	March–May	Engels publishes *Socialism: Utopian and Scientific*
1881	March 13	Assassination of Alexander II
1882	December 3	Death of Nechayev
1883	March 14	Death of Marx
1883	Autumn	Plekhanov forms Emancipation of Labor group in Switzerland
1884		Engels publishes *The Origin of the Family, Private Property and the State*
1885		Engels publishes volume two of Marx's *Capital*
1887	May 20	Execution of Lenin's brother Alexander Ulyanov for plotting assassination of Alexander III
1888		Engels publishes *Ludwig Feuerbach and the Close of Classical German Philosophy*
1888	October 9	Birth of Nikolai Ivanovitch Bukharin
1889	July 14	Founding Congress of the Second International
1890	March	Bismarck's dismissal as chancellor of Germany
1890	September 30	Antisocialist laws expire in Germany
1891	January	Engels and Kautsky publish Marx's *Critique of the Gotha Program*
1891	October	SPD adopts the Erfurt Program
1892		Plekhanov publishes Russian translation of Engels's *Ludwig Feuerbach*
1894		Engels publishes volume three of Marx's *Capital*
1895		Plekhanov publishes *The Development of the Monist View of History*
1895	March	Engels publishes his Introduction to Marx's *The Class Struggles in France*, declaring revolution outmoded
1895	August 5	Death of Engels
1898		Bernstein's "Revisionist" articles begin to appear
1898		Plekhanov publishes *The Role of the Individual in History*
1898	March 13–15	First Congress of the RSDLP
1898		Bernstein publishes *The Presuppositions of Socialism and the Tasks of Social Democracy* (later translated into English as *Evolutionary Socialism*)

1899		Rosa Luxemburg publishes article "Reform or Revolution?" excoriating Bernstein
1902	March	Lenin publishes *What Is to Be Done?*
1903	July 30–August 23	Second Congress of the RSDLP. Split between Bolsheviks and Mensheviks
1904		Rosa Luxemburg publishes article "Organizational Questions of the Russian Social Democracy" (*Leninism or Marxism?*) criticizing Lenin
1905		Alexander Bogdanov publishes *Empiriomonism*
1905–1910		Kautsky publishes *Theory of Surplus Value* (fourth volume of Marx's *Capital*)
1905	January	Beginning of a year of revolution in Russia
1905	July	Lenin publishes *Two Tactics of Social Democracy in the Democratic Revolution*
1906		Rosa Luxemburg publishes *The Mass Strike*
1907		Otto Bauer publishes *The National Question and Social Democracy*, initiating the Social Democratic debate on imperialism
1908		Plekhanov publishes *Fundamental Problems of Marxism*
1909	May	Lenin publishes *Materialism and Empiriocriticism*
1910		Franz Hilferding publishes *Finance Capital*
1913		Rosa Luxemburg publishes *The Accumulation of Capital*
1914	August 4	War credits voted in Reichstag with unanimous support of SPD. Outbreak of World War I
1914	Autumn	Lenin writes article "Karl Marx" for *Granat Encyclopaedia*
1914	Autumn	Lenin works on "Conspectus of Hegel's *Science of Logic*"
1914	November 1	Lenin publishes "The War and Russian Social Democracy," calling for policy of "revolutionary defeatism"
1915		Lenin works on "The Question of Dialectics"

1915	April	Rosa Luxemburg completes the "Junius Pamphlet" in prison
1915	September 18– 21	Zimmerwald Conference in Switzerland. The "Junius Pamphlet" fails to arrive in time
1916		Bukharin publishes article "On the Theory of the Imperialist State"
1916	January– June	Lenin writes *Imperialism—The Highest Stage of Capitalism*
1916	April	The "Junius Pamphlet" finally published
1916	October	Lenin's criticism of the "Junius Pamphlet" appears
1917	March 8	The "February Revolution" [N.B. All dates for events in Russia are given according to the Western (Gregorian) calendar]
1917	March 15	Abdication of Nicholas II
1917	April 16	Lenin arrives in St. Petersburg
1917	April 17	Lenin delivers "April Theses"
1917	April 22	Lenin's article "The Dual Power" published in *Pravda*
1917	July 17–18	Abortive Bolshevik coup
1917	Summer and Autumn	Lenin hides in Finland and writes *State and Revolution*
1917	September 25– 27	Lenin writes "Marxism and Insurrection"
1917	October 23	The Bolshevik decision to seize power
1917	November 7	The "October Revolution." Bolsheviks control Soviet government
1917	November 8	Decree on Peace; Decree on Land
1917	November 9	Declaration of Workers' and Peasants' Government
1917	December 20	Formation of the Cheka (Soviet secret police)
1918		Rosa Luxemburg writes *The Russian Revolution*
1918	January 18– 19	Constituent Assembly meets and is dissolved
1918	January 20	Lenin writes "Theses on the Question of the Immediate Conclusion of a Separate and Annexationist Peace"
1918	February 8	Gregorian Calendar adopted in Russia
1918	March 14–16	Ratification of the Treaty of Brest-Litovsk
1918	March	Bolsheviks change their name to Communists
1918	Spring	Outbreak of Civil War in Russia

1918	May 30	Death of Plekhanov
1918	July	Left Socialist Revolutionaries attempt coup against Communists
1918	July 17	Romanov family assassinated
1918	Summer	Beginning of Red Terror
1919	January 5–13	Spartacus uprising in Germany
1919	January 15	Assassination of Rosa Luxemburg and Karl Liebknecht
1919	March 2–6	First Congress of the Third (Communist) International
1920		Bukharin publishes *The Economics of the Transformation Period*
1920		Trotsky publishes *Terrorism and Communism*
1920	May	Lenin publishes *Left-Wing Communism: An Infantile Disorder*
1920	July	Lenin submits his "Twenty-one Conditions" for admission to the Communist International
1921	February	Stalin orders invasion of Georgia
1921	March 1–18	Kronstadt uprising
1921	March	Lenin moves to end factions within RCP
1921	April	Lenin inaugurates "New Economic Policy"
1922	March	Stalin appointed General Secretary of the RCP
1922	April 11	Trotsky refuses Lenin's offer to be his designated second-in-command
1922	May 26	Lenin's first stroke
1922	November 20	Lenin announces triumvirate, omitting Stalin and Trotsky
1922	December 16	Lenin's second stroke
1922	December 23–25	Lenin dictates "Letter to the Congress"
1922	December 27–29	Lenin dictates his plan to expand Central Committee and to subordinate it to the State Planning Commission
1922	December 30–31	Lenin moves to end Stalin's "Great-Russian chauvinism" in the Georgian affair
1923	January 4	Lenin dictates postscript to "Letter to the Congress" recommending Stalin's removal as Party General Secretary
1923	March 2	Lenin moves to eliminate Stalin's Workers' and Peasants' Inspectorate
1923	March 5	Lenin appeals to Trotsky for help against Stalin

1923	March 5	Lenin's ultimatum to Stalin
1923	March 6	Lenin promises aid to Georgian foes of Stalin
1923	March 9	Lenin's third stroke
1923	April 17–25	Twelfth Party Congress. Emergence of Stalin as dominant figure
1923	May	Formation of Labor and Socialist International, successor to Second International
1923	December 8	Trotsky publishes open letter on "The New Course"
1924	January 16–18	Thirteenth Party Conference condemns Trotsky
1924	January 21	Death of Lenin
1924	April	Stalin's lectures on *The Foundations of Leninism*
1924	December	Stalin stresses "Socialism in One Country" against Trotsky
1928	January 16	Trotsky exiled to Central Asia
1929	January 18	Trotsky banished from the U.S.S.R.
1929	February	Condemnation of Bukharin. Stalin unchallenged leader of RCP
1929	April	Adoption of First Five-Year Plan. Forced industralization and collectivization of agriculture begin
1929	April	Purge of Soviet philosophers
1929	December	Beginning of Stalin's attacks on the kulaks
1931		Growth of managerial elite
1932	December 18	Death of Bernstein
1933	January 31	Hitler appointed chancellor of Germany
1933		Trotsky founds Fourth International
1934	July	Stalin's attacks on egalitarianism in the U.S.S.R.
1934	July	Comintern approves policy of "United Front" against Fascism
1934		Revival of Russian patriotism in the U.S.S.R.
1934	August 17	Zhdanov delivers Party Line on "Socialist Realism"
1934	December 1	Assassination of Sergei Kirov, Stalin's heir apparent
1935	August 30–31	Stakhanov breaks coal-mining quota; beginning of "Stakhanovite" movement
1936		Trotsky publishes *The Revolution Betrayed*

1936	July 17	Rising of the generals and the start of the Spanish Civil War
1936	August 19–24	Show trial of Zinoviev and Kamenev, who are immediately executed
1937	March 3	Stalin's speech justifying the purges
1938	March 2–13	Show trial of Bukharin, Rykov, and others, who are immediately executed
1938	September	Stalin publishes *Dialectical and Historical Materialism*
1938	October 17	Death of Kautsky, long since forgotten as an active socialist leader
1939	August	Signing of Nazi-Soviet Pact
1939	September 1	Germany invades Poland. World War II begins
1940	August 20	Assassination of Trotsky
1946	August	Zhdanov's condemnation of Soviet writers
1947	June	Zhdanov's condemnation of Soviet philosophers
1953	March 5	Death of Stalin
1956	February 24–25	Khrushchev's denunciation of "Crimes of the Stalin Era"

SUGGESTIONS FOR FURTHER READING

The works listed below have been selected for the reader who wishes to further pursue his studies of Marxism. For the sake of convenience the list has been limited to sources available in English. Items of special interest are indicated with an asterisk.

PRIMARY SOURCES

MARX AND ENGELS

Unfortunately, there is at present no complete English edition of the works of Marx and Engels. The following works, however, contain the most important of their writings:

*Marx, Karl. *Capital.* 3 vols. Moscow: Progress Publishers, 1965–1966.
*———. *Early Writings.* Trans. and ed. by T. B. Bottomore. New York: McGraw-Hill, 1964.
*———. *Karl Marx: The Essential Writings.* Ed. by Frederic L. Bender. New York: Harper and Row, 1972.
*———. *Marx's Grundrisse* (selections). Trans. by David McLellan. New York: Harper and Row, 1972.
*———. *Theories of Surplus Value* (the "fourth volume" of *Capital*). 3 vols. Moscow: Progress Publishers, 1963–71.
*———. *Writings of the Young Marx on Philosophy and Society.* Trans. and ed. by Loyd D. Easton and Kurt H. Guddat. Garden City, N.Y.: Doubleday, 1967.
*Engels, Friedrich. *The Dialectics of Nature.* Moscow: Foreign Languages Publishing House, 1966.
*———. *Herr Eugen Dühring's Revolution in Science* (the so-called *Anti-Dühring*). Moscow: Foreign Languages Publishing House, 1962.
*———. *The Origin of the Family, Private Property and the State.* New York: International Publishers, 1964.
*Marx and Engels. *The German Ideology.* Moscow: Progress Publishers, 1968.
*———. *The Holy Family.* Trans. by R. Dixon. Moscow: Foreign Languages Publishing House, 1956.
*———. *Selected Correspondence.* Moscow: Progress Publishers, 1965.
*———. *Selected Works.* 2 vols. Moscow: Co-operative Publishing Society of Foreign Workers in the U.S.S.R., 1935–1936.

SUGGESTIONS FOR FURTHER READING

GERMAN MARXISM TO 1914

*Bernstein, Eduard. *Evolutionary Socialism* (*The Presuppositions of Socialism and the Tasks of Social Democracy*). Trans. by Edith C. Harvey. New York: Schocken, 1970.

Kautsky, Karl. *The Class Struggle.* Trans. by William E. Bohn. New York: Norton, 1971.

———. *The Dictatorship of the Proletariat.* Trans. by H. J. Stenning. Ann Arbor: University of Michigan Press, 1964.

Luxemburg, Rosa. *The Accumulation of Capital.* Trans. by Agnes Schwarzschild. New York: Monthly Review Press, 1964. Her magnum opus.

*———. *Rosa Luxemburg Speaks.* Ed. by Mary-Alice Waters. New York: Pathfinder Press, 1970. Contains most of the important essays.

SOVIET MARXISM

Bukharin, Nikolai. *Historical Materialism.* Ann Arbor: University of Michigan Press, 1969. For 15 years the basic Soviet textbook of Marxism.

Lenin, V. I. *Collected Works* (in 45 vols.). Moscow: Progress Publishers, 1963–70.

———. Articles on the First World War, the collapse of the Second International, etc. *Collected Works,* vol. 21.

———. *The Development of Capitalism in Russia. Collected Works.* vol. 3.

*———. *Imperialism: The Highest Stage of Capitalism. Collected Works,* vol. 22.

———. "Karl Marx" (article for *Granat Encyclopaedia*). *Collected Works,* vol. 21.

———. *"Left-Wing" Communism: An Infantile Disorder. Collected Works,* vol. 31.

———. Letters, articles, speeches of the pre-Bolshevik Revolution period (April–Sept. 1971). *Collected Works,* vols. 24, 25.

———. Letters, articles, speeches, and decrees of the early days of the Bolshevik Revolution. *Collected Works,* vols., 26–28.

*———. *Materialism and Empiriocriticism. Collected Works,* vol. 14.

———. "Philosophical Notebooks." *Collected Works,* vol. 38.

*———. *The State and Revolution. Collected Works,* vol. 25.

———. "The Three Sources and Three Component Parts of Marxism." *Collected Works,* vol. 19.

*———. *Two Tactics of Social Democracy in the Democratic Revolution. Collected Works,* vol. 9.

*———. *What Is to Be Done? Collected Works,* vol. 5.

———. *Selected Works in One Volume.* New York: International Publishers, 1971. This is the best of the readily available collections.

Plekhanov, G. V. *Fundamental Problems of Marxism.* Trans. by Eden and Cedar Paul. New York: International Publishers, 1929.

———. *Selected Philosophical Works,* Vol. I. Moscow: Foreign Languages Publishing House, n.d. (This is the only volume ever released in the projected series of 5 vols.)

*Stalin, Joseph. *Dialectical and Historical Materialism.* New York: International Publishers, 1940.

———. *The Foundations of Leninism.* New York: International Publishers, 1939.

———. *Problems of Leninism.* Moscow: Foreign Languages Publishing House, 1947. Selected articles by Stalin.

———. *Works.* 13 vols. (incomplete). Moscow: Foreign Languages Publishing House, 1952–55.

Trotsky, Leon. *The New Course.* Trans. by Max Schachtman. Ann Arbor: University of Michigan Press, 1965.

———. *The Revolution Betrayed.* Trans. by Max Eastman. Garden City, N.Y.: Doubleday, Doran & Co., 1937.

———. *Terrorism and Communism: A Reply to Karl Kautsky* (i.e., Kautsky's *Dictatorship of the Proletariat,* above). Ann Arbor: University of Michigan Press, 1969.

Zhdanov, Andrei A. *Essays on Literature, Philosophy and Music.* New York: International Publishers, 1950.

SECONDARY SOURCES

INTERPRETATIONS OF MARX

*Avineri, Shlomo. *The Social and Political Thought of Karl Marx.* Cambridge: Cambridge University Press, 1969. One of the outstanding recent works on Marx, stressing the unity of his earlier and later periods.

*Fetscher, Iring. *Marx and Marxism.* New York: Herder and Herder, 1971. Essays by one of Germany's foremost interpreters of Marx. Especially important is "The Relationship of Marxism to Hegel."

Kamenka, Eugene. *The Ethical Foundations of Marxism.* New York: Frederick A. Praeger Co., 1962. A study of the early Marx, emphasizing his relation to the traditional problems of ethics.

*Korsch, Karl. *Marxism and Philosophy.* Trans. by Fred Halliday. New York: Monthly Review Press, 1970. A thorough assessment of the Marxists' misreadings of Marx. When published in 1923 this book provoked great controversy, its author being eventually expelled from the German Communist party.

*Lukacs, Georg. *History and Class Consciousness.* Trans. by Rodney Livingstone. London: The Merlin Press, 1971. The first "rediscovery" of the "humanist" Marx. Provoked a major storm upon its first publication in 1923. The outstanding work of Marxist theory in the twentieth century.

McLellan, David. *Marx Before Marxism*. New York: Harper and Row, 1971. Documents the development of Marx's thought through the "Paris Manuscripts" of 1844.

————. *The Young-Hegelians and Karl Marx*. London: Macmillan & Co., 1969. A recent work of considerable scholarly interest.

*Meszaros, Istvan. *Marx's Theory of Alienation*. London: The Merlin Press, 1970. The most thorough study of Marx on alienation yet published.

Ollman, Bertell. *Alienation: Marx's Conception of Man in Capitalist Society*. Cambridge: Cambridge University Press, 1971. A recent and scholarly study.

Rotenstreich, Nathan. *Basic Problems of Marx's Philosophy*. Indianapolis: Bobbs-Merrill, 1965. Thorough examination of Marx's "Theses on Feuerbach."

STUDIES OF DIALECTICAL MATERIALISM

Bochenski, J. M. *Soviet Russian Dialectical Materialism*. Trans. by Nicolas Sollohub. Dordrecht: D. Reidel Publishing Co., 1963. A thorough study of the principles and development of Soviet philosophy.

*Jordon, Z. A. *The Evolution of Dialectical Materialism*. New York: St. Martin's Press, 1967. Outstanding study of the history of dialectical materialist philosophy from Marx through Stalin.

Lefebvre, Henri. *Dialectical Materialism*. Trans. by John Sturrock. London: Jonathan Cape, 1970. A standard interpretation by a leading French Marxist theoretician.

Marcuse, Herbert. *Soviet Marxism: A Critical Analysis*. New York: Random House, 1961. Documents the poverty of Soviet philosophy.

*Wetter, Gustav A. *Dialectical Materialism*. Trans. by Peter Heath. New York: Frederick A. Praeger, 1958. A classic study of the historical and systematic aspects of dialectical materialism through Stalin.

GENERAL HISTORIES OF MARXISM

*Lichtheim, George. *Marxism: An Historical and Critical Study*. New York: Frederick A. Praeger, 1961. A basic work on the development of Marxism. Focus is on politics rather than philosophy.

Wolfe, Bertram D. *Marxism: One Hundred Years in the Life of a Doctrine*. New York: Dell, 1967. A critical presentation of the history of Marxism.

BIOGRAPHICAL STUDIES

Marx

*McLellan, David. *Karl Marx: His Life and Thought.* New York: Harper and Row, 1974. A recent biography distinguished for its thoroughness.

Mehring, Franz. *Karl Marx: The Story of His Life.* Ann Arbor: University of Michigan Press, 1962. The standard biography by a leading Social Democrat and admirer of Marx. Quite dated, especially as regards the early Marx.

Payne, Robert. *Marx.* London: W. H. Allen, 1968. A rather critical biography which concentrates more on the man than on his thought. A valuable source on the many personal controversies involving Marx.

Engels

Mayer, Gustav. *Friedrich Engels: A Biography.* Trans. by Gilbert and Helen Highet, ed. by G. D. H. Cole. New York: Alfred A. Knopf, 1936. An abridged version of the standard biography of Engels.

Bernstein

Gay, Peter. *The Dilemma of Democratic Socialism: Eduard Bernstein's Challenge to Marx.* New York: Collier, 1970, The standard biography of Bernstein.

Luxemburg

Frohlich, Paul. *Rosa Luxemburg.* New York: Monthly Review Press, 1973. Written by an admirer, with a tendency to defend her uncritically.

*Nettl, J. P. *Rosa Luxemburg.* 2 vols. London: Oxford University Press, 1966. The standard biography.

Plekhanov

Baron, Samuel H. *Plekhanov: The Father of Russian Marxism.* Stanford University Press, 1963. Generally accurate but weak on Plekhanov's contributions to Marxist philosophy.

Lenin

*Fischer, Louis. *The Life of Lenin.* New York: Harper and Row, 1964. The best biography of Lenin thus far.

Payne, Robert. *The Life and Death of Lenin.* New York: Avon Books, 1967. A fine biography, in which is discussed the evidence for the possibility that Stalin had Lenin murdered.

Stalin

Deutscher, Isaac. *Stalin: A Political Biography.* New York: Oxford University Press, 1967. A thorough biography by a distinguished scholar.

Payne, Robert. *The Rise and Fall of Stalin.* New York: Simon and Schuster, 1965. An interesting and exciting biography.

*Trotsky, Leon. *Stalin: An Appraisal of the Man and His Influence.* Trans. by Charles Malamuth. New York: Stein and Day, 1967. Trotsky's polemical appraisal of his rival.

Trotsky

*Deutscher, Isaac. *The Prophet Armed, The Prophet Unarmed, and The Prophet Outcast.* New York: Random House, 1965. The standard biographical study.

Trotsky, Leon. *My Life.* New York: Pathfinder Press, 1917. Trotsky's autobiography until his exile in 1929.

The Second International

Cole, G. D. H. *Socialist Thought: The Second International.* London: Macmillan, 1956. The standard history of the period.

Roth, Günther. *The Social Democrats in Imperial Germany.* Totowa, N.J.: Bedminster Press, 1963. A sociological approach to the history of the German labor movement.

The Russian Revolution

Browder, Robert P., and Kerensky, Alexander F. *The Russian Provisional Government,* 1917. 3 vols. Stanford: Stanford University Press, 1961. Documents of the provisional government, March–November 1917.

Carr, E. H. *The Bolshevik Revolution.* 3 vols. New York: Macmillan, 1951–53. The most complete study of the period 1917–1926.

Kerensky, Alexander F. *The Catastrophe.* New York: Appleton, 1927. A classic eyewitness account by the leading figure of the provisional government.

Reed, John. *Ten Days that Shook the World.* New York: Modern Library, 1935. Eyewitness account of the October Revolution by an American journalist.

*Trotsky, Leon. *The History of the Russian Revolution.* Trans. by Max Eastman. London: Sphere Books, 1967. The classic eyewitness account from the Bolshevik perspective. Covers only events culminating in the October Revolution.

*Wolfe, Bertram. *Three Who Made a Revolution.* New York: Dell, 1964. Study of Lenin, Stalin, and Trotsky to 1917.

HISTORIES OF THE COMMUNIST PARTY OF THE SOVIET UNION

A Commission of the Central Committee of the CPSU (B). *History of the Communist Party of the Soviet Union (Bolsheviks).* Moscow: Foreign Languages Publishing House, 1939. Official Stalin era version of party history based upon "confessions" of purge victims and falsifications by Stalin's writers. An extremely interesting study in the technique of the "big lie."

Ponomaryov, B. N., et al. *History of the Communist Party of the Soviet Union.* Trans. by Andrew Rothstein and Clemens Dutt. Moscow: Foreign Languages Publishing House, n.d. The official version produced during the Khrushchev period. Should not be accepted as historically accurate.

Schapiro, Leonard. *The Communist Party of the Soviet Union.* New York: Random House, 1970. The standard history of the CPSU by a noted Western scholar.

THE STALIN PERIOD

*Medvedev, Roy A. *Let History Judge: The Origins and Consequences of Stalinism.* Trans. by Colleen Taylor. New York: Alfred A. Knopf, 1972. The first full-length study of the Stalin era by a Soviet historian. This work was forbidden publication in the U.S.S.R.

People's Commissariat of Justice of the U.S.S.R. *Report of Court Proceedings in the Case of the Anti-Soviet "Bloc of Rights and Trotskyites."* Moscow: People's Commissariat of Justice of the U.S.S.R., 1938. Verbatim account (edited) of the trial of Bukharin, Rykov, Yagoda, and others, based upon "evidence" obtained by torture and police fabrication. Especially interesting is Bukharin's last plea and "confession."

*Solzhenitsyn, A. *The Gulag Archipelago.* Trans. by Thomas P. Whitney. New York: Harper and Row, 1974. Chilling exposé of Stalinist forced labor camps.

The Communist International

Degras, Jane (ed.). *The Communist International (1919–1943): Documents.* 3 vols. London: Oxford University Press, 1965.

The basic documentation of the history of the Third International.

Sobolev, A. E. (ed.) . *Outline History of the Communist International.* Trans. by Bernard Isaacs. Moscow: Progress Publishers, 1970. The official version written by Soviet historians. To be read with considerable scrutiny.

INDEX